MICROCOMPUTERS IN EDUCATION TODAY

MICROCOMPUTERS IN EDUCATION TODAY

Gary G. Bitter

MP **Mitchell Publishing, Inc.**
Innovators in Computer Education
55 Penny Lane, #103 • Watsonville, California 95076
(800) 435-2665 • In California (408) 724-0195

Cover design:	JUAN VARGAS
Printer:	R. R. DONNELLEY & SONS
Product development:	RALEIGH S. WILSON
Production management:	BOOKMAN PRODUCTIONS
Sponsoring editor:	ROGER HOWELL
Text design:	HAL LOCKWOOD, BOOKMAN PRODUCTIONS
Photo research:	MONICA SUDER & ASSOCIATES

Printed in the United States of America
10   9   8   7   6   5   4   3   2

Library of Congress Card Catalog No.: 88-061872

ISBN: 0-07-558009-8 (text alone)
     0-07-558229-5 (text, plus 0-07-558228-7 *APPLEWORKS in the Classroom* by Bitter, with data software)

CONTENTS

PREFACE

Microcomputers in Education Today was written for the preservice or inservice educator who wants to become "computer literate." The book introduces microcomputers and emphasizes productivity tools and the use of computers in learning and the curriculum, today as well as in the future. It assumes no prerequisite computer skills but presents the microcomputer as an effective tool for instruction, focusing on the integration of the microcomputer into the curriculum. A comprehensive coverage of application software, including databases, word processing, spreadsheets, graphics, telecommunications, and integrated software, is included. Suggested roles of the computer for various curriculum areas are outlined. Computer-assisted and computer-managed instruction are discussed, including references for popular educational software. The book uses an education orientation throughout, and thus serves as a valuable aid for the preservice or inservice teacher in preparing to use the microcomputer in the classroom.

ORGANIZATION

Chapter 1 focuses on applications of the microcomputer in education. It discusses why computers are so popular and why they can be invaluable as learning tools. Computer-assisted and computer-managed instruction are explored and their advantages and disadvantages discussed.

Chapter 2 outlines the history of computers in education. The computer "family tree" is discussed, including the standard "generations." Early educational computing activities are explored, and their significance to current practices is explained.

Chapter 3 describes the components of a computer system. Numerous photos and illustrations explain the parts of a computer and its peripheral devices. The concept of software as the necessary instructions that run a computer is introduced. Programming, including techniques to plan programs, is outlined. The chapter concludes with the types of software required to operate a microcomputer system.

Chapter 4 concentrates on integrating the computer into the curriculum. Proper care of hardware, steps in writing a lesson plan (including computer uses), discussion of types of software, and software programs for the various curriculum areas are all discussed. The chapter concludes with a description of tool software.

Chapter 5 carefully details the specifics of common word processing terms and capabilities, as well as factors to consider in choosing a word processor, and concludes with a discussion of several commercial educational word processing programs.

Chapter 6 defines and provides a brief history of spreadsheets. Educational applications, as well as a listing of several educational software packages, are included. Terms and capabilities of common spreadsheet packages are discussed.

Chapter 7 provides a definition of "databases," including terms and capabilities. Commercial educational databases are introduced. The chapter carefully describes how to create a database and enter data.

Chapter 8 outlines graphics capabilities and explains how graphics are used in education. Several popular educational graphics programs are listed, outlined, and illustrated.

Chapter 9 examines the role of telecommunications in education. The requirements for telecommunications, including terms, equipment, and networking are discussed. The advantages of integrated software packages are reviewed. The chapter's conclusion investigates desktop publishing, including educational implications.

Chapter 10 examines the benefits of computer-assisted instruction (CAI) in education, with the characteristics of effective CAI software provided. The advantages and disadvantages of drill-and-practice, tutorial, simulation, and problem-solving software are covered.

Chapter 11 discusses the characteristics, advantages, and disadvantages of computer-managed instruction (CMI). The electronic gradebook is described; test generation is reviewed; and networked CMI is introduced. CMI examples are produced to illustrate their role in education. How to choose and implement CMI programs concludes this chapter.

Chapter 12 includes sources of software information. User groups and public domain software are discussed. The chapter concentrates on techniques and procedures for reviewing educational software, including what makes CAI software effective.

Chapter 13 examines social and ethical concerns such as software piracy, computer fraud, and privacy. All topics are related to education.

Chapter 14 explores technology of the future such as optical disks, video disks, CD-ROM, telecommunications, digital video interactive software, HyperCard, robotics, artificial intelligence, and expert systems.

Each chapter concludes with a bibliography, review exercises (including multiple choice, true-false, and short-answer questions), and five to ten educational activities.

SUPPORT TEXT

Appleworks in the Classroom Today (Mitchell Publishing, 1989) is a step-by-step tutorial with educational applications, which was designed to be an accompanying support text to *Microcomputers in Education Today*. It provides hands-on use of the applications of word processing, databases, and spreadsheets. The two texts together can be coordinated with related supporting assignments. The assignments depend on course length and on the rigor desired. Ideally, these two books match the teacher certification requirements of many states and were specifically designed to meet this need.

ACKNOWLEDGMENTS

I would like to thank Roger Howell for encouraging me to write this book. His professional approach to publishing will not be forgotten. My special thanks to Linda Evans for her efforts in this project. Without her expertise, dedication, and patience, this project would never have been completed. Thanks also to Diane Doyle and Gladys Bennett for proofing the manuscript pages, and special thanks to my wife and sons, who have been patient with me during the writing process. Their encouragement of my efforts is appreciated.

It is my hope that the enlightened application of technology in the teaching and learning process will help improve our educational system.

Gary G. Bitter
February 2, 1989

MICROCOMPUTERS IN EDUCATION TODAY

CHAPTER 1

THE MICROCOMPUTER IN EDUCATION

Objectives

- List features of the computer that make it an effective teaching tool
- List several ways in which computers are used in schools
- Explain how computers assist in special education
- Describe various ways of setting up computers in the schools
- List a number of hints to help teachers use computers most effectively

Key Terms

analog computer
applications software
CAI (computer-assisted instruction)
CMI (computer-managed instruction)
computer
computerphobia
data
data processing
digital computer
downloading
graphics
load
memory
nanosecond
network/networking
programs
software
speech synthesis
stand-alone systems
terminal systems
tool software
uploading

When we visualize a classroom, we usually imagine blackboard-lined walls, rows of desks and chairs, books lined up on shelves, bulletin boards, and a teacher's desk located prominently in the room. Most classrooms look this way—you have to look very closely to see that the ordinary-looking classroom is undergoing a quiet but powerful revolution.

Did you notice the microcomputer in the corner? Not at first glance, perhaps, but that is where the revolution is taking place. Computers may not change the way the classroom looks—although in some applications they do just that—but they *are* changing the way education happens. Even in classrooms without computers, the revolution touches teachers who debate what and how much they teach their students about computers to prepare them for our highly computerized society.

This is a classroom with a microcomputer.

In this chapter, we will examine the features of the computer that make it an effective tool for both teaching and learning. We will also look at some real-world applications of computers in schools—as tutors, as laboratory instruments, as electronic gradebooks and filing cabinets, and as aids in special education. Then we will consider some of the different ways in which computers are set up for use in schools today.

WHAT IS A COMPUTER?

First, let's consider the term computer and what it really means. A **computer** is a machine that takes in and processes information—called **data.** The data, which can be numbers, letters, symbols, or even sound, is turned into electrical impulses so that it can be processed by sorting, collating, deleting, mathematical calculation, or other forms of data **processing.**

The computer has a number of characteristics that distinguish it from other machines, as follows:

1. *Computers are electronic.* They rely on electrical impulses—"on" and "off" signals—to read and process information.
2. *Computers can compare statements.* After a computer compares two statements, it can make a decision about which statement is "true." This basic ability has made possible most of the successful applications of computers today. (For further explanation, see Chapter 3.)
3. *Computers can be programmed to do what people want them to do.* **Programs** are written sets of instructions that tell the computer what to do. Some of the programs used to operate the computer are stored permanently inside the computer. The people who operate the computer never see the actual programs, in this case. Other programs are written by students and professional programmers and are stored outside the computer. The operator must **load** these programs into the computer before it "knows" how to do its work. The specific work a computer is programmed to do is called **software.** Software is a set of instructions or programs that allow a computer to do a particular job.
4. *Computers can perform arithmetical functions.* Besides comparing statements, computers can also add, subtract, multiply, and divide. Whether the arithmetical formula is complicated, tedious, difficult, fun, time-consuming, or simple, the computer follows instructions to perform the arithmetic.
5. *Computers are either analog or digital.* An **analog computer** measures quantities (such as temperature, air pressure, or voltage) and converts these quantities into electrical impulses in order to run other

devices. For example, a computer that senses when to turn on a furnace or air conditioner is an analog computer.

In contrast, a **digital computer** counts discrete data or numbers that are changed into electrical impulses. The digital computer lends itself to processing business data and other information that relies more on numbers and letters than on physical conditions. Most computers that are used today, especially those in the classroom, are digital computers.

WHY ARE COMPUTERS SO POPULAR?

Understanding what a computer is and how it works still does not explain the technological explosion we have seen in our lifetime. Computers are so commonplace in our world that we barely notice them in our homes, offices, classrooms; they are everywhere, even in our cars and home appliances. They are no more unusual in a business office than a typewriter or a copy machine. Let's examine why.

Computers are fast. Information can be processed so quickly that the terms used to describe their speed are hard for humans to comprehend. For example, one second contains one billion **nanoseconds.** The same information that took several hundred nanoseconds to process just twenty years ago now takes only a few nanoseconds. To the person operating the computer, this seems like no time at all.

Computers are accurate. Computers do exactly what they are programmed to do. If a program is accurate the computer will carry out the instructions correctly. If a computer program contains errors, the computer will not be able to produce correct results. Whether we like it or not, the mistakes we blame on computers are usually the result of mistakes in computer programs.

Computers can work twenty-four hours per day. Computers never get tired, nor do they require coffee breaks or sleep. They operate whenever people need them to, whether daytime or nighttime, weekday or weekend.

Computers can perform repetitive tasks without becoming bored. In spite of the science fiction movies that show smart computers bossing people around, computers actually do not know or care about what kind of work they do. Therefore, the same program can be run hundreds or thousands of times with large amounts of data and many repetitive calculations. Computers do not require challenge or creativity as human workers do.

Computers are able to work under conditions hazardous to or difficult for people. Computer-controlled robots, for example, can work in conditions that would be unhealthy, uncomfortable, or dangerous to human workers. Computers thus can save people from injury or even death. The computer in the space vehicle that flew past Saturn followed all its instructions, oblivious to the fact that this was a one-way trip.

The microcomputer is an integral part of most offices.

Computers are becoming smaller and more portable. Some computers are small enough now to be held in your hand. And it is certainly not unusual to see a business traveler on an airplane writing reports with a briefcase-sized computer. The more portable that computers are, the more useful they are to people on the go.

Computers are becoming less expensive. In an age of inflation, the prices of computers have decreased markedly in the last two decades. A computer that would have cost $25,000 a few years ago may cost only $5,000 today. As costs have diminished, the size of **memory**—how much information a computer can hold at one time—has increased dramatically. So has the speed at which computers operate. This means that while computers cost

Computerized robots are used in automobile production lines to assemble and weld together the parts.

less, they can do more work in a shorter period of time—and more people have access to them.

THE COMPUTER AS A TEACHING AND LEARNING TOOL

The same features that have skyrocketed the computer to its current popularity also make it an effective tool for both teaching and learning. Let's look at some of those features again and consider their implications in the classroom.

Computers are fast. Students working with computers get immediate feedback on their performance. The computer works much faster than the people who operate it, so students don't lose interest. Also they don't have

Teachers use the microcomputer to keep track of grades and to provide problem-solving experience for students.

to wait for papers to be graded and returned to them. Teachers can save a great deal of time by using the classroom computer to keep track of grades, write reports and bulletins, and perform other paperwork tasks.

Computers are accurate. Assuming that they are programmed with correct information, they will always perform correctly and consistently. Thus, students receive correct information when working with the computer. The accuracy of the computer also makes it a reliable record-keeping tool for the teacher.

Computers can work twenty-four hours a day. The computer in the classroom can be available to students at all times during the school day. After hours, the teacher can use the same computer to keep attendance records or write notes to parents.

Computers perform repetitive tasks without becoming bored. No matter how long it takes a student to master multiplication tables, for example, the computer will continue to drill the student without becoming bored or impatient. This makes the computer especially useful in special education where students may require extra time to practice new skills. The computer allows students of all levels to work at their own pace.

Computers are able to work under conditions hazardous or difficult for people. In a high school science lab, for instance, computer programs allow students to conduct simulated experiments involving dangerous materials (say, radioactive elements)—something they could not do if they had to actually handle such materials.

Computers are becoming smaller and more portable. Microcomputers fit easily into the classroom, unlike the early computers that had to be housed in huge rooms under special conditions. Portable computers can even be shared among several classrooms. Some schools are experimenting with permitting students to take computers home to do assignments.

Computers are becoming less expensive. Since school districts continually struggle with limited budgets, the cost of computer hardware and software is an important factor in how widely computers are used in schools. With decreasing costs, computers become more affordable and therefore more accessible to schools. More computers in the schools mean that more students have access to the advantages of educational computing.

There's no doubt about it: computers help teachers do their jobs more effectively; they do this in three basic ways. First, they help teachers instruct their students through special programs known as **computer-assisted instruction (CAI).** These programs include games, tutorials, simulations, and other programs for teaching new concepts and skills to students. Along with CAI software designed especially for use in the classroom, teachers can also use tool software to facilitate learning. **Tool software,** also called **applications software,** includes word processors, database managers, spreadsheets, graphics, and telecommunications. (Applications of tool software are discussed in detail in Chapters 5, 6, 7, 8, and 9.)

Second, computers help teachers cope with mountains of paperwork that may otherwise take time away from classroom activities. Programs that help teachers manage their record-keeping tasks are called **computer-**

Laptop computers make it possible to do computing almost anywhere.

managed instruction (CMI). Finally, computers have also taken over many administrative functions in the classroom and office, such as generating reports and maintaining files. From preschool to graduate school, computers are used widely throughout education.

A major cause of **computerphobia**—the fear of using computers—is the anxiety that computers will make human skills obsolete. Some people fear that they will lose their jobs if computers are programmed to work more quickly, efficiently, and less expensively than human workers are capable of doing. For many, this fear is not merely a figment of the imagination: In the past decade especially, we have seen or heard about manufacturing jobs taken over by programmable robots.

Will Computers Replace Human Teachers?

As human beings, teachers are not immune to this anxiety and often have mixed feelings about computers in the classroom. On the one hand, teachers are excited about any technology that promises to help them provide better education for their students. On the other hand, they may be afraid that the computer can perform their job as well as they can.

However, a computer *cannot* do many of the most important acts that a human teacher performs every day. Although computers can present material in a methodical and patient way, they cannot provide an encouraging smile or congratulatory pat on the shoulder at just the right moment. They cannot listen to students' problems or facilitate cooperation among groups of students. And they cannot know and understand students as individuals with different goals, hopes, and dreams. Simply put, computers cannot be human. The human factor that teachers bring to education cannot be mechanized by even the most gifted computer programmer.

Another factor that contributes to teachers resisting computers in the classroom is that most teachers haven't received adequate training in the use of computers. Many fear that they will have to spend too much time struggling through complex manuals before they can train their students to work with computers. Already burdened with reams of reports, lesson plans, and grading, teachers must budget their time carefully. Computer training may not be at the top of their lists of priorities, especially if they are unconvinced that it will directly benefit their students. School districts can begin to overcome this resistance by offering workshops in computer literacy for teachers.

Finally, educational software packages are not always designed by people who understand the needs of the classroom teacher. Some teachers have been frustrated by trying to use software that performs miserably in the classroom. Even very good software is ineffective unless it can be integrated into the regular curriculum—and software publishers often leave this task to the busy teacher. Fortunately this is changing, as publishers hire experts in education to help design and produce curriculum-oriented software and related materials such as workbooks, textbooks, and teacher guides.

Great strides are now being made in the development of hardware and software for education, as in all other areas where computers are used. Smaller, simpler, and affordable computers are becoming available to teachers and students. At the same time, more creative and practical educational software and courseware are appearing on the market to help teachers integrate computer use into the curriculum. Computers do not threaten to replace teachers, then, but promise to provide them with an array of new tools for encouraging their students to learn.

Computer-Assisted Instruction (CAI)

Computer-assisted instruction helps teachers to instruct their students in a number of ways: It introduces new materials, teaches lessons, allows practice of new skills, tests for mastery of skills, and provides review and remediation when necessary.

Computers can teach just about anything and at any level of difficulty, from the most basic to the most advanced. Although there's no limit to the range of topics that computers can teach, the following list includes subjects of special interest to teachers:

Alphabet skills	Literature
Art	Mathematics
Biology	Music
Business applications	Nutrition
Chemistry	Physical education
Economics	Physics
Foreign languages	Reading
Geography	Speed reading
Grammar	Typing
Language arts	

The amount of material, the complexity, and the degree of detail presented in a lesson can be adjusted to the level of individual students. (For specific examples of how computers are used to teach different areas of the curriculum, see Chapter 4.)

The computer program interacts with the student by presenting material and by asking questions that the student must answer before continuing; the program then analyzes the student's responses. Students who respond correctly are rewarded before advancing. Students whose answers are incorrect are given another try or allowed to review information they do not understand completely. The program may even be able to present information in a different manner for students who respond incorrectly. The computer teaches, evaluates, and reteaches as often as students require and on an individual basis, which is often difficult for teachers to do who have many students.

Educational computers use a variety of methods to do their teaching. Some use a video screen with photoelectronic sensors that react to the pressure of a finger. With one of these, all the student has to do is touch the place on the screen where the answer appears, and the computer analyzes the response to see if it is correct. Some computers use standard keyboards that require students to type in their answers. Computers that include voice recognition can understand and process oral responses from students. Consequently, students of all ages, abilities, and limitations can use computers as tools for learning.

The special abilities of computers allow them to teach in interesting and innovative ways. Many CAI programs use **graphics** (pictures or other images on the screen), music, color, **speech synthesis** (creation and assembly of human sounds into recognizable words), and animation to present educational material. This helps to attract and hold the attention of even the youngest students. Especially when students feel that they are actively involved in the process, computer-assisted instruction can motivate them to learn concepts and skills they might otherwise dismiss as routine or boring. Sometimes they become so interested in working with the computer that learning seems to occur almost automatically.

Touchscreens make computer use available to young children.

A handy and attractive feature of most educational computer systems is their ability to store and display color pictures. This can be very helpful, for example, in presenting basal reading materials. For students with difficulties in reading, there are even computers that talk. A student may listen to an entire passage or may ask the computer to read aloud only a particularly troublesome word.

Most computers can play music. A student of musical theory can view a piano keyboard on a computer screen. The computer can play notes as they are selected so that the student can compose simple or elaborate musical pieces.

Computers that offer this versatility and uniqueness have one major drawback: They are expensive. However, as technology advances and its cost decreases, systems such as these will find their way into more and more classrooms.

There are many advantages of using a computer to teach. First, it can provide individualized attention to students who need it. These students might need specialized remedial work or may be ready to progress beyond the scope and sequence of regular lessons. Gifted students can be challenged with higher-order thinking simulations. The computer does not discriminate between the slow learner and the gifted learner.

Second, educational computers can be used outside the classroom. For example, homebound students need not miss their lessons when a computer is available. In higher-education applications, students can take correspondence courses via computers, allowing them to study with scholars at universities across the country or even around the world.

Third, students with special needs—such as those with physical handicaps—can benefit from computers that are programmed especially to help them overcome their limitations. For example, speech-impaired students

Computers can be used to compose music.

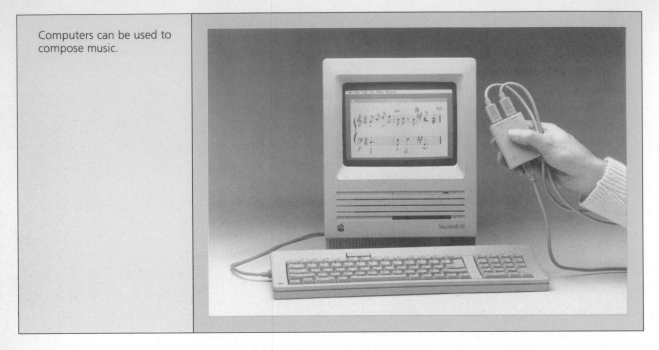

can communicate with the help of the computer keyboard. For those who cannot type with their fingers but must use other methods of data entry, keyboards can be adapted. The computer is very patient, which makes it especially well-suited for special education. Unlike its human counterpart, it can present a lesson over and over again without becoming frustrated, tired, or irritable.

Computers in the Science Lab

An exciting and innovative use of microcomputer power has been implemented by science teachers in their laboratories. In the "real world," computers have long been used as laboratory instruments, taking precise measurements and compiling data. However, these uses were generally funded by private industry or the federal government, and the cost of using a computer in a high school laboratory was prohibitive to the average science teacher.

The microcomputer has changed all that, however, because it is small and affordable. Some teachers program their classroom computers to perform or assist in performing experiments in the laboratory. Most hardware and software systems used in the lab are designed for high school and college students and often require some expertise in computer use by teachers and their students. Other packages, such as Science Toolkit (see Chapter 4), are designed for use by younger, less experienced students.

Why use a computer as a lab instrument? First, the computer can function in situations that are dangerous or uncomfortable for humans. This

The microcomputer can be used in conjunction with science laboratory experiments and can simulate dangerous experiments.

greatly increases the range of experimentation that can be done when computers rather than students gather data. Second, the computer works so quickly to gather data that it can make hundreds or thousands of measurements per second—an impossible task for even the most gifted student. This results in a much more detailed record of the results of the experiment being performed. Also, students have time to replicate the experiment and confirm results, often in a single class period. Third, in calculating the data it has gathered, the computer follows the formulas it is given; it will not deviate from its instructions or make errors in simple mathematics, thus guaranteeing more accurate results.

But perhaps the greatest advantage of using the microcomputer in the science lab is that students are given hands-on experience in working with computers for research. Since most of the research done in government, commerce, and universities involves computers, it makes sense to teach students to use computers to gather, compile, and report scientific data. These are very practical skills that budding scientists will require throughout their careers.

The cost of using microcomputers as laboratory instruments can be offset by considering that computers can replace other instruments that are standard in the lab. In other words, the purchase of one computer may be more cost-effective than the purchase of a dozen other instruments that measure the same data that the computer measures. In some cases, the computer actually performs *better* than the lab instruments it imitates, thus making it an even more attractive investment.

HOW COMPUTERS WORK IN SCHOOLS

Now that we have seen how useful computers can be in the classroom, we should discuss the options for setting them up. As we have pointed out, computers can be expensive, especially to schools contending with limited funding and budget cuts. Some districts choose to purchase many stand-alone, or independent, microcomputers. However, others choose to purchase larger systems that can communicate with microcomputers. Computer programs and information for these larger systems can be downloaded to run on a smaller microcomputer system. **Downloading** simply means transferring information from a larger system to a smaller one. The information may be programs or data files. Often the information consists of programs that will not even run on a larger system but are simply stored there by microcomputers. This storage transfer is called **uploading.** The larger system may be maintained in a district office, where it can also be used for administrative and record-keeping functions for all schools in the district. Whichever option is chosen, a school system can have access to a large number of programs via a telephone line connecting the microcomputer to the larger or main computer. (For a more detailed description of how computerized information is transferred across telephone lines, see Chapter 9 on telecommunications.)

Computer-Managed Instruction (CMI)

Along with teaching, computers can also help to manage the instructional process. The use of computers to help teachers maintain records and plan lessons is called computer-managed instruction (CMI). Even if the computer does not actually teach, much of the management of students' educational progress can be computerized. Two major CMI applications are keeping records of students' progress and planning students' instructional programs. Many CAI packages include built-in CMI components that track student progress through pretests and posttests.

Records that document how students are doing at all times during the school term help teachers make decisions about educational programs. The traditional gradebook is the most obvious way in which to track student progress. Most teachers continue to manually enter a letter or numerical grade for each assignment that students complete. At the end of the grading period, teachers must average and evaluate scores before assigning final grades. They must then complete report cards or progress reports, all by hand. Most teachers spend many hours tabulating and recording grades.

With the advent of the microcomputer and specially designed CMI software, all this tedious work can be done rapidly. Grades can be assigned as usual and then typed into the computer to be stored in its memory. At any time, the teacher can add to a record and instantly obtain an updated grade without having to average grades by hand. Thus, cumulative grades are available at any point in the grading period. In addition, computer-

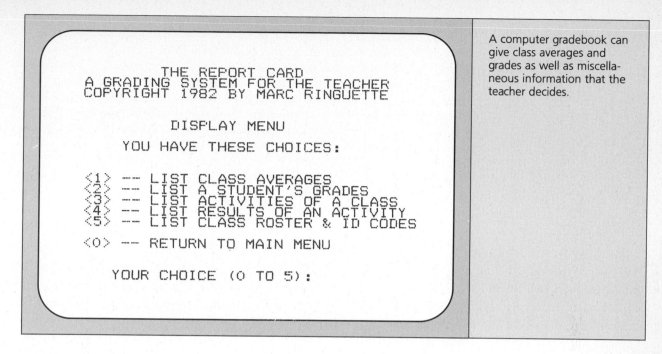

```
                    THE REPORT CARD
          A GRADING SYSTEM FOR THE TEACHER
          COPYRIGHT 1982 BY MARC RINGUETTE

                    DISPLAY MENU
             YOU HAVE THESE CHOICES:


          <1> --- LIST CLASS AVERAGES
          <2> --- LIST A STUDENT'S GRADES
          <3> --- LIST ACTIVITIES OF A CLASS
          <4> --- LIST RESULTS OF AN ACTIVITY
          <5> --- LIST CLASS ROSTER & ID CODES

          <0> --- RETURN TO MAIN MENU


             YOUR CHOICE (0 TO 5):
```

A computer gradebook can give class averages and grades as well as miscellaneous information that the teacher decides.

```
File: Ind Grades            REVIEW/ADD/CHANGE          Escape: Main Menu
======V----W----X----Y======Z======AA=======AB=======AC-----AD---AE==AF==AG==AH=
  1|                     1| Name    Gary Bitter     A     90   Weights
  2|                     2| Grade   5th             B     80
  3|Tot Wt   Tot  Wt     3| Period  First Qtr 1989  C     70   Asgm .80
  4|Asgm Asgm Test Test  4|                         D     60   Test .20
  5|------------------   5| -----------------------------------------------
  6|                     6| <-- Assignment   Average    English
  7| 502       371       7| <-- Points Recvd          A  B  C  D  F
  8| 550 73.0 400 18.6   8| <-- Tot Points      91.6   1  0  0  0  0
  9|------------------   9| -----------------------------------------------
 10|                    10| <-- Assignment   Average    Math
 11| 362       307      11| <-- Points Recvd          A  B  C  D  F
 12| 455 63.6 400 15.4  12| <-- Tot Points      79.0   0  0  1  0  0
 13|------------------  13| -----------------------------------------------
 14|                    14| <-- Assignment   Average    Science
 15| 886       334      15| <-- Points Recvd          A  B  C  D  F
 16|1000 70.9 400 16.7  16| <-- Tot Points      87.6   0  1  0  0  0
 17|------------------  17| -----------------------------------------------
 18|                    18| <-- Assignment   Average    Soc Studies
                           -----------------------------------------------
Y7: (Label, Protect-N)

Type entry or use 9 commands                        9-? for Help
```

Gradebooks can be designed on spreadsheets to show individual student progress by subject.

stored grades can be used to form statistics that show how an entire group, class, or grade level is doing. The teacher can also compare the progress of one student to the progress of the whole class. Not only does the computerized gradebook make the teacher's record keeping simpler, but it also helps the teacher determine whether lessons are effective and when remedial work is needed. In addition, parent-teacher conferences can be scheduled at any time, since all the information is at the teacher's fingertips.

In many areas, teachers are required to write up a schedule of academic objectives for each student in their class. To make this an easier task, a teacher can enter information on each student into the computer, such as scores on standardized tests, progress to date, expected level of performance, and goals and objectives for the school year. The computer can then determine whether the student is ready to go on to more difficult material, skip lessons, review previous material, or relearn material through different strategies.

Since the computer is capable of storing and remembering data on many students at the same time, the task of individualizing instruction becomes much easier. Although this kind of programming can be complicated, it reaches a higher level of individualization than a teacher can be expected to reach. Whether we are speaking of a single lesson or an entire course, the sequence of the program can be managed by the computer through preestablished guidelines, making the educational process more relevant to the learner.

Administrative Uses of Computers

Teachers and students are not the only people in the educational community. Administrators can and do use computers extensively in their work. Let's explore some of these uses.

Grades assigned to students at every grade level must be recorded in some fashion, and these records must be easily and readily accessible to appropriate individuals. In the past, storage of such records has caused files to bulge in almost every school system. Now, however, administrators can keep these records on computer storage devices, which saves a great deal of space, and access them as needed. Printouts of records can be made almost instantaneously.

Records showing the costs involved in running a school or university must be kept up to date in a thoroughly accurate manner. Computers can be tremendously helpful in this capacity, especially when administrators track their budgets with spreadsheet software. (For more detail on spreadsheets, see Chapter 6.)

Computers help with many administrative functions that are difficult to manage on paper. They can help to schedule classes without room or time conflicts. They also enroll students in classes, making sure that the student has taken prerequisite exams or placement tests. The computer can assign teachers to classes and, of course, make sure those teachers are compensated by processing payroll calculations as well.

Imagine the record-keeping tasks faced by the school librarian! Keeping files on films, books, periodicals, pictures, and other library materials can be an awesome responsibility. Once again the computer comes to the rescue. Not only does it keep an accurate file, but it also monitors the borrowers, due dates of materials borrowed, and reservations of materials in great demand. The computer can also generate overdue notices automatically.

Library computers can give students at all levels access to an unlimited range of research materials. No longer are students restricted to the collections in their school libraries. Using databases and telecommunications, students can locate and order materials from libraries in other schools within the district or across the country, for that matter. As more library collections become computerized, students will be able to request printouts of materials from other libraries. This makes the traditional process of research obsolete and speeds the flow of information to students. These are only a few of the ways in which computers can and are being used by school administrative personnel, as well as by students.

INTRODUCING COMPUTERS INTO THE CLASSROOM

Think back to the imaginary classroom at the beginning of the chapter. Was there room for a computer? How about a computer laboratory? One of the challenges that teachers and school administrators face is how to set up

Libraries use computers to keep records of all their transactions.

computers in classrooms and schools. Let's look at several common arrangements of computers in educational settings.

Where school budgets are limited or teachers are not prepared to incorporate many computers into the classroom, there may be only one computer in the classroom. This is often true in elementary schools where classrooms are self-contained. In other words, children study several subjects in the same classroom and the computer may be used for a wide range of topics and purposes. In this case, the teacher usually puts the computer close to his or her desk. This makes it easier to help students run the computer and to make sure that the equipment and the software are handled properly. The teacher must also devise a system for sharing computer time since the computer area may become the most popular spot in the classroom. Depending on the age of the students, a sign-up chart may solve this problem. The teacher can also use the computer, with the help of a projection system, to demonstrate contexts and activities.

Some classrooms are fortunate enough to have several computers. Often, the teacher chooses to place the computers close to each other. It is practical to do this because cables, printers, and other related equipment can be isolated in one area of the classroom. Also, students can work in groups and assist each other, which can allow the teacher to continue with other activities without interruption.

Advance planning for computer use is necessary for classrooms with only one computer.

Computers in the classroom can be either terminal systems or stand-alone systems. **Terminal systems** consist of data input and output devices that send information to a central system for processing. Since they do not process data themselves, terminals are often less expensive than microcomputers. By far the more popular choice, **stand-alone systems** are microcomputers that accept input, process data, and generate output independently. Like terminals, they can be made to communicate directly with other computers; unlike terminals, they can process information without requiring the presence of other equipment.

The main advantage of terminal systems is that they can be connected to very large, extremely powerful central computers that work much faster and store much more data than microcomputers and have access to all the student and school information. On the other hand, when the central computer is not operating, terminal users cannot compute. Also, they must depend on the programs that are stored in the central computer.

Stand-alone microcomputer systems are quite reliable and can run a wide range of software on the market. However, because they are not as powerful as larger computers, they are available to fewer users at one time and may be limited to programs written in less powerful and sophisticated languages. Still, the trend in most schools is to opt for stand-alone microcomputer systems. In some classrooms where monitors or large screens are

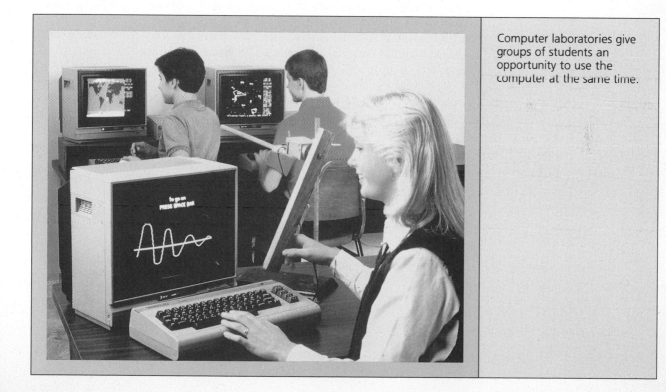

Computer laboratories give groups of students an opportunity to use the computer at the same time.

used to show students what is being done on a stand-alone system, a small microcomputer can teach a whole class at once.

In some schools, computers are not placed in individual classrooms but are housed in a special area of the school designated as a computer center or computer laboratory. This is often the case in secondary schools where students are accustomed to moving from classroom to classroom to study different subjects.

The computer laboratory offers a number of advantages in teaching computer skills. First, in schools where one teacher who is a computer expert manages the laboratory, students benefit from this instructor's specialization in computer science. Second, in the lab students learn computer skills as a group, which allows them to assist and learn from each other as well as from the teacher. Finally, it is usually true that students in a computer laboratory spend more time at the computer than is possible with one or a few computers in the regular classroom. Of course, the more computer time students receive, the more they can practice valuable computer skills.

Unfortunately, there are some disadvantages to locating computers outside the regular classroom. If schools purchase more computers for the laboratory than they would purchase for each classroom, they may have to buy additional copies of software for each computer in the laboratory, thus limiting the number of different packages they can afford to buy. In laboratories without a teacher designated as lab manager, computers and related equipment may not be cared for properly, which can result in a higher incidence of hardware repair and software replacement—costs the school budget may not support. In addition, students may have to interrupt their work to wait for computer repairs to be done, which can be frustrating in the middle of an exciting project.

The teacher may also experience some problems when students work in a computer center outside the regular classroom. It may be more difficult for teachers to integrate computer activities into the classroom curriculum when students must leave the classroom for the computer laboratory. The teacher must also devise a system for reading and compiling results from many computers rather than from a single computer or system.

One method to eliminate or at least minimize these problems is to **network** computers in the lab. **Networking** establishes communication among computers through cables so that they can share software and data. With networked computers, it is not necessary to purchase and load software separately for each machine. Instead, one copy of a program can be loaded into all computers at one time, saving schools considerable time and expense. Software that can be networked may cost more initially than single-computer software, but it costs less than purchasing thirty or forty copies of software for individual machines.

Another money-saving option may be purchasing a license agreement from the software publisher. The licensing agreement permits the school to make as many copies of the software as required so that all computers can run the software at the same time. Again, it may cost more initially, but in the long run the school will probably save a considerable amount of money. The problem with this arrangement is that numerous copies of software must still be loaded into the individual computers—a task that may be time consuming and require assistance from a teacher or lab manager. Networking eliminates this task. In secondary schools especially, student volunteers can be trained to help with some routine procedures such as loading software into computers.

Some drawbacks involved in networking may discourage school administrators from establishing a network of computers in the computer lab. First, depending on the computer hardware selected and the degree of computer expertise among teachers in the school, networking may present some technical difficulties. Enabling computers to "talk" to each other requires special cabling, software, and computer knowledge. The lab may need to be modified (in terms of electrical outlets and so on) to ensure that the networked system will operate properly. If possible, networking should be done by someone who has experience with the particular hardware being used. Because of the additional hardware and software required, networking can also be an additional expense in the computer budget. Adding to the cost is the need for a specially designated computer teacher or aide who has the expertise to manage the networked system.

Another option available to schools is to install one or several computers in or near the library or media center. A teacher, librarian, or aide can be assigned to manage these computers. Given the location, only a few students will be able to work here at any one time, and they will work quietly and individually.

Cooperative group learning is popular with computers.

School libraries and media centers are popular locations for computers.

The advantage of this system is that it can be highly individualized to meet student needs. The gifted student can be excused from regular classes in order to receive more challenging instruction from the computer. Similarly, slow learners can receive patient remediation from the computer while their classmates progress to other areas. Working alone and away from class, special students do not need to feel isolated or different from their classmates, which they may feel while doing extra work in the classroom. On the other hand, this separateness can be a disadvantage. Since the computer offers unique opportunities for group cooperation, teachers may prefer the computer lab or classroom to the media center or library.

Because students leave their regular classrooms for the media center individually (rather than en masse as they would for a lab), teachers must set up a system of computer passes that indicate that students have permission to work with computers in the media center. Included on the pass should be the particular program or topic the student is to work on. This allows the librarian or aide to manage software in an organized fashion and to ensure that students benefit from computer time.

However, computers in the media center may become a headache for the overburdened librarian unless a thoughtful system for scheduling computer time is in place. When many students compete for time on a few computers, the librarian or computer aide may get caught in the middle. It is essential that teachers and students understand and use the scheduling system designed for computers in the media center. Also, close communication between the classroom teacher and the librarian or aide is vital. The librarian cannot be expected to know each student's individual needs, so teachers must indicate clearly what software or topics the student needs to concentrate on.

Whatever the arrangement of computers in the school, administrators and teachers should strive to ensure that all students have as much access as possible to computer power. Not only do students learn the material presented by CAI and tool software packages, but they also develop and hone computer skills that will make them more effective adults in the Information Age.

SUMMARY

Computers are machines that accept information, process it, and then output it in some form. They are characterized by the following traits:

1. Computers are electronic.
2. Computers can compare statements.
3. Computers can be programmed to perform different tasks.
4. Computers can perform arithmetical functions.

Computers have increased in popularity dramatically in the past thirty years. They are now used in nearly every facet of our society. The following qualities have contributed to their immense popularity:

1. Computers are fast.
2. Computers are accurate.
3. Computers can work twenty-four hours per day.
4. Computers perform repetitive tasks without becoming bored.
5. Computers can work in conditions that are dangerous or uncomfortable for humans.
6. Computers are becoming smaller and more convenient.
7. Computers are becoming less expensive.

Computers are used in education for three major purposes: to teach students (computer-assisted instruction and tool software), to keep records and help teachers plan educational programs (computer-managed instruction), and to perform administrative functions such as budgeting, scheduling, and record keeping.

Computers can be located in different places throughout the school. One or more computers may be placed in regular classrooms for use by one class. The school may have a computer center or laboratory where students work in groups with computers. Or several computers may be installed in or near the library or media center where students can work independently. Each of these systems has advantages and disadvantages. Schools must consider cost, efficiency, accessibility, and teacher and student needs before installing computer systems.

Although computers are becoming more prevalent in education, some teachers still resist computers in the classroom. These teachers may fear that they will be replaced by cold, unfeeling machines, or worry that they haven't the time to train themselves so that they can then assist their students. Finally, a lack of good educational software and hardware that are both affordable and convenient has been a stumbling block to introducing computers into schools. Fortunately, this situation is correcting itself as software publishers and hardware manufacturers alike are working to meet the needs of teachers and their students.

REVIEW EXERCISES

Multiple Choice

1. A computer is
   a. a magic box with flickering lights
   b. a machine that takes in and processes information
   c. a tool for performing mathematics manually
   d. a device that will replace human teachers in the future
2. A program is
   a. a set of instructions that tells the computer what to do
   b. a schedule of events for the day
   c. a set of instructions to the computer operator
   d. computer hardware
3. A computer *cannot*
   a. perform calculations
   b. carry out instructions
   c. save time
   d. act without instructions
4. Analog computers are designed to
   a. manipulate data
   b. perform physical tasks such as measuring temperature or pressure
   c. be used by teenagers
   d. perform logical operations
5. Which trait is *not* characteristic of a computer?
   a. it performs with speed
   b. it performs with accuracy
   c. it executes instructions
   d. it tires quickly
6. A video screen capable of accepting input by human touch on the screen is a
   a. television screen
   b. color monitor
   c. CRT with a photoelectric sensor around the screen
   d. plate-glass screen
7. When a program is loaded from a large or main computer into a smaller microcomputer, the process is called
   a. transfer downward
   b. uploading
   c. downloading
   d. unloading
8. Networking is the process of
   a. establishing communication among computers
   b. giving workshops in computer literacy
   c. corresponding with other computer users
   d. teaching students to load computer software
9. A stand-alone computer system *can*
   a. accept information
   b. process information
   c. be used as an educational tool
   d. all of the above
10. Computerphobia refers to
    a. eyestrain from too many hours of computer use
    b. fear of electrocution by computer
    c. fear of using a computer
    d. malfunctioning of the computer

True/False

1. Computers are seldom electronic.
2. The cost of computers has risen with inflation.
3. CAI stands for computer-authored instructions.
4. Computers have not yet been used to help educate the handicapped.
5. Computers can be used in the laboratory to replace many standard pieces of laboratory equipment.

6. Teachers use electronic gradebooks to save time and prevent errors in calculating grades.
7. School budgets should not be kept on computers.
8. Computers should never be placed in the library because students working in groups are too noisy.
9. Computers will eventually replace human teachers.
10. Educational software is improving all the time.

Short Answer

1. Define the word *computer.*
2. What are some limitations of computer capabilities?
3. Why are computers helpful in special education?
4. Name the three major uses of computers in education.
5. List some reasons teachers might give for resisting computers in their classrooms.

Activities

1. List five ways that computers have affected your life.
2. Visit a local classroom to see how CAI software is being used, or invite a computer sales representative to speak to your class about CAI packages available today.
3. Investigate the computing activities of your local school district to find out some of the administrative uses of computers.
4. Visit a school computer center or lab and see how computer time is scheduled and how software is organized and managed. Report your findings to the class.
5. Interview five people in different professions, including one teacher, about their attitudes toward computers.

BIBLIOGRAPHY

Becker, H. J. "Instructional Uses of School Computers." *The Computing Teacher* 15 (no. 7): 8.

Bitter, Gary G. "The Road to Computer Literacy: A Scope and Sequence Model." *Electronic Learning* 2 (no. 1, September 1982): 60–63.

Bitter, Gary G., and Ruth Camuse. *Using a Microcomputer in the Classroom.* 2d ed. Englewood Cliffs, N.J.: Prentice-Hall, 1988.

"Computers for the Masses." *U.S. News and World Report* 93 (no. 26, December 27, 1982): 64–72.

Harper, Dennis O., and James H. Stewart. *Run: Computer Education.* Monterey, Calif.: Brooks/Cole, 1983.

Kalbecker, Warren. "The Digital Age." *Science Digest* 90 (no. 3, March 1982): 66–70, 96.

Schwartz, Helen J. "'But what do I write?'—Literary Analysis Made Easier." *The Computing Teacher* 10 (no. 1, August 1983): 16–18.

Woerner, Janet J. "The Database as a Resource in the Earth Science Classroom." *The Computing Teacher* no. 15 (no. 4): 20.

REVIEW ANSWER KEY

Multiple Choice

1. b	5. d	9. d
2. a	6. c	10. c
3. d	7. c	
4. b	8. a	

True/False

1. F	5. T	9. F
2. F	6. T	10. T
3. F	7. F	
4. F	8. F	

Short Answer

1. A computer is a machine that follows instructions one at a time, is reprogrammable, helps people do their work more quickly and accurately, stores a great deal of information in a small space, and so on.
2. A computer cannot think or make sophisticated judgments. It has no conscience or feelings.
3. The computer is patient; it can repeat a lesson many times without becoming tired or frustrated. It can also present challenging lessons to gifted students.
4. Teaching, classroom management, and administrative functions.
5. Some fear being replaced by computers; some feel they don't have time for computer training; some are dissatisfied with the software and hardware on the market.

CHAPTER 2

THE HISTORY OF COMPUTER USE

Objectives

- Identify the generations of computers and technological advances
- Define and discuss vacuum tubes, transistors, integrated circuits (IC), and large-scale integrated circuits (LSI)
- List three basic improvements in computer technology since 1950
- Understand the progression of computers in education from mainframe- and microcomputer-based systems to microcomputers
- Describe the contributions of innovators such as Papert and Bitzer to computer-based education

Key Terms

Atanasoff
authoring language
binary arithmetic
chip
CRT (cathode ray tube)
data processing
ENIAC
IC (integrated circuit)
Logo
LSI (large-scale integrated circuit)
memory
Papert
PLATO
stored program
supercomputer
TICCIT
time sharing
transistors
Von Neumann

Computers have been used commercially for more than thirty years, but their development is a result of events spanning thousands of years. (See Table 2.1 for an outline of the origins of the computer.) In this chapter, we look at the most important events in the development of computers, with special attention to the advent of computers in education.

Table 2.1 *Historic Origins of the Computer*

1000 B.C.E.		*300 B.C.E.*
Counting with fingers and toes Counting with pebbles and stones Base 10 numeration system		Counting with abacus

1617 C.E.		
John Napier Introduction of logarithms Invention of Napier's rods		

1642 C.E.		*1692 C.E.*
Blaise Pascal First mechanical adding machine		Gottfried Wilhelm Von Leibnitz First mechanical calculating machine

1821 C.E.	*1850 C.E.*	*1880 C.E.*
Charles Babbage Difference machine	George Boole Boolean algebra	Herman Hollerith Tabulating machine

B.C.E. = Before Common Era
C.E. = Common Era

THE COMPUTER AGE BEGINS

In 1939, John V. **Atanasoff** and Clifford Berry designed the first electronic digital computing device. As a result of the relatively low costs of mass-producing electronic components, the Mark I was developed at about the same time by a group of Harvard University scientists headed by Howard Aiken in cooperation with International Business Machines (IBM) Corporation. This machine, completed in 1944, was electromechanical—operated by mechanical switches which were opened and closed by electrical currents. The Mark I was classified as a computer because it followed coded instructions that were punched onto paper tape. Instructions could be changed merely by changing the tape. The Mark I was fifty-one feet long and eight feet high. No less than one million components, over 500 miles of electric wire, and 3,000 electrically activated switches constituted the machine. It was noisy because of the kicking of relays, but it was also capable of adding three eight-digit numbers per second. In spite of its noise and size, Mark I made IBM an American leader in computer technology.

The next computer was called the **ENIAC** (Electronic Numerical Integrator And Computer). Its designers were John W. Mauchly and J. Presper Eckert, Jr., at the Moore School of Electrical Engineering at the University of Pennsylvania. The system was designed for the military to calculate the firing tables of new weapons. It was programmed by means of electrical switches and connections, weighed 60,000 pounds, and used almost 20,000 vacuum tubes. These tubes created tremendous heat and the system required large amounts of electricity. However, the machine did work fast, performing up to 5,000 additions in one second, a speed 1,000 times faster than the Mark I. ENIAC was used at the Aberdeen Proving Grounds for many years, even though it stored only a limited amount of information and errors were difficult to detect.

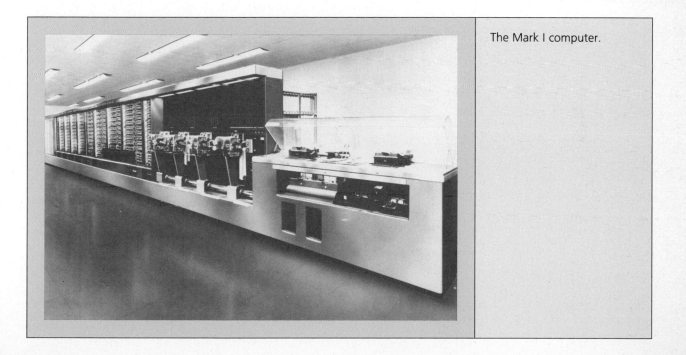

The Mark I computer.

The ENIAC computer.

A major contributor to the modern computer age was John **Von Neumann.** After fleeing from a Communist uprising in 1919 in Hungary, he became an international expert in mathematics. He served as a consultant to the ENIAC project (and later to the EDVAC project) and made several important contributions to the computer revolution. Perhaps the most fundamental of his theories is his description of what a computer ought to be. Von Neumann said that a computer should have three parts: an arithmetical part, a control part, and a memory. The arithmetical part should be a calculating machine, capable of performing basic arithmetic functions. The control part should regulate the ways in which the machine deals with the orders given it and the sequence of its instructions. This part should also have the ability to read from the outside world (computer input) and to inform the outside world of its results (computer output). The **memory** part should be capable of storing information for later use. This could be done by coding programs as numbers and storing them as data in the computer memory. (Indeed, it was the stored-instructions feature that distinguished EDVAC, completed in 1949 but not operational until 1952, as a true computer).

Electronic digital computers are sometimes called stored-program computers because they store sets of instructions in their memories. These stored programs are used to direct the step-by-step operation of the computer upon command.

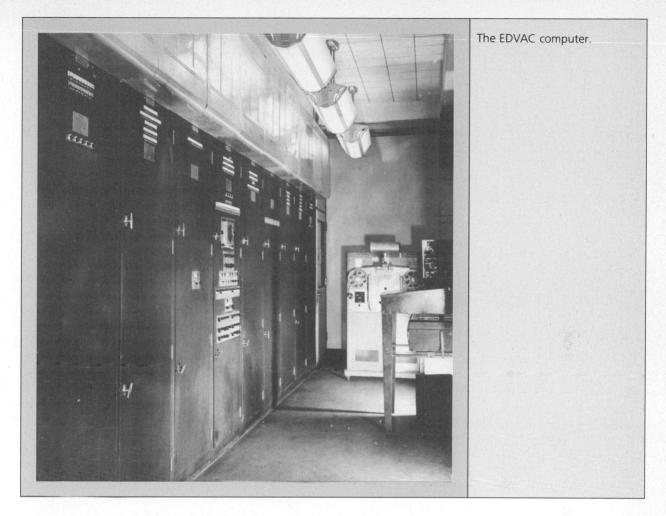

The EDVAC computer.

Another of Von Neumann's major contributions was adapting **binary arithmetic**, the numerals 0 and 1, to represent all decimal numbers. An "on" electrical switch was represented by "1" and an "off" electrical switch by "0." Thus, by arranging zero and one switches in sequence, all computation could be reduced to simple on-off switching. This greatly improved the reliability of transferring information and calculations.

At about the same time, several major European countries were also making technological advances, many inspired by the work being done by American scientists. In Germany, for example, Konrad Zuse constructed relay calculators; by 1943, he had his own company, which built three successful machines, making Zuse the premier builder of electromechanical computers. In England, Kathleen H. V. Britten and Andrew D. Booth developed the concept of the magnetic core which stores numbers as electrical charges in magnetic material. During World War II the European allied countries received money from the United States for computer projects to help the war effort. However, up until the 1950s computers were used mainly by the U.S. government. In 1951, UNIVAC (Universal Automatic Computer) I became the first commercially available stored-program computer. In 1964, just thirteen years after its initial installation, the UNIVAC I was turned over to the Smithsonian Institution because of its historical significance.

THE COMPUTER'S FAMILY TREE

The events leading to the early phases of computer development spanned thousands of years. However, since ENIAC, the first actual electronic computer, was built in the mid-1940s, a number of tremendous technological changes have occurred. The facts that a student learned in the 1950s about computers are radically different from those learned today. We now divide computer development into four generations based on significant technological advancements.

The First Generation   The first generation of computers was born with the use of vacuum tubes (in contrast to the electromechanical switches and gears of the Mark I), which marked the beginning of the computer age.

The ENIAC was the first completely electronic computer. No moving parts were required to process data. ENIAC's major advantage over electromechanical devices was speed. The Mark I, the fastest electromechanical machine of the time, could perform one multiplication per second, but ENIAC was capable of 300 multiplications per second. In one day, ENIAC could process what would have taken one person 300 eight-hour days to process manually.

The underlying principle of vacuum tube computers is that the vacuum tubes carry and control the weightless electrical current that serves to indicate numerical values in the computer's memory. The large amount of electrical energy required to power such a system generated excessive heat. Special air conditioning was developed to keep these systems from overheating and, consequently, from shutting down. (When a computer shuts down, information is lost and the system must be started or "booted" up again.)

The next machine, the EDVAC (Electronic Discrete Variable Computer), was smaller and more powerful than its predecessors, the Mark I and the ENIAC, and had two additional features: use of binary numbers and internal storage of instructions as electronic states. These two features were the

The IBM Model 701 computer.

forerunners of modern computer technology; today, all data and program storage are binary. EDVAC's internal storage allowed programs to be stored in the computer's internal memory devices and to be run based on the program's instructions. This means of storage was much faster than paper-tape storage used in earlier devices, such as the Mark I.

Another application of internal storage was the EDSAC (Electronic Delayed Storage Automatic Computer), built at Cambridge University in England. Its main feature was the concept of the **stored program**. Before EDSAC, when a company wanted to process inventory instead of payroll on the computer, the computer had to be shut down and rewired with different programs. But with EDSAC and the development of plug-in boards, programs could be changed more easily. Stored programs enhanced the practicality of computers in businesses. Also, the cost was reduced as handling programs became more efficient.

In the early 1940s, computers were built primarily for military projects to aid the war effort and funded by the federal government. In 1946, the Eckert-Mauchly Computer Corporation, later known as the UNIVAC division of Remington Rand, began building computers for commercial use. Eckert and Mauchly designed their computers to perform commercial data processing in private industry. Their introduction of UNIVAC into the business field in 1951 triggered the growth of the computer industry in the private sector.

Soon to follow was IBM Corporation, which entered the field with the IBM 701 in 1953, followed by the IBM 650 in 1954. Both were business-oriented computers. The IBM 650 became the most widely used computer between 1954 and 1959. As a result of this system's popularity, IBM became a trend-setter in the computer industry.

Not only was developing and building computer systems expensive, but maintaining them was costly to the organizations that used them. Until a few years ago, most organizations leased computer systems, which had to be maintained by company-trained technicians.

To summarize, the first generation of computers was characterized by the use of vacuum tubes. These computers were large, expensive to operate, and often difficult to maintain. Nevertheless, they initiated the Computer Age.

The Second Generation

The second generation of computers (from approximately 1959 to 1963) was made possible by the development of **transistors**. Transistors were developed in 1947 by John Bardeen and others at the Bell Laboratories in New Jersey and soon replaced vacuum tubes. Transistors were instantly

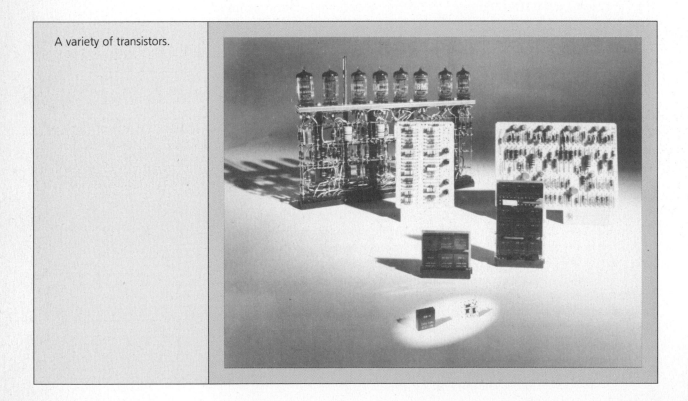

A variety of transistors.

successful, primarily because of the advantages of using them instead of vacuum tubes.

Although vacuum tubes were far superior to anything previously used, such as mechanical relays in the Mark I, they still presented many problems. They were much larger than transistors, and a great many were needed, which resulted in very large computers. With the advent of transistors, the age of miniaturization had begun. The transistor (a semiconductor) was originally called a transfer resistor, shortened to transistor. One transistor replaced one vacuum tube in much less space—two hundred transistors could fit into the same amount of space required for one vacuum tube. With the second generation, computers became solid-state (which means that electrical impulses travel through the solid part of a semiconductor, in this case a transistor, rather than through the void space in a vacuum tube).

The development of transistors produced scientific- and business-oriented computers that were smaller, more energy efficient, more powerful, and more reliable than those of the first generation. Second-generation computers could operate with programming languages that made communication between user and computer easier. Punched cards (cards with punched holes to represent data) could be read at a reasonably fast speed, allowing high-quality reports to be produced.

With these innovations, computers became physically smaller. Power

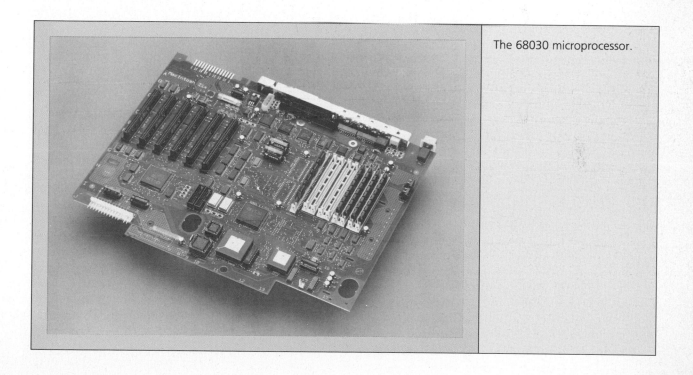

The 68030 microprocessor.

requirements were reduced also since transistors require much less energy to run than do vacuum tubes. As a result, transistors were manufactured in large quantities in response to increasing demand, and by 1958, the second generation of computers was rushing forward.

However, transistors presented several problems. They were expensive: Each transistor and its related parts had to be inserted individually into holes in a plastic board. Also, wires had to be fastened by floating the board in a pool of molten solder. Although this was done automatically, a large number of parts was required for even simple computations. Another problem was that the distance between individual transistors, although physically small, was still large enough to limit the speed of computer operations.

The Third Generation

When the **integrated circuit** was developed in 1963, a new generation of computer systems was born. Integrated circuitry means that many tiny transistors were put together on a very small piece of silicon. This small piece resembles a thin wafer and is called a **chip**.

The computer systems that developed as a result of integrated circuits were faster and could store more data than could second-generation computers. In addition, peripherals became more widely used. These included magnetic tape drives and disk drives. Programming languages that were developed in the second generation were used more widely; some are still used today on large computer systems. (For a discussion of programming languages, see Chapter 3.) Another distinguishing feature was that multiple users could access the same computer at approximately the same time.

Actually, time was shared by users, hence the term **time sharing**, which is the cooperative use of a computer system by multiple users. The computer is available to users one by one, but the time that lapses between contacts is so small that a person entering data is unaware of the gap. With the advent of time sharing, computers were installed in businesses where it was necessary for many users to access the system.

Third-generation computers represented another step forward in the handling, manipulation, and storage of data (all of which is called **data processing**). Not only were speed and reliability increased, but power consumption was decreased. Computers were now being used worldwide in business, government, and science. While some computers were being developed in smaller packages that made them accessible to more users, other computers were growing larger to handle greater burdens of arithmetical operations, increased data storage, and faster speeds. During these developments, a new generation of computer was germinating. Work begun in 1966 led to the fourth generation of computers characterized by large-scale integrated circuits.

Table 2.2   *Developments in Computer Technology*

1944	*1946*	*1949*
Howard Aiken (Harvard University) Mark I Automatic digital computer	John Mauchly and J. Presper Eckert, Jr. (University of Pennsylvania) ENIAC First actual electronic computer	EDVAC (University of Pennsylvania) EDSAC (Cambridge, England) First truly electronic computers with internally stored programs

1946–1959	*1959–1963*
First-generation computers: Vacuum tubes Magnetic core memory UNIVAC I, II IAS First commercially available stored-program computer IBM 701, 704 IBM 650	Second-generation computers: Discrete transistors IBM 1620, 1401 CDC 3600 IBM 7090–7094 LARC Stretch Honeywell 800 RCA 3301, 501 Development of PLATO

1963–1975	*1975–early 1980s*
Third-generation computers: Integrated-circuit (IC) chips IBM 360, first family of computers UNIVAC 1108, 1110 CDC 6000, 7000 DEC PDP-10 Development of TICCIT Founding of MECC Seymour Papert develops Logo	Fourth-generation computers: Very-large-scale integration (VLSI) IBM 3081 CRAY 1 CDC CYBER 176, 205 Micro-PLATO Jobs and Wozniak introduce Apple Computers IBM-PC

1980s–
IBM-PC XT and AT Fifth-generation computers: Thinking machines Artificial intelligence

The Fourth Generation

Engineers were not satisfied with the degree of miniaturization that resulted from the integrated circuit. In addition, they were dissatisfied with chips of the third generation that could perform only one function. (For example, these chips might perform calculations or amplify weak currents in a television or radio.) But as chips were manufactured more readily, engineers tried grouping an assortment of functions on a single chip, thus creating a microelectronic system that could perform a complete job. With these **large-scale integrated circuits (LSI)**, the fourth generation of computers was born, in the late 1960s.

One of the first LSIs to reach the market was the calculator-on-a-chip. The chip consisted of a single block containing 6,000 transistors capable of adding, subtracting, multiplying, and dividing. Thus, the pocket calculator was born.

Another device employing the LSI chip was the digital watch. It contained several thousand transistors on a single chip. Still another creation resulting from the chip was the video games that are now so popular.

Not far behind was the computer-on-a-chip. Manufacturers created a masterpiece of miniaturization by compressing nearly all the subsystems of a computer into one-twentieth of a square inch. Over 15,000 transistors were combined to form a tiny device that could store, process, and retrieve data with a capacity rivaling room-sized computers of a decade earlier.

The large-scale integrated circuit resulted in lower prices of electronic devices. Digital watches, originally introduced at $2,000, are now available for less than $10. Prices of pocket calculators started at $300 but have now dropped to less than $5. Citizens'-band radios using LSI chips originally sold for $250, but are now around $50.

As we've seen, at one time cost hindered the fast growth of computer sales. Now this is changing. Let's look at the change of cost per calculation during the computer revolution.

The first generation of vacuum tube computers cost an estimated $1.25 per 100,000 computations. The second generation, using transistors, could perform the same 100,000 calculations at a cost of 25 cents. In the third generation, with the introduction of integrated circuits, the cost dropped as low as 10 cents for 100,000 computations. Today, with very-large-scale integrated circuits, the cost for the same 100,000 calculations is less than 1 cent.

Indeed, as computer capabilities have increased, costs have decreased. The average computer hobbyist, small-business owner, school district, or other organization can now look to computers as a viable means of handling the ever-increasing flow of paper work.

After being on the computer scene for 100 years, punched cards were phased out. Terminals replaced keypunch machines as the most common device for inputting data. The terminal was constructed with a keyboard and a **cathode ray tube (CRT)**, which displays input data on a screen. The

Digital watches that include calculators are now available in all price ranges and styles.

Table 2.3 The Computer Revolution

First Generation	Vacuum Tubes	$1.25
1946–1959	40,000 additions per second	100,000
Second Generation	Transistors	$0.25
1959–1963	200,000 additions per second	100,000
Third Generation	Integrated Circuits	$0.10
1964–1977	1,250,000 additions per second	100,000
Fourth Generation	Large-Scale Integration (LSI)	$0.01
1978–1983	Up to a billion computations per second	100,000
Fifth Generation	Very Large-Scale Integration (VSLI)	?
1984–	Computations in nanoseconds (billionths of a second)	100,000

terminal, keyboard, and CRT are referred to as an interactive system, also called a visual or video display unit.

The LSI chip also created another breakthrough that was unexpected: the development of the desktop computer. These machines changed the face of data processing. No longer was it necessary to monopolize a large computer with jobs that could be handled just as easily, or even more easily, by a smaller computer. These small computers, called microcomputers, now perform many tasks for education, business, and industry personnel.

Increasing sales of these smaller systems encouraged manufacturers to develop their electronics further. This, in turn, resulted in lower prices to consumers. Originally priced at $20,000, soon these computers could be purchased for a few thousand dollars. Lower prices of LSI chips resulted in even more experimentation and the addition of new features, spawning today's microcomputer revolution.

More people, including young children, are now using computers. In many cases, the big, mysterious machine once residing only in a computer room has now become the small, friendly computer that sits on a desk, ready to perform the work it is given.

The need has continued for large mainframes, or **supercomputers**, to handle intricate problems involving large databases. The outstanding supercomputers of the early 1980s were the Cray-1 built by Cray Research and CYBER 205 built by Control Data Corporation.

The price of these supercomputers ranged from $10 million to $15 million, but even at these prices the price per calculation was dramatically lower than that of comparable systems that were available in 1950. These supercomputers successfully addressed many problems of earlier computers, including that of speed. Speed was increased by putting several hundred thousand transistors on a single chip, decreasing the actual size of the circuits. However, heat remained a continuing problem: The Cray-1 and CYBER 205 were virtual refrigerators, with coolant circulating near the central processing unit of the computer.

COMPUTERS IN EDUCATION

Early in the development of computer technology, the many advantages of computer use in education were recognized. As early as 1959, Donald Bitzer led a group of educators, computer specialists, and psychologists at the University of Illinois in developing a powerful computer system for educational applications. Still in use today—particularly in universities—this system is known as PLATO. **PLATO** is based on the mainframe, since microcomputers were nonexistent when Bitzer and his team began their project.

PLATO uses a special authoring language called TUTOR. An **authoring language** is a code of commands that enables a nonexpert user to write special programs. Many classroom teachers use authoring languages to write or customize software for their students. Bitzer's team produced approximately 200 lessons that demonstrated PLATO's effectiveness in the classroom.

The hardware of the PLATO system includes a terminal that was designed especially for classroom applications. The terminal has a plasma panel display as well as a microfiche projector, touch panel, and keyboard for entering data. The plasma panel display makes it possible to display very sophisticated graphics to enhance the lessons presented through PLATO. The transparent screen enabled users to display slides. Because of its unique design and sophistication, PLATO was extremely costly to produce. For this reason, it took some time to gain wide popularity in school settings.

In the 1960s, Control Data Corporation purchased the rights to sell PLATO. Soon after this, they installed a number of PLATO systems in the United States and abroad. They also poured resources into further development of PLATO. Since all PLATO systems use compatible courseware, PLATO users can share a variety of programs and information. PLATO also uses telecommunications so that users can send messages to each other in seconds—across the country or around the world.

In 1977, the Micro-PLATO system was introduced, reflecting the trend of educators toward smaller computer systems. Micro-PLATO enables microcomputer users to exchange courseware and other information without going through a host computer. Today there are more than 1,000 Micro-PLATO terminals in 200 installations and many more than the original 200 lessons written for use with PLATO. PLATO software is also available for many other computers commonly found in school installations.

Another significant development in educational computing occurred in 1964 when the CAI Laboratory was created at Pennsylvania State Uni-

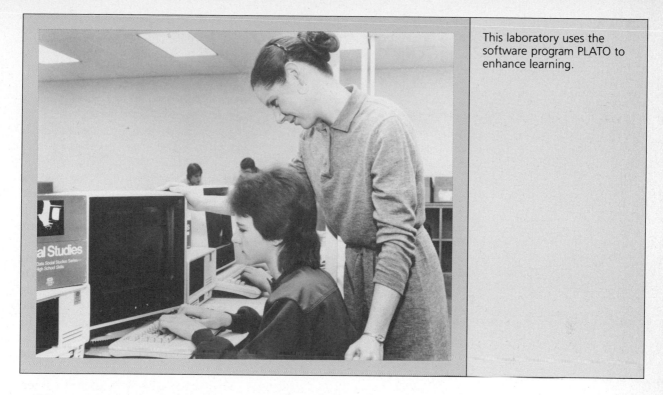

This laboratory uses the software program PLATO to enhance learning.

versity. The lab was directed by Harold E. Mitzel. Three years later in 1967, an IBM 1500 Instructional System was installed in the lab. The system, used in conjunction with an authoring language called Coursewriter, had one important drawback: Student terminals had to be located near the host computer. This problem was solved by equipping vans with complete systems that could be moved around the state and eventually around the country.

In 1969 at the University of California at Irvine, Al Bork began creating CAI software to be used in teaching physics. Bork believed that innovative programming techniques including graphics and simulation would make CAI software more effective. His software has been well received, and Bork continues to be a respected CAI developer. His courseware is in use in many schools.

During this same period, educators saw the need to consider how computers might best be used in education. One pioneer in educational technology, Seymour **Papert** of the Massachusetts Institute of Technology, developed an educational tool in the 1970s that allows students to interact with computers in a nonthreatening manner. Using a simple programming language called **Logo**, the student instructs a computer-drawn figure to move about on a video screen. The figure—called a "turtle"—leaves a visible trace of its path, allowing the student to draw pictures on the screen. Other commands in Logo enable the student to change the color of drawings, set them in motion, or copy them.

In his book *Mindstorms,* Papert asserts that Logo is "more than fun. Very powerful kinds of learning are taking place. Children working with an electronic sketchpad are learning a language for talking about shapes and fluxes of shapes, about velocities and rates of change, about processes and procedures. They are learning to speak mathematics, and acquiring a new image of themselves as mathematicians." Logo has been used successfully by children as young as three years of age.

TICCIT (Time-shared, Interactive, Computer-Controlled Information Television) was developed in 1971 under the direction of C. Victor Bunderson. This minicomputer-based system was intended originally for teaching mathematics and English courses to college freshmen. It has since been used with younger students and deaf students, and for enhancing basic skills among military personnel. A special version for microcomputers, Micro-TICCIT, is also available. Like PLATO, TICCIT uses an authoring system so that users can create their own software. It also includes color television and sophisticated graphics. TICCIT is distinguished from earlier systems by two basic principles. First, TICCIT attempts to present concepts and to teach the use of rules rather than presenting drill-and-practice activities. Second, it is designed to give the learner control over the lesson. Students decide when they wish to proceed, review, test, and so on.

Students find Logo challenging.

In 1972, a group calling themselves the Minnesota Educational Computing Consortium (MECC) joined forces to try to improve the use of computers in education throughout Minnesota. Their influence has grown beyond state bounds, and MECC is now a leader in educational computing across the country. MECC operated a vast time-sharing system and made it available to virtually all students in Minnesota schools. With the advent of microcomputers in the classroom, MECC began to develop software with a reputation for excellence and reasonable cost. In fact, MECC makes its software available free of charge to Minnesota educators; to those outside the state, the software is available at extremely low cost.

Another group dedicated to improving the use of computers in education is WICAT (the World Institute for Computer-Assisted Teaching). Formed in 1977 under the leadership of Dustin H. Heuston, WICAT was created to develop high-quality software for teaching basic skills such as reading and mathematics. It is also a leader in developing the theory of educational computing and has contributed to our knowledge of how computers can best help students to learn.

In the early generations of large and expensive computers, most schools could not afford to install computer systems. When they did, they usually purchased mainframe systems to which terminals could be connected through

Microcomputers in the classroom became a reality in the early 1980s.

cables. Generally, only secondary and university students had access to these systems and usually only for the purpose of learning computer programming. But the picture changed dramatically with the introduction of microcomputers into the classroom in the late 1970s and early 1980s.

Thanks to two computer wizards, Steve Jobs and Steve Wozniak, microcomputers are now commonplace in elementary and secondary schools. Pooling their limited resources and working in a garage, Jobs and Wozniak developed the Apple computer, which proved to be ideally suited to the educational environment. The Apple was an overnight success, bringing Jobs and Wozniak fame and wealth. It also began the race to produce high-quality software and peripherals for classroom use. As the educational market grew, other computer manufacturers such as IBM, Commodore, Radio Shack, and Atari recognized the potential of classroom computers. Some companies even donated computer equipment to schools to encourage the use of high technology in schools. Today CAI software is available for many brands of computers including IBM, Apple, Atari, Commodore, and Radio Shack.

Given the many improvements in hardware and software for education and the decreases in costs of computers, almost every school system in the United States can take advantage of computer power. Students at all grade levels and with all levels of ability and disability are learning to use computers. In some schools computer literacy courses are now required for graduation. Teacher surveys indicate that most teachers either use computers or express an interest in using them to improve their effectiveness as educators. Although it is a relatively new teaching tool, the computer promises to change forever the nature of teaching and of learning.

SUMMARY

By the 1940s, technological advances gave birth to the modern computer age. The work of such people as Mauchly, Eckert, and Von Neumann triggered research and development resulting in the first true computer systems. Using their discoveries and successes as a starting point, the industrialized countries of the world began successful computer development.

From this point on, the world of computers would never be the same. The first generation of computers had almost died out. The next generation produced machines that were easier to operate. Speedy processing suddenly became a goal, but computers were still large and temperamental, and produced excessive heat.

Even though Von Neumann provided crucial ideas, the process was just beginning to be refined. The acceleration of new technologies would quickly produce several generations of computers, including the introduction of transistors, integrated circuits, and microprocessors.

Computer development has come a long way in a short span of time. The major computers of the 1940s and 1950s have evolved from vacuum tubes to integrated circuits and then on to large-scale integrated circuits and very large-scale integrated circuits. Their speed has been enhanced and their cost greatly lowered. Performance has become so reliable that there are few major problems, and separate systems are no longer needed to handle different applications. Indeed, computers have become general-purpose machines for use in science, education, and business.

Educational computing began with the development of PLATO in 1959. PLATO is a specially designed mainframe-based computer system that uses the authoring language TUTOR to allow users to create their own PLATO lessons. A microcomputer version, Micro-PLATO, is in wide use today. Another educational system, TICCIT, was developed in 1971. Using color television and graphics, TICCIT seeks to present concepts and teach the use of rules rather than concentrate on drill-and-practice.

Many groups have formed to develop theory and materials for teaching with computers. Two such groups are the Minnesota Educational Computing Consortium (founded in 1972) and the World Institute for Computer-Assisted Teaching (founded in 1977). Both contributed toward the distribution of exemplary CAI software.

Educational computing followed the trend of using smaller and smaller computers. From early systems based on mainframe and minicomputers, microcomputer systems have developed and enjoyed much wider popularity because they are more affordable and easier to use. Seymour Papert, a pioneer in educational technology, proved that the youngest of students can gain valuable learning experiences from computers. He developed Logo, which is still used widely to introduce students to computers. The Apple microcomputer, designed by Jobs and Wozniak in the late 1970s, established educational computing as a viable market. Other computer manufacturers, such as IBM, Atari, Commodore, and Radio Shack, recognized the new market and began to tailor some of their products to classroom applications.

Today it is unusual to find a school district in the United States that does not make extensive use of computer power. Computers are available to students at all grade levels, and surveys indicate that in-service and preservice teachers are eager to make use of the microcomputer as a powerful teaching tool.

REVIEW EXERCISES

Multiple Choice

1. The machine that first made IBM a recognized leader in computer technology was the
   a. Mark I
   b. ENIAC
   c. UNIVAC
   d. EDVAC

2. The concept of stored-program instructions was developed by
   a. Steve Wozniak

b. Donald Bitzer
c. John Von Neumann
d. Seymour Papert

3. The development of computers has been divided into
   a. generations
   b. years
   c. companies
   d. skills

4. The first generation of computers began with the use of
   a. vacuum tubes
   b. electromechanical springs and gears
   c. electrical currents
   d. wires and switches

5. The concept of grouping an assortment of functions on a single chip is called
   a. an integrated circuit
   b. an electronic chip
   c. large-scale integration
   d. large-sized integrated circuits

6. The microcomputer was introduced during which generation?
   a. second
   b. third
   c. fourth
   d. fifth

7. A code of commands designed to help nonexpert computer users write their own programs is
   a. BASIC
   b. an authoring language
   c. yet to be developed
   d. CAI software

8. The PLATO system was originally created for use with
   a. a mainframe computer
   b. a minicomputer
   c. a microcomputer
   d. an Apple microcomputer

9. In 1972 a group called _____ formed to improve computer-assisted teaching in Minnesota.
   a. WICAT
   b. MS-DOS
   c. MECC
   d. TICCIT

10. The Apple microcomputer was designed in the late 1970s by
    a. John Von Neumann
    b. Steve Jobs and Steve Wozniak

c. Dustin H. Heuston
d. Harold E. Mitzel

True/False

1. Binary arithmetic uses the numbers 1 and 2.
2. The EDVAC is considered the first true computer rather than merely a calculator because it stores instructions.
3. The ENIAC was capable of adding up to 500 numbers per second.
4. Vacuum tubes create problems for designers because they generate excessive amounts of heat.
5. It took 6,000 transistors to create the calculator-on-a-chip.
6. Computers have become less expensive to operate over the years.
7. Because it was too expensive to build, the PLATO system was never installed in an educational setting.
8. Seymour Papert designed the TICCIT system to introduce young children to computers.
9. MECC offers high-quality CAI software at little or no cost to educators.
10. Today most schools are still resistant to installing computer systems.

Short Answer

1. List the approximate inclusive dates of the generations of computers.
2. What problems did first-generation computers present?
3. Describe the characteristics of third-generation computers.
4. What distinguished the TICCIT system from its predecessors?
5. According to teacher surveys, how do most teachers feel about computers in the classroom?

Activities

1. Prepare a report describing in detail one of the following machines: ENIAC, EDVAC, Mark I, Apple.
2. Invite a representative from a computer company such as IBM, Apple, Tandy-Radio Shack, Control Data, or Honeywell-Bull to speak to your class about the history of their computers.

3. Research the contributions of key women to the development of computers.
4. Locate a nearby PLATO installation, perhaps at your university, and arrange for a demonstration of the system.
5. Conduct an anonymous survey of your class members or other colleagues to discover their attitudes about computer-assisted teaching.

BIBLIOGRAPHY

Bitter, Gary G. *Exploring with Computers*. New York: Julian Messner, 1981 (rev. 1983).

Bitter, Gary G. "Hardware: Portable Computers, Software." *Computers in the Schools* 1 (no. 2, Spring 1984): 19–29.

"Chips for the Making." *Popular Computing* 1 (no. 3, January 1982): 54–57.

Evans, Christopher. *The Micro Millennium*. New York: Viking, 1979.

Gardner, W. David. "The Independent Inventor." *Datamation* 28 (no. 10, September 1982): 12–22.

Hungate, Harriet. "Microcomputers in the Early Childhood Classroom." *The Computing Teacher* 10 (no. 2, September 1983): 9–10.

Killmon, Peg, and Joseph Aseao. "Computer Design Today: Processor Technology." *Computer Design* 21 (no. 12, December 1982): 101–126.

Merrill, Paul F., et al. *Computers in Education*. Englewood Cliffs, N.J.: Prentice-Hall, 1986.

Metropolis, E., et al. *A History of Computers in the Twentieth Century*. New York: Academic Press, 1981.

Moursund, Dave. "Looking Forward and Backward." *The Computing Teacher* 15 (no. 9): 4.

Papert, Seymour. *Mindstorms*. New York: Basic Books, 1980.

Poroit, James, and David Groves. *Computers and Mathematics*. Manchaca, Tex.: Sterling Swift, 1979.

Sassi, Anthony, and Richard Alan Smith. "Bridging the Gap Between Elementary and Middle School." *The Computing Teacher* 15 (no. 3): 45.

Stern, Nancy. *From ENIAC to UNIVAC*. Bedford, Mass.: Digital Press, 1981.

"Super Computers." *Scientific American* 246 (no. 1, January 1982): 118–135.

REVIEW ANSWER KEY

Multiple Choice

1. a	5. a	9. c
2. c	6. c	10. b
3. a	7. b	
4. a	8. a	

True/False

1. F	5. T	9. T
2. T	6. T	10. F
3. F	7. F	
4. T	8. F	

Short Answer

1. First: 1946–1959; Second: 1959–1963; Third: 1963–1975; Fourth: 1975–early 1980s.
2. Costly breakdowns, overheating, and slow operating speed.
3. IC chips, fast calculation speeds, low cost per computation, and mass storage devices.
4. Presented concepts and taught rule usage rather than relying on drill-and-practice; promoted learner control of lesson presentation.
5. Most are either currently using computers in the classroom or are interested in doing so.

CHAPTER 3

THE MICROCOMPUTER SYSTEM: HARDWARE AND SOFTWARE

Objectives

- Describe input, process, and output
- Explain the use of secondary storage and the types of secondary storage available
- List three types of computer output
- List three methods of computer input
- List the advantages of using various programming languages

Key Terms

arithmetic/logic unit
CPU (central processing unit)
COM (computer output microfilm)
control unit
data entry
disk
dot matrix printing
flowchart
formed character printing
hardware
impact and nonimpact printing
MICR (magnetic ink character recognition)
microfilm
OCR (optical character recognition)
output
pseudocode
random access
semiconductor memory
software
structured design
system software
tool software
top-down design

Several basic components compose a microcomputer system. The physical machinery—called **hardware**—includes input units, processing and storage units, and output units. As their names imply, these devices allow computer users to enter data into the computer, enable the computer to process and store the data, and provide a means for the computer to return the processed data to the user. In this section, we examine the various devices that make up each of these categories.

DATA ENTRY (INPUT) UNITS

Display terminals come in many styles and with varying capabilities.

"The computer has made an error" may be an easy response to a teacher who is complaining about a schedule error; however, a statement such as this ignores an important characteristic of computers. Computers are machines that do only what they are instructed to do and process only the data given them by the humans who operate them. The importance of a properly written program and accurate input into any computer system cannot be overemphasized. Keep this important fact in mind as you read this chapter and, indeed, whenever you participate in a discussion of computers.

The first step in the use of any computer is **data entry** (input). At this point, data is translated from a form in which it can be understood by humans into a form in which it can be understood by machines. The data can be program instructions, such as a word processor, or it can be information the user has created, such as the text of an essay.

A person usually enters data into the computer from a keyboard similar to that of a typewriter. It includes the alphabet, numerals, and a variety of special characters, such as the percent sign and the quotation mark. Usually it includes other keys as well, which are used to communicate with the computer. The keyboard may also include a numeric pad like that of a calculator for efficient entry of numerical data.

Data entry requires a display device that allows the user to see what is being entered. The most popular of these display devices is the monitor, which is a screen similar to a television's, on which data appears as it is typed. Monitor displays range from simple models that display alphanumeric data (letters, numbers, and symbols) to more sophisticated models that can display more complex graphics and pictures. Monitors are either monochrome (one color only) or color.

Computer terminals are also input devices. They employ a keyboard and monitor to enter data. Once entered, data can be transmitted directly to the processor or to a disk or tape.

Some data entry devices can read data directly from a source document. Optical scanning devices are used for **optical character recognition (OCR),** that is, for sensing readable marks, characters, or bar codes. The OCR device simply passes over marks and senses the data. These sensations may

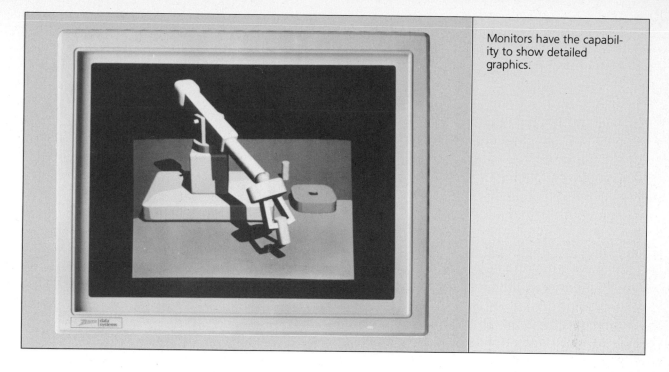

Monitors have the capability to show detailed graphics.

then be read by a processor. Another system for machine-readable data is called **magnetic ink character recognition (MICR).** MICR devices, widely used in the banking industry, sense markings written in magnetic ink. (MICR devices are used in banks, for example, to read account numbers from checks.)

Some users need alternate methods of inputting information into the computer. This is especially true for the physically handicapped and young children who have not yet learned to type. In fact, as more and more software became available for very young computer users, the need for easy-to-use input devices became more critical. The joystick was one of the first user friendly input devices. It looks something like a gear shift and permits the user to move the cursor on the screen to draw figures, play games, and select options from a menu.

The light pen is another device that requires no typing. When touched to the monitor screen, the light pen causes points on the screen to light up. Engineers may use light pens to design new products, for example. It can also be used in the classroom for a variety of purposes since students do not need typing skills to use a light pen.

Many home and school microcomputer systems are able to use a "mouse" for inputting data. The mouse is a small box that the user rolls over a flat

Light pens allow the user to communicate with the computer.

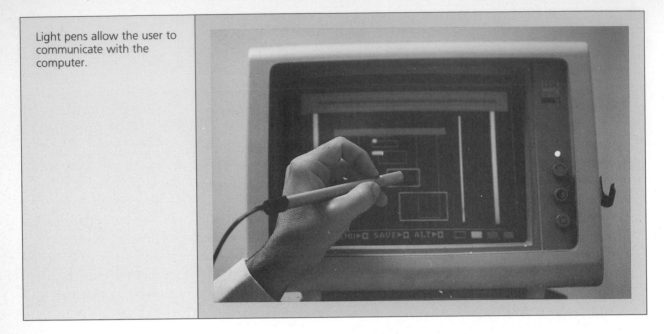

The mouse is a popular way of providing input to the computer.

surface. As the mouse rolls, the cursor moves on the screen. When the cursor is positioned at a particular command, the user presses a button to choose that command and send the information to the computer. The mouse can also draw figures with graphics programs that are designed to accept its commands and data.

Touch screens help people who cannot type or even read to use the computer. Touch screens are designed to respond to the touch of a finger: The user simply touches the screen to select a command, which is then sent automatically to the computer to be carried out. With devices such as these, almost anyone can use a computer.

Increasingly sophisticated data entry allows us to present data to the computer in more complex and efficient ways. Some optical sensing devices can read items as nonstandard as medical X-rays. Others can actually interpret voice commands and enter corresponding data directly into a processor. Exactly how these devices work is beyond the scope of this book, but the point must be made that there is a constant effort to expand the capabilities of input devices to increase their convenience and speed and to allow the entry of increasingly complex and varied data.

Data can also be entered into a computer from a disk, which can store programs as well as data. Data from a disk can be entered ("loaded") into the computer's main memory, from which the user can then access it. The disk is the most popular way of entering commercial software into the microcomputer.

PROCESSING AND STORAGE UNITS

Now that data has been fed into the computer, the processing unit receives it, stores it, and performs all necessary functions to manipulate and prepare it for the user. The processing unit is made up of two parts: the **central processing unit (CPU)** and main computer storage, or memory. Within the CPU are the *control unit* and the *arithmetic/logic unit,* both of which consist of electronic circuitry.

Just as a teacher manages classroom activities, the **control unit** synchronizes and regulates the operations of all parts of the computer system, including input-output devices, the arithmetic/logic unit, and the movement of data to or from main memory.

The **arithmetic/logic unit (ALU)** receives data and instructions from the control unit, performs necessary operations, and then returns results to the control unit. The ALU performs calculations with numbers, such as addition and multiplication, and logical operations with data, numerical or otherwise. The computer's logical ability is often considered its most valuable asset.

The processing of data within the computer occurs as follows:

Action	*Unit Involved*
1. OBTAIN data and programs from main memory	Control unit
2. PROCESS data according to program instructions	Arithmetic logic unit
3. STORE processed data	Main memory

Although this process may seem lengthy, the fastest computers now available can perform millions of these operations each second.

Main Memory

Main memory stores all the instructions (programs) necessary to process data. In addition, it stores all data during processing.

Most systems today use **semiconductor memory** devices within the main memory. Semiconductor memory uses integrated-circuit devices that retain and represent data in a manner based on the presence or absence of electrical current. Although semiconductor memory offers increased access speeds and decreased costs and storage size, most have one major disadvantage: If electrical current is removed, stored data is lost. To minimize this danger, backup power systems are being designed into computers with semiconductor memory.

Secondary Memory

To understand the need for secondary, or auxiliary, storage, let's examine a particular classroom situation. Think of a student writing an essay with a word processor. Initially, the student inputs (keys) the data into the computer and receives a rough draft as output. The student then submits the essay to the teacher for comments. But what about subsequent drafts? Since main memory is not designed to save data (the essay) while performing its other functions, the data is lost. However, the student doesn't want to retype the entire essay each time it's revised. To avoid such repetition, secondary memory was developed. Secondary memory media store data for future access and processing by the user and the computer. When the student is ready to revise the essay, it is easily accessed and edited.

The most common data storage medium is the **disk,** of which there are two types: floppy disks (diskettes) and hard (fixed) disks. A floppy is a flexible Mylar disk, coated with a substance that allows electronic storage of data. It looks a lot like a phonograph record and, like a phonograph record, is stored in a jacket until needed, when it is inserted into a floppy disk drive for use. A hard disk is usually installed inside the computer and consists of a stack of disks. Because of increased storage space, a hard disk holds much more data than a single floppy. Most education software is stored on either type of disk.

The method of file organization on disk is called **random** (or direct) **access.** Each file is identified by its file name, which allows the computer to locate and directly access it from among the many files stored on each disk.

OUTPUT UNITS

Without a means to receive processed information, the computer would be of little use. The user must be able to receive processed data in some comprehensible form. **Output** is processed data sent from the main memory of a computer's processor unit to a receiving device that allows it to be translated into an understandable, useful form. For many years, the printed document was the major form of output, but today a greater variety of output forms exists. Many of the input units discussed earlier in this chapter serve equally well as output devices.

Monitors

The monitor is one such dual-purpose device. In addition to serving as an input device, it can conveniently display processed data as well. For example, an automobile manufacturer may have a graphic display terminal that

Expansion cards increase the capabilities of the microcomputer.

This diagram shows the steps that data entered into a computer go through in processing.

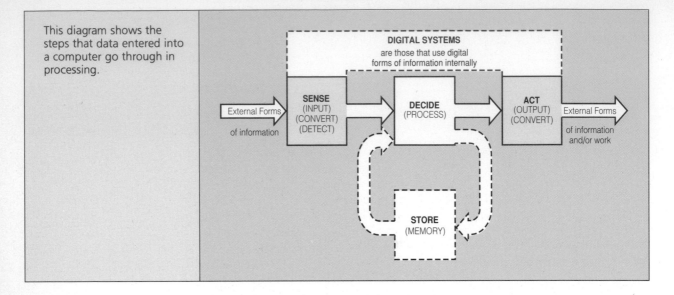

allows engineers to enter data for a new car design. The computer can process the data and then display a picture of the design on the monitor. Users don't have to wait for a printout to view the outcome of their actions. In addition, changes can be made instantly, so that users can quickly glance at the different outcomes that result. These features are useful for spreadsheets, art designs, page arrangements, and many other tasks.

Printers   While a monitor may provide quick access to output, in many instances a permanent form of output is desirable. Printers are the most widely used devices that meet this need. Most types of printers are not part of the data entry system, but are separate units that receive print instructions from the computer's processor unit. The wide variety of printers today meets the many and varied demands of computer users. The point-of-sale (POS) system in the grocery store, for example, requires a printer to simply record prices on a cash register tape—the printing need not be fancy, only legible. In contrast, the school literary magazine requires a higher quality of printing that closely resembles typeset material. This high-quality printing reproduces easily and enhances the appearance of important data.

The two distinguishing features among various types of printers are print speed and print method. Print speed is normally measured in lines per minute and can range from less than thirty lines per minute to more than 3,000. Some printers can print bidirectionally, that is, from both left-to-right and right-to-left, which improves speed. Other factors that affect print speed include the rate at which data is transmitted from the processor unit to the printer and the type of printing method being used.

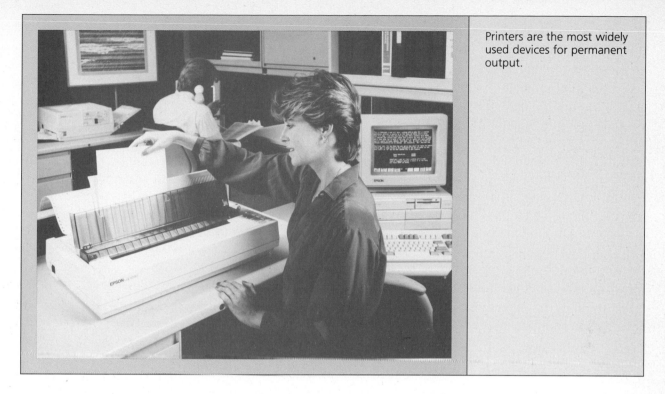

Printers are the most widely used devices for permanent output.

Printing method also affects the quality of the printing. Currently there are two primary methods of printing in use.

1. **Impact printing,** which closely resembles that of a typewriter because characters are formed on paper as a result of the impact of character key and inked ribbon on paper
2. **Nonimpact printing,** which uses thermal, ink-jet, xerography, or laser techniques to form characters on paper

Impact printing uses either formed or dot matrix characters. In **formed character printing,** the actual shapes of the characters are pressed against the paper; **dot matrix printing** creates characters by series of dots from pins pressed against the paper. Dot matrix printers are less expensive, faster, and sometimes more reliable than formed character printers. However, the quality of their print is usually inferior to that of formed character printers.

Nonimpact printers do not rely on the impact of characters or pins on paper. Early methods incorporated electrosensitive and thermosensitive papers, but these proved too expensive, too fragile, and too poor in quality.

Today's more popular nonimpact printers use techniques similar to those of copy machines. Laser technology has been incorporated into some of these. Because they can print over 20,000 lines per minute, nonimpact printers have been developed to meet high-volume printing needs. The quality is good but they are expensive; therefore, they are found primarily in installations that require large amounts of data to be printed.

Special printing devices include those that can print unusual or large-sized characters and plotters that can prepare complex illustrations such as geographical maps.

Ink-Jet Printers Ink-jet printers, which form characters by spraying ink onto paper, are much quieter and faster (as much as ten times) than impact printers. Ink is forced through nozzles that may produce up to 117,000 droplets per second. The ink travels toward the paper at 40 miles per hour!

Laser Printers Laser printing is a hybrid of xerographic technology and television. The process involves assembling all characters on a line together and then printing them simultaneously. The laser beam forms an electrostatic television image on the paper. As the paper passes through the printer, the toner particles are attracted to the regions where the laser has not struck. The paper then passes between a pair of hot rollers that press and bake the toner image onto its surface. Laser printing is of excellent quality.

Microfilm In many schools and classrooms, paperwork becomes an enormous problem. Paper reports are expensive to produce, time consuming to generate, and cumbersome to store. **Microfilm** was developed to resolve these problems. Microfilm is a film on which documents are photographed in miniaturized form—up to forty-eight times smaller than the original document. **Computer output microfilm (COM)** systems transfer computer output directly from the processor unit to microfilm. In most of these systems, data is displayed on an internal CRT and is then photographed onto film by a camera. The film is subsequently developed into microfilm or microfiche.

Texts can be typeset from a variety of typefaces.		
	Bookman-Demi	**The quick brown fox jumps over the lazy dog.**
	Bookman-DemiItalic	***The quick brown fox jumps over the lazy dog.***
	Bookman-Light	The quick brown fox jumps over the lazy dog.
	Bookman-LightItalic	*The quick brown fox jumps over the lazy dog.*
	Courier	The quick brown fox jumps over the lazy dog.
	Courier-Bold	**The quick brown fox jumps over the lazy dog.**
	Courier-BoldOblique	***The quick brown fox jumps over the lazy dog.***
	Courier-Oblique	*The quick brown fox jumps over the lazy dog.*

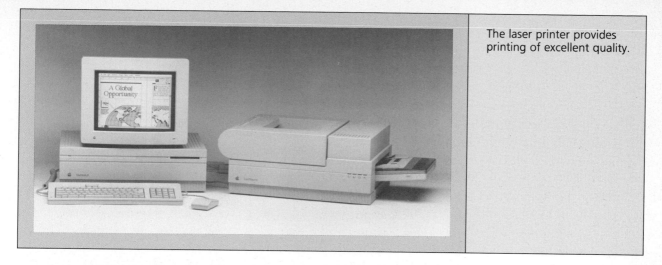

The laser printer provides printing of excellent quality.

Although COM systems seem more complex than systems that generate printed output, they are actually much faster and less expensive than paper printing systems. COM speeds approach 30,000 lines per minute, and COM output may cost an estimated eight times less than traditionally printed reports. Many libraries and media centers have replaced their cumbersome card catalogs with COM systems.

Computers linked directly to a wide variety of machines instruct them to perform work. These machines include computer hardware that places processed data on any of the input devices previously discussed. Also, some computer-controlled devices place data on disks.

Computer Output to Machines

Many assembly-line functions can now be performed by computer-controlled machines. For instance, spot-welding functions in an automobile factory can be accomplished by computer. Within the electronics industry, computer-aided drafting systems create designs in response to computer commands. In telephone networks, systems that create vocal responses are now used. For example, the recording that tells a caller that a particular line is no longer in service may very well be a computer-generated voice.

There are several reasons for using computer-controlled machines—or robots, as they are called. These machines often perform tediously repetitive tasks more cost effectively and consistently than can be done manually. They also undertake work that is physically dangerous or difficult for human workers to perform, such as lifting very heavy objects. In some instances, computers simply perform work *better* than people do, especially where great precision or detail is required.

Robots are very popular in industry.

COMPUTER SOFTWARE

To operate efficiently, computer hardware requires **software**, which consists of sets of instructions (programs) written by people (programmers). However, a computer can *only* do what the program tells it to do—it is incapable of judgment and therefore cannot tell a good program from a poor one. And because it works so quickly, when mistakes occur in a poorly written program they happen almost instantaneously (and may go undetected for a long time).

For a program to run correctly, the programmer must develop a plan that will produce a systematic scheme that solves the problem logically. The importance of the planning stage cannot be overemphasized. Consider the case of building a house. In the blueprint stage, several more electrical outlets in each room and two more doors at the back of the house may be added to the plan at little or no cost. But once the house is completed, those changes cannot be made so easily: Walls must be altered and several workers hired while the expense and inconvenience mount. This situation is analogous to computer programming in which foresight and careful planning pay off. Unnecessary expenses of time, inconvenience, labor, and money result from poor planning.

To help programmers plan and write programs, several techniques have been developed: top-down and structured design, flowcharts, and pseudocode. An experienced programmer usually uses one of these techniques.

Flowcharts (or diagrams) are like road maps. They help us find our way through unfamiliar territory by showing the most direct path. In this case, they guide us through a program's logic. To make this easier, they use certain standardized symbols to represent the different parts and functions of a program. Mapped out this way, programming steps are easy to verify and errors in logic can be readily found.

Top-down design begins with the general statement of a problem and sequentially breaks the statement down into smaller and smaller steps, until a program can be written directly from the flow diagrams generated by this process. In **structured design,** the programmer constructs a program logically into several independent tasks or subtasks. This allows for relatively easy location of errors in logic. Structured design also expedites program maintenance and the revision necessary when computing equipment is changed, or specifications are altered (such as changing from five-digit to nine-digit zip codes).

Pseudocode is another tool that helps the programmer plan a program (see example below). Simply put, **pseudocode** is ordinary language that the programmer uses to write out the steps in a program. Once this is done, the program can then be actually coded in any of a variety of programming languages. (Since ordinary language is not the code used in programming languages, the process is called pseudocode, or false code.)

```
Read student record
Do while not "end of file"
     add grades
     divide to final average
     print record
End do
```

Some programmers prefer flowcharts, others work best with decision logic tables (a listing of all possible conditions within a program along with

Sample flowchart symbols and a sample flowchart used in planning a software program.

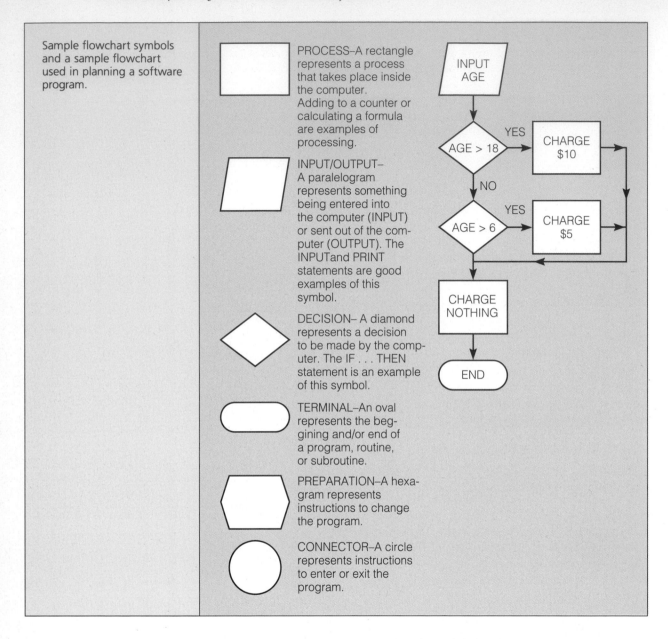

PROCESS–A rectangle represents a process that takes place inside the computer. Adding to a counter or calculating a formula are examples of processing.

INPUT/OUTPUT– A paralelogram represents something being entered into the computer (INPUT) or sent out of the computer (OUTPUT). The INPUT and PRINT statements are good examples of this symbol.

DECISION– A diamond represents a decision to be made by the computer. The IF . . . THEN statement is an example of this symbol.

TERMINAL–An oval represents the beggining and/or end of a program, routine, or subroutine.

PREPARATION–A hexagram represents instructions to change the program.

CONNECTOR–A circle represents instructions to enter or exit the program.

appropriate actions to be taken), and still others write pseudocode. All agree, however, that initial planning is essential to successful programs. Although meticulous planning may seem time consuming to a new programmer eager to begin writing code, it can actually save time and energy in the long run. Careful planning prevents problems from developing when the program is put into use.

Every program must be explained concisely and clearly so that others can read it with ease. Good documentation assures a flow of efficient programs in any setting where computers are used and allows a program written today to be read and understood five years from now. Each programming language has a system for including explanations of program steps.

Although words differ from programming language to programming language, they all have several structures in common. Some of the most important are the following:

START. Each program is begun by a special word or words that initiates the program.

READ. Every program must read input data in some manner. Likewise, every high-level programming language has a definite manner in which records are read.

DECISION. Each language contains words that determine whether conditions are true or false. Based on the theories of Boole and the on/off capabilities of the computer, each language has a particular method for testing conditions.

LOOP. The ability to perform repetitive operations based on some test condition is so important that almost all languages include a special word or words for this structure.

Common Structures in Programming

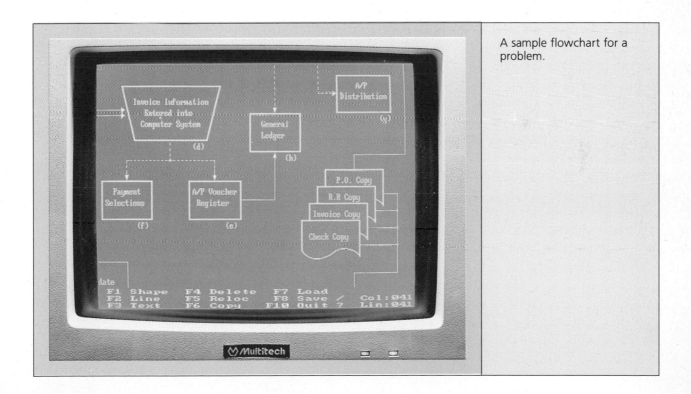

A sample flowchart for a problem.

PROCESS. Arithmetical calculations must be performed in all languages. Consequently, each language has been developed so that arithmetical operations flow smoothly and accurately.

WRITE. Every program that calls for printed output must include steps that direct output to be written to some output device. Each language has the capability of writing records.

END. Every program must end, so programming languages contain a way to tell the computer that the end of the program has arrived and that the computer can stop processing the program.

Types of Software

Broadly speaking, there are two major types of software: system software and applications, or tool, software. **System software** controls common computer functions, such as copying the contents of one disk to another or displaying characters on the screen in a particular format. System software must be in place before the computer can operate. Computer compatibility relies on compatible system software, which is also called the operating system. Two common microcomputer operating systems are MS-DOS and CP/M.

Tool software instructs the computer to do specific jobs such as word processing, graphics, payroll, record keeping, and so on. Tool software includes the five most common applications of computer power, whether in schools, industry, government, or the home: word processing, database management, spreadsheets, graphics, and telecommunications. (Each of these applications is discussed in later chapters.) In addition, there are applications programs that perform very specialized functions, such as CAI software that teaches geography or inventory control software used in retail stores.

Both system and tool software are essential components of the microcomputer system.

SUMMARY

Computers are designed to handle data in the following manner:

$$\text{Input} \longrightarrow \text{Processing} \longrightarrow \text{Output}$$

Accordingly, various types of hardware, or computer equipment, have been designed to handle these functions. Input is usually done by keyboard, disk, terminal, mouse, light pen, or joystick. There are other less commonly used methods of data entry. Processing is done by the central processing unit (CPU) of the computer, made up of the control unit and the ALU. The computer stores data (programs and information) in main memory during processing and in secondary storage (usually floppy or hard disks) for retrieval. Output is often accomplished by the same devices that perform input. Monitors provide quick access to output data, but printers—impact or nonimpact—generate lasting, physical copies. Other machinery can be connected to computers and instructed by them to do work that humans might find difficult, dangerous, or boring.

Computer hardware cannot function without corresponding software, or programs. The process of planning a program, coding it in an appropriate programming language, and producing accurate output is exacting. To ensure accuracy, programmers must pay close attention during planning; they may use several planning aids, such as flowcharts, top-down and structured design, and pseudocode. If the planning is meticulous, the program should be successful.

System software gives instructions to the computer that allow it to operate. These instructions tell the computer how to communicate with a disk drive, disk, peripherals, other software, and the human user. Tool software gives the computer instructions for applications such as word processing, graphics, databases, and spreadsheets.

Hardware and software are the components of a computer system. Good hardware and good software are necessary to fully realize the computer's power.

REVIEW EXERCISES

Multiple Choice

1. The part of the computer that does the processing is called
   a. a CRT
   b. a CPU
   c. an ABC
   d. a disk
2. Disks can be used as
   a. printers
   b. tapes
   c. a storage medium
   d. a processing unit
3. A printer that uses a ribbon similar to a typewriter's is
   a. a nonimpact printer
   b. a CRT
   c. an impact printer
   d. a POS

4. A computer-controlled machine can be called
   a. an OCR
   b. an ALU
   c. a CPU
   d. a robot
5. A CPU contains
   a. the arithmetic/logic unit only
   b. the arithmetic/logic and control units
   c. the control unit only
   d. the printer and tape drive
6. A written narrative that briefly describes the flow of a program is
   a. a flowchart
   b. pseudocode
   c. a decision table
   d. a loop
7. The microcomputer operation system is
   a. system software
   b. hardware
   c. tool software
   d. arithmetic/control

8. The most important stage of programming is
   a. operating
   b. executing
   c. compiling
   d. planning
9. A symbolic plan of a program's flow is
   a. a debugging device
   b. a planning board
   c. a flowchart
   d. an output table
10. The part of a program that provides detailed explanations of the program is called the
    a. accumulation
    b. interpretation
    c. explanation
    d. documentation

True/False

1. The arithmetic/logic unit performs all the calculations in the program.
2. To input means to print data.
3. A terminal is an input device.
4. Optical scanning devices read bar codes.
5. Output may be done by a printer.
6. COM stands for computer-operated memory.
7. READ is the term used to instruct the computer to accept input.
8. Computer programs do not require careful planning.
9. Pseudocode is written in ordinary human language.
10. Computer disks can be hard or floppy.

Short Answer

1. Define computer hardware and identify the three basic categories of hardware.
2. List the types of OCR and MICR marks seen in everyday business situations. On what items do they appear?
3. What are the two basic types of software?
4. What are the two basic printing methods of computers?
5. Discuss the merits of flowcharting a problem before writing the computer code.

Activities

1. List and discuss the advantages and disadvantages of floppy disks and hard disks for storing data.

2. Identify and describe the major units of the computer.
3. Describe the differences among types of printers and discuss their advantages and disadvantages.
4. List and describe different types of input media.
5. If you were purchasing a microcomputer for a classroom teacher, what kind of memory and what kind of printer would you select? Why?
6. List and describe several different types of systems and applications, or tool, software.

BIBLIOGRAPHY

Angler, Natalie. "The Organic Computer." *Discover* 3 (no. 5, May 1982): 76–79.

Bitter, Gary G. "Basic Differences in BASIC." *AEDS Monitor* 10 (no. 7, 1972): 8–9.

———. *Beginning BASIC.* Menlo Park, Calif.: Addison-Wesley, 1988.

———. *Introduction to Programming in BASIC.* New York: Random House, 1985.

Bitter, Gary G. (with A. Cameron, A. Walters, and V. Satya). "Pascal: The New Word on High School Computers." *Curriculum Review* (May/June 1986): 136–142.

Bitter, Gary G. (with R. Goodberlet). *Macintosh BASIC for Business.* Englewood Cliffs, N.J.: Prentice-Hall, 1987.

Bitter, Gary G. (N. Watson.) *Apple Logo Primer.* Reston, Va.: Reston, 1983.

Bitter, Gary G. (with N. Watson). *Commodore 64 LOGO Primer.* Reston, Va.: Reston, 1984.

Bitter, Gary G. (with N. Watson). *IBM Logo Primer.* Reston, Va.: Reston, 1986.

Brown, Chris. "Software Technology." *Computer Design* 21 (no. 12, December 1982): 187–206.

Camuse, Ruth. "An Apple PILOT Primer: Part I." *Educational Computer* 2 (no. 5, September-October 1982): 20–23.

Dock, Thomas V., and Edward Essick. *Principles of Business Data Processing.* Chicago: Science Research Associates, 1978.

Hassell, Johnette, and Victor J. Law. "Tutorial on Structure Charts as an Algorithm Design Tool." *AEDS MONITOR* (September-October 1982): 17–32.

Heller, Dorothy. "User Friendly Languages of the Future." *Interface Age* 7 (no. 12, December 1981): 78–82.

Krajcik, Joseph S., and Craig Berg. "Exemplary Software for the Science Classroom." *School Science and Mathematics* (October 1987): 494.

Massey, C. "Preschoolers and Mathematics Software." *The Computing Teacher* 15 (no. 8): 36.

Prelle, Walter V. "Hard Disk Data Storage." *The Computing Teacher* 10 (no. 3, October 1983): 39–40.

Rose, Raymond. "Identifying Equitable Software." *The Computing Teacher* 11 (no. 8, April 1984): 51.

Shell, Ellen Ruppel. "The Brain Behind BASIC." *Technology Illustrated* 2 (no. 6, December-January 1983): 83–90.

Stern, N., and R. A. Stern. *Structured COBOL Programming.* New York: John Wiley, 1980.

"Systems Software Survey." *Datamation* 28 (no. 13, December 1982): 96–138.

Veit, Stanley, "Computer Language Confusion . . . Sorting it Out." *Popular Electronics* 19 (no. 12, December 1982): 39–56.

ADDITIONAL READING

Other helpful sources are the following periodicals:

A+
Business Week
Byte
Communications of the ACM
Compute!
Computer Design
Computerworld
Datamation
High Technology
InCider
Information Week
INFOWORLD
MACUSER
MACWEEK
MACWORLD
Mini-Micro Systems
MISweek
Nibble
PCWeek
PCWORLD
Personal Computing
Software News
Technology on Campus
T.H.E. Journal

REVIEW ANSWER KEY

Multiple Choice

1. b	5. b	9. c
2. c	6. b	10. d
3. c	7. a	
4. d	8. d	

True/False

1. T	5. T	9. T
2. F	6. F	10. T
3. T	7. T	
4. T	8. F	

Short Answer

1. Hardware is computer equipment, which consists of input units, processing and storage units, and output units.
2. OCR: readable marks—library cards, groceries; MICR: magnetic ink—checks.
3. System software and applications, or tool, software.
4. Impact and nonimpact.
5. Steps are easy to verify; missing logic or poor logic is discovered.

CHAPTER 4

METHODS, CURRICULUM, AND THE COMPUTER

Objectives

- Describe several common arrangements of computers in the school setting
- Explain how to organize and care for software media, such as floppy disks
- Write lesson plans for use with CAI (computer-aided instruction) software
- Describe how CAI software can be integrated into the curriculum
- Suggest ways of using tool software such as word processors, databases, and spreadsheets to teach across the curriculum

Key Terms

antistatic mat
computer lab
data disk
down time
drill-and-practice
floppy disk
games
objective
probeware
problem solving
program disk
simulation
surge protector
teacher utilities
tool or applications software
tutorial

Computers have brought about phenomenal changes in the way educators teach and the way students learn. In this text we are considering some of the challenges facing the educational system today. For example, how can we best train teachers to work with computers in their classrooms? What constitutes an adequate education in computer literacy? And how can teachers of all grade levels and all curriculums best use computers to teach their students?

Currently, teachers and students have many unanswered questions about the use of computers for learning. While some teachers are experimenting enthusiastically with this dynamic medium for learning, others are wary of such unfamiliar technology. Students, although curious, may also be intimidated by the technology. Unfortunately, in some cases, computer equipment goes unused or underused because of this confusion.

In this chapter, we consider some practical hints for making the most of educational computing. We will begin with a look at some of the more common arrangements of computer hardware in schools. This expensive, sophisticated equipment requires special care in order to operate efficiently. We will also explore how computer technology can be applied across the curriculum to help teachers and students meet their goals.

People viewed early computers as electronic math wizards capable of calculating great strands of inexplicable formulas. Even today, it is not unusual to hear people call computers "number crunchers." But with the advent of other applications of computer power—for example, word processing, database management, graphics, and telecommunications—people are beginning to broaden their vision of what computers can do. In education, the best reason to use computers is that they are effective teaching tools across the curriculum: They can be used to teach writing as well as accounting.

Another reason for using computers across the curriculum is to expand and reinforce students' computer literacy skills. Whether they use the computer to write essays, compile historical statistics, or simulate scientific experiments, students develop a comfortable familiarity with computer terminology and operations. This knowledge can be as valuable to them as the specific concepts they learn in any given area of the curriculum. It can inspire in them a desire to learn more about computers and to write programs of their own.

Even teachers who believe in teaching their students computer skills may feel uncertain about where and how to begin. Integrating any new methods into the curriculum is a gradual process, accomplished partly by trial and error and partly by careful planning and training. Computers present a unique challenge because they require that teachers receive some degree of special training in order to operate them. This training may be as concise as an after-school seminar offered by a computer manufacturer or as extensive as a special course offered at a local college or university. Teachers need to know how to operate computer equipment, choose educational software, and write lesson plans that incorporate the traditional **objectives**, or goals, of learning with nontraditional methods.

We begin our discussion by looking at some of the more common ways that computer equipment is arranged in schools. To a large degree, the physical arrangement of computers has an impact on how teachers present computer lessons and how much computer time is available to students.

SETTING UP AND CARING FOR COMPUTER HARDWARE

In most schools, it is the principals and other administrators, not the teachers, who make final decisions about computer purchases. Although teachers' input may be important to these decisions, rarely do teachers have the budgetary freedom to purchase computer hardware and software of their choice. Instead, they are limited to the equipment available and where it is placed in the school.

As discussed in Chapter 1, schools commonly arrange their computer equipment in a **computer lab**, which is centrally located and available to all students. Teachers may be assigned a regular time slot for their classes to attend the lab, or they may need to schedule time as their students need it. In either case, students must leave their classroom to work with computers. The school may employ a special computer teacher or aide to manage the lab and see that the equipment is maintained properly. This alleviates the classroom teacher of the responsibility of caring for the computer. On the other hand, computer labs may suffer occasional **down time** (periods when the equipment is out of order) because so many people use the equipment.

If there are enough computers in the lab, a whole class of students can work on a lesson at the same time. But in most cases computer time is more limited, because one lab must accommodate all of the classes in a school. Of course, the amount of time available to students determines the length and number of lessons that teachers can plan.

When schools can afford only a few computers, they often put them in the library where students perform research and other tasks that require computer power. A librarian or aide may supervise the use of the computers as well as the organization of the software. Again, this relieves the classroom teacher of the duty of caring for hardware and software. Usually there are too few computers to accommodate an entire class, so students work alone or in small groups. The teacher must give out passes that indicate clearly what the student needs to work on, what software is to be used, and so on. Lesson plans that involve the whole class at once are more difficult to handle.

Computer laboratories with networking allow students to work at their own pace without constantly changing disks.

Most classroom teachers probably prefer having one or more computers in the classroom. This arrangement gives teachers more freedom: They can use the computer when it is convenient rather than during scheduled periods only. Depending on the number of computers in the classroom, individual students, small groups, or sometimes an entire class may work on computer projects at the same time. The obvious benefit of this is that students can assist each other. Teachers can plan lessons of any length and can present computer lessons at any time. In addition, the computer is available to the teacher for managerial tasks when students are not using it.

Because students stay in the classroom to work with the computer, the teacher is always available to assist them. Software is often maintained within the classroom, so that it too is available, whenever the students and teacher wish to use it. The library or media center may also have a collection

Computers are often available in libraries.

A computer laboratory often has a computer specialist available for help as well as computer preparation and maintenance.

of software that can be checked out for classroom use. Although computers in the classroom help students learn to handle computer equipment and software responsibly, they present an additional organizational task for the teacher. (When software is housed in the computer lab, some schools minimize the risk of damage by not allowing students to handle it. However, this prevents students from learning to handle software correctly.)

When teachers are responsible for maintaining hardware and software, they must make sure that their students understand how to treat these materials. In other words, teachers and students need to cooperate in order to keep computers and software up and running as much of the time as possible. Several basic rules apply to caring for computer hardware.

1. *Install* **antistatic mats** over carpet to prevent static electricity from damaging hardware and software. Most discount, electronics, and computer stores sell antistatic mats.
2. *Install* **surge protectors** to prevent loss of data or software caused by fluctuations in the supply of power to the computer. Surge protectors are commonly available at hardware and electronics stores as well as at many discount stores. They are relatively inexpensive to purchase and will prevent the frustration that occurs when students lose the data they have worked so hard to create.
3. *Protect the computer from dust*, which is another major cause of malfunctioning. There are several ways to do this. You can either purchase dust covers for computers and printers, or you can make sure the equipment is dusted on a regular basis. Special cloths and cleaning solutions are available for this purpose. The manufacturer of your computer will probably recommend a product to you.
4. *Clean disk drive and cassette recorder heads often.* There are special devices available to do this. You can purchase them inexpensively at discount or electronic stores. This ensures that the disk drive or cassette recorder sends accurate data and instructions to the computer for processing.
5. *Do not allow food, drinks, paint, or other similar substances near the computer.* Liquids around the computer are easy to avoid, but once spilled, can cause tremendous damage to the inside of the computer.

ORGANIZING AND CARING FOR COMPUTER SOFTWARE

Like hardware, software is also vulnerable to physical damage unless it is cared for properly. Software can be stored on any of several media—for example, floppy disks, cartridges, or, less commonly, the cassette tapes used to record music. A **floppy disk**, or diskette, is similar to a phonograph

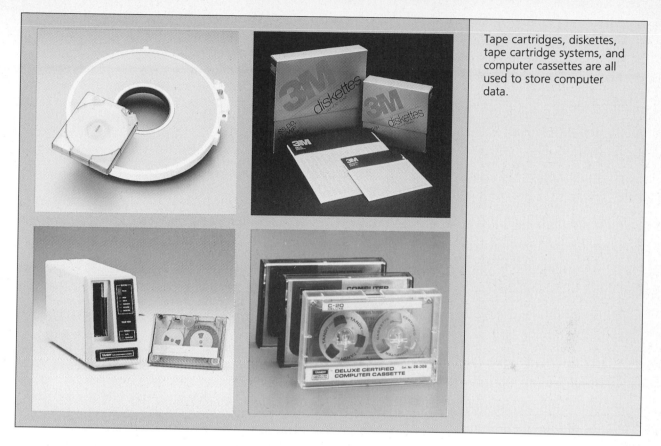

Tape cartridges, diskettes, tape cartridge systems, and computer cassettes are all used to store computer data.

record that is sealed inside a protective plastic envelope. Floppy disks come in a variety of sizes and can store vast amounts of information in a very small space.

Sometimes users can choose the type of storage medium they wish to use. The same package may be available on either disk or cartridge to accommodate different computer systems. For younger children, many software publishers offer software in self-contained cartridges that take more abuse than disks.

When working with software stored on disk, teachers often have two kinds of disks to organize and store: program disks and data disks. The **program disk** comes with the software package and contains all the program instructions for the computer. The **data disk** is used to store data that students generate while operating the program. For example, when stu-

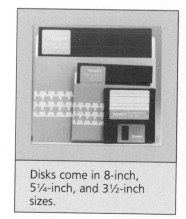

Disks come in 8-inch, 5¼-inch, and 3½-inch sizes.

dents use word processing software, they usually need a program disk to run the word processor and a data disk to store their essays, poetry, or short stories. Data disks need to be marked carefully and stored in a safe place. Older students may want to maintain their own file of data disks.

The disk is a fairly sensitive medium that can be damaged by improper handling. The result of this damage will be loss of programs or data. Since good software is usually expensive, it is advisable to follow several basic rules to avoid damage and loss:

1. *Do not touch the exposed recording surfaces of a disk.* The exposed recording surfaces are the circular center and any other areas that show through the protective plastic envelope. Fingerprints can interfere with the way the computer reads data from and records data onto the disk.
2. *Do not bend floppy disks.*
3. *Use only felt-tip pens to label floppy disks.* It is preferable to write on a self-adhesive label and then place the label on the disk so that the disk is not damaged by a sharp pen or pencil point. To write on a disk, be sure to use only soft-tipped pens. Pencils and ball point pens can damage the disk.
4. *Keep disks away from metallic objects* such as scissors, paper clips, and so on. Metallic objects may have a magnetic field that can erase data stored on disks.
5. *Do not store disks in direct sunlight* as this may have a damaging effect on the disk.
6. *When not in use, store disks in the paper envelopes provided to protect them.* The envelopes help to protect disks from dust, spills, and fingerprints.
7. *Store disks at a moderate temperature, between 50°F and 125°F.* Extreme temperatures will cause damage to the disk and the data it contains.
8. *It is best to file disks in plastic cases designed especially for this purpose.* These cases—available at discount, electronics, and computer stores— are the proper size and shape for storing disks vertically. Usually they also contain dividers so that the user can devise a sensible filing system.

These rules apply primarily to the use of 5¼-inch and 8-inch disks, which are especially vulnerable to physical damage. In recent years, the 3½-inch disk has become increasingly popular in schools. Its smaller size makes it easier to store. Also, it is encased in a thick plastic covering, which makes it much sturdier than a floppy disk.

Before students begin working with the computer, it's a good idea to introduce them to these rules for caring for disks and computer equipment. Students can even be encouraged to design colorful posters on disk care to be displayed near the computer.

The smaller size of the 3½-inch disk makes it a popular storage medium.

WRITING LESSON PLANS

Now that the computer is installed and the software ready to load, there is still one important task that the teacher must perform before running a program with students: writing a lesson plan that demonstrates what objectives will be met and how. CAI lesson plans are quite similar in format to traditional lesson plans. They must account for many of the same factors, as follows:

1. *Grade level.* For what grade level is this lesson designed? Although software publishers usually write their programs for a specific level, teachers may find that a particular program is either too simple or too sophisticated for the targeted grade. In this case they may sometimes find that a program designed for one level may work well with students above or below that level.
2. *Objective.* What skills or concepts is this lesson intended to teach or reinforce? The objective(s) of a lesson should be stated simply and clearly.
3. *Materials required.* Will the student need any supplementary materials to complete the lesson successfully? Such materials might include textbooks, worksheets, and research materials.
4. *Preparation.* What background information, vocabulary, skills, and concepts must the student have *before* the lesson is presented? This factor also includes tasks that the teacher must perform beforehand, such as copying dittos, copying or formatting disks, preparing the printer, and so on.
5. *Activity.* What will occur during the lesson? The teacher must include both the steps that involve the computer, such as keying in data, and those that do not, such as collecting and verifying data.
6. *Evaluation.* How will the success of the lesson be measured? Will students take posttests? If so, what mastery will they be expected to demonstrate?
7. *Follow-up.* What activities can be done *after* the lesson to reinforce the skills and concepts learned? How can students be encouraged to apply these skills and concepts in other areas of the curriculum? Follow-up activities are vital in helping students retain the knowledge that they have acquired during the lesson.
8. *Teacher's notes.* In this section, teachers can record any notes that do not fall under the previous headings. These may include ideas for related lessons, problems and solutions, or suggestions for relating the lesson to other classroom activities.

Teachers can adapt any lesson plan they choose to those that involve the computer. However, there are some special conditions that apply to the computer that may affect how successful a given lesson is. Teachers must consider these conditions when planning a lesson to make sure that the plans are reasonable and practical. The more thought that goes into the lesson plan, the more learning will result.

An important consideration is the length of the lesson. Teachers should try to estimate how long a lesson will take, since its length must be appropriate for the level of the participating students. If inappropriate, even the most brilliant lesson will fail.

In general, most educators find that several short lessons a week are better than one long lesson. However, this is not always easy for teachers to manage, unless they have control over the availability of computers to their students. Let's say, for example, that each class in a school is assigned a one-hour period in the computer lab each week. The classroom teacher must work within this limit: one weekly lesson not to exceed one hour in length. On the other hand, where there are several computers in a classroom, the teacher can plan several shorter lessons to occur at any time during the week.

Another consideration, also dependent on computer availability, is whether students will work alone, in small groups, or as a large group. If there is only one computer in the classroom or if students must report to the media center to use a computer, then most of the class will be working on other activities that require teacher attention, while one or a few students complete a computer lesson. When students work in cooperative groups, however, they can often help each other and answer questions that arise without needing assistance from the teacher. Group activities can also foster competition and cooperation. All of these factors have an impact on how a teacher plans and presents a lesson.

COMPUTERS ACROSS THE CURRICULUM

For teachers who are not expert programmers, the success of computer lessons depends to a large extent on the variety and quality of software available to them. In the early days of CAI (computer-aided instruction), much of the software on the market was geared toward teaching mathematics. As the educational software market became more competitive and educators became more involved with computers, the picture changed dramatically. Today teachers can choose from software designed for all areas of the curriculum as well as a wide range of special interest topics. The challenge that teachers face at present is to select and integrate CAI software into the traditional curriculum so that it reinforces rather than interferes with more traditional methods of teaching. Educational software has many different approaches. The following is a summary of the more common:

Type of Education Software	Description
Drill-and-practice	Allows learner to practice facts, relationship problems, and vocabulary until the material is committed to memory or until a particular skill has been learned. Usually provides practice on the basic skills in the curriculum.
Games	Present instruction using game formats. May follow format of popular video games.
Problem solving	Uses various problem-solving strategies such as too much information, too little information, graphs, tables, and so on to solve problems and manage situations. Emphasizes thinking and reasoning skills.
Tool or applications	Includes databases, spreadsheets, word processors, supposers (series of programs by Sunburst to assist a teacher with mathematics presentations), graphs, spell and grammar checkers, and so on that manipulate information and produce a finished product.
Tutorial	Uses written explanations, descriptions, questions, problems, and graphic illustration for concept development similar to a human tutor. Presents the concepts and theories behind a specific concept or problem.
Simulation	Allows students to explore situations that would be difficult, impractical, or impossible to duplicate in a classroom setting. Often uses problem-solving strategies.
Teacher utilities	Highly specialized software such as electronic gradebooks, test, puzzle and worksheet generators, mailing lists, statistical packages, readability analysis, and so on.

In this section, we will explore some of the many CAI software choices for classroom teachers. Following is a sampling of some software packages available for teaching mathematics, science, social sciences, language arts, special education, and early childhood education. (At the end of this chapter, you will find a list of mailing addresses for the software publishers mentioned here.)

Mathematics

The computer's ability to process numbers quickly and accurately makes it an excellent mathematics tutor. In fact, a great deal of the CAI software on the market is still aimed at teaching mathematics. There are packages available to teach the most fundamental concepts to young children and far more advanced skills to older students. Using interesting graphics and game formats, CAI can help even the most mathphobic student master mathematic principles.

An example of a program for very young students is Arithmetic Critters, published by MECC (Minnesota Educational Computing Corporation). The program is based on both drill and educational game format and holds the interest of kindergartners through second graders. Arithmetic Critters teaches counting, simple addition and subtraction, one-to-one correspondence, and writing numerals to represent from ten to twenty-nine objects. The package includes a teacher guidebook and a CMI (computer-managed instruction) component that keeps score for as many as 100 students.

Arithmetic Critters comprises four lessons or games, which require about fifteen minutes each to complete. "Animal Addition" displays sets of animals to illustrate basic addition and subtraction problems. "Fowl Play" requires that students perform simple subtraction as they watch birds leave their nests. Students use a caterpillar to measure length and perimeter in the game "Unit Worm." "Egg Plant" drills students in counting with tens and ones as they count the number of boxes of eggs on a truck.

For middle school students, there are math packages such as McGraw-Hill's Problem Solving, which teaches strategies and concepts. Problem Solving is a simulation and tutorial package that stresses situational math. Students learn to simplify problems by breaking them down into their parts, identifying what information is missing, and making a model of the problem. The program offers several levels of problems that can be solved by this process. Problem Solving has a built-in note pad for student use. Because the program is conducive to students working in groups, it is excellent for cooperative learning. Students learn effective methods of problem solving that they can apply to many areas of their curriculum. The package includes a teacher guide, student worksheets, and CMI functions for record keeping.

EduCalc (from Houghton Mifflin) is a software package that teaches students to use a popular computer application—spreadsheets. It also reinforces mathematical skills. Aimed at grades five through twelve, EduCalc is based on tutorial, simulation, and problem-solving formats. The package includes a teacher guidebook, user manual, and practice templates (sample spreadsheets). Students can save their work on disk for future reference.

Some of the activities that students can perform with EduCalc are population comparisons, budgeting, scheduling leisure activities, and scientific calculations. Students work at their own pace by selecting options from a series of menus. They can create, store, edit, and print spreadsheets as large as twenty-six columns by ninety-nine rows.

Another approach to teaching mathematics is the Supposer Series from Sunburst Communications. This series includes Geometric Presupposer; Geometric Supposer: Circles; Geometric Supposer: Quadrilaterals; and Geometric Supposer: Triangles. These programs allow the teacher or stu-

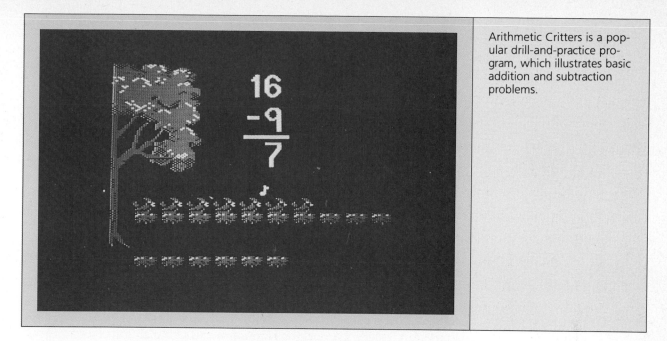

Arithmetic Critters is a popular drill-and-practice program, which illustrates basic addition and subtraction problems.

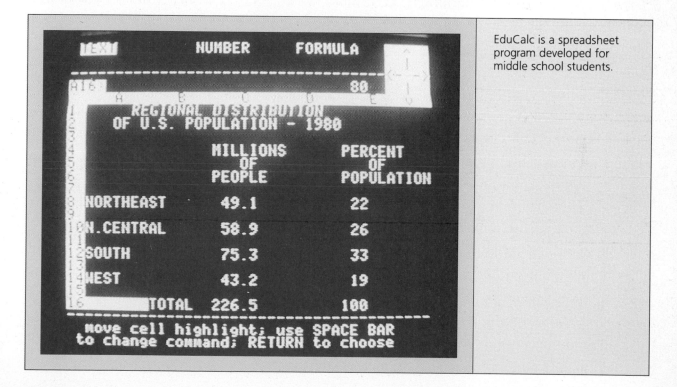

EduCalc is a spreadsheet program developed for middle school students.

dent to experiment with and hypothesize about the characteristics of the various shapes. The user can make constructions, manipulate information, and make conclusions. The series is excellent for demonstrations on an overhead computer projector.

Science   Science is another area of the curriculum that computers can enhance. In Chapter 10, "Computer-Assisted Instruction," we see how simulation software, for example, can bring dangerous or expensive experimentation into the classroom where students can observe the scientific process firsthand. With appropriate software, the computer can perform many functions in the science classroom: laboratory tool, tutor, and simulator. Some packages turn the computer into a laboratory instrument capable of measuring physical qualities such as temperature and speed. These packages are known as **probeware**. *Science Toolkit* from Broderbund is one popular probeware package that enables the computer to perform the functions of a host of expensive laboratory instruments.

The Secrets of Science Island, published by Houghton Mifflin, drills students on facts compiled in the book *Science Facts You Won't Believe*, which comes with the package. As students learn amazing new facts, they also gain research skills that include skimming and using an index and table of contents.

Aimed at grades three though eight, the Secrets of Science Island uses an interesting game format to motivate students. Students must travel around a magical island and build a shelter to protect themselves from hurricanes. To earn stones to build their shelters, they must answer scientific questions correctly. There are three different adventures on the island, each of which requires approximately ten minutes to complete. At any point in the game, students can exit the program and reenter it at the same place the next time they play. There is no CMI component for scorekeeping, but the package includes a user manual and the reference book, *Science Facts You Won't Believe*. The research skills that students acquire through The Secrets of Science Island can be applied to any other area of the curriculum.

An example of a simulation program designed for science students in grades seven though twelve is Robot Odyssey I, published by The Learning Company. The program teaches logic, problem solving, observation, forming and testing hypotheses, and collecting and analyzing data. In addition, Robot Odyssey I introduces the basic principles of electricity.

Students find themselves wandering around Robotropolis, where they must enlist the aid of programmable robots to get home. There are five levels of Robotropolis, and students encounter more danger at each level. Clues are provided by a three-dimensional map of the city sewer. As students attempt to escape from Robotropolis, they learn the process of designing, building, and testing robot circuits and chips. The package includes a robot tutorial for students with limited knowledge of robotics.

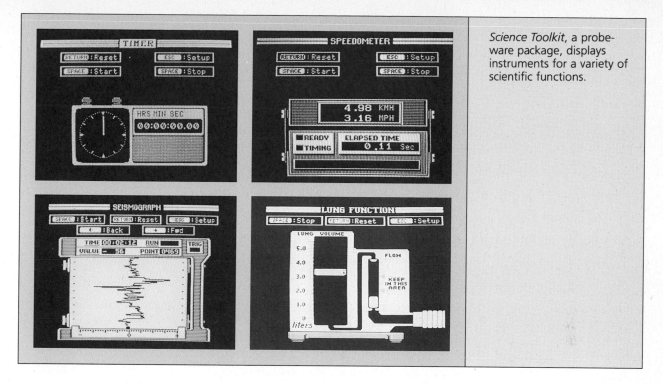

Science Toolkit, a probe-ware package, displays instruments for a variety of scientific functions.

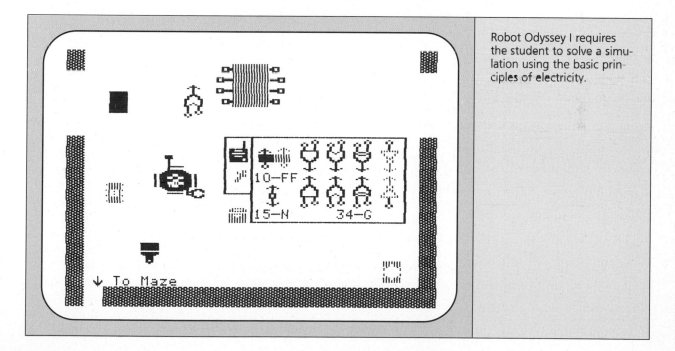

Robot Odyssey I requires the student to solve a simulation using the basic principles of electricity.

Also included in the package are a scope and sequence chart, teacher's manual, worksheets, and specification sheets for building robots. A CMI component stores each student's progress on disk.

To display the data that students gather during their scientific investigations, utility programs such as Easy Graph II from Houghton Mifflin Publishing are available. Designed for grades three through nine, Easy Graph II is used to create tables and graphs from all kinds of data. Students can create pictographs, bar and line graphs, and pie charts, all of which can be printed on a dot matrix printer and saved on disk. As many as six items can be included in a pictograph or bar graph; eight items can be included in a pie graph. The package includes a teacher guidebook and user manual. The program can be used with any type of data. Students in a social science class, for example, can use the package to display results of opinion polls or demographic data. Other programs with similar characteristics are Exploring Tables and Graphs I and II from Optimum Resource.

Social Sciences An impressive variety of software is available for teaching many topics in the social sciences. For grades four through eight, for example, The Voyage of the Mimi: Maps and Navigation from Sunburst teaches concepts of longitude, latitude, bearings, angles, and ecology. The program is comprised of four simulations based on the adventures of the crew of the Mimi presented in the video series *Voyage of the Mimi*, also available from the same publisher.

In "Pirate's Gold," students locate a sunken pirate ship based on its longitude and latitude and dive for gold. Another simulation, "Hurricane!," challenges students to escape an impending hurricane by guiding their ships to a safe island. "Lost at Sea" leaves students in a thick fog with a broken engine; their only hope is to triangulate their location on the basis of two known radio beacons so that they can radio for help. The fourth simulation, "Rescue Mission," gives students the opportunity to save a trapped whale. The program uses sophisticated graphics to hold student attention.

The Voyage of the Mimi: Maps and Navigation is part of a series that includes three other software packages as well as a selection of video cassettes. Included in the package are a teacher guidebook and student workbook that explains techniques of navigation. No CMI component is included.

CAI software can also make it possible for students to relive historical events that occurred centuries before they were born. For example, seventh through twelfth graders can experience the major decisions faced by George Washington with the program Washington's Decisions, published by Educational Activities. The two-part program presents specific information about the challenges Washington faced. Students are asked to anticipate Washington's decisions and can thus weigh various factors and compare their own judgment to that of Washington. Students score points for answering

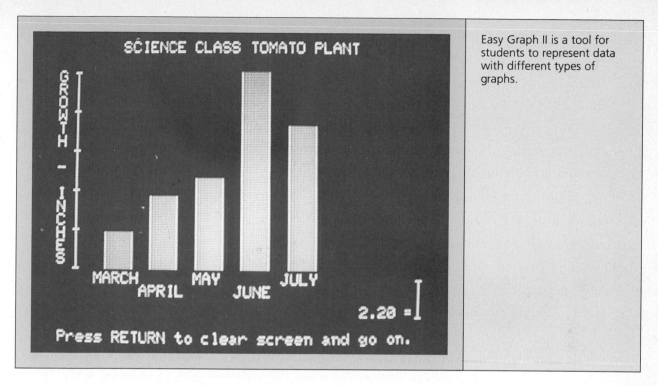

Easy Graph II is a tool for students to represent data with different types of graphs.

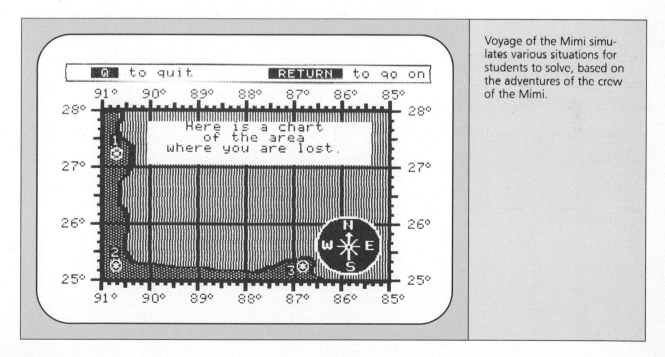

Voyage of the Mimi simulates various situations for students to solve, based on the adventures of the crew of the Mimi.

questions correctly; their scores are tracked by the management component of the system.

Washington's Decisions includes support materials such as guidebooks and worksheets. A glossary and a time line help students understand the factors that influenced Washington's decision making. The program encourages cause-and-effect thinking and includes related activities such as crossword puzzles and suggested topics for essays.

Since the social sciences entail a great deal of research, many utility programs have been developed to help students conduct research. One such program is NoteCard Maker from Houghton Mifflin. Designed for grades five through twelve, this program contains functions that allow students to create, edit, sort, and search up to 100 bibliographic entries and up to 200 note cards on any topic. As an added bonus, students learn to work with databases as they write bibliographies and note cards to use in essays and other research projects.

Language Arts

The computer is more than a sophisticated calculator; it can also store and process large amounts of text. This makes it an effective tool for teaching reading and writing. Word processing applications are changing the way students perceive writing. Students who compose at the computer are able to write and edit more easily than they can with pencil and paper. This often results in better, more thoughtful writing.

Word processing is available to even the youngest students through programs such as LogoWriter (from Logo Computer Systems), aimed at kindergartners through eighth graders. LogoWriter teaches writing, word processing, and programming fundamentals and encourages students to experiment with language and the computer. It makes extensive use of graphics, sound, and database and text manipulation. Students can save their work on disk for future reference, and the package contains a range of support materials including a teacher guidebook, student work cards, keyboard templates, posters, and videotapes.

A similar word processing tool designed for classroom use for grades three through twelve is FrEdWriter, a public domain package available from CUE Softswap at a nominal fee. Teachers can make as many copies of this program as they wish, which is an attractive feature. Students can use FrEdWriter to create, edit, store, and print their writing, and teachers can insert special prompts in files to provide guidance to students.

For vocabulary development, programs like The Game Show take advantage of entertaining game formats to hold students' interest and encourage them to run a program repeatedly. The Game Show, published by Advanced Ideas, involves students in grades three through eight in a two-player game show in which students score by guessing vocabulary words. The program includes sixteen subject files, but teachers and students can create additional subject files on any topic they choose, making

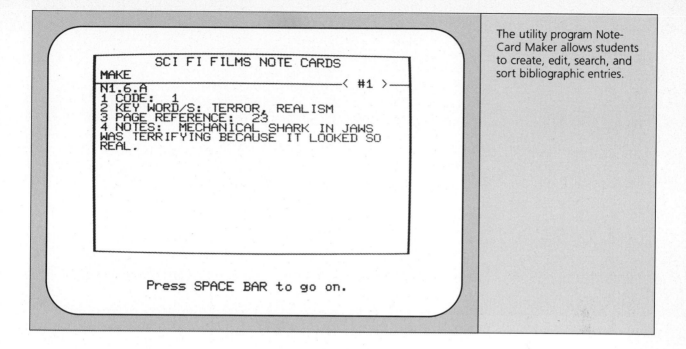

```
            SCI FI FILMS NOTE CARDS
MAKE
N1.6.A ─────────────────────────< #1 >──
1 CODE:    1
2 KEY WORD/S: TERROR, REALISM
3 PAGE REFERENCE:   23
4 NOTES:  MECHANICAL SHARK IN JAWS
WAS TERRIFYING BECAUSE IT LOOKED SO
REAL.




          Press SPACE BAR to go on.
```

The utility program Note-Card Maker allows students to create, edit, search, and sort bibliographic entries.

this program applicable across the curriculum. Each game takes from twenty to thirty minutes to complete. Because students must base their guesses on clues given by the computer, the program sharpens problem-solving skills as well as builds vocabulary.

To teach spelling and vocabulary in grades two through five, another program, Magic Castle from Mindscape, uses a game format. In this game, students try to climb to the top of a magic castle to get Merlin's wand. To do this, students must answer vocabulary questions from Merlin. The program comes with a list of 140 words, and teachers can add three more sets of the same size. Magic Castle has a management component that records how many times a student tries to answer a question, how many correct answers are given, and a percentage score for as many as forty students. The results can also be printed.

Simulation programs can also be effective in bringing language to life. An outstanding example of this is The PlayWriter's Theater, published by Educational Technology. This package enables students in grades four through eight to write, produce, direct, and present their own plays on the computer screen. Students can save their plays on disk for future reference. Students use music, characters, sets, and dialogue to produce entertaining plays of their own creation. It takes from twenty to sixty minutes to complete a lesson once students have planned their plays carefully. The package includes a teacher guidebook, student worksheets, and reference cards.

The Game Show uses a game format to encourage vocabulary development.

Magic Castle is another game format to teach spelling and vocabulary.

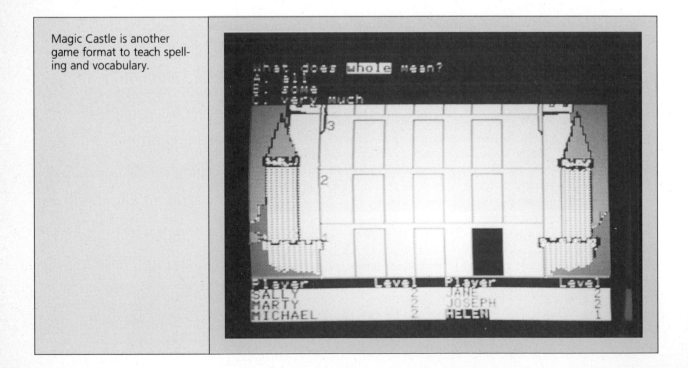

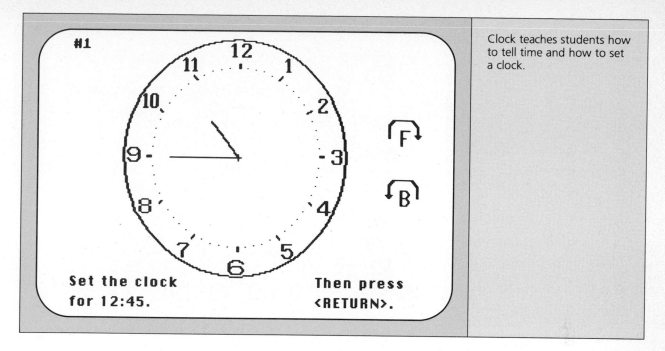

Clock teaches students how to tell time and how to set a clock.

Special Education

Almost any type of educational software can be adapted for the special education classroom. Depending on the age and skill level of students, teachers may choose from a wide variety of CAI packages. This section will focus on packages that teach practical skills such as telling time and counting money.

Clock is a package designed for the regular or special education classroom by Hartley Courseware. It teaches students to tell time and to set a clock. Using graphics and animation, Clock displays the face of a clock so that students can practice converting digital time to analog time. Other activities include reading digital time by the position of the hands on the clock and setting a clock when the time is given in words rather than digital form.

Clock includes four lessons that take from five to ten minutes to complete. (Short lessons are appropriate for students with short attention spans.) After students complete a lesson, the program tracks their progress for as many as fifty students at a time. A teacher guidebook is included with the program.

Garfield, Eat Your Words (from Random House) is another package designed for either regular or special education classrooms. (Other Garfield programs are available from DLM.) Based on the popular cartoon cat, Garfield, Eat Your Words uses a game format to teach word recognition, sight vocabulary, spelling, and letter patterns. Playing alone or in teams, students

Garfield, Eat Your Words teaches word recognition, sight vocabulary, spelling, and letter patterns.

try to guess a mystery word based on clues presented by Garfield. If students answer correctly, Garfield loses weight; if students are unsuccessful, Garfield indulges in lasagna and gains weight.

The game takes from three to ten minutes to complete, and teachers and students can add both vocabulary words and clues to keep the game interesting. A teacher guidebook is included, but the program contains no CMI component. Because it functions as a vocabulary builder, this programs is also useful in teaching English as a second language.

Money! Money!, published by Hartley Courseware, can be used to teach students to count money, decide if they have enough money to purchase an item, and make change. The program comprises fifteen lessons that last from five to ten minutes each and are of varying levels of difficulty. Money! Money! makes effective use of graphics to help students visualize the coins and bills they are manipulating. A CMI component keeps scores for as many as fifty students, and teachers can change or add word problems as they choose. (Note: Hartley Courseware offers a Canadian version of this program.)

Early Childhood Education

No one is too young to learn from and enjoy working with computers. In fact, many educators feel that when it comes to children and computers, the sooner the better. With the advent of peripheral devices such as the mouse and the touch-sensitive screen, children no longer need to read or

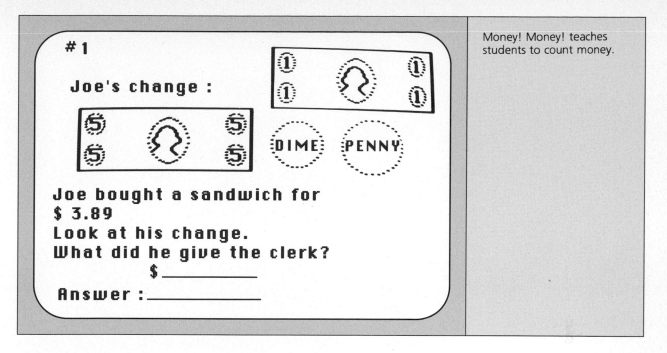

Money! Money! teaches students to count money.

to type before they can use the computer. CAI software is available to teach all sorts of concepts and skills to even the youngest computer enthusiasts.

For example, Giant First-Start from Troll Associates is a series of CAI packages that promote computer literacy skills and reading readiness. Play Ball, Kate teaches alphabetical order, classification, and word/picture identification through three different games. Each activity takes from ten to fifteen minutes to complete. The package includes a book and read-along cassette. Children are enticed to play the games by colorful and entertaining graphics.

Young children can learn about months and the numbers of days in each month, holidays, different seasons, and abbreviations for months and days with Calendar Skills, published by Hartley Courseware. The program is a tutorial made up of fifteen lessons that take from five to ten minutes to complete. The package includes a teacher guidebook, student worksheets, and behavioral objectives. Students can exit the program at any point and are given a report of their progress at the end of each lesson. A CMI component enables teachers to track student progress for up to fifty students and print reports. They can also change lessons and add lessons of their own.

The Flying Carpet from Learning Technologies helps students develop skills in shape recognition, matching, one-to-one correspondence, counting, and figure-ground relationships. The computer displays a figure made up of different-sized geometric shapes. Students then calculate the number

Play Ball, Kate teaches alphabetical order, classification, and word/picture identification.

With Calendar Skills, students learn about the calendar, including months, days of the week, and holidays.

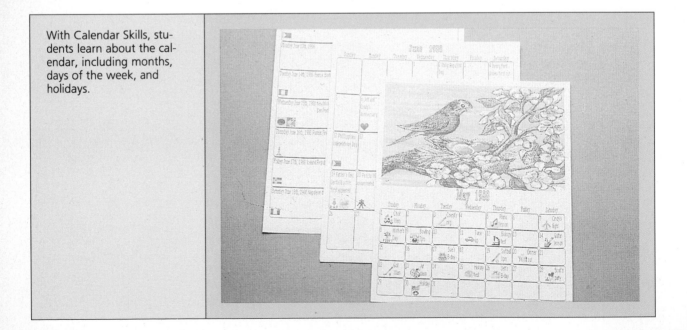

of each shape contained in each figure. The lesson takes from five to fifteen minutes to complete. This drill program can be used effectively in special education as well.

Very young children learning English as a second language are aided by the Harmony series from Educational Technology. Each package in the series features vocabulary enhancement on a specific topic and highlights grammar rules. In Croaker's Cafe, for instance, students learn vocabulary related to foods and the three daily meals. Also stressed are sentence structure, verb tenses, and positions of prepositions. Each lesson takes from ten to twenty minutes to complete, and there are three tutorials. Two games are included to provide drill of the concepts presented. The package also contains student worksheets.

USING TOOL SOFTWARE IN THE CLASSROOM

So far our discussion has focused on software that is designed specifically for classroom use. CAI software and support materials such as workbooks and teacher guides are convenient because they were written with the special needs of students and teachers in mind. However, this is not the only type of software available to educators.

As discussed in Chapter 1, software designed to perform more general tasks is called applications, or tool, software. As the term implies, tool software helps computer users perform all sorts of jobs. For example, a word processing program can be used in a law office to create a contract, in the classroom to produce a research paper, and in the home to compile a family newsletter. While tool software does not come with lesson plans, worksheets, and visual aids, it can be used as effectively in the classroom as in the business world.

There are five types of tool software: word processing, database, graphics, spreadsheet, and telecommunications. In the chapters that follow, each of these applications is discussed in detail. Examples of how these tools are used in the school setting are also presented.

With so much CAI software on the market, why do some teachers prefer to use "all-purpose" tool software? There are several advantages. First, tool software can be used across the curriculum. Because it is not based on a given topic or subject, students can use the same software in many different curriculum areas. For example, the same database program can be used to save notes on Edgar Allen Poe for a term paper, store data gathered during an experiment in chemistry class, and survey results from a poll of the students in a sociology class.

Second, when software is integrated (that is, when different applications can work together to process the same data), students can use several applications simultaneously. This promotes computer use across the curric-

Geometric Supposer introduces students to geometric shapes.

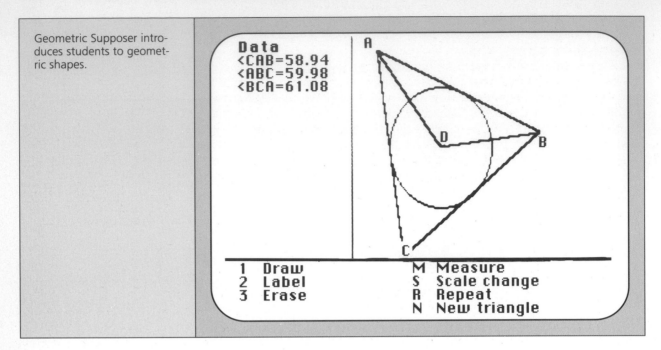

```
Data
<CAB=58.94
<ABC=59.98
<BCA=61.08
```

```
1   Draw          M   Measure
2   Label         S   Scale change
3   Erase         R   Repeat
                  N   New triangle
```

Another screen from Geometric Supposer.

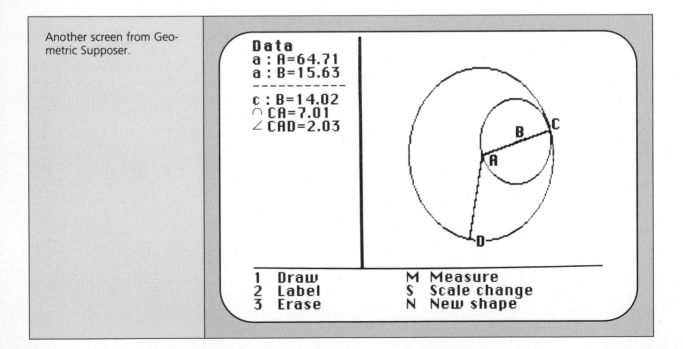

```
Data
a : A=64.71
a : B=15.63
----------
c : B=14.02
⌒ CA=7.01
∠ CAD=2.03
```

```
1   Draw          M   Measure
2   Label         S   Scale change
3   Erase         N   New shape
```

ulum. For instance, after using a spreadsheet to compile the results of a survey, students can use a word processor to compose a report of their findings—complete with graphs and charts created with a graphics program.

Third, students who use tool software become familiar and comfortable with computer applications in use outside the school environment. Thus, they gain valuable and marketable hands-on experience with computers. In many cases, students may have access to the same or compatible tool software on a home computer, allowing them to reinforce practical skills and to complete school assignments at home.

The main disadvantage of using tool software in the classroom is that students may sometimes require more time and assistance to learn to operate the software. Software designed for use in the business environment, for example, may not be as user friendly as some CAI software. Also, it is left to the teacher to integrate tool software into the curriculum since it does not arrive with lesson plans and worksheets. Many teachers find this appealing because tool software is unlimited in the ways it can be used in the classroom.

SUMMARY

Today while some teachers and students fear computer technology, others embrace it enthusiastically. The computer has proved an excellent tool for teaching all curriculums. In addition, its use in the curriculum expands and reinforces computer literacy skills. Whether they use the computer to write essays, compile historical statistics, or simulate scientific experiments, students develop a comfortable familiarity with computer terminology and operations. This knowledge can be as valuable to them as the specific concepts they learn in any given area of the curriculum.

Often, computer equipment in a school is housed in a computer lab that is centrally located and available to all students. Teachers may be assigned a regular time slot for their classes to attend the lab, or they may need to schedule time as their students need it. When schools can afford only a few computers, they often put them in the media center or library, where students perform research and other tasks that require computer power. However, if feasible, most classroom teachers probably would like one or more computers in their classrooms. This arrangement gives teachers more flexibility in integrating the computer with the curriculum.

When teachers are responsible for maintaining hardware and software, they must make sure that their students understand how to treat these materials. Computer hardware and software are subject to damage or data loss from static electricity, power surges, dust, and substances like food and drink. Teachers must create an environment conducive to computer maintenance and operation, and teach their students the appropriate guidelines.

Because floppy disks are especially sensitive, teachers must show their students how to properly handle and store these disks.

Whether the computer environment is a lab or a classroom, the teacher's main task is to provide instruction using the computer. CAI lesson plans are quite similar in format to traditional lesson plans. When planning a CAI lesson, teachers must make the lesson's length appropriate to the students' level. They must also plan with computer availability in mind—whether students will work alone, in small groups, or as a large group.

For teachers who are not expert programmers, the success of computer lessons depends to a large extent on the variety and quality of software available to them. Today teachers can choose from software designed for all areas of the curriculum as well as a wide range of special interest topics. The challenge that teachers face at present is to integrate CAI and tool software into the traditional curriculum so that it reinforces rather than interferes with other methods of teaching.

REVIEW EXERCISES

Multiple Choice

1. CAI is an effective tool in teaching
   a. math
   b. social sciences
   c. special education
   d. all of the above
2. A major challenge facing the schools of the future is
   a. training teachers to work with computers
   b. phasing out teachers who cannot work with computers
   c. eliminating central computer labs
   d. all of the above
3. Which of the following is *not* a reason for using computer technology across the curriculum?
   a. students see how versatile the computer is
   b. students gain valuable computer literacy skills
   c. teachers who do not wish to use computers will find other professions
   d. all of the above
4. What skill(s) must teachers possess in order to use CAI effectively?
   a. operate computer equipment
   b. select high-quality software
   c. write lesson plans that include work on the computer
   d. all of the above

5. Decisions about what computers to buy and how to set them up in the school are usually made by
   a. teachers
   b. administrators
   c. parent/teacher organizations
   d. none of the above
6. Which of the following is *not* a characteristic of a central computer lab in a school?
   a. teachers must schedule class time in the lab
   b. students must leave the classroom to complete computer projects
   c. software is usually kept in the lab
   d. all of the above
7. Many teachers prefer to have computers set up in their classrooms because
   a. students can work on computer projects whenever it is convenient
   b. software can be maintained in the classroom
   c. the computer will replace the teacher
   d. a and b
8. CAI software can be stored on
   a. disk
   b. cartridge
   c. cassette tape
   d. all of the above
9. Floppy disks should always be
   a. stored vertically
   b. folded neatly before storing
   c. cleaned with window cleaner
   d. all of the above

10. Most CAI packages designed for regular classroom use can be adapted for
    a. the special education classroom
    b. early childhood education
    c. on-the-job training
    d. none of the above

True/False

1. Students develop valuable computer literacy skills whenever they use CAI programs.
2. Teachers can be trained to work with computers in seminars, workshops, and special courses offered at local colleges and universities.
3. Down time refers to the hours when the computer lab is closed.
4. The amount of computer time available to students determines the length and number of lessons that teachers can plan.
5. Teachers and students need to cooperate in order to keep computers and software up and running as much of the time as possible.
6. A floppy disk is similar to a phonograph record sealed inside a protective plastic envelope.
7. Data disks contain program instructions that tell the computer what to do.
8. Extremely high or low temperatures can cause damage to disks.
9. Students who use the computer for writing tend to hurry through their work and produce sloppy results.
10. Computer technology should not be used in the primary grades.

Short Answer

1. What are three common arrangements of computers in the school setting?
2. What are the advantages of setting up computers in a self-contained classroom?
3. What steps can be taken to care for computer hardware?
4. List the rules that apply to handling and caring for disks.
5. What factors should be included in a lesson plan for computer projects?
6. List the seven types of education software.

Activities

1. Design a poster that shows students how to handle disks properly.
2. Choose one area of the curriculum and research what CAI software is available in this area. Report your findings to the class.
3. Create a format for writing lesson plans. Then write a lesson plan that uses one of the CAI packages described in this chapter.
4. Choose one major computer application—database, word processing, spreadsheet, graphics, or telecommunications—and list ways that this application can be used across the curriculum.
5. Invite an expert in special education to speak to your class about how computers are used to assist and teach exceptional students.

BIBLIOGRAPHY

Anderson-Inman, Lynne. "Teaching for Transfer: Integrating Language Arts Software into the Curriculum." *The Computing Teacher* 15 (no. 1): 24.

AppleAccess Curriculum Software Guide: Mathematics. Apple Computer, 1987.

AppleAccess Curriculum Software Guide: Reading, Writing, and Language Arts. Apple Computer, 1987.

Balajthy, Ernest. "Keyboarding, Language Arts, and the Elementary School Child." *The Computing Teacher* 15 (no. 5): 40.

Bitter, Gary G. "Back to Basics with Math for the Future." *Electronic Education* 69 (no. 4, January 1987): 22–24, 26.

———. "Calculus with Computers." *Two Year Mathematics Journal* 1 (no. 2, 1970): 41–49.

———. "Computer Literacy Across the Curriculum." *SIGCUE Bulletin: Association of Computing Machinery* 17 (November 4, 1983): 7–12.

———. *Computer Literacy: Awareness, Applications, and Programming.* Menlo Park, Calif.: Addison-Wesley, 1986.

———. "Computer Literacy for Teacher Certification." *Educational Computer* 3 (no. 7, January/February 1983): 22.

———. "Computer Oriented Calculus." *Journal of Education Data Processing* 7 (no. 3, 1970): 193–195.

_____. "Creating an Effective Computer Literacy Training Model." *Educational Computer* 2 (no. 5, September 1982): 42, 74.

_____. "Education in the Microcomputer Revolution." *The Principal* 24 (no. 4, March/April 1984): 1–10.

_____. "Educational Technology and the Future of Mathematics." *School Science and Mathematics Journal* (October 1987): 454.

_____. *Exploring with Computers.* New York: Julian Messner, 1981 (rev. 1983).

_____. "The First Step in Utilizing Microcomputers in Education: Preparing Computer Literate Teachers." *The Monitor* 21 (nos. 5–6, November/December 1982): 19–21.

_____. "Involving Pre-Service Teachers with Microcomputers." *99er Magazine* (May/June 1981): 80–81.

_____. "Kindergarten Teachers Use Computers, Too." *Educational Computer* 3 (no. 3, May/June 1983): 46–53.

_____. "Microcomputers in the Classroom: Direction Needed." *Contemporary Education* 59 (no. 2, Winter 1988): 109–111.

_____. "The Road to Computer Literacy: A Scope and Sequence Model." *Electronic Learning* 2 (no. 1, September 1982): 60–63.

_____. "The Road to Computer Literacy Part II: Objectives for Grades K–3." *Electronic Learning* 2 (no. 2, October 1982): 34–37, 85–86.

_____. "The Road to Computer Literacy Part III: Objectives and Activities for Grades 4–6." *Electronic Learning* 2 (no. 3, November/December 1982): 44–48, 90–91.

_____. "The Road to Computer Literacy Part IV: Objectives and Activities for Grades 7–9." *Electronic Learning* 2 (no. 4, January 1983): 40–42, 46–48.

_____. "Survey of Arizona Public School Practices and Needs for Computer Assisted Instruction." *The Computing Teacher* 8 (no. 4, 1981): 31–34.

_____. "Who's in Control Here—You or the Computer?" *Educational Computer* 2 (no. 6, November/December 1982): 25–26.

Bitter, Gary G. (with D. Craighead). *Teaching Computer Literacy: Lesson Plans and Activities for Your Classroom.* Vols. 1–4. Austin, Tex.: Sterling Swift, 1984.

_____. *Teaching Computer Literacy: Lesson Plans and Activities for Your Classroom.* Vols. 5–8. Austin, Tex.: Sterling Swift, 1985.

Bitter, Gary G. (with K. Gore). "Computer Labs—Fads?" *Electronic Education* 4 (no. 7, May/June 1985): 17–35.

Bitter, Gary G. (with Stephen Rossberg). "Computer Literacy Requirement Professional Teacher Preparation Program." *Collegiate Microcomputer* 6 (no. 3, August 1988): 201.

Bitter, Gary G., and Ruth Camuse. *Using a Microcomputer in the Classroom.* Englewood Cliffs, N.J.: Prentice-Hall, 1988.

Burke, Robert L. *CAI Sourcebook.* Englewood Cliffs, N.J.: Prentice-Hall, 1982.

Computers in Mathematics Education. Reston, Va.: National Council of Teachers of Mathematics, 1984.

Kent, W. A., and R. Lewis, eds. *Computer-Assisted Learning in the Humanities and Social Sciences.* Boston: Blackwell Scientific Publications, 1987.

Krolick, Bettye. "Computer Access for the Visually Impaired." *The Computing Teacher* 11 (no. 8, April 1984): 48–50.

Nave, Gary, Philip Browning, and Jeri Carter. *Computer Technology for the Handicapped in Special Education and Rehabilitation.* Vols. 1 and 2. International Council for Computers in Education, University of Oregon, 1983, 1985.

Savas, Stephen D., and E. S. Savas. *Teaching Children to Use Computers.* New York: Teachers College Press, Columbia University, 1985.

Solomon, Cynthia. *Computer Environments for Children.* Cambridge: MIT Press, 1986.

Trollip, Stanley, and Stephen M. Allessi. "Incorporating Computers Effectively in the Classroom." *Journal of Research on Computers in Education* 21 (no. 1, Fall 1988): 70–81.

REVIEW ANSWER KEY

Multiple Choice

1. d	5. b	9. a
2. a	6. d	10. a
3. c	7. d	
4. d	8. d	

True/False

1. T	5. T	9. F
2. T	6. T	10. F
3. F	7. F	
4. T	8. T	

Short Answer

1. Computers in central lab; computers in or near library or media center; computers in self-contained classroom.
2. Teacher maintains control of equipment, software, and computer time; students do not have to leave classroom to complete computer projects; students can work in groups and assist each other.
3. Install antistatic mats and surge protectors; protect the computer from dust and spills; clean disk drives and cassette recorder heads regularly.
4. Do not touch recording surfaces; do not bend; use only felt-tip markers to write on disks; keep disks away from metal objects; do not store in direct sunlight or under extremely high or low temperatures; store disks in paper envelopes and plastic cases to protect them.
5. Grade level, objective, materials required, preparation, activity, evaluation, follow-up, and teacher's notes.
6. Drill-and-practice; games; problem solving; tool, or application; tutorial; simulation; teacher utilities.

SOFTWARE PUBLISHERS

Advanced Ideas
2902 San Pablo Ave.
Berkeley, CA 94702

Broderbund Software
17 Paul Dr.
San Rafael, CA 94903

CUE Softswap
San Mateo County Office of Education
333 Main RC
San Mateo, CA 94401

DLM
One DLM Park
Allen, TX 75002

Educational Activities
P. O. Box 392
Freeport, NY 11520

Educational Technology
6150 N. 16th St.
Phoenix, AZ 85016

Hartley Courseware
123 Bridge St.
Dimondale, MI 48821

Houghton Mifflin Co.
Dept. 67
Mount Support Rd./CN 9000
Lebanon, NH 03766–9000

The Learning Company
6493 Kaiser Dr.
Fremont, CA 94555

Learning Technologies, Inc.
Suite 131
4255 LBJ Fwy.
Dallas, TX 75244

Logo Computer Systems, Inc.
1000 Roche Blvd.
Vaudreuil, P. Q.
J7V683 Canada

McGraw-Hill Book Co.
8171 Redwood Hwy.
Novato, CA 94947

Mindscape
3444 Dundee Rd.
Northbrook, IL 60062

Minnesota Education Computing Corporation (MECC)
3490 Lexington Ave. No.
St. Paul, MN 55112–8097

Optimum Resource, Inc.
10 Station Pl.
Norfolk, CT 06058

Random House
201 E. 50th St.
New York, NY 10022

Sunburst Communications
39 Washington Ave.
Pleasantville, NY 10570–9970

Troll Associates
100 Corporate Dr.
Mahwah, NJ 07430

CHAPTER 5

WORD PROCESSING

Objectives

- Define the term *word processing*
- List various applications for word processors and their impact on education
- Describe how to create, revise, print, and store a document

- Describe columns and tables to be included in documents and how they can be used in classroom teaching
- Define the term *merge* and describe the applications for which it is used

Key Terms

columns
commands
copy
cursor draw
dedicated
footnote
format
grammar check
header
justify
macro
merge
move
note pad
pagination
print
save
search
spell check
thesaurus
type style
underline
variable
word processing
word wrap

Advancements in the data processing world appeared after the punched card was replaced by the display terminal. The ability to store information on a disk, store the disk for later use, and print the output stored on the disk at an even later date provided the basis for using the computer for textual material as well as mathematical calculations. Along with data processing, word processing has become an everyday function in classrooms and offices that handle large quantities of written text. **Word processing** refers to writing, manipulating, and storing textual material in a computerized medium.

WORD PROCESSING: ITS HISTORY AND POPULARITY

IBM introduced the Magnetic Tape/Selectric Typewriter (MT/ST) in 1964. Because MT/ST stored characters entered by the operator on magnetic tapes, this was the beginning of word processing. The tape was used to store manuscripts, portions of which could be corrected and reused. Another advance occurred in 1973 when IBM introduced the Magnetic Card Selectric Typewriter. Typed documents were stored on magnetic cards that could be revised more easily than could be done on previous machines. This system also contained an electronic main memory.

The first word processor for microcomputers was developed by Seymour Rubinstein and Bob Barnaby. Other early word processors were Electric Pencil, Scripsit, and WordStar. After the mid-1970s, the field of word processing blossomed as many different companies began to develop programs to suit various needs. During the 1980s word processors became the most popular microcomputer software.

Word processing is popular because writing, editing, storing, and copying text can all be done much more efficiently by computer than by typewriter. Although text is usually entered via the keyboard (as with a typewriter), changes during entry can be made much more easily than with a typewriter, either before printing the document or after. (The user does not have to retype an entire document to accommodate changes. The printer simply prints out the new version.) The document can also be saved and retrieved later, simply with a few keystrokes. Once retrieved, the text can be edited if desired—changes, additions, and deletions can be made easily to the file; the file can then be printed out and saved for future use. The document or portions of it can be copied and printed as many times as the user likes and can be used in the original form or combined with other documents.

Obviously, the advantages over simple typing make word processing useful in almost every field. Business and government use word processing to prepare letters, reports, instructions, and advertisements. Educational uses include teacher preparation of written material for students; student preparation of reports, newspapers, and letters; and administrative paper work.

SYSTEMS FOR WORD PROCESSING

Word processing is performed in one of four ways: on a time sharing system, on a shared logic system, on a dedicated word processor, or on a microcomputer. In time sharing, the user operates a terminal that interfaces with a large computer at a remote location, sharing access to its word processing software with many other terminals, which are often in other locations as well. In shared logic situations, a small business computer is used by several terminals in an office environment for a variety of applications, including word processing. The computer and terminals form a network. Often, a cluster of terminals is located in a work area with the computer nearby.

Stand-alone word processing systems do not need to interface with a large computer and require only one terminal. With the advent of greater-capacity chips and improved diskettes, stand-alone systems have become more popular. These systems are also called **dedicated** word processors, meaning that they serve no other function but word processing.

The microcomputer is an alternative to the dedicated word processor. Available software can turn any microcomputer into a sophisticated word processor. The primary advantage of the microcomputer is that it can perform many other functions as well, such as database management, spreadsheets, and graphics. (See Chapter 9 for a discussion of integrated software.)

The various word processing systems meet the needs of different users. Word processing technology now pervades almost every area of society. Following are some of the ways in which we use word processing in the educational environment.

WORD PROCESSING IN EDUCATION

Elementary and high school students can use word processing equipment to compose text. They can enter and edit essays before and after teachers have critiqued the material on paper; they can adjust prose or poetry on the screen and then reprint the text. Word processing activities can include the following:

Writing letters
Writing introductory sentences and paragraphs

The dedicated word processor only performs that function.

With the right software, micro computers also make powerful word processors, but they can still perform other functions as well.

In classrooms with word processors, students can practice writing, and they can also run interactive programs created by the teacher.

Writing closing statements or paragraphs
Creating a group story
General writing
Describing a person, place, or thing
Writing a biography
Writing an autobiography
Writing a news article
Writing an essay
Writing a fantasy story
Writing an editorial
Writing a review
Writing a play
Writing a poem
Writing instructions for using a device
Editing an article or story

Word processors in the classroom can expand the horizons of learning in ways not possible before this technology was available. In writing, for example, students learn far more than just how to create text. As they create a document, the word processor prompts them to consider how the material will appear on the printed page. This includes choices about margins, spacing, and type style, to name a few.

Spelling and vocabulary are other areas where students can have instant feedback. By using the spell check feature now available with most word

**Sample Lesson Plan—
Word Processing**

> Objective: Organize and write a short introduction and conclusion to a given paragraph.
>
> Application: Word processor.
>
> Assumption: The teacher has prepared a word processing file with a given paragraph.
>
> **Discussion:**
> Using a word processor, the student enters into the computer no more than three introductory and three closing sentences for the given paragraph.
> > Have students share their stories with the class.
> > Discuss similarities and differences in the introductions.
> > Discuss similarities and differences in the closings.
> > Discuss other options for introductory and closing sentences.
>
> **Activity—Higher-Order Thinking:**
> Assemble class writings into a creative word-processed newsletter.
> > The teacher can prepare a demonstration disk of examples and students can make comments about each example.

processors, students can tell if a word is spelled incorrectly; the word processor may even give them the correct spellings. This immediacy is especially advantageous: It promotes learning and prevents students from repeating their errors.

Another option now offered by many word processors is a thesaurus, which can expand students' vocabulary when properly used. Just as spell check offers a list of correctly spelled words, a **thesaurus** provides a list of words with similar meanings. Thus, students are able to write in a more diverse and interesting manner and learn new words at the same time.

Also available on many word processors is a **grammar check**. This feature examines sentences for grammatical correctness. The user can make the appropriate changes to avoid grammatical errors. Gram.mat.ik II is one such program. (See the end of the chapter for addresses of software publishers.)

By using a word processor's many functions, students can produce better first drafts that are also eye pleasing and easy for the teacher to read and grade. When revising and rewriting, students retrieve the original and make the necessary changes, without having to reproduce the whole text.

The teacher might prefer to evaluate the text on a screen display rather than from a printed copy, have the student make revisions on screen, and print a copy only after all desired changes have been made. The time saved for both students and teachers is one of the positive aspects of word processing.

Subjects other than creative writing benefit equally from the use of word processing in the classroom. For example, teachers can create interactive documents that require student response. History, social studies, English, foreign languages, science, and the arts are all adaptable to this kind of instruction. In addition, teachers can administer and grade exams and quizzes using a word processor.

Some education-oriented word processing packages are Magic Slate (Sunburst Communications), AppleWorks (Claris), First Choice (Meizner Business Machines), Writing Workshop (Milliken), Microsoft Works (Microsoft), Multiscribe (Scholastic), Bank Street Writer (Scholastic), First Writer (Houghton Mifflin) for young children, and FrEdWriter. FrEdWriter is public domain software, which means that it can be copied by anyone without charge. Teachers should evaluate the available software and determine their particular needs based on the students and subjects to be taught. Chapter 12 offers assistance in evaluating software.

In addition to the above, let's not overlook one of the most obvious areas of learning—computer literacy itself. While creating, editing, storing, printing, and later retrieving written text, students learn a great deal about the computer system, its hardware and software. Because of computer technology's impact on society, computer literacy is being taught at increasingly lower grade levels. In the future, it's possible that computer literacy courses will be unnecessary in college or high school because they will have become an established part of the elementary curriculum.

In addition to its uses for teaching, word processing can help educators meet their scholarly and administrative needs. At the university level, word processors are used to write manuscripts, research reports, grant proposals, and public relations materials. Much of this information remains the same over an extended period of time and only changes need to be incorporated. On any level, teachers can prepare lesson plans, examinations, and other classroom material on the word processor. Again, the material can be updated from year to year as necessary without having to recreate the whole body of information.

Whatever the application and whoever the user may be, certain characteristics are common to most word processing systems. Generally, the user enters text on a typewriterlike keyboard. Instead of a sheet of typing paper inserted into a typewriter, a CRT displays each character (letter, numeral, or symbol) as it is typed. A **cursor**—a small marker of space—moves along the line of type, indicating the position at which the next character typed will be entered. In addition to common typewriter symbols, the keyboard includes directional arrows that, when pressed, move the cursor up and down, and to the left or right, at the discretion of the user. Other keys allow the user to insert or delete characters, spaces, or lines. Further adjustments to a text are possible by giving different commands to the system. Although these commands are given different names in different systems, the various word processors perform similar tasks.

Using a word processor to write a memo.

```
 Folder  Edit  Search  Format  Style  Fonts
                    Sales Memo
|1 . . . . |2 . . . . |3 . . . . |4 . . . . |5 . . . . |6 . . . . |

Date: February 24, 1983

To: Fred Ames

From: Allan Johnson

Subject: Sales Conference Display

As we agreed in the sales meeting last week, I have committed to prepare an
explanation on why the design of our Sales Conference Display will effectively
communicate the benefits of our new product to the sales force.  This is not an
easy issue.  We must resolve it immediately!

We have three things that we would like to communicate:

1.  The forecasted sales for the next three years.
```

In the following sections, some of the more frequently used terms and commands are discussed. Although different software packages do not use identical terms, teachers and students will soon become familiar with the terminology of their software. The following examples do not define commands for every application; rather they are approximations of terms to be found in most word processing packages.

WORD PROCESSING TERMS

Word Wrap   On a conventional typewriter, typists must press a carriage return key at the end of each line to return the carriage to the left margin of the next line. However, in most word processing systems, the cursor moves there automatically. This is often called **word wrap**.

Justify   The word processor can easily produce text with equal, or **justified**, right and left margins. Before the advent of word processors, justified margins were only available for typeset material. (Electronic typewriters, with proportional spacing can produce justified margins also.)

Spacing   Spacing refers to how many blank line spaces there are between lines of text. The usual options are single spacing and double spacing; however, many systems also offer the option of half-line spacing.

Margins   The size of margins may be specified, left and right as well as top and bottom. On most word processors, margins may also be changed within the document.

Tab   Similar to a typewriter tab, the cursor moves a predetermined number of spaces to the right each time the tab key is pressed. This is useful for typing tables or columns. Many programs also include tab left.

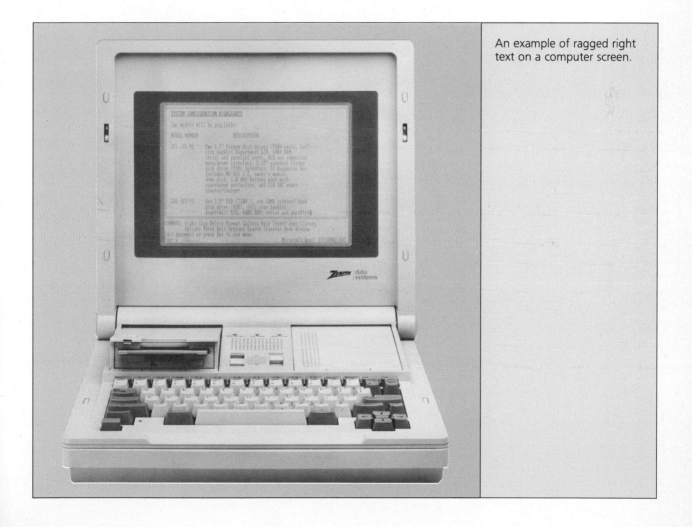

An example of ragged right text on a computer screen.

An example of text that is right justified.

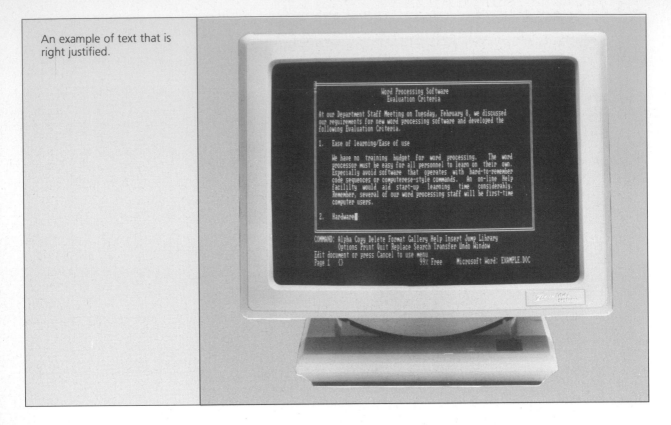

Column   Many school systems have a sophisticated procedure for setting up **columns** (vertical arrangement of printing), which allows two or more columns per page. Text or numbers in one column can be changed without affecting other columns of information.

Type Style   **Type style** refers to typeface and pitch. In word processing, typeface refers to the design of the characters; these are usually pica or elite, as on a typewriter. Pitch refers to the number of characters printed per inch and ordinarily is either ten or twelve. However, on some word processors, fifteen and seventeen pitch options or five and eight for primary grades are also available.

Header   The **header** is the first few lines at the top of a page; this space can be used to create headings, page numbers, or any other text that the user wishes to have appear on every page or specified pages of a document.

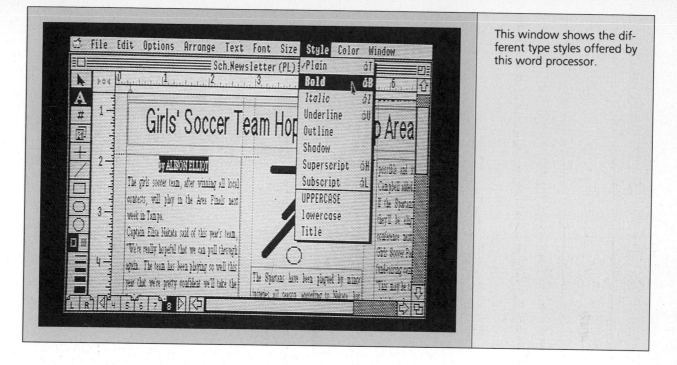

This window shows the different type styles offered by this word processor.

Footer The footer is the last few lines at the bottom of a page and, like the header, may be programmed to appear on all or any number of specified pages.

Footnote With some sophisticated word processing programs, **footnotes** can be added as they occur within the document. During pagination, they are automatically numbered and placed at the bottom of the appropriate page with a line inserted to separate them from the body of the document. If a footnoted document is revised, footnotes are automatically renumbered and repositioned as necessary.

WORD PROCESSING COMMANDS

In addition to cursor movement and the editing features offered by the keyboard, word processors employ **commands**, which tell the program to perform various tasks. Depending on the program, the user implements these commands in various ways (for instance, by selecting them from a menu or by typing them on a command line). Users will become familiar with the language and methods of their particular word processor (in education, AppleWorks is one of the most popular word processors).

The following is a summary of AppleWorks' word processor commands. Regardless of how the commands are activated, most word processors provide the commands that we discuss below.

AppleWorks Word Processor Command Summary

OPEN APPLE [?]	=	Help screen
OPEN APPLE [C]	=	Copy test (includes cut-and-paste)
OPEN APPLE [D]	=	Delete text
OPEN APPLE [F]	=	Find occurrences of . . .
OPEN APPLE [K]	=	Calculate page numbers
OPEN APPLE [M]	=	Move text (includes cut-and-paste)
OPEN APPLE [N]	=	Change name of file so that different versions can be saved under the different names
OPEN APPLE [O]	=	Options for print formatting
OPEN APPLE [P]	=	Print
OPEN APPLE [R]	=	Replace occurrences of . . .
OPEN APPLE [T]	=	Set and clear tab stops
OPEN APPLE [Z]	=	Zoom in or out to display or not display printer options (e.g., margins, characters per inch)
OPEN APPLE [SPACE BAR]	=	Sticky space
CONTROL B	=	Begin or end boldface
CONTROL L	=	Begin or end underline
RETURN	=	Mark end of paragraph
DELETE	=	Delete preceding character
ARROWS	=	Move the cursor
OPEN APPLE [UP ARROW]	=	Back up a full screen
OPEN APPLE [DOWN ARROW]	=	Go forward a full screen
OPEN APPLE [RIGHT ARROW]	=	Go to next word
OPEN APPLE [LEFT ARROW]	=	Go to previous word
TAB	=	Go to next tab stop
OPEN APPLE [TAB]	=	Go to previous tab stop
OPEN APPLE [1] through	=	Go to beginning of file through
OPEN APPLE [9]	=	Go to end of file

Format The **format** of a document defines how the text will be arranged on a single page or for the entire document. Formatting also can be implemented for a single line or group of lines, for instance, to set a paragraph apart from others. Among other things, formatting covers size of margins, type style, single or double spacing, justification, and headers and footers.

Go To The Go To command allows the user to move quickly from one page to another within a document. This is particularly useful when it's necessary to move backward and forward in a very long document.

Bold   An individual character, a word, or a block of text may be printed in **bold** type for emphasis. To accomplish bold print, most systems print over the text two or more times.

Underline   Characters, words, or blocks of text may be **underlined**. Sometimes the user can specify that underlining be either continuous (words and spaces) or separate (words only).

Copy   The user can **copy** text already entered in one part of a document to another part of the document automatically without having to retype it.

Move   The user can **move** rather than copy text. Text is moved to a new location and no longer appears in its original location.

Note Pad   To save text for another document or file, the user can copy or move it to a holding file by activating a **Note Pad** or similar command. At a later time when creating or revising another document, the text can be retrieved from the note pad and inserted where desired.

Spell Check   Systems with **spell checking** have a dictionary of common words programmed into them. The size of the dictionary (the number of words it contains) varies with each program (the larger the dictionary, the more efficient the spell checker). When activated, the spell checker will highlight words that are spelled incorrectly or that it doesn't recognize; it may also supply a list of similar words. The user may then choose the correct word from the list and instruct the system to insert it in place of the misspelled one. If the correct word does not appear on the list, the user may type it in.

Thesaurus   The **thesaurus** is one of the newer additions to word processing. It works much like the spell checker. The computer will, upon command, produce a list of words of similar meaning that may be substituted for a given word. If the list contains a more appropriate word, the user may then instruct the computer to exchange one word for another.

Grammar Check   The **Grammar Check** command finds grammatical mistakes in the word processed document. For instance, it can detect split infinitives, confusing language, incorrect punctuation, and jargon.

Search   Given the **Search** command, the word processor will find and pause at every occurrence of a particular word, phrase, or number in a text. This allows changes in text to be made quickly and accurately throughout an entire document. Usually the system offers both automatic and prompted changes. If a word or number is to be changed in some instances but not in others, the user selects the prompted option to decide each instance.

Left, top to bottom: sample screens showing a thesaurus and two Search programs. Right, top to bottom: text-and-graphics displays, including two-page spreads and a double-column format (bottom).

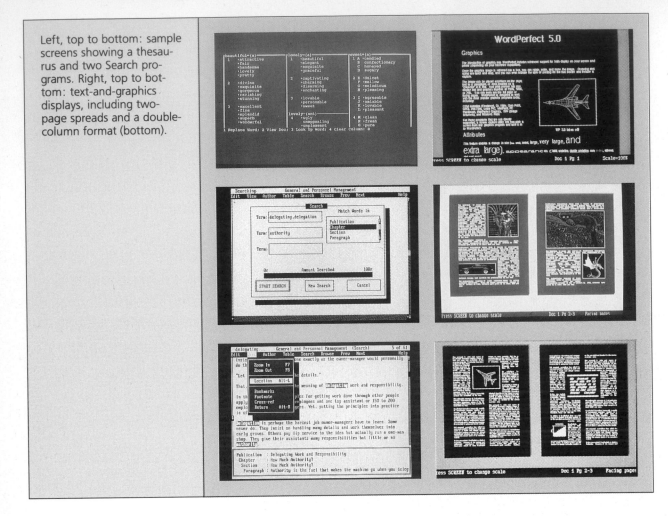

With the Search feature, some programs count the number of times a given word appears in the text, thus allowing the writer to determine whether there has been too much repetition.

Merge   Most word processors can **merge**, or combine, the contents of more than one document. For instance, when part of a letter must be placed in another letter, retyping is unnecessary—the appropriate texts can simply be merged with the Merge command.

Documents may also be created for the specific purpose of merging. For example, if an identical letter must be sent to different individuals or organizations, the document containing the letter can be combined with a document containing any number of names and addresses. The computer may then be instructed to print one letter for each addressee.

Center   The word processor can speedily center titles and other text when given the **Center** command.

Paginate   The word processor's **pagination** can rearrange text on pages after additions and revision. It also automatically numbers and renumbers pages of a text when given the proper command.

Math   Some word processors contain a **math** function that allows numbers to be added, subtracted, multiplied, and divided. This is helpful for calculating numbers within the document while typing, or for checking totals on columns of numbers to eliminate typographical errors.

Cursor Draw   **Cursor draw** creates box or line drawings. It may be used to set text apart for emphasis, or to divide blocks of text for clarification. In addition to the straight line, other characters may be substituted to create interesting boxes and borders. This feature may also be used to create simple line or bar graphs within the text.

Save   The **Save** command ends the document and copies it to a disk for storage. When revising documents, some systems allow saving with or without the current revisions. The more sophisticated systems also copy a document to file in ASCII (American Standard Code for Information Interchange) format for use on other computer systems or with other software programs.

Print   The **Print** command directs the computer to print an entire document or only a portion of it. The user may be able to select the number of copies desired; other print options may be available, depending on the program.

In addition to the above terms, which are basic to most word processors, there are numerous other functions and capabilities for the user to consider. The following section contains a list of these, which should help novices to determine what best fits their needs.

Word Processing Command Checklist

This checklist summarizes the commands offered by popular word processing software packages. By using it—or a customized version that reflects individual priorities—prospective buyers can compare the capabilities of different word processing packages. Purchasing should be based on price, vendor reputation, documentation quality, and classroom needs. For example, ease of use, help screens, and prompts will help the teacher to instruct and the student to learn. New features appear every day.

DOCUMENT CREATION
Cursor Movement
Move cursor left and right by character/word
Move cursor to left and right on a line
Move cursor up and down one line
Move cursor to top of screen (first space of first line)
Move cursor to bottom of screen
Move cursor to beginning/end of document
Move cursor to next screen
Move cursor to start of next line
Move cursor to a specified page
Scrolling
Scroll text up and down one line
Scroll text up and down one screen
Screen Formatting
Set/clear all tabs
Set/clear single tab
Set left and right margins
Margin release
Word wrap
Variable word wrap
Reformat paragraph
Automatic page breaks
Manual page breaks
Automatic hyphenation

EDITING
Inserting and Deleting
Insert character
Delete character/next character
Delete preceding character
Delete next word
Delete remainder of line
Delete entire line
Delete to end of document
Delete through specified character
Delete paragraph
Block Operations
Copy block (of text)
Move block
Delete block
Erase all block markers
Print block
Hide/display block
Write block to file

Search and Replace Operations
Find string
Find string and replace
Find string and replace with verification
Find string and replace *n* times
Global find and replace
Repeat last find operation
Ignore a specific string occurrence when searching
Match only whole words
Search and replace operations using "wild cards"
Search and delete

DOCUMENT FORMATTING
Page Layout
Set top, bottom, left, right margins
Insert page headings
Insert page footings
Set heading margin
Set footing margin
Set physical page length
Set number of characters per inch
Set number of lines per inch
Temporary left margin offset
Indent first line of paragraphs
Indent lines of paragraphs after first line
Number paragraphs
Insert <LF> between paragraphs
Suppress headings and footings
Page numbering
Page number suppression
Book style page numbering (odd numbers on right)
Force new page
Two-column printing
Create tables
Justification
Right justify
Center
Ragged left margin
Hard spaces (cannot be closed up)
Hard hyphens (cannot be separated from preceding and following text)
Automatic alignment of decimal data
Character Attributes
Underline
Boldface
Shadowed (double strike)

Variable intensity boldface
Superscript
Subscript
Overprint
Combined attributes (i.e., ribbon color shift)
Proportional spacing
Continuously variable character spacing
Explicit alternate character pitch
Pitch-independent line lengths

UTILITIES AND SPECIAL FEATURES
Document/File Operations
Display file directory
Save file
Exit file without saving
Save file and continue editing
Automatic backup—one generation
Automatic backup—n generations
Read file
Read part of file
Delete file
Delete files with "wild cards"
Rename file
Link/merge WP documents and non-WP documents (i.e., VisiCalc)
Move text blocks from document to document
Copy text blocks from document to document

Printer Control
Print a specified page
Print starting from a specified page
Print through a specified page
Print starting from cursor position
Print with values from a specified disk record
Print until a specified record is read
Print multiple copies of a document
Interrupt/resume printing
Display/change print format
Pause and display message
Continuous printing of multiple documents (print spooling)
Convert to all upper case
Convert to upper/lower case

Miscellaneous (mostly new) Features
Grammar check/correct
Business graphics (character graphics)
Display options (screen colors)
Mail list create/update/select/sort routines

Columnar math
Automatic table of contents
Automatic index
Macros (keystroke programming)
"What you see is what you get" display (print enhancements on screen)
Security passwords by library, by document
Electronic mail packages
Columnar math
Spelling check/correct
Phone index, appointment calendar, card file routines
Syntax check
Thesaurus

All the options we've discussed are useful; however, it may be necessary to choose among them depending on the school's computer system and the needs of individual teachers and students. In the following sections we will discuss in more detail some of the features that are most advantageous.

COLUMNS AND TABLES

Often it is desirable to present text and numbers in columns and in tables. Many word processors allow the user to design columns and tables to fit their data. Most systems offer two types of columns—tabular (or parallel) and text (or newspaper). Creating either involves three basic steps: 1) defining the columns, 2) activating the column feature, and 3) typing text and numeric data into each column.

Tables consist of parallel columns, which keep blocks of text next to (parallel to) each other on the same page. A history teacher could use parallel columns to display descriptions of historical events from different time periods. By placing these descriptions in columns side by side on a page, students can compare them more easily and efficiently. (If a parallel column continues from one page to another, the user must define a page break, or create a new set of columns for each page, depending on the software in use.)

Parallel columns would also be useful to display scientific formulas and other information. Such information displayed side by side for comparison and explanation makes it easier for the student to comprehend and simplifies the teacher's task of presenting the material.

As the name implies, newspaper columns are used for text (or numbers or both) that continues from one column to another on the same page, and can continue onto subsequent pages. Newspaper columns use the word wrap function to do this, keeping the text within the defined column width.

The creation and publishing of a class or school newspaper would be an excellent use for newspaper columns. Such a project offers students opportunities far beyond the lessons in journalism that are apparent in this application. For example, students might learn that communication between varied groups requires presenting different kinds of information in different ways. Publishing a newspaper, even with the limited scope of a single classroom, provides experiences that mirror the political, civic, and academic environments of the larger world.

For both parallel and newspaper columns, the number of columns is limited only by the width of the document itself. The document width, of course, is determined by setting the left and right margins. Column width may also vary. For example the user may need a two-character column for a number and a forty-character column to contain a paragraph of text.

It's also possible to create columns for existing data. This procedure varies from one software program to another. Some allow users to create the columns with the data in place, whereas others instruct the user to create columns and then retrieve data into them. Usually either way is simple and is explained by on-screen messages during the process.

Columns can be manipulated in much the same way as other text. They can be inserted, deleted, moved, and copied. When revising a document, each column is treated as a separate block of text and can be changed without affecting other columns. Printing enhancements such as boldface type and underlining can be used in columns.

Some word processors allow the user to set up reference areas, either at the top of a table of columns or at the left side. Reference areas identify what a column or row of data contains and are especially helpful when revising the contents. Top reference areas identify columns, and side reference areas (appearing at the left side of the screen and document) identify rows.

MERGE

Many word processing software programs have a merge function that allows for two or more documents to be combined. One of the most common applications of the merge function is to create form letters that appear to be individualized. The basic form letter is typed once, with special codes inserted where data will differ for each letter. This is called the primary document.

A secondary document is then created that contains a page for each letter that is to be produced. Each page in turn contains the variable data for a particular letter. (Examples of **variable** data are name, address, phone number, salutation, account balance, and so on.)

When the two documents are merged, the system will print one letter for each page in the secondary document. Each letter will contain the variable data from the secondary document page plus the complete basic letter from the primary document. In this way, names, addresses, and salutations can be inserted at the beginning of a form letter, which then looks as if it were originally created only for the addressee.

The classroom teacher can use merge to create a form letter that, when printed, would appear to be a personalized letter addressed to the parents of each student. In addition to a different name, address, and salutation for each letter, other variable information can be inserted as desired. This function can save the teacher a great deal of time in communicating with parents without sacrificing the ability to make each letter pertinent to the individual student's situation.

The secondary document can also be used to print lists of names, addresses, or virtually any text contained within the document. It can be used to generate mailing labels. If there is a large amount of variable information, it can be contained in a database that can be merged with a word processed document in the same way. (See Chapter 7 on databases.)

Another way to create documents for merging is to type one paragraph per document page. During the merge process, the user can then specify which paragraphs are to be included in a particular document by specifying page numbers to be merged. Teachers can use this method for writing up objectives for individual students.

In addition, many word processors allow the user to type information at predetermined locations within the document. This eliminates the step of creating a secondary file. However, since it doesn't save the variable data for future use, it's most useful for one-time situations. For instance, teachers could create documents in which students insert the appropriate information, to teach or reinforce spelling, vocabulary, and grammar concepts.

MACRO

A **macro** is a simple process of recording and saving a sequence of keystrokes in a file that can be recalled for future use. It is a shortcut for entering frequently used commands. Data, or a combination of data and commands, can also be entered in this way. Macros can range from short, simple entries to elaborate chains of commands. Obviously the more complex the function, the more time is saved by creating and using a macro, if it is needed often enough to warrant it.

A macro is assigned a name that the user types in to implement the series of keystrokes or data that it represents. Instead of names, macros can be assigned to specific keys; this is sometimes called keystroke programming. To activate the macro, the user presses the specified key (or more often a combination of two keys) rather than typing in a macro name.

The macros described above are permanent and will remain on the disk on which they have been saved. Temporary macros may also be created

This school newspaper was written and laid out on a word processor.

The Apple Core

Vol. 1 No. 2   *Park Tudor Middle School*   *October 1988*

Sixth grade takes mystery trip

by
Catherine Price

On Wednesday, September 28, at about 9:30, 59 sixth graders were told to go to the Commons to pick up sack lunches. Soon we were told we were going on a mystery trip. No matter how much we begged, no teacher informed us where we were going.

After being loaded into a bus, we were shipped downtown to the Hawthorne Railroad Yards at Prospect Street and Southeastern Avenue. We were told to eat lunch while standing on the train tracks. The food was salty and it seemed nobody brought enough to drink.

Mrs. Schafer finally revealed that we were waiting for the circus train. Some of us imagined what it was like for children 100 years ago who waited, like us, for the arrival of the circus train.

An ice cream truck saved us from the stifling heat. After everyone got ice cream, the train unloaded its cargo and the animals marched past us on the way to perform at Market Square Arena for five days.

We saw llamas, horses, ponies, a camel, elephants, and most important of all, King Tusk, a forty-two year old, 7 ton pachyderm.

Jim Combs said, " It was really hot, and the elephants smelled, but the ice cream was refreshing."

Our mystery trip gave us a taste of the excitement people felt who lived in small towns a century ago.

Afterwards, we went to the Natatorium to get drinks (not from the pool), and to Broad Ripple park to play. We got back very tired at 2:30 p.m.

Mr. Nordby brings quintet to P.T.

by
Sarah Cohen

Gorgeous sounds floated out of the Middle School's new library Tuesday afternoon. DePauw's Woodwind Quintet, which consists of an oboe, flute, french horn, clarinet, and a bassoon, played to a very appreciative audience.

Sharon Lange played the oboe at this assembly. She plays for the Indianapolis Symphony Orchestra and has performed in many festivals.

Larry Philpott played the french horn. Even though the french horn is a brass instrument, it blends very nicely with the rest of the woodwinds. Larry Philpott is the principle

See DEPAUW Page 2

for use during one word processing session and are deleted automatically when the session ends.

Macros may also be combined with merges. The possible combinations are numerous and differ greatly from one software program to another.

With use, it will become apparent which of the available options and combinations of options will be of most benefit.

One of the concerns inherent in using microcomputers and word processing software in the classroom is the amount of time needed to implement the various functions. Using macros is an ideal way to decrease the time needed for all students to arrive at a particular point in the lesson. By pressing one or two keys instead of many, the time saved can be devoted to the lesson itself.

DISADVANTAGES OF WORD PROCESSING

While word processing allows fast, accurate text editing, it has several disadvantages. Fluctuations in electrical current can damage disks or keep text that is being entered from going into memory. In this case, the text must be entered (retyped) again. Also, diskettes are fragile and easily damaged. If damage occurs, text will not be properly stored on the disk and must be retyped. Damage to hardware can result in text being removed unexpectedly from memory or disk.

To minimize the risk of data loss, the user can create backup disks. This is a simple matter of copying one or more files (or the entire contents) from the original disk to a new disk. Text stored on a computer's hard disk should always be backed up on diskettes as a safeguard in the event of power failure or system malfunction.

While creating a document of some length, it's a good practice to save the data after several pages are input. In this way, large amounts of data will not be lost in case of system failure.

Many software programs allow the user to save the document without leaving it; they can then continue to create or revise it. This helpful feature allows for quick and easy protection of data while the cursor remains at the same place in the document; the user can resume input immediately without having to exit and reenter the document.

SUMMARY

Word processing refers to writing, manipulating, and storing text in a computerized medium. The use of computers to input and output text is one simple definition of word processing. Word processing allows text—such as essays or reports—to be entered by means of a keyboard similar to that of a typewriter. Further adjustments of a text are possible by giving different commands to the system.

Word processing began in 1964 when IBM introduced the Magnetic Tape/Selectic Typewriter, which stored characters entered by the operator on magnetic tapes. The first word processor for a microcomputer was developed by Seymour Rubinstein and Bob Barnaby. Word processing software has become the most popular use of the microcomputer. After the mid-1970s, the field of word processing blossomed as many different companies began developing programs to suit various needs.

Four types of word processors are available: time-sharing, shared logic, stand-alone systems (dedicated word processors), and the microcomputers with word processing software. An alternative to the dedicated word processor, the microcomputer uses software that turns it into a sophisticated word processor. Since it can use other software (such as databases, spreadsheets, and graphics), the microcomputer is a good choice for the classroom.

School districts purchase word processing equipment for elementary and high school classrooms where students compose text. Universities purchase word processors for many uses, including the writing of manuscripts, research reports, grant proposals, and public relations materials.

Word processing is useful in teaching many subjects in addition to writing. Through the process of computer instruction, students also learn about how things work in the world beyond school. Teachers gain time to teach concepts, while letting the computer perform some of the more routine tasks that previously were part of their responsibilities.

This chapter provided an overview of word processing terms and commands. A checklist, covering document creation, editing, formatting, utilities, and special features, summarized the commands offered by popular word processing software packages. Teachers and administrators can use the checklist to help them choose a package that meets their needs.

More detailed descriptions of some of the highly sophisticated and valuable functions of word processing were also discussed. The columns and tables function allows users to create columns and tables to fit their data. Merge allows two or more documents to be combined. Common applications of the merge function are creating form letters that appear to be individualized and creating documents of paragraphs that can then be merged in any combination. Macros, which record and save a sequence of keystrokes in a file that can be recalled for future use, are a shortcut for entering frequently used commands.

While word processing allows fast, accurate text editing, it has several disadvantages. Fluctuations in electrical current can damage disks or keep text that is being entered from going into memory. Also, diskettes are fragile and easily damaged. Damage to hardware can result in text being removed unexpectedly from memory or disk.

To minimize the risk of data loss, the user can create backup disks. Text stored on a computer's hard disk should always be backed up on diskettes as a safeguard in the event of power failure or system malfunction.

A wide variety of hardware and software is available to classroom teachers who wish to incorporate word processing into their teaching. Many factors must be considered when choosing a word processor, such as the teacher, the student population, the curriculum, the school district, and the funds available and how they are allocated. However, once a decision is made and equipment is in place, both teachers and students will benefit greatly from this newest classroom tool.

REVIEW EXERCISES

Multiple Choice

1. IBM introduced the Magnetic Tape/Selectric Typewriter, a forerunner of current word processors, in
   a. 1954
   b. 1964
   c. 1974
   d. none of the above
2. Word processing allows the creation of documents with more
   a. speed
   b. accuracy
   c. professional appearance
   d. all of the above
3. Which of the following is *not* a type of word processing system?
   a. dedicated
   b. shared logic
   c. top down structure
   d. time sharing
4. The advantage of using word processing software on a microcomputer is that
   a. it is faster than a dedicated word processor
   b. it costs less than buying a typewriter
   c. the computer can be used for other functions as well
   d. all of the above
5. Word processing is useful in
   a. government
   b. business
   c. education
   d. all of the above
6. The ability of the cursor to move automatically to the beginning of the next line in the document is called
   a. word wrap
   b. justification
   c. spacing
   d. none of the above
7. Which word processing command is used to move backward or forward in a document quickly?
   a. Search
   b. Merge
   c. Format
   d. Go To
8. Columns and tables are created during word processing for the purpose of
   a. setting information apart for emphasis
   b. placing data side by side for comparison
   c. printing text in columns
   d. all of the above
9. Two or more documents are merged to
   a. create individualized form letters
   b. form a document outline
   c. save disk space
   d. none of the above
10. Word processing offers math functions for the purpose of
    a. checking totals of rows and columns of figures
    b. making numeric calculations within a document
    c. counting number of pages in a document
    d. a and b

True/False

1. The cursor marks spaces on the video screen.
2. Time sharing systems require users to wait until the computer is free.
3. Students can use word processors to type and edit their essays.
4. Justification is the process of renumbering pages after text has been edited.
5. The copy command causes extra copies of a document to be printed.
6. The search command locates every occurrence of a particular word, phrase, or number within a document.

7. A table may contain no more than four columns.
8. A word processed document may be merged with databases and spreadsheets.
9. When using the math function, a numeric pad on a computer acts as a calculator.
10. Documents should *never* be copied from a hard disk to a floppy disk.

Short Answer

1. Define the term *word processing*.
2. List some applications of word processing in universities.
3. What is the difference between a header and a footer?
4. Why is it useful to merge several documents?
5. Explain the purpose of math functions in word processing software.

Activities

1. Visit a local computer retail store to compare several popular word processing packages.
2. Make a list of the ways you could use a word processor at school, work, or home.
3. Research how computers are being used to teach writing skills in elementary and secondary schools and in colleges and universities.
4. Consult the want ad pages of a local newspaper to see what job opportunities are available in word processing. Report on your findings.
5. Invite a legal secretary, journalist, teacher, or business person to speak to your class about word processing applications in his or her career field.
6. Find at least ten help-wanted advertisements that require word processing knowledge or experience.
7. List several job titles for positions that require word processing knowledge or experience.
8. List educational or training opportunities to learn word processing.
9. For a specific curriculum topic, develop a detailed lesson plan that requires word processing.

BIBLIOGRAPHY

Baer, Vicki E. "Attitudes Toward Writing with Different Tools." *The Computing Teacher* 15 (no. 5): 16.

Bitter, Gary G. *Computers in Today's World.* New York: John Wiley, 1984.

Bitter, Gary G. (with Stephen Rossberg). "Microcomputer Infusion Project: A Model." *Tech Trends* (October 1988): 24–28.

Bitter, Gary G., and Ruth Camuse. *Using a Microcomputer in the Classroom.* Englewood Cliffs, N.J.: Prentice-Hall, 1988.

Bright, George W. *Microcomputer Applications in the Elementary Classroom.* Boston: Allyn & Bacon, 1987.

Coburn, Edward J. *Learn to Compute!* Albany, N.Y.: Delmar, 1988.

Daiute, Colette. *Writing and Computers.* Menlo Park, Calif.: Addison-Wesley, 1985.

Gerlach, G. J. "The Effect of Typing Skill on Using a Word Processor for Composition." *The Computing Teacher* 15 (no. 7): 7.

Grauer, Robert T., and Paul Sugrue. *Microcomputer Applications.* New York: McGraw-Hill, 1987.

Johnston, Randolph. *Microcomputers: Concepts and Applications.* Santa Cruz, Calif.: Mitchell, 1987.

Kelly, Susan Baake. *Mastering WordPerfect.* Alameda, Calif.: Sybex, 1987.

Knapp, Linda Roehrig. *The Word Processor and the Writing Teacher.* Englewood Cliffs, N.J.: Prentice-Hall, 1986.

Mehan, Hugh, et al. *The Write Help.* Glenview, Ill.: Scott, Foresman, 1986.

O'Brien, George E., and Edward L. Pizzini. "Word Processing/Text Editing and the Quality of Student Abstracts." *School Science and Mathematics Journal* (March 1986): 223.

Palmer, Adelaide. "Changing Teacher and Student Attitudes Through Word Processing." *The Computing Teacher* 11 (no. 9, May 1984): 45–47.

SOFTWARE PUBLISHERS

Claris Corp.
440 Clyde Ave.
Mountain View, CA 94043

FrEdWriter
(public domain software) available at:
CUE Softswap
San Mateo County Office of Education
333 Main RC
San Mateo, CA 94401

Gram.mat.ik. II
Suite 31
330 Townsend St.
San Francisco, CA 94107

Houghton Mifflin Co.
Dept. 67
Mount Support Rd./CN 9000
Lebanon, NH 03766–9000

Meizner Business Machines, Inc.
4771 Boston Post Rd.
Pelham, NY 10803

Microsoft Corp.
16011 N.E. 36th Way
Box 97017
Redmond, WA 98073

Milliken Publishing Co.
P.O. Box 21579
St. Louis, MO 63132–0579

Scholastic Inc.
730 Broadway
New York, NY 10003

Sunburst Communications
39 Washington Ave.
Pleasantville, NY 10570–9970

True/False

1. T	5. F	9. T
2. F	6. T	10. F
3. T	7. F	
4. F	8. T	

Short Answer

1. Writing, manipulating, and storing text in a computerized medium.
2. Writing manuscripts, research reports, grant proposals, and public relations materials.
3. A header appears at the top and a footer appears at the bottom of a page.
4. To create individualized form letters; to include lengthy portions of different documents in a new document without retyping.
5. Calculations may be performed while typing a document; totals of rows and columns of numbers may be checked for accuracy.

REVIEW ANSWER KEY

Multiple Choice

1. b	5. d	9. a
2. d	6. a	10. d
3. c	7. d	
4. c	8. d	

CHAPTER 6

SPREADSHEETS

Objectives

- Define the term *electronic spreadsheet*
- List educational applications of spreadsheets
- Describe how to create a spreadsheet and input data
- Describe how to perform an analysis of spreadsheet information
- Describe how a teacher might use an electronic spreadsheet in the classroom

Key Terms

active cell
cell
column
command mode
copy
current cell
delete
edit
electronic spreadsheet
erase
formula
function
heading
hierarchy
insert
justification
label
modeling
move
projection
range
scrolling
template
title
window

One of the most widely used computer applications is the **electronic spreadsheet**. Perhaps the best way to describe an electronic spreadsheet is to visualize on the computer screen an accountant's ledger sheet with its array of horizontal rows and vertical **columns**. Each row and column contains information (which can be both letters and numbers) that may be organized in such a way as to be easily understandable to the viewer. The term *spreadsheet* itself implies material spread before the eye of the user for quick and easy reference.

While the electronic spreadsheet performs exactly such a function, that is only the beginning of what it can do. Each piece of data entered into the spreadsheet is considered in its relationship to all the other data contained therein. In this way, any change made in one part can affect the whole spreadsheet. Information can be manipulated to reflect potential change in any or all sections of the spreadsheet.

The electronic spreadsheet can automatically recompute and change any data affected by an entry, almost instantaneously. It takes little imagination to recognize the time saved over doing the same task on a ledger sheet, with an eraser and calculator at hand. In addition, since computers do not make mistakes in calculations as humans are apt to do, the potential time saved in looking for errors is even more impressive. The spreadsheet has presented speedy solutions to many tasks. As it develops further, it continues to present ever more sophisticated capabilities.

The beginning screen of a popular spreadsheet. Rows are numbered 1–18 and columns A–H.

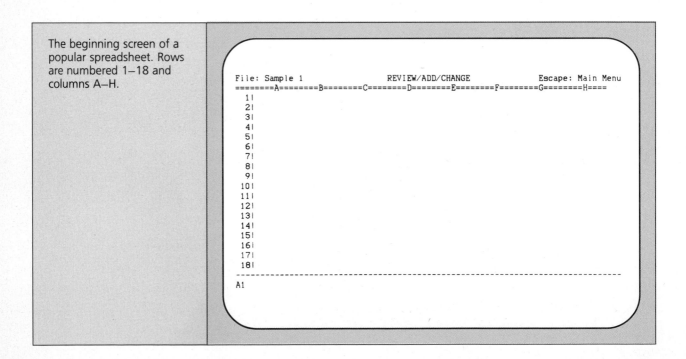

```
File: Sample 1                  REVIEW/ADD/CHANGE              Escape: Main Menu
========A=========B=========C=========D=========E=========F=========G========H====
  1|
  2|
  3|
  4|
  5|
  6|
  7|
  8|
  9|
 10|
 11|
 12|
 13|
 14|
 15|
 16|
 17|
 18|
-------------------------------------------------------------------------------
A1
```

SPREADSHEETS: THEIR HISTORY AND USE

The electronic spreadsheet made its debut in 1979, a creation of two Harvard Business School graduate students, Daniel Bricklin and Robert Frankston. They named their program VisiCalc, and it became the prototype for many other software programs that formed the first generation of electronic spreadsheets.

The second generation came on the scene with the introduction of Lotus 1-2-3. This program was unique in that it was the first integrated software program. An integrated software program blends several different programs so that information can be presented in various forms (see also Chapter 9). For example, a graphics option allows the user to create visual aids, such as line graphs, vertical and horizontal bar graphs, and pie-shaped charts. In this way, the figures from the spreadsheet can be converted to graphs that show at a glance what the user wishes to communicate about the financial picture. (See Chapter 8 for a discussion on graphics software.)

Another option contained in Lotus 1-2-3 is database management. A database is an electronic filing system in which large volumes of data (information) can be stored and organized. For instance, names, addresses, phone numbers, and account numbers can be entered into a database. That information can then be sorted alphabetically, numerically, or in any other way that will be helpful to the user. In an integrated program, when any of the stored information is needed, it can be retrieved from the database and inserted into the spreadsheet. The time saved in locating and adding data to a spreadsheet made this new generation of software a welcome addition to the electronic spreadsheet family. (See Chapter 7 for a detailed discussion of databases.)

The most recent addition to this family, and the beginning of the third generation, is the integrated software program with extended capabilities, adding word processing, expanded spreadsheet size, and communications between computers. Word processing allows text to be added to the report. In this way an explanation of the spreadsheet figures or the graphic pictures can complete a financial report.

Another improvement is the potential size of spreadsheets. Spreadsheet programs vary in the numbers of rows and columns available, but average size is much larger now than what was originally offered. Any number of these columns and rows may be used, depending on the needs of the user and the memory capacity of the computer. While only a small portion of this total picture appears on the computer screen at one time, the user may move around within the spreadsheet to display any part of it.

The other improvement in this latest generation of spreadsheet programs is the ability of computers to communicate with each other. Through the new technology of telecommunications, computers in different locations can communicate by telephone lines and exchange data as needed. (See Chapter 9 on telecommunications.) Examples of programs combining all of the above options are Enable and Microsoft Works.

With these enhancements and increased options available to the user, many more educational applications became apparent. Following is a discussion of some of those applications.

Spreadsheets in Education

One of the most obvious uses for spreadsheets in education is to teach accounting, both principles and practical applications. Math and science also have a similar need to teach concepts and theories, as well as to manipulate vast amounts of numerical and statistical information. Additionally, math teachers find the spreadsheet helpful in teaching students to write and use mathematical formulas.

In a math class using spreadsheets, students can see displayed on a computer screen the logical relationship between numbers and mathematical operations. Other lessons are also enhanced by teaching math on spreadsheets. For example, the logic of transferring a problem written in

This spreadsheet represents a page of a teacher's gradebook for seven students. Each student has five test scores, a total score, and an average score.

```
File: Gradebook                REVIEW/ADD/CHANGE              Escape: Main Menu
===========A==========B=====C=====D=====E=====F=======G========H========I====
 1IGradebook
 2I
 3INames          #1   #2   #3   #4   #5   Total    Ave.
 4I
 5IAndrews, R.    82   99   78   84   98    441     88.2
 6IBarker, M.     76   79   99   76   65    395     79.0
 7IFisher, M.     88  100   98   76  100    462     92.4
 8IJohnson, D.    96   95   99   96  100    486     97.2
 9IMichaels, D.   56   77   99   88   79    399     79.8
10IParker, T.     89   97   79   76   99    440     88.0
11IRobertson, J.  94   85   92  100   88    459     91.8
12I
13ITest Averages  83   90   92   85   90    440     88.1
14I
15I
16I
17I
18I
------------------------------------------------------------------------------
A1: (Label) Gradebook
```

text, usually called "story problems," to a spreadsheet sharpens students' cognitive skills.

By entering instructions in the form of formulas, students reinforce the learning of mathematical symbols and the standard order of precedence. Decimals, percentages, and the computation of simple and compound interest are other areas of math study that are expedited and explained more fully when displayed in spreadsheet format.

In addition to math, other subjects may also be better explained, as well as made more interesting, with the use of spreadsheets. The analysis of social studies data (such as population growth, income distribution, census information) and the results of scientific studies are only a few of the potential uses for spreadsheets in classroom teaching.

Spreadsheets can be used to maintain student records and specifically grade reports. To most effectively use the computer's ability to manipulate data, grades can be combined to compute their average, mean, median, and various ranges in a class, or group of classes. On the other hand, specific data can be isolated from the rest (for instance, to view an individual student's records). Virtually any piece of information desired is at the user's fingertips.

Schools, colleges, and universities are organizations with employees, income, and expenses just like any other business. Therefore, all uses of computer technology in general and spreadsheets in particular that apply to business and industry apply also to educational organizations. For example, employees' personnel and payroll records, the organizational budget, balance sheets for income and overhead, and reports supporting need for additional funding are only a few of the many administrative tasks for which the spreadsheet can be helpful. Various special interest groups and clubs also exist in the educational environment. They, too, have budgets, income, and expenses that can be managed through the use of spreadsheets.

Still another educational function for spreadsheets is the management of data by researchers. Large amounts of demographic and statistical information can be gathered through survey questionnaires and entered into a computer's database. Then the computer's spreadsheet compiles and analyzes the data in whatever way fits the purpose of the researcher.

Spreadsheets for Individuals

While all of the above activities affect us as individuals, there are even more personal ways in which the electronic spreadsheet serves us. It can balance the checkbook, manage household expenses, organize and store income tax records, project interest income, and aid in budgeting and planning for the future.

Students will be working in the real world—in business and industry, education, or in government or nonprofit agencies. Spreadsheets will inev-

**Sample Lesson Plan—
Spreadsheet**

Spending Time

Objective: Determine how much time you spend doing your activities.

Application: Spreadsheet

Assumptions: There are 24 hours in a day and 7 days in a week.

For calculation purposes, a month is measured as 4.3 weeks.

Students typically spend 5 days a week in school and engage in other activities during the weekend.

Discussion:

There are times when you may wish to find out how much time you spend doing your daily tasks. You or your friends may have heard adults complain that kids spend too much time watching TV or not enough time studying. It is surprising to some people how much time they spend doing a particular task in a week, a month, or even a year. The spreadsheet that follows can be used as a template for the lesson.

```
    A======B======C======D======E======F======G======H======
  1 │Time Spent on Activities
  2 │
  3 │          Weekday  Weekend  Week Tot  Mon. Tot  % Spent
  4 │
  5 │School       6        0        30       129     17.9%
  6 │Sleep        8        8        56       240.8   33.3%
  7 │Hobbies      2        4        18        77.4   10.7%
  8 │Exercise     1        2         9        38.7    5.4%
  9 │Study        1        2         9        38.7    5.4%
 10 │Meals        2        2        14        60.2    8.3%
 11 │TV           4        6        32       137.6   19.0%
 12 │
 13 │Totals      24       24       168       722.4  100.0%
 14 │
 15 │
 16 │
 17 │
 18 │
    ─────────────────────────────────────────────────────────
```

The template lists activities typical of most junior high students and the amount of time each student might spend doing each task. The Weekday column is for daily times and the Weekend column for weekend times. The Week Tot. column computes the total for the week. Since there are five weekdays and two weekend days, the formula used to obtain the total weekly time is to multiply (the weekday time for each activity * 5) (each weekend activity * 2). The monthly figure (Mon. Tot column) is obtained by multiplying each activity's time in the weekly column by 4.3. Finally the % Spent column determines the percentage of time spent on each activity during the week. Each cell's value in column D (Week Tot) is divided by the weekly time total in cell D13. That is: The percentage in cell F5 = D5 / D13, cell G5 = D6 / D13, and so on.

Enter the template into a spreadsheet program such as AppleWorks with the values shown and save it.

Questions and Activities:

1. How many hours does this student spend sleeping in a week? In a month? What percentage of time does the student spend sleeping?
2. How many hours are there in a week? How many hours are there in a month? How close is the figure to the approximate figure in cell E13?
3. How many hours a week does this student spend watching television?
4. The student's grades are not very good. What changes might be made to the spreadsheet when you increase the number of hours spent for studying?
5. Revise the spreadsheet by entering the hours you spend doing various activities. Change task names to suit your needs. Save your personal spreadsheet under a new file name.

Activity—Higher-order Thinking

I. The spreadsheet only calculates for the months that you are in school. Add your summer schedule to your personal spreadsheet. If you have tasks that you do during the summer months, but not during the school year, you must include them in both lists. The same is true if you do things during the school year but not during the summer. If you don't go to school during the summer, you simply enter the value 0 for the amount of time spent in school. Calculate the total for all 52 weeks of the year. Save this new template under a new file name. Make conjectures on how you could improve your time management.

itably be a part of their world. For that reason students will benefit from hands-on, classroom training with the spreadsheet.

Some education-oriented spreadsheets are Educalc (Houghton Mifflin), AppleWorks (Claris), Microsoft Works (Microsoft), and First Choice (Meizner Business Machines). Teachers should evaluate the available software and determine their particular needs. Chapter 12 offers assistance in evaluating software. (Addresses for software publishers are at the end of this chapter.)

Now that we know how helpful a spreadsheet can be, let's look at the practical application and fundamentals of electronic spreadsheets.

FUNDAMENTALS OF SPREADSHEETS

The spreadsheet has three modes of operation: ready, entry, and command. It always begins in the ready mode, in which the user presses the directional, or arrow, keys to move around within the spreadsheet. When the user begins to enter data into the spreadsheet, the entry mode is activated automatically. The **command mode** is used to manipulate data for various purposes that we will explore later. The command mode is also invoked when the user is ready to perform calculations on the data entered. A third function of this mode is to instruct the computer what to do with the spreadsheet once it is completed.

In the past, the typical ledger sheets used by accountants and others who deal with figures were already laid out in a specific pattern and preprinted on paper. The electronic spreadsheet, on the other hand, is a blank computer screen that may be designed by the user to suit a particular need. Number and arrangement of columns and rows to accommodate the data to be entered are the first items to be considered. These considerations also determine the size of the finished spreadsheet.

Spreadsheet Size

The size of a spreadsheet is limited by the software program being used. Some spreadsheets are as small as sixty-three columns by 255 rows. One of the best-selling spreadsheet programs has 254 columns by 2,048 rows. Other programs have varying numbers of columns and rows. The size of the formatted spreadsheet is determined by the number of rows and columns needed to perform a specific task. Only a small portion of the entire spreadsheet is visible on the display screen at one time. However, the user can view any other portion of the spreadsheet by using the *cursor* keys to bring other areas into view.

Cursor Movement

Cursor keys are the ones with directional arrows that move the cursor to the left or right and up or down. Some programs allow the cursor to move more rapidly when the Home, End, Page Up, or Page Down keys are pressed. In addition, most programs allow the user to move directly to any specific area of the spreadsheet with a Go To command. The most common key used to activate the Go To command is the equal sign (=). After pressing the Go To key, the user must tell the computer where to go. This is accomplished by designating a *cell* location.

Cells

A **cell** is the point on the spreadsheet at which a row and column intersect. Most programs provide letter designations for columns, for example A, B, C . . . on to Z, then AA to AZ, BA to BZ, and so on for as many columns as the spreadsheet contains. Rows, on the other hand, are numbered beginning with one. Thus, a cell location might be D3, meaning the intersection of column D and row three.

There are some programs that use numbers for both rows and columns. In that case, the above cell location would be designated as C4 R3, again meaning the intersection of column number four and row number three.

When the user activates the Go To command and enters a cell location, the program instantly moves the cursor to that position. The cell where the cursor is currently positioned is referred to by most programs as the **current**, or **active**, **cell**.

Two different kinds of entries are possible at the current cell position. Either text (letters) or numeric data (numbers) can be entered from the keyboard. Numeric data is used to make calculations. Text, of course, cannot be used in this way.

To ensure accuracy as entries are made, many programs provide a line, sometimes called a *data entry line,* where the information appears as it is typed. The data does not go directly into the cell but remains on the entry data line until the Enter, or Return key is pressed. If there are errors, they can be corrected on this line before the data is placed in the cell. When the Enter key is pressed, the computer transfers what appears on the entry line into the current cell.

After information is entered into cells, some programs move automatically to the next cell. If the program in use does not have this feature, the user must move to the next cell with one of the cursor keys.

In addition to number and arrangement of columns and rows, other decisions must be made by the user regarding headings, labels, values, formulas, and commands. We discuss these one at a time in the following sections.

Headings

Headings appear at the top of the spreadsheet. Headings are titles, names, or any identifying information that describe the contents of the spreadsheet. A heading should give an accurate picture of what the spreadsheet was created for and what it contains. The heading should be clear and concise, as shown in the example below, so that anyone who receives a copy of or works with the spreadsheet can easily see what it contains.

> **Example:**   EMC522 PERSONALITY DEVELOPMENT
> (INSTRUCTOR'S NAME)
> SEMESTER GRADES FOR SPRING 1989

This heading makes it quite clear that this spreadsheet contains students' grades for the Spring 1989 semester in a specific course taught by the identified instructor. More detailed identification of the spreadsheet contents may be made by the use of *labels*.

Labels   Like headings, **labels** are titles, names, or other identifying information that describe the contents of rows or columns. They need to be descriptive, informing the viewer of exactly what is contained in each row and column. For example, in the spreadsheet for students' grades, the row labels might consist of students' names while column labels would contain identifying names of what will be graded (tests, papers, class participation).

Labels may consist of both letters and numbers. However, if the label begins with a number, the user must make it clear to the computer that this is indeed a label. This is done by pressing a key defined by the software program to indicate that what follows is a label. The data is then typed and entered into the cell. The most common character used to designate a label is the quotation mark ("). If a distinction is not made in some manner for a label that begins with a number, the computer will confuse it with a value.

Values   Values are numbers entered into any cell. The computer always interprets numeric entries as values, unless indicated otherwise (as described above). Values are used to enter financial and statistical information into cells. It is crucial that only entries that are true representations of values be input as numerical data. It is also important that the values be entered accurately.

An aid for entering data correctly is the status line. The status line tells you where the cursor is located and what the cell contains. In addition, the status line of some programs indicates what kind of entry is being made. If numbers are being entered, the line will read "value," and if letters are typed, it will say "label," or "text."

Formulas   Once the columns and rows are labeled and the financial or statistical information is entered into cells, the user must tell the computer what is to be done with this data. This is accomplished by the use of **formulas**. The formulas used in spreadsheets are much like the mathematical formulas used elsewhere.

Most spreadsheets use the standard mathematical order of precedence. That is, mathematical functions are performed in the same order that they are done on paper. Higher orders of precedence are performed before the lower orders. For instance, multiplication and division are calculated before addition and subtraction. Also, whatever is enclosed in parentheses is always calculated first.

However, some spreadsheets do not use the order of precedence but calculate from left to right. It is necessary to determine how the spreadsheet program being used handles calculations. Formulas may then be written to perform calculations in the order desired. Consider the following equation:

$$2 + 8 * 9 = ?$$

The asterisk (*) is used by many programs to indicate multiplication. Therefore the standard order of precedence is multiplication first, then addition,

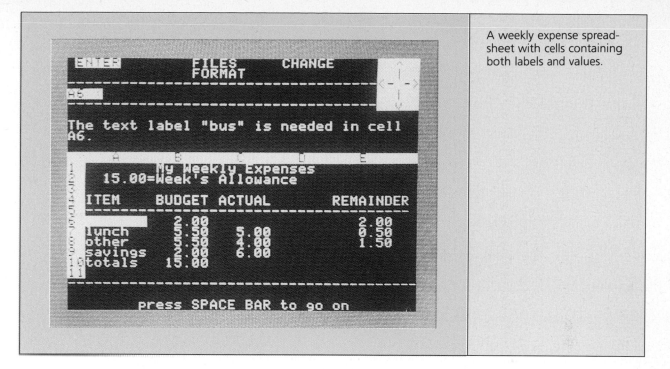

A weekly expense spreadsheet with cells containing both labels and values.

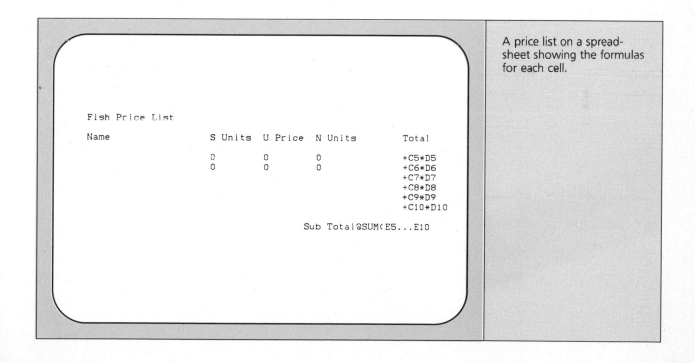

A price list on a spreadsheet showing the formulas for each cell.

This spreadsheet displays cells with formulas as well as tax and total computation formulas.

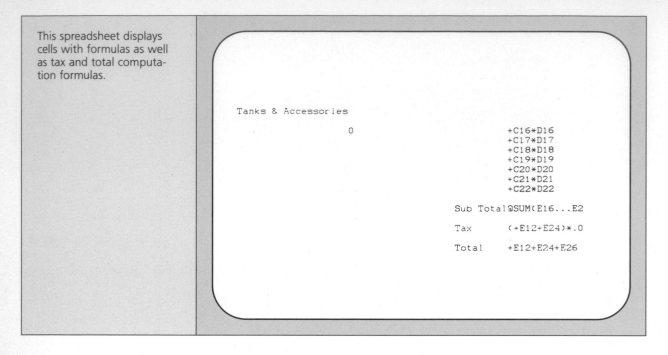

```
Tanks & Accessories

                 0                              +C16*D16
                                                +C17*D17
                                                +C18*D18
                                                +C19*D19
                                                +C20*D20
                                                +C21*D21
                                                +C22*D22

                               Sub Total@SUM(E16...E2

                               Tax      (+E12+E24)*.0

                               Total    +E12+E24+E26
```

giving a total of 74 (8 times 9 = 72, plus 2 = 74). On the other hand, a left to right calculation results in a total of 90 (2 plus 8 = 10, times 9 = 90).

Since there is an obvious discrepancy in the two answers, it is easy to see the importance of knowing how your spreadsheet program performs calculations, in order to ensure accuracy. It is also necessary to know how your program designates specific math functions. Usually the plus (+) sign is used for addition, the minus (−) sign for subtraction, the asterisk (*) for multiplication, and the slash (/) for division.

To make these procedures easier, most spreadsheets have preprogrammed formulas, called **functions**, which consist of those formulas that are most commonly used in spreadsheets. They are preprogrammed for convenience and speed. In addition, on many keyboards there are special function keys, usually called F or PF keys and numbered from one to the maximum number the keyboard contains. By pressing one of these keys, its specified function is brought into play, thus eliminating the need to input formula information over and over.

The names of function keys are descriptive of the calculations that they perform. For instance, Sum adds numbers in a designated group of cells. Count, as its name implies, counts the number of entries in a specified group of cells. Avg performs two tasks: It will total the numbers in a group of cells and calculate the average.

Different spreadsheet programs have different names assigned to the various functions. These names are then reserved, or restricted, and may not be used for other purposes within that program. The user must become familiar with the names and functions unique to the spreadsheet program being used.

Formulas are entered into the cell where the result is to be displayed. Although the cell actually contains the formula, the user sees not it but its numeric result on the screen. Because the formula remains in the cell, whenever a value is changed in any of the cells that the formula uses, the resulting numerical value changes automatically. Let's consider a formula for simple addition.

Example: Column B contains ten numbers in cells B2 through B11.

It is always a good idea to leave a blank row between the total and the column being added. A blank row separates the total from the other numbers and makes it more visible. Therefore, leave cell B12 blank, place the cursor on cell B13, and enter a formula. The formula tells the computer to add the numbers and display the total in cell B13. This may be done as follows:

SUM(B2 + B3 + B4 + B5 + B6 + B7 + B8 + B9 + B10 + B11)

However, as in this instance, there may be lots of numbers to add and this method would be cumbersome. For that reason, the formula may be written in an easier and quicker way by defining a **range** of cells as follows:

SUM(B2 . . . B11)

The three periods (. . .), also called ellipses, are used by many programs to separate the first and last cell designations. The colon (:) or period (.) is also commonly used for this purpose.

After the formula is entered into the cell, the computer adds the numbers in cells B2 and B11 plus all the cells in between. It will then display the total in the cell containing the formula. As long as the formula remains in cell B13, if the value of any cell between B2 and B11 is changed, the total in cell B13 will automatically be changed and displayed.

Many spreadsheets use the "at" symbol (@) along with the function name to indicate a function or predefined formula. However, this is not true of all spreadsheet programs. The user must learn the language of the particular program in use in order to input words and symbols that the computer will understand.

Commands

Each spreadsheet program also has its own group of commands. Commands are an additional method of manipulating data within the spreadsheet to accomplish the user's purpose. Users will become familiar with the language and methods of their particular spreadsheet (for education, AppleWorks is one of the most popular spreadsheets).

This spreadsheet gives range of cells and some layout possibilities.

```
File: Buy.Rent plans          REVIEW/ADD/CHANGE              Escape: Main Menu
========A========B========C========D========E========F========G========H====
  1|Best Time Buy/Rental Plans
  2|
  3|Item              Clarinet      Totals
  4|Cash Purchase       376.00                   Base    + lessons
  5|
  6|Lessons               9.00      Music Lessons    216.00
  7|Number of lessons      24
  8|                                Cash             376.00    592.00
  9|Installment Rate    34.50
 10|                                Installment Plan 414.00    630.00
 11|
 12|          Rent Rent/Buy         Reltal Plan      378.00    594.00
 13|
 14|1rst Per.     3        3        Rent - Buy       504.00    720.00
 15|Rate      45.00    45.00
 16|2nd Per.      9        9
 17|Rate      27.00    41.00
 18|
-------------------------------------------------------------------------------
A1: (Label) Best Time
```

The most common way to access commands is to type a slash (/). The command line then appears with a list of options. Some of these options are Format, Edit, Insert, Delete, Erase, Copy, Move, Title, Scroll, Window, Save, and Print, which are discussed below. The following summarizes AppleWorks' spreadsheet commands.

OPEN APPLE [A]	=	Arrange (sort) a columnn
OPEN APPLE [B]	=	Blank an entry or entries
OPEN APPLE [C]	=	Copy entries (includes cut-and-paste)
OPEN APPLE [D]	=	Delete rows or columns
OPEN APPLE [F]	=	Find coordinates or information
OPEN APPLE [I]	=	Insert rows or columns
OPEN APPLE [J]	=	Jump to other split view
OPEN APPLE [K]	=	Calculate all values
OPEN APPLE [L]	=	Change layout of entries
OPEN APPLE [M]	=	Move entries (includes cut-and-paste)
OPEN APPLE [N]	=	Change name of file
OPEN APPLE [O]	=	Options for print formatting
OPEN APPLE [P]	=	Print
OPEN APPLE [T]	=	Set/Remove fixed titles
OPEN APPLE [U]	=	Edit contents of an entry
OPEN APPLE [V]	=	Set standard values and rules
OPEN APPLE [W]	=	Windows: split view of screen
OPEN APPLE [Z]	=	Zoom in to show formulas
		Zoom out to show values

[RETURN]	=	Accept
[ARROWS]	=	Move the cursor
[TAB] or	=	Move the cursor
OPEN APPLE [TAB]		
OPEN APPLE [ARROWS]	=	Move to another full screen
0–9 + −.	=	Type a value
"or letters	=	Type a label
OPEN APPLE [1]	=	Go to the beginning of file through
OPEN APPLE [9]	=	Go to the end of file

Most programs have so many applications for individual commands that they cannot be shown on the screen all at once. Therefore, choosing one command option may lead the user to other levels of options for that command. Once in this **hierarchy** of commands, you may back out if necessary by pressing the Escape key as many times as needed. Pressing the Escape key will usually retrace your path, level by level, to where you began. Now that we have a way of getting in and out of the command mode, let's look more closely at what the different commands do.

Format The Format command is used to define the arrangement and placement of data within the spreadsheet. The Format command does not change the data, only the way it appears on the spreadsheet. The user can initiate the format command in several ways, the most common being the slash (/). Several options will then be presented.

The first choice defines how much of the spreadsheet will be affected by the format settings. Choosing Global establishes a format setting for the entire spreadsheet. **Column** specifies changes for designated columns. Likewise, Row defines changes for designated rows. Another choice might be Entry, which changes the format for the current cell only.

One way to arrange data is to choose the width of columns. Column width can be adjusted to accommodate the data that the cells will contain. Obviously some information requires more than the nine-character width commonly assigned to a column. By choosing a wider format for column width, the additional space can be added to one column, or to more than one, as needed.

Another reason for changing column width is to enable the user to view more columns at one time on the screen. If less than nine characters are needed for the values and labels in a column, it can be narrowed to the required number of characters, thus allowing extra columns to occupy the display area.

An additional format option is alignment of data. This is a method of arranging data by defining how and where the data is to be placed within the cell. The Format command can instruct that the text and numbers be centered. They can also be placed at the extreme left or the extreme right position in a cell, which is called **justification**. The data is then said to be right or left justified.

In addition to data alignment in each cell the user can decide how the data will look once placed there. Numerical data, for instance, can contain commas to make long numbers more readable. They can begin with a dollar sign ($) to indicate money values. They can contain up to four decimals, to indicate dollars and cents, percentages, or highly accurate numbers. All these choices, as we have already learned, may be defined for the entire spreadsheet or for specified ranges (columns, rows, or cells) by using the Format command.

Edit   Often, in addition to changes in the appearance of data, the user wishes to make changes (**edit**) in the data itself. It is possible to simply retype the data in a particular cell and replace what is there. However, there is an easier way, and that is to change or modify what has already been entered. The Edit command is used for this purpose. The cursor may be placed on the cell to be changed, the edit command entered, and characters inserted, deleted, or changed as necessary.

Insert   Sometimes the user may wish to add (**insert**) an entire row or column. If data has already been entered, this can be done without disturbing what the spreadsheet already contains. The user can call up the Insert command, which allows you to insert an entire blank row or column. By placing the cursor at the point where the new row or column is desired, and by choosing Row or Column, the Insert command instantly places the user's choice at that location.

Delete   On the other hand, perhaps the user wishes to remove (**delete**) a row or column. The Delete command works in the same way as Insert. A word of caution is necessary here. The entire row or column will be deleted, along with all the data contained in it. In most cases, once this information has been deleted, it is gone forever. There are some programs with an Undo command that retrieves the last block of information deleted, in case of error. However, since most programs do not, the delete command should be used carefully.

Most spreadsheet programs contain an interesting automatic feature that is helpful when using the Insert and Delete commands. It automatically adjusts formulas that have been moved into different columns or rows as the result of an insert or delete. That is, the column letters or row numbers within the formula will be changed to those of the new position. This is a great time saver and eliminates much editing and possible errors.

Erase   The **Erase** command is similar to the Delete command. Unwanted information can be deleted from one cell or a range of cells with Erase. It is activated in the same way as the Insert and Delete commands.

The Erase command can also erase the entire spreadsheet. This is quite a drastic action, and for that reason most programs will ask for verification that this is the action desired. Thus, if the command has been initiated in error, the user has a way out. The command can be reversed by responding with a "no" answer when asked for verification. This is very important because, as with the Delete command, many programs do not have a procedure for retrieving the information once it is erased. Unless the program contains an Undo command, caution is necessary when using Erase.

Copy   Sometimes the user wants information to appear in the same form in more than one area of an electronic spreadsheet. The **Copy** command saves many hours of duplicating information in different areas. Copying is done in two ways: duplicating (or exact copying of data) and replicating (sometimes called relative copying).

Exact copying is self-explanatory. A block of data, which can be defined by cell, row, column, or a range of these, is copied exactly as it appears. In some programs, a space must be prepared before data can be copied there. This is done by inserting blank rows or columns where the information is to appear.

The other option, replication, applies to formulas and functions. Replicating adjusts the formula to reflect its new position. This process changes the column letters or row numbers so that, when performed, the calculation will operate on the data contained in the correct column or row. The term *relative copying*, then, refers to copying the data relative to its position after copying is complete.

Move   The **Move** command is very similar to the Copy command. However, when information is *copied*, it not only appears in a new position but also in its original position; when information is *moved*, the original position is then blank and the information appears only in the new position. As with copying, it may be necessary to insert blank rows and columns to receive the data when moved.

Title   With all this copying, replicating, and moving within a spreadsheet, the cursor may end up at a cell many rows below, or many columns to the right of, the labels that identify cell contents. Without labels as guideposts, it's easy to become confused and not know what a cell should contain. This can be avoided by use of the **Title** command. Invoking the Title command enables the user to fix the labels in place. This can be done with vertical (column) labels or horizontal (row) labels, or both. Once titles, or labels, are fixed, they remain in view as the cursor moves through columns and rows. The columns and rows in between the labels and the cursor position temporarily disappear from view, but they can be restored simply by moving the cursor in the opposite direction.

Scroll **Scrolling** is a term used for moving quickly through the spreadsheet. Most spreadsheets will be larger than a display screen can accommodate at one time. Display screens are usually twenty-four rows long and eighty characters wide. This allows for approximately six or eight columns by twenty rows. The entire spreadsheet, including the part that is not displayed, may be thought of as a long and wide scroll. Scrolling then refers to moving the spreadsheet vertically or horizontally to display another portion.

Window Occasionally the user wants to view two separate portions of a spreadsheet at the same time for purposes of comparison. This can be accomplished by a procedure called *windowing*. A **window** is a portion of the spreadsheet that is displayed on the screen at the same time that another portion appears. This may be done at the top or bottom of the screen, or side by side. This display is very similar to the split screen we are accustomed to seeing on our television sets. Many programs allow two or more windows at one time to display portions of a spreadsheet.

Save Once the spreadsheet has been formatted, all the data entered, the calculations performed, and the desired results obtained, the user will want to save the entire project. This can be done in different ways. The Save command copies the spreadsheet to a specified disk drive. The spreadsheet can be placed on a hard disk, if the computer contains one. (A hard disk is a permanent part of the computer.) If the computer does not have a hard disk, the file can be saved on a floppy disk (which is removable). It is always wise to make a backup copy on floppy disk in any case. The disk copy can be stored in a safe place, and can be used on a different computer if necessary.

When needed again, a Load, or Retrieve, command brings the spreadsheet back to the display screen for viewing or revising.

Print The Print command causes a printed copy (often called a *hard copy*) to be made. Spreadsheets can be printed in two different versions. Display Print, a copy of the displayed data and calculation results, is the obviously useful option. It contains financial or statistical information that is meaningful to those involved with it.

Contents Print, the other option, prints precisely what appears in each cell, including formulas. This printout is especially useful for checking the accuracy of formulas for calculation. An error may have occurred during entry of a formula that causes calculations to be performed incorrectly. The user can also make sure that all the data was entered and that it was entered correctly.

The spreadsheet should always be saved before printing. This will avoid loss of data in the event of an electronic failure.

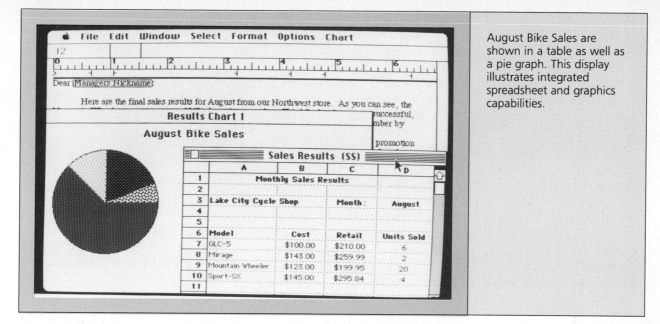

August Bike Sales are shown in a table as well as a pie graph. This display illustrates integrated spreadsheet and graphics capabilities.

Help   Another aid for creating spreadsheets is the Help key. One of the function keys (which were discussed earlier), this key may be activated at any location within the spreadsheet. The user can scroll through screens full of information or select a specific topic for further exploration. Most help screens offer comprehensive information and a quick way to find an answer without having to refer to a manual. To the computer novice, having a function key that offers instant help is like having a safety net.

Another helpful and very effective time saver is a **template**, which is a formatted spreadsheet that has not yet had data entered. If, for instance, a spreadsheet is being created for a report that is generated periodically, the same format will be needed again. The formatted spreadsheet can be saved and copied to a disk before any information is entered. Then, the next week, month, quarter, or year when the same report needs to be generated, a blank spreadsheet containing the basic format is available.

Template

When saving the template and indeed any file, the user must assign a name to it. Its name identifies it and allows it to be retrieved as needed. As with all file names, a descriptive name helps the user identify the file for retrieval.

After saving the template under one name, its blank spreadsheet can be used to enter data and perform calculations. This spreadsheet is then saved as well (under a different name).

Another use for the template is to generate reports that are similar but not identical. For example, a monthly report may be combined with two other monthly reports to generate a quarterly (three-month) report. The template saved from the monthly report format can be modified to satisfy the requirements for a quarterly report.

ANALYSIS AND PROJECTION

Now that we know how spreadsheets are created and saved, let's explore how they are used. Spreadsheet information is essential in analyzing the financial condition of any organization. Spreadsheets also make analysis of statistical information more manageable and much faster. Analysis then, is one of the more important uses of electronic spreadsheets. A natural outcome of analysis is projection for the future. Let's look now at the value of spreadsheets in these two areas.

Analysis   In business and other organizations, analysis is the examination and evaluation of data to measure its impact on the particular organization for which it is being performed. Spreadsheets are an excellent way to compare data. To accomplish this, spreadsheets can be combined, both in part and in total. By defining a range of cells, rows, or columns, any part of a spreadsheet may be retrieved and made a part of others. In this way, very complicated data can be displayed for comparison. Windowing, discussed earlier, is most helpful for these operations.

Another way to analyze data is to use **modeling**. As its name implies, this technique—which employs what-if statements—creates a model of what might occur if certain conditions existed. Modeling may be likened to the actual building of a physical model, such as architects do when designing a building. A spreadsheet model is created and its figure displayed; the user then asks the computer "what if" a specific value were to be changed. The value can be a change in actual numbers or an increase or decrease by a specified percentage rate.

Again, it is easy to envision the time saved over hand calculations when the computer can display instantly how a change in one number affects all other numbers relating to it. The ways in which this is helpful to any organization and its decision makers are virtually endless.

Modeling is especially effective in education. Due to changes and shifts in population, it is important for educational institutions to assess their immediate future needs, as well as long-term ones. By asking what-if questions based on census information and other known statistics, school districts, colleges, and universities can be better prepared to offer quality education. In the classroom, probability situations can be modeled with a spreadsheet. By experimenting with various probabilities, students can examine the basic theories of probability.

As in education, planning for other public and social programs is dependent upon knowing what will happen if certain changes take place within society. Changes in the political climate, for instance, have an impact on almost every area of life. The educational community will obviously benefit quite as much as private business and industry by using the analytic properties of electronic spreadsheets.

By combining the information gained from analysis of a spreadsheet with expectations for the future, it is possible to project what may happen.

Projection is the predicting, or forecasting, of what may be logically expected to occur in the future based on what we know about the past. There are three basic types of planning for the future: *operational, tactical,* and *strategic.* There are also two basic areas where planning is necessary—expense and income.

Projection

In the area of expense, operational planning is the simplest and covers a period of only a few months at a time. It deals with day-to-day operations. Usually done by lower-level managers, this type of planning obviously is short-term and therefore requires less complex spreadsheet information than other types. An example of operational planning is the adjustment of teaching staff and classroom space.

Tactical planning is for an intermediate period, perhaps covering a time span of one to three years. This includes planned stages of development working toward long-term goals. An example of this type of planning is the revision of school budgets in response to projected increased enrollment.

Strategic planning occurs at the highest level of management and addresses the overall, long-range welfare of the organization. Examples of this level of planning are direction of growth, curriculum development, and expansion of school districts.

Future income also requires planning and projection on the part of school administrators. For instance, expected changes in income due to school bond issues can be included in planning.

For higher-level educational institutions, administrators must predict potential changes in student population and project income based on tuition and fees. For instance, funds allotted from other agencies may change from time to time. For this and other reasons, planning for the future is essential to a smooth operation.

Government agencies have a similar need to make projections based on changes in population, income, and societal needs. One of the most obvious areas of public service is transportation. How many freeways to build? What is the projected need for public transportation? This is only one of many services provided by local, state, and national government agencies that may be better analyzed through the use of electronic spreadsheets.

SUMMARY

Computers have been used by business, education, government, and individuals to organize and analyze all kinds of information. The spreadsheet is a useful tool for managing financial and statistical information in this manner. Called an electronic spreadsheet when done by a computer, this technique has become one of the most effective timesavers of our new technology.

From the prototype created by two Harvard students in 1979, to the latest sophisticated integrated software packages, electronic spreadsheets have grown from a useful tool to an indispensable fact of life. All areas of daily existence have been influenced by this development.

In education, spreadsheets are used in various ways. Some of those ways are teaching (for example, accounting, math, and science classes); maintaining student records; budgeting for both the entire school and various groups within it; and management of data by research groups.

Government agencies are also big users of electronic spreadsheets. They manage and manipulate vast amounts of data, analyze changes in all areas of society, and plan for the future needs of communities and the nation.

We as individuals benefit from this new tool as well. We use electronic spreadsheets for personal banking, household management, tax records, and budgeting.

Each of us is influenced in either direct or indirect ways by the widespread use of spreadsheets in the real world. For this reason, the practical application of spreadsheets has been stressed in this chapter. To implement a spreadsheet, a user must be familiar with the terms, modes, commands, formulas, and functions presented here.

Once a spreadsheet has been created and data entered, it may be used to analyze the data it contains, and to make projections for the future based on that data and other knowledge and expectations. What-if statements may be used to set up theoretical conditions; the spreadsheet then calculates the potential results. The instant answers given by this method save many hours of tedious labor, without mathematical error.

Spreadsheets serve us all in many ways. In some cases, we use them to make our individual tasks easier. In other instances, we benefit from their use in business, government, and education.

REVIEW EXERCISES

Multiple Choice

1. The electronic spreadsheet is a computerized version of a
   a. scratch pad
   b. sketch pad
   c. ledger sheet
   d. none of the above
2. The first electronic spreadsheet was called
   a. Lotus 1-2-3
   b. MS-DOS
   c. Daisy
   d. VisiCalc
3. Schools can use spreadsheets for
   a. calculating grades
   b. budgeting
   c. teaching mathematical principles
   d. all of the above
4. A cell is
   a. a point on the spreadsheet where a row and column intersect
   b. a group of related spreadsheets
   c. a title on the spreadsheet
   d. none of the above
5. In designing a spreadsheet, the user must make decisions about
   a. headings and labels
   b. values
   c. formulas and commands
   d. all of the above
6. Which symbol usually designates multiplication in a spreadsheet formula?
   a. @
   b. ×
   c. *
   d. none of the above
7. What is the Avg command used for?
   a. to total the values in a group of cells
   b. to calculate averages
   c. all of the above
   d. none of the above
8. Which command is used to change the value of data in the spreadsheet?
   a. Format
   b. Edit
   c. Justify
   d. Delete
9. A template is
   a. a preformatted, blank spreadsheet
   b. a calculating device similar to a slide rule
   c. an electronic compass
   d. none of the above
10. The process of modeling enables users to
    a. test what might happen under different conditions
    b. answer what-if statements
    c. all of the above
    d. none of the above

True/False

1. Information in a spreadsheet can be changed to show different conditions.
2. Electronic spreadsheets cut down on errors in calculating numeric data.
3. The first generation of spreadsheets appeared in 1959.
4. Unfortunately, spreadsheets are not yet practical for personal use.
5. Cursor keys move the cursor left, right, up, or down.
6. Either text or numbers can be entered in a spreadsheet cell.
7. A value is a formula used to calculate spreadsheet data.
8. The Format command changes the appearance but not the value of data in the spreadsheet.
9. The Erase command is used to eliminate an entire spreadsheet.
10. The Copy command is used to print a hard copy of the spreadsheet.

Short Answer

1. List several ways in which classroom teachers can use spreadsheets.
2. Name the three modes of operation of the spreadsheet.
3. How are cells usually identified on a spreadsheet?
4. Define the term *spreadsheet function*.
5. List two ways in which projection based on spreadsheets can be used in a school system.

Activities

1. Visit a local computer retail store to compare the features of several popular spreadsheet programs.
2. Research at least one use of spreadsheets to compile statistics from a survey.
3. Make a list of ways you might use a spreadsheet for your own financial records.
4. Invite a teacher to speak to your class about the use of spreadsheets in teaching accounting, science, or mathematics.
5. Contact a local school district to learn how spreadsheets are being used for instructional or administrative purposes.
6. Make a list of the information that a teacher could place in a spreadsheet gradebook.
7. Prepare a template for a teacher gradebook.
8. Develop a detailed lesson plan that uses the spreadsheet to teach a lesson on a specific curriculum topic.

BIBLIOGRAPHY

Arganbright, Deane E. *Mathematical Applications of Electronic Spreadsheets*. New York: McGraw-Hill, 1985.

Beamer, James E. "Using Spreadsheets in the Mathematics Classroom: Loan Repayment Schedules and Compound Interest." *School Science and Mathematics Journal* (April 1987): 316.

Bennett, Randy E., ed. *Planning and Evaluating Computer Education Programs*. Columbus, Ohio: Merrill, 1987.

Bitter, Gary G. *Computers in Today's World*. New York: John Wiley, 1984.

Carland, Jo Ann C., et al. "Spreadsheets: Placebos or Panaceas?" *Journal of Research on Computing in Education* 21 (no. 1, Fall 1988): 112–119.

Coburn, Edward J. *Learn to Compute!* Albany, N.Y.: Delmar, 1988.

Grauer, Robert T., and Paul Sugrue. *Microcomputer Applications*. New York: McGraw-Hill, 1987.

Johnston, Randolph. *Microcomputers: Concepts and Applications*. Santa Cruz, Calif.: Mitchell, 1987.

Karlin, Marty. "Beyond Distance = Rate * Time." *The Computing Teacher* 15 (no. 5): 20.

Miller, Martin. "Using NFL Statistics To Teach the Spreadsheet." *The Computing Teacher* 15 (no. 4): 45.

Russell, John C. "Probability Modeling with a Spreadsheet." *The Computing Teacher* 15 (no. 3): 58.

Spencer, C. "Weeding Out Spreadsheet Errors." *Personal Computing* 10 (no. 11, 1986): 160–162.

Stewart, Jenice, and Thomas P. Howard. "On the Use of Electronic Spreadsheet Assignments in the Cost Accounting Class." *Journal of Research on Computing in Education* 20 (no. 4, Summer 1988): 384–391.

SOFTWARE PUBLISHERS

Claris Corp.
440 Clyde Ave.
Mountain View, CA 94043

Houghton Mifflin Co.
Dept. 67
Mount Support Rd./CN 9000
Lebanon, NH 03766–9000

Meizner Business Machines, Inc.
4771 Boston Post Rd.
Pelham, NY 10803

Microsoft Corp.
16011 N.E. 36th Way
Box 97017
Redmond, WA 98073

Troll Associates
100 Corporate Dr.
Mahwah, NJ 07430

REVIEW ANSWER KEY

Multiple Choice

1. c	5. d	9. a
2. d	6. c	10. c
3. d	7. c	
4. a	8. b	

True/False

1. T	5. T	9. T
2. T	6. T	10. F
3. F	7. F	
4. F	8. T	

Short Answer

1. Electronic gradebooks; modeling science and math topics; illustrating populations; geographical area and census data in social studies; exploring consumer costs in mathematics; planning the least expensive class party; illustrating formulas; forecasting populations and weather; tabulating statistical information.

2. Ready; entry; command.

3. By letter (column) and number (row). For example, cell B3 is located at the intersection of column B and row 3.

4. A function is a preprogrammed formula that performs a commonly used operation. Functions are preprogrammed for convenience and speed.

5. To predict class size and future income.

CHAPTER 7

DATABASES

Objectives

- Define the term *database*
- List various educational applications of databases
- Describe how to create a database and enter data
- Describe how data is managed within a database management system
- Describe some databases available to the classroom teacher for specific curricula

Key Terms

ascending order
data items
DBMS (database management system)
descending order
edit
enter
fields
file
hierarchical model
index
join
joining
merge
network model
project
projection
querying
records
relational model
report
retrieve
select
selection
sort
union

Before the advent of computer technology, organizations and individuals had no choice but to maintain their files manually. In a manual system simple files are often kept on index cards stored alphabetically (or numerically) in a box or drawer. More complex files are maintained in file folders and stored in drawers of file cabinets.

A manual system requires much physical manipulation of the files themselves, since it is often necessary to add to, delete from, or modify them. A library card catalog, for example, is continuously updated as new acquisitions are added and outdated material is removed. Classroom teachers keep many different kinds of records pertaining to their students that require updating. Here again, the physical manipulation and revision of records takes much time and energy.

When computers came on the scene, programs were developed that allowed people to store information electronically. For instance, a company might run inventory accounts using information originated and updated with each set of transactions. Another program might keep track of the company's sales (requiring the same information as the inventory program, but entered independently). While these programs were an improvement to manual record keeping, the redundancy of their methods became obvious to programmers during the third generation of computers. At this time, the concept of databases—programs that tie the various files together—was developed.

With the creation of database programs, files can be manipulated by the computer, thus saving hours of physical labor in handling, updating, and moving them when changes are made. Database programs enable users to

- create new files
- add, delete, or change entries in files
- perform limited calculations using files
- sort files
- merge two or more files into one
- select records that have specific attributes for further use

A **file** is created when information such as identification numbers, names, social security numbers, grades, and other pieces of data are gathered. As with manual files, the file must be revised constantly to be useful. New information must be added; records that are no longer needed must be removed from the file. Name changes, statistical updates, and corrections of errors are just a few of the factors that require file updates.

After new records are added to a file, it is usually necessary to change the order of records in the file so that they are once again in correct sequence. The computer can perform a **sort** to accomplish this task—often in a matter of seconds. Sometimes it is necessary to **merge,** or **join,** two or more files into one. Usually, a **sort** is done while files are being merged to put the new files into proper sequence.

At times, it is helpful to **select** only certain records within a file for processing. For example, a principal may want to generate a mailing list of parents of a specified segment of the student population; however, the database files contain addresses of parents of *all* the students. The computer can be instructed to search for only the specified parents and to print out all relevant address information.

DATABASES IN EDUCATION

The educational community has been one of the primary beneficiaries of the database's ability to compile, store, and manipulate huge amounts of demographic and statistical information. Student records, for example, once entered into a database can then be accessed by whatever criteria the user wishes and compiled to generate specific and individually designed reports. School districts and universities have built databases to handle student files, which can include currently enrolled students, classes, financial accounts, grades, and schedules.

Databases are also an invaluable new tool for the classroom teacher. A database can be created for members of an individual class and used to arrange information as the teacher requires. Curriculum enhancements are also available through the use of databases created by libraries and other sources of reference materials. By implementing a search in one of these databases for information relevant to the subject being taught, a teacher can locate many different sources of material in much less time than that required for a physical search.

The suppliers of educational software have recognized the need for commercially produced educational database products and are working toward meeting that need. Two of the first databases designed for schools were AppleWorks and PFS. Other databases are Bank Street Filer (Scholastic), Friendly Filer (Houghton Mifflin), HyperCard (Apple Computer), and MicrosoftWorks (Microsoft). Teachers should evaluate the available software and determine their particular needs. Chapter 12 offers assistance in evaluating software. (Addresses for software publishers are located at the end of this chapter.)

In the early days, the only database programs available were database managers. These programs provided the format and computer power for creating a database, but required the user to gather and enter the information. This was a great deal of work, especially for busy classroom teachers. Then database programs were developed that contained data files as well. In education, these programs even included suggestions on how to implement them in specific teaching situations.

Now there are software programs that teach students how to use a database. These programs are self-contained: They have a built-in database manager, a database containing data, and tutorials that ask questions about the data and its implications. The following are some examples (all from AppleWorks data files) of these tutorial databases:

- "States" consists of the name of each state, its area in square miles, its population, the number of electoral votes, and the number of representatives.
- "British Monarchs" contains the monarch's name, chronological order of reign, family, age at ascending the throne, first and last year of reign, number of years of reign.
- "Notable German Authors" includes name, historical time frame, types of literary works, most notable works, location where author lived, when the author was born and died, and prominent contemporaries.
- "Immigrant" (developed by the Educational Technology Center at the Harvard Graduate School of Education) is public domain software for elementary and secondary social studies courses; included are spreadsheets, word processed text, and databases on the Irish immigration to Boston between 1840 and 1870. Students "adopt" an immigrant family and make decisions about living and working such as that family might have made. In large part, these decisions are based on actual data taken from city and historical records.

From these few examples, it is obvious that the lessons cover many subjects. The wide variety of subjects allows students to learn much more utilizing a database than they would from a singular approach.

Following are more ideas for lessons using a database as a tool, which teachers can have students prepare and then implement in the classroom:

- *Space Travel Database*
  Contains spaceship name, date launched, number of miles traveled, number of astronauts, number of days in space, discoveries, other data.
- *Weather Chart Database*
  Contains date, daily high and low temperatures, and yearly high and low temperatures.
  Students can search for temperatures for specific days and see the overall weather pattern for a specific time period and specific area of the country, or find yearly lows and highs.
- *Dinosaur Database*
  Contains name, period of time it existed, length, weight, food, distinctive features.
  Students might search for the largest, longest living, most unusual features.
- *Presidents Database*
  Contains name, political party, dates term(s) began and ended, age, state of birth.

```
File:    Space
Report:  Table List
Date          Spacecraft    Country-      Event
-----------   -----------   -----------   -----------
1958          Explorer 1    US            First scient
1959          Explorer 6    US            First televi
1962          Mariner 2     US            First sci. d
1962          Mariner 2     US            First scient
1962          OSO-1         US            First observ
1968          Apollo 8      US            First manned
1969          Apollo 11     US            First humans
1969          Apollo 11     US            First sample
1971          Apollo 15     US            First manned
1971          Marner 9      US            First spacec
1973          Pioneer 10    US            First fly-by
1973          Pioneer 10    US            First spacec
1974          Mariner 10    US            First dual p
1976          Viking 1      US            First succes
1976          Viking 1      US            First spacec
1974          Mariner 10    US            First fly-by
1979          Pioneer 11    US            First fly-by
1979          Voyager 1     US            Discovery of
1979          Voyager 1     US            Discory of J
1979          Voyager 1     US            First close
1980          Voyager 1     US            First close
1980-84       Solar Maximu  US            First satell
```

Space Travel database on U.S. space exploration.

```
Date          Spacecraft    Country-      Event
===========================================================
1957          Sputnik 1     SU            First satellite
1957          Sputnik 2     SU            First animal in
1959          Luna 1        SU            First spacecraf
1959          Luna 2        SU            First artificia
1959          Luna 2        SU            First spacecraf
1959          Luna 3        SU            First spacecraf
1961          Volstok 1     SU            First human in
1961          Volstok 1     SU            First human to
1961          Ventura 1     SU            First spacecraf
1962          Mars 1        SU            Second spacecra
1963          Vostok 6      SU            First woman in
1964          Voskhod 1     SU            First multipers
1965          Voskhod 2     SU            First space wal
1966          Venera 3      SU            First entry int
1966          Luna 9        SU            First successfu
```

Space Travel database on U.S.S.R. space missions.

Weather Chart database showing day of month, high and low temperature, and average daily temperature.

```
File:    Temperatures
Report: Ave Temp
Day              High Temp       Low Temp        Average
------------     ------------    ------------    ----------
1                75              43              59.0
2                80              55              67.5
3                72              62              67.0
4                80              60              70.0
5                77              47              62.0
6                82              55              68.5
7                84              70              77.0
8                88              45              66.5
9                75              55              65.0
10               77              45              61.0
11               80              65              72.5
12               85              60              72.5
13               88              62              75.0
14               89              70              79.5
15               87              52              69.5
16               80              62              71.0
17               83              54              68.5
18               85              55              70.0
19               89              70              79.5
20               85              65              75.0
21               88              59              73.5
22               83              70              76.5
23               75              55              65.0
24               79              64              71.5
25               81              61              71.0
```

Weather Chart database for January 1, 1988, providing weather records for that date as well as comparative information from previous years.

```
Record 1 of 31
=================================================================
RC: 1                                          1988 Low Temp: -
Date: Jan  1 88
Day: Friday
Sun Rise: 7:32
Sun Set: 5:31
1987 Prcp: -
1987 Hum Hi: 73
1987 Hum Low: 23
Temp Hi: 81
Year Hi: 1981
Temp Low: 24
Year Low: 1919
1987 Hi Temp: 68
1987 Low Temp: 42
1988 Hi Temp: -
```

```
RC    City          High         Low          Pcp.
=====================================================
1     Geneva        38           29           55
1     Helsinki      6            17           65
1     Hong Kong     65           56           13
1     Jerusalem     56           42           29
1     Lisbon        57           46           58
1     London        43           36           48
1     Los Angeles   67           47           20
1     Madrid        47           35           26
1     Miami Beach   74           61           29
1     Moscow        15           3            58
1     Nairobi       77           54           20
1     New Delhi     71           44           6
1     New York      37           24           40
1     Paris         43           34           56
1     Peking        34           14           10
```

Weather Chart database of temperatures and rainfall for cities of the world. This is similar to a daily newspaper weather listing.

```
RC    Name          Period  Length  Weight  Eats  Features
==========================================================
1     Allosaurus    -       -       -       -     -
1     Ankylosaurus  -       -       -       -     -
1     Apatosaurus   -       -       -       -     -
1     Brachiosaurus -       -       -       -     -
1     Coelophysis   -       -       -       -     -
1     Corythosaurus -       -       -       -     -
1     Cryptocleidus -       -       -       -     -
1     Deinonychus   -       -       -       -     -
1     Diplodocus    -       -       -       -     -
1     Euparkeria    -       -       -       -     -
1     Fabrosaurus   -       -       -       -     -
1     Ichthyosaurus -       -       -       -     -
1     Iguanadon     -       -       -       -     -
1     Kentrosaurus  -       -       -       -     -
1     Megalosaurus  -       -       -       -     -
```

Dinosaur database is an interactive template for students to research information and complete

A database on U.S. Presidents.

```
File:    Presidents                                              Page 1
Report: Lists
RC   No.  Name           Party  Term Beg  Term End      Years  Age  State Born
---  ---- ------------   ------ --------- ----------  ----------  ---- ----------
 1   37   Nixon          R      1969      1974            5     56   CA
 1   39   Carter         D      1977      1981            4     52   GA
 1   31   Hoover         R      1929      1933            4     54   IA
 1   40   Reagan         R      1981      1988            7     69   IL
 1   16   Lincoln        R      1861      1865            4     52   KY
 1   35   Kennedy        D      1961      1963            2     43   MA
 1   6    Adams, J. Q    DR     1825      1829            4     57   MA
 1   2    Adams, J.      F      1797      1801            4     61   MA
 1   33   Truman         D      1945      1953            8     60   MO
 1   11   Polk           D      1845      1849            4     49   NC
 1   17   Johnson, A.    U      1865      1869            4     56   NC
 1   38   Ford           R      1974      1977            3     61   NE
 1   14   Pierce         D      1853      1857            4     48   NH
 1   22   Cleveland      D      1885      1889            4     47   NJ
 1   24   Cleveland      D      1893      1897            4     55   NJ
 1   26   Roosevelt, T   R      1901      1909            8     42   NY
 1   13   Filmore        W      1850      1853            3     50   NY
 1   32   Roosevelt, F   D      1933      1945           12     51   NY
 1   8    Van Buren      D      1837      1841            4     54   NY
 1   18   Grant          R      1869      1877            8     46   OH
 1   20   Garfield       R      1881      1881                  49   OH
 1   27   Taft           R      1909      1913            4     51   OH
 1   19   Hayes          R      1877      1881            4     54   OH
 1   25   McKinley       R      1898      1901            3     54   OH
 1   23   Harrison, B    R      1889      1893            4     55   OH
 1   29   Harding        R      1921      1923            2     55   OH
 1   15   Buchanan       D      1857      1861            4     65   PA
```

The U.S. President database listing all presidents born in Virginia.

```
File:    Presidents                                              Page 1
Report: Lists
Selection: State Born equals VA
RC   No.  Name           Party  Term Beg  Term End      Years  Age  State Bor
---  ---- ------------   ------ --------- ----------  ----------  ---- ---------
 1   10   Tyler          W      1841      1845            4     51   VA
 1   28   Wilson         D      1913      1921            8     56   VA
 1   3    Jefferson      DR     1801      1809            8     57   VA
 1   4    Madison        DR     1809      1817            8     57   VA
 1   1    Washington     F      1789      1797            8     57   VA
 1   5    Monroe         DR     1817      1825            8     58   VA
 1   12   Taylor         W      1849      1850            1     64   VA
 1   9    Harrison, W.   W      1841      1841                  68   VA
 8*                                                            45*
```

Student can search for youngest, oldest, how many from each party, who served during periods of war, and so on.

- *Batting Average Database*
Contains name, number of hits, number of times at bat, will compute the batting average. Student can compare batting averages and search for highest, lowest, number of hits, as well as compute "what if" situations. (For example, what if we increased the number of bats or number of hits—what is the outcome?)

These are only a few examples of how databases can be created and used for teaching. Students more interested in space than math will perhaps see a relevant relationship between the two when space travel numbers are explored. In studying about presidents, students may become interested in the political process of today, how it has changed, and how it might be changed for the better.

From these few examples, it is easy to see that the possibilities are endless. Whatever a teacher may want to convey to the students can be better presented and covered more comprehensively by the use of a database.

In teaching computer classes and many other disciplines, databases can save hours of routine and repetitive data entry into the computer. That time may be better used to teach the concepts and practical applications of the particular subject. In the case of quantitative subjects, such as math

```
File: Batting Percent            REVIEW/ADD/CHANGE              Escape: Main Menu
=======A=======B=======C=======D=======E=======F=======G=======H=======I====
  1|Name            Hits At Bats Singles Doubles Triples H. Runs   Slug %  Average
  2|
  3|Daniel            4     28      1       2                 1     .321     .143
  4|Danny             3     14      1       1       1               .429     .214
  5|Daryl             6     29      2       2       1         1     .448     .207
  6|Dave              5     25      1       1       3               .480     .200
  7|Donna             5     20      2       1       2               .500     .250
  8|Jay               4     25      1       2                 1     .360     .160
  9|Mark D.           4     24      1       1       1         1     .417     .167
 10|Mark S.           5     15      1       2       1         1     .800     .333
 11|Mary N.           5     30      2       2       1               .300     .167
 12|Mary R.           4     28      1               2         1     .393     .143
 13|Nick              3     12              1       1         1     .750     .250
 14|Tommy             4     30      1       1       1         1     .333     .133
 15|
 16|Totals           52    280     14      16      14         8     .429     .186
 17|
 18|
```

A database for a baseball team that lists batting information for each player, including slugging percentage and batting average. Team totals are also provided.

Dinosaurs

Objective: Research and enter data for a database file that contains information about dinosaurs. Use the database to group the dinosaurs by characteristics; for example, by the type of food they ate.

Application: Database

Assumption: There are over 300 known kinds of dinosaurs; 30 of the best known are listed in the database file.

All dinosaurs lived during the Mesozoic era which is made up of three periods:

Triassic	225 to 180 million years ago
Jurassic	180 to 130 million years ago
Cretaceous	130 to 65 million years ago

Dinosaurs were either meat or plant eaters.

Some had unique features, such as physical characteristics or unusual habits.

Discussion:

Dinosaurs fascinate children as well as adults. Yet it is sometimes hard to remember all of the creatures that had a particular characteristic. Records in a database file can be retrieved based on such a characteristic. The partial Dinosaurs database file that follows shows the information already entered (under Name) as well as the five categories for which information must still be added.

```
Name            Period      Length      Weight      Eats      Features
=========================================================================
Ankylosaurus    -           -           -           -         -
Apatosaurus     -           -           -           -         -
Brachiosaurus   -           -           -           -         -
Coelophysis     -           -           -           -         -
Corythosaurus   -           -           -           -         -
Cryptocleidus   -           -           -           -         -
Deinonychus     -           -           -           -         -
Diplodocus      -           -           -           -         -
Euparkeria      -           -           -           -         -
Fabrosaurus     -           -           -           -         -
Ichthyosaurus   -           -           -           -         -
Iguanadon       -           -           -           -         -
Kentrosaurus    -           -           -           -         -
Megalosaurus    -           -           -           -         -
Monoclonius     -           -           -           -         -

-------------------------------------------------------------------------
```

Go to the library for information about dinosaurs. The following list shows the most well-known dinosaurs:

```
Allosaurus
Ankylosaurus
Apatosaurus
Brachiosaurus
Coelophysis
Corythosaurus
Cryptocleidus
Deinonychus
Diplodocus
Euparkeria
Fabrosaurus
Ichthyosaurus
Iguanadon
Kentrosaurus
Megalosaurus
Monoclonius
Ornithosuchus
Pachycephalosaur
Parasaurolophus
Piesiosaurus
Protoceratops
Psittacosaurus
Pterodactylus
Quetzalcoatlus
Scelidosaurus
Spinosaurus
Stegosaurus
Styracosaurus
Triceratops
Tyrannosaurus
```

Because there are three periods (Triassic, Jurassic, and Cretaceous) you only need to enter the first letter of the age in the period column. The length should be recorded in feet and the weight should be recorded in pounds. The Eats category should describe whether that kind of dinosaur ate meat (flesh eating) or plants. The Features column should contain some interesting fact; for example, that the pterodactylus was a flying dinosaur.

Questions and Activities:
Design your own reports to answer the following questions:
1. What was the longest dinosaur?
2. What was the lightest dinosaur?
3. List the dinosaurs by age from the oldest to the youngest. **Hint:** arrange the Period category in reverse alphabetical order.
4. How many dinosaurs belong to each of the three periods?
5. Which dinosaurs could fly?
6. Which dinosaurs were meat eaters?
7. Which dinosaurs were less than twenty feet long?

Activity—Higher-Order Thinking
Find data on five more dinosaurs and enter them into the database file. Make conjectures about dinosaurs and how they lived.

and science, much basic information can be contained in databases, in this way eliminating human error in transferring it to specific problems to be worked on.

The individual student can also benefit from the timesaving potential of a database. In writing research papers, for example, a database of references is very useful. Often blocks of written information pertaining to one subject also relate to other subjects; if retained in a database, they can be called up at will for reference or inclusion.

School administrators must deal with a great amount and variety of information. For instance, personal information about students and their families, courses completed and grades attained, class schedules, and financial information are just a few areas that generate large amounts of data. The computer's ability to store data as well as to manipulate it for various purposes serves to expedite and simplify these tasks.

Information about courses and class schedules, for instance, is needed to generate student and instructor schedules. With the ability to access a database containing thousands of pieces of information, much time is saved, with a resulting saving of both private and public monies.

DATABASES IN SOCIETY

In addition to their uses in education, databases are widely used in other sectors of society. Government agencies, nonprofit organizations, businesses, and private individuals all use them.

Federal, state, and local governments make extensive use of databases. Vast bodies of information can be accessed easily for a number of purposes. For example, information collected and updated periodically by the U.S. Census Bureau is accessible to university scholars for research, to government officials who must determine allocations of grants, and to many others.

Law enforcement agencies rely on databases to help coordinate their efforts across the nation. Agencies on the East Coast have access to information on crimes committed on the West Coast by virtue of nationwide databases. This can help law enforcement in many ways, for instance, to capture criminals who cross state boundaries to avoid prosecution.

Databases also help us cope with several pressing social issues. For example, in recent years, databases with information on runaway adolescents have been established. Similarly, databases about children who have been abducted by parents who do not have legal custody have helped find these children, who are often taken out of state. Many families have been reunited, thanks to the advent of databases.

In business, databases have expedited many procedures, especially in the airline industry. Enormous databases are now shared by all the airlines; since each airline no longer has to input separate sets of information, records are not duplicated and computer processing time is reduced. This allows travel agents to determine fares, flight schedules, and connections for various airlines, with lightning speed.

While airlines are no doubt the largest passenger-carrying organizations to use databases, the same concept applies to ships, trains, and buses. Other carriers, such as those in the trucking industry, also benefit from database technology in moving goods from place to place and maintaining schedules and inventory.

All of the uses mentioned so far are advantageous to us as citizens and individual recipients of goods and services. However, the database can be used in a more personal manner.

For many years, large computers handled databases. However, with the advent of chips that can accommodate large amounts of data, databases on microcomputers have become a reality.

A home microcomputer and a database can help its owner to keep track of medical appointments, visits to the veterinarian, dinner engagements, upcoming cultural events, vacations, school conferences, birthdays, anniversaries, or other events that, if forgotten, could cause embarrassment or inconvenience. A database can also be used to store and update a personal mailing list and to keep track of personal finances.

File: Personnel
Report: scslvl
Selection: All records

First Name:: Deborah   Last Name:: Harrold
Street:: 1227 Aptos Way
City: State:: CA   Zip Code:: 92245

Job Title:: English Instructor
Hire Date:: Aug 15 85
Salary Grade:: 40   Tax Exemptions:: 2

Sick Leave Allotted:: 5
Sick Leave Taken:: 0
Vacation Allotted:: 5
Vacation Taken:: 0
-----------------Each record will print 12 lines-----------------

Use options shown on Help Screen   ô-? for Help

Databases are useful for keeping personnel files like the one shown here. These records might include such information as salary grade, address, job title, sick leave, vacation, and tax exemption information.

DATABASE STRUCTURES

A database is not constructed haphazardly but by concepts defined by the Conference of Data Systems Languages (CODASYL). Its report in 1971 contained information that is helpful in understanding how to build a database.

Generally all databases are organized into **records**, each of which contains categories, called **fields**, which hold **data items** (a data item is an individual unit of alphanumeric data that is entered into each field). For instance, a college application could translate into records for individual students: Each category on the application—student name, address, social security number, and so on—would become a field in the record; each completed application would result in responses that could be entered as data items in the appropriate fields.

A group of related records is called a **file**. One file, on admissions for instance, may contain students' names and other pertinent information. Another file, for class enrollment, will show who is enrolled in which classes as well as other related facts. A third file for finances could hold students' payment records. All three files have at least one identical field (in this case, student name), which allows them to be organized into a database (a group of related files).

Although all databases share the above characteristics, there are several different methods of data access. These methods divide database programs into those that are hierarchical, network, or relational models.

Hierarchical Databases

The simplest database is the **hierarchical**, or tree-structured, **model**. By the nature of its organization, information is accessed from the top down. For example, a social security number may be used to identify a record. It would therefore be the first data item entered and would be placed at the top of the tree-like structure. Following it might be a student's name and address, which would be placed on lower branches of the tree. Therefore, if the known data is a student's name, the system must follow the hierarchical path (starting from the top) to reach that particular item.

This method is said to be a parent/child relationship, that is, each item relates only to the one above and below it in the hierarchy. This procedure naturally suits many business management functions, such as organizational tables, charts of accounts, and personnel records.

However, the necessity to follow the hierarchical structure can be cumbersome and ill suited to other kinds of needs. For this reason network models were developed.

To meet the needs of users who wanted more flexibility of access, the **network model** was devised, where multiple, explicit relationships exist. In other words, the relationships are numerous, not necessarily from top to bottom, and are explicit because a *pointer* is established to direct the computer from one item to another.

The network model differs from the hierarchical because the search structure is less rigid. Through the pointers, or links, set up within the system, the shortest distance to the required information is followed, rather than a top-to-bottom route, which is unchangeable. While this is an improvement over the previous model, it is still cumbersome.

The complexity of the system makes modification also a complex procedure. When modifying data within such a system, great care must be taken to maintain all the pointers that join the relationships so that none of the links in the chain are lost. Since the relationships are explicit, the route from one relationship to another must be consistently maintained.

This model works well for standardized operations where transactions predictably follow a preconceived path. For instance, banking transactions, airline reservations systems, and inventory control are examples of transactions that remain the same for each occurrence. Therefore, defining an explicit relationship with pointers from one step to the next is a practical application.

When transactions are not so predictable, a less explicit path from one record to another is desirable. For that purpose, the relational model was developed.

A **relational model** is set up in a table format. Thus, it is two dimensional, with rows and columns. What was formerly referred to as a file is now a relation. A record is now a row; a field is now a column. In order to avoid confusion, we will continue to refer to files, records, and fields.

The relational database performs three basic functions:

1. Two files may be **merged** into one; this is called **joining**.
2. Fields may be extracted from various files to form a new file; this is called **projection**.
3. Various records may be chosen according to the user's own criteria; this is called **selection**.

A relational database is useful in situations such as our school records example. Student information, course information, class information, instructor information, and financial information can all be stored in a database, then managed according to the desired results. Schedules can be created and modified for a student, for an instructor, for a department, or for the whole institution. Grades can be maintained, averaged, compared, printed, and mailed to students.

Libraries are another area where relational databases are used with extreme effectiveness. Huge volumes of text, as well as scientific data, can be stored in a database and accessed according to the interest of the user.

One disadvantage of the relational model is that there is no practical way to link one field with many others that may relate to it. Its very flexibility in mixing and managing fields limits its ability to establish explicit links. Files can be created by the user using any number of fields, limited only by the contents of the database. However, the user must define and implement the creation of the files; it is not done by the system. For this reason most database systems are not strictly relational.

There are advantages and disadvantages to the three models discussed. The user must choose the one that best meets his or her needs. There is no best way to do it, except as defined by the desired end result.

CREATING A DATABASE

After determining the structural model to be used, the next step is to actually create a database and enter data. The data can then be modified and managed to accomplish the user's objectives.

Because fields, records, and files are added, modified, joined, projected, and selected, an obvious question arises: What happens when a piece of data is changed, for instance a name, an address, or telephone number? The database system manages this with a *data dictionary*. A data dictionary keeps track of the names of all fields and their widths, types, and file locations in the database. When a change is necessary, the change is made in the data dictionary. Since all other occurrences of the field are dependent on the dictionary, accuracy is maintained.

Creating a Data Dictionary

When the user begins to create a file, some systems ask for data dictionary information regarding fields. *Name, type, width*, and *number of decimal places* are to be defined by the user. *Name* is most functional when it identifies the field's contents. In the example we have been using, name might be student name or address, or class name.

Type indicates whether the information entered will be alphanumerical or numerical. Alphanumerical means that the entry has no numeric value although it may contain characters (including numbers) other than letters of the alphabet. This type accommodates entries that contain nonalphabetic characters, such as names with apostrophes or hyphens, or addresses with street numbers.

Width refers to number of spaces in the field and is determined according to what the field will contain. Obviously, the field needs to be wide enough to accommodate the longest anticipated entry. Standard length for names, for example, is thirty spaces.

Number of decimal places refers only to numeric fields and does not need to be specified for others. Most systems allow from two to four decimal places. If dollar signs, commas, or decimal points are to be included in the number, they must be taken into account when defining the field width.

Once the user has defined the format of a file by entering all of the above information, data can be entered into the various fields. This is done with an Enter command. This and other commands will be explained further in the following section.

While the command function remains constant, the specific word used to implement it may differ from one program to another. For instance, AppleWorks refers to fields as *categories*. *Sort*, in some programs, is referred to as *arrange*. The user will learn the language of the particular applications program in use and become comfortable with it in a relatively short time.

AppleWorks Database Command Summary

OPEN APPLE [A]	=	Arrange (sort) this category
OPEN APPLE [C]	=	Copy records (includes cut-and-paste)
OPEN APPLE [D]	=	Delete records
OPEN APPLE [F]	=	Find all records that contain . . .
OPEN APPLE [I]	=	Insert new records before the current record
OPEN APPLE [L]	=	Change record layout (e.g. column width, placement of categories) functions differ depending on whether you are in single-record or multiple-record display
OPEN APPLE [M]	=	Move records (cut-and-paste)
OPEN APPLE [N]	=	Change name of file; insert, delete, and rename categories
OPEN APPLE [P]	=	Print records
OPEN APPLE [R]	=	Change record selection rules
OPEN APPLE [V]	=	Set/remove standard values for a category
OPEN APPLE [Z]	=	Zoom in to one record, zoom out to multiple-record display
OPEN APPLE ["]	=	Copy entry directly above (multiple-record layout only)
[RETURN]	=	Accept
[TAB]	=	Go to next category
OPEN APPLE [TAB]	=	Go to previous category
[UP ARROW]	=	Go up one line at a time
[DOWN ARROW]	=	Go down one line at a time

OPEN APPLE [DOWN ARROW]	=	Go forward a full screen
OPEN APPLE [UP ARROW]	=	Back up a full screen
OPEN APPLE [1]	=	Go to the beginning of file
through		through
OPEN APPLE [9]	=	End of the file

Database Commands

As with any program, users will become familiar with the language and methods of their particular database (for education, AppleWorks is one of the most popular databases).

To avoid confusion in distinguishing between database commands, it helps to remember that fields are equivalent to columns and records are the same as rows. In the relational mode, files are also called *relations*.

Enter   When the user chooses the **Enter** command, the system displays the format established in the data dictionary, with spaces provided for entering the data. Each time the Enter command is activated and data entered, a new record is created and stored in the file. Most systems give the user an opportunity to correct any errors before the data is stored on disk. Once the user signals that the data is correct and complete, it becomes a permanent part of the file.

Edit   The **Edit** command is used to change or modify data that is already part of the file. The system displays the entire record; any field can be altered as necessary. Entered changes replace the earlier entries.

Sort   **Sort** can be used to arrange records in a specific order. It operates on any one field in each record of a file. For example, records can be arranged alphabetically according to students' names, or, numerically according to zip codes, for mailing purposes.

Sorting can be done in ascending or descending order. **Ascending order** is from lowest to highest (A to Z or one to nine). **Descending order** is from highest to lowest (Z to A or nine to one). Since the Sort command operates on only one field at a time, data is sorted by the field chosen. For instance, it may be necessary to have all students' names in alphabetical order or it may be more desirable to have them listed according to class standing. The choices are limited only by the number of fields designated when creating or modifying a database.

Index   The **Index** command creates an index used to find records within a file. It is used by the computer system much as we would use an index card file in the library to direct us to a specific location containing the item we are looking for.

Select   The **Select** command searches for and copies into a working file all the records (rows) containing the specified data. For instance, the user could select all students whose major is computer science and copy those records into a new file.

Project   The **Project** command works the same way as Select except that it locates and copies fields (columns) into a new file.

Join   The **Join** command helps create new composite files. Columns (fields) from one file may be placed in a new file alongside columns from another. This is useful in comparing and analyzing data from various fields.

Union   A **Union** command performs the same function as a Join command except that it works on rows (records) rather than columns (fields).

Retrieve   The **Retrieve** command displays the data stored in a file on the computer display screen. This command allows both managers and computer personnel to review the contents of a database.

Print   The Print command tells the computer to print the contents of a file. Each record is printed as a row; fields are printed in a series of columns.

Report   Similar to the Print command, **Report** differs in that it allows the user to select and organize data into a desired format before printing. In other words, Print reproduces on paper the entire contents of a file, while Report allows selected data to be printed in a specific format.

Analysis and Testing

Once a database is created, it is necessary to analyze the system, its structure, and how it will work. An accepted practice is to construct a set of test data to be processed by the database. The primary purpose is to determine whether the database will do its job. In addition to providing information, the database should be capable of formatting the data for printing reports in precisely the manner requested.

In order to be a comprehensive test of the system's capabilities, the test should execute all functions, including input, processing, output, and storage. To assure the best results at this stage of the process, the user would have had to exercise analytical skills from the very beginning.

To create, test, and manage a successful database, it is necessary to have a thorough understanding of the data to be stored, the reason for its existence, and how it can be managed to provide the end product desired. Only then will the user have the full advantage of the many benefits provided by a database.

DATABASE MANAGEMENT

The term **database management system (DBMS)** signifies the use of a database within an organization. DBMS saves a great deal of time for programmers and others who access the database for many different needs. For example, a programmer may write a program to find all the students enrolled in the university who have a grade-point average higher than 3.5. Or a clerk may call up a list of all students who live off-campus. Accessing the database in this manner is called **querying**; the clerk *queries* the database. Usually a management system employs a query language for database access. The user must initiate the query commands and the query program will execute them.

Database Access

We are living in the midst of an information explosion. It is incomprehensible how this vast amount of information might have been managed before the advent of computer technology. Since we are fortunate to have the technology, the availability of information changes life in ways not even imagined a few short years ago. Now we can access encyclopedias, airline

A special-interest database providing access to commercial ordering for N.F.L. teams.

reservations, and research data in a few minutes. Before databases, these activities were long, tedious processes. A look into the future would probably reveal a computer in every home with access to huge databases. In the meantime, there are other methods of access for groups and individuals.

Access to special-interest databases can be achieved through telecommunications, using a computer terminal and a telephone with a modem. (Telecommunications will be discussed in greater detail in a later chapter.) Fees for access range from $100 to $5,000. An additional hourly fee is standard. As use increases, cost should decrease. Medical databases include MEDLINE and RTECS, CANCERPROJ, and BIOTHICSLINE. Legal databases include LEXIS and WESTLAW. Farmers can access AGNET. Financiers and money managers can use MONEY MARKETS, COMMODITY, COMPUSTAT, and ENERGYNET. Individuals can look for books through BAMBAM and antiques through UTOPIA. Libraries use databases such as OCLC, NEXIS, and MAGAZINE INDEX.

Social Implications of Databases

While many Americans naively believe that any computer-directed activity is good, without considering the possibility of adverse consequences, some people fear the misuse of databases. Consider the huge database that the Internal Revenue Service maintains on taxpayers. Might not a family's financial situation be of interest to businesses or other government agencies? Nowadays, corporations maintain databases on personnel, schools maintain databases for academic records, and credit bureaus maintain databases on financial status. Any of these databases accessed by an individual or group for purposes other than originally intended could endanger an individual's right to privacy and perhaps cause real harm. During the next decade, our legislators will be charged with the responsibility of determining the legal and illegal uses of databases based on their potential threat to the privacy of the individual. (See Chapter 13 for a further discussion of ethics and social concerns.)

SUMMARY

The concept of databases has expanded computer capability, making it possible to store large amounts of data for repeated use in many different applications. Business and industry, educational institutions, and government agencies all use databases to expedite their many functions. This has resulted in reduced costs and eliminated tedious manual data management. While organizations have probably benefited the most from databases, they are by no means the only recipients of the advantages. With the addition of databases to microcomputers, individual users have benefited as well.

The three most commonly used database models are hierarchical, network, and relational. Each model has advantages and disadvantages depending on the application for which it is intended.

All databases contain files that consist of individual records. The records contain fields of various types of information. This information can then be combined to create new files, revise existing files, perform limited calculations, and prepare reports in varied formats by organizing the data in different ways.

Data is stored in a data dictionary created within the database. All information is stored there; therefore when changes are necessary they are made in the data dictionary. This allows accuracy to be maintained, since all other files are dependent on the dictionary for information. A database management system (DBMS) stores, manipulates, formats, and displays data on a video screen or on paper.

The use of databases is controversial. The benefits are obvious. However, there is apprehension on the part of some that large amounts of personal and confidential information centrally maintained and easily accessible may bring with it a temptation for its misuse.

Lawmakers are being asked to anticipate potential problems with database use. They must pass legislation to prevent the abuse of this technology while preserving its benefits for society.

REVIEW EXERCISES

Multiple Choice

1. The need to store information on the computer was recognized during which generation of computers?
   a. first
   b. second
   c. third
   d. fourth
2. Database programs allow users to
   a. create files
   b. edit files
   c. delete files
   d. all of the above
3. CODASYL is
   a. a programming language for creating databases
   b. the Conference of Data Systems Languages
   c. a cold remedy
   d. none of the above
4. Which of the following is *not* a method of building a database?
   a. informational
   b. relational
   c. network
   d. hierarchical
5. A relational database
   a. is set up in a table format
   b. is two-dimensional
   c. includes rows (records) and columns (fields)
   d. all of the above
6. A data dictionary keeps track of
   a. file locations of all fields in the database
   b. spelling of all words in the database
   c. both of the above
   d. neither of the above
7. The Sort command
   a. operates on any one field in each record of a file
   b. arranges records in a specific order
   c. neither of the above
   d. both of the above

8. To query a database means to
   a. purge records no longer needed
   b. consult the database for information
   c. sort database records
   d. none of the above
9. To test a database means to
   a. measure the electric current
   b. see how much data it contains
   c. construct a set of test data to determine whether the database is doing the job it was designed to do
   d. all of the above
10. Test data should require execution of
    a. fields
    b. files
    c. video display
    d. all functions

True/False

1. A file is a collection of information located in one place.
2. Database files cannot be changed easily.
3. Databases save many hours of repetitious data entry.
4. Students can use databases in writing research papers.
5. Databases are not yet practical for microcomputer use.
6. A data item is the smallest unit of data and may be of any value.
7. In a hierarchical database, information is accessed from the top down.
8. Database systems are all relational.
9. Sorting can be done in ascending or descending order.
10. In a database, information is stored in a data dictionary.

Short Answer

1. Describe how law enforcement agencies can use databases to solve crimes.
2. List several applications of network model databases.
3. Name the three basic functions of a relational database.
4. Explain the difference between the Join command and the Union command.

5. Why do some people consider databases a threat to personal privacy?

Activities

1. Locate a database that pertains to a special interest of yours (a career or hobby, for instance); find out how to access the database.
2. Visit a local library (or your school library) to discover what database tools are available for helping patrons locate research materials.
3. Visit a local computer retail store to see what database programs are available for personal use.
4. Design a data dictionary that you could use to store the names, addresses, telephone numbers, and birthdays of your family and friends.
5. Choose one curriculum area (for example, language arts, social studies, science, and math) to research how databases can be used to teach this subject.
6. List occupations that require a familiarity with databases.
7. Collect several help-wanted ads that require database management skills.
8. Develop a detailed lesson plan that uses a database to teach a lesson in a specific curriculum topic.

BIBLIOGRAPHY

Bitter, Gary G. "Application Skill Software Helps for Math Instruction." *Electronic Education* 6 (no. 4, January 1987): 24–25.

Bitter, Gary G. *Computers in Today's World.* New York: John Wiley, 1984.

Bitter, Gary G., and Ruth Camuse. *Using a Microcomputer in the Classroom.* Englewood Cliffs, N.J.: Prentice-Hall, 1988.

Bryan, Marvin. "1988 The Year of the Database." *Personal Computing* 12 (no. 1, January 1988): 100–109.

Budin, Howard. "Teacher Training for Using Databases." ACM-SIGCUE paper, January 18, 1988.

Coburn, Edward J. *Learn to Compute!* Albany, N.Y.: Delmar, 1988.

Date, C. J. *Database: A Primer*. Menlo Park, Calif.: Addison-Wesley, 1983.

Fife, Dennis W., W. Terry Hardgrave, and Donald R. Deutsch. *Database Concepts*. Cincinnati, Ohio: Southwestern, 1986.

Grauer, Robert T., and Paul Sugrue. *Microcomputer Applications*. New York: McGraw-Hill, 1987.

Hannah, Larry. "The Database: Getting to Know You." *The Computing Teacher* 15 (no. 1): 17.

Hunter, Beverly. "American Indian Data File." *Teaching and Computers* (November-December 1985): 10–14.

Hunter, Beverly, and Mary Furlong. "Meet the Press." *Teaching and Computers* (February 1986): 12–17.

Johnston, Randolph. *Microcomputers: Concepts and Applications*. Santa Cruz, Calif.: Mitchell, 1987.

Warner, Michael. "Developing Database Files for Student Use." *The Computing Teacher* 15 (no. 7): 44.

Woerner, Janet. "The Database as a Resource in the Earth Science Classroom." *The Computing Teacher* 15 (no. 4): 20.

SOFTWARE PUBLISHERS

Apple Computer, Inc.
19525 Mariani Dr.
Cupertino, CA 95015

The Educational Technology Center
The Harvard Graduate School of Education
Cambridge, MA 02138

Houghton Mifflin Co.
Dept. 67
Mount Support Rd./CN 9000
Lebanon, NH 03766-9000

Microsoft
16011 N.E. 36th Way
Box 97017
Redmond, WA 98073

Scholastic Inc.
730 Broadway
New York, NY 10003

REVIEW ANSWER KEY

Multiple Choice

1. c	5. d	9. c
2. d	6. a	10. d
3. b	7. d	
4. a	8. b	

True/False

1. T	5. F	9. T
2. F	6. T	10. T
3. T	7. T	
4. T	8. F	

Short Answer

1. Law enforcement agencies nationwide have access to information in databases that can help them apprehend criminals who cross state boundaries.

2. Banking transactions, airline reservations, inventory control.

3. Merging files, projection (extracting fields from various files to form a new one), and selection (combining various records according to user's needs).

4. The Join command combines columns; Union combines rows.

5. Because they are afraid that personal and confidential information contained in databases—for example, financial information maintained by the Internal Revenue Service—may be misused.

CHAPTER 8

GRAPHICS

Objectives

- Define the term *computer graphics*
- Explain how graphics are used in education and by individuals
- Describe different types of graphics and their uses
- Describe how graphs are created from spreadsheets
- Describe ways in which graphs are displayed and distributed

Key Terms

coordinates
digital mouse
digitizer pad
exploded pie chart
font
graphics editor
high resolution
histogram
icon
image digitizer
legend
light pen
line graph
low resolution
optical mouse
pixel
plotter
resolution
screen memory
slide show
stacked bar chart
text resolution
trac-ball
type
X-Y axes

We are all familiar with graphic art, whether or not we recognize it as such. Advertisements in newspapers and magazines as well as television commercials are some of the more common uses of graphic art that we come in contact with daily. In the past, this type of art, commonly called *graphics*, was created by hand by a person called a graphic artist. Today, although most of us would not be aware of the difference when looking at a picture, computers are often used to create in minutes or hours what would take an artist days or weeks to create.

Another type of graphics with which most of us are familiar is the graph, or diagram. Graphs are often used to make complicated information more understandable or to make comparisons easier among different items. There is a familiar saying that "a picture is worth a thousand words"—graphs are a demonstration of that theory. A large amount of data can be condensed into a few figures and formulated into a graph. The graph can then display a manageable picture of the overall situation. In this way, a large amount of data can be viewed all at once and comparisons made.

By using graphics you can conveniently reach more people at one time. You can either project graphics on a screen for an audience to view, or reproduce them in print for many people. What would be extremely cumbersome to copy and distribute in its original form can often be translated to a one-page graph for reproduction. The resulting ease of distribution, even to a large group, is one of the benefits of using graphics.

Computer graphics is one of the fastest growing computer applications today. Software has been available for some time, and it's becoming more sophisticated as new and diverse ways are discovered for using graphics in everyday life. Since there are three types of graphics available on computers—presentation, design, and entertainment graphics (each of which will be discussed later in this chapter)—computer graphics are widely applied in our society. They benefit business, government, and individuals, and education as well.

GRAPHICS IN EDUCATION

Most of us can recall our math and science teachers using graphs to teach us about numbers, formulas, and graphs themselves. Nowadays, with the computer's ability to create complex presentation graphics in short periods of time, other subjects can be made more easily comprehensible.

For example, a social science teacher might use presentation graphics to display the results of a sociological study or the relationship between weather conditions and crops produced in a given region. A political science instructor might use a graph to demonstrate how the voting process works in a democratic society.

Presentation graphs can be used to compare anything that is relevant to the subject being taught in the classroom. More learning probably takes place when students' attention is held by an interesting graphic presentation than by the traditional presentation of written material.

Design graphics can be used in the classroom as well. In geometry, students creating geometric forms on a computer will no doubt learn more about them than by simply looking at the same illustrations in a book. The teaching of art itself benefits from design graphics in the classroom. A whole new world of creativity is open to everyone, even those with minimal artistic skills. Indeed, the classroom teacher is limited only by his or her imagination in creating lesson plans using presentation and design graphics to enhance the curriculum. Popular classroom graphics programs are Print Shop (Broderbund), MacPaint (Claris), Easy Graph (Houghton Mifflin Co.), Delta Drawing (Spinnaker Software), Create with Garfield (DLM), MECC Graph (MECC), and Award Maker Plus (Baudville). (Addresses for software publishers can be found at the end of this chapter.)

School administrators, as well as classroom teachers, can benefit from computer graphics. One of the major record-keeping and comparison tasks of any educational institution is the assigning and accumulation of grades. Graphics can translate individual and class grades into a table for comparison that is easily understood and readily displayed to any number of observers.

As with any other organization, schools, colleges, and universities can use graphics to expedite information for meetings, track financial transactions, make projections for the future, and perform other information functions necessary to managing a large organization.

While computer graphics applications benefit classroom teachers, their students, and school administrators, they definitely have their place in the larger society as well.

GRAPHICS IN SOCIETY

The myriad uses of graphics in business and industry make the advent of computer-generated graphics a technological wonder. For example, imagine a large national firm, with offices all over the country. The volume of information vital to managing such a business is huge and constant. By reducing this vast amount of data to graphics that can be sent through the mail or communicated through computers (see Chapter 9 on telecommunications), employees all over the nation can have the information they need in a timely manner. In addition to the use of graphics in meetings and presentations, the medium is also used in new product design, advertising, publishing, electronic media, and all forms of entertainment.

The user is creating and editing graphics on the display using a mouse.

Our government uses graphics to inform us as citizens. We receive bulletins, pamphlets, newsletters, and instructional material from the government that often contain graphic illustrations. It's likely that most of us can better process the information in this way, by looking at a picture rather than reading lengthy reports.

Government agencies can also use graphs to demonstrate how a budget is apportioned. The money collected and distributed by public agencies belongs to all of us, and therefore we are entitled to know how it is spent. A simple way to give us this information is to use graphics. A well-designed graph will show how much money was spent for what purpose, the percentage of the total, and compare the percentages spent in different areas.

The government can use graphics to help interpret extremely large amounts of data, like census information. The information can be listed by state, by area of the country, by ethnic population, by socioeconomic group, or any number of other criteria. It can be organized and categorized in various ways to demonstrate whatever the user desires. When it is presented in graph form, it will be much more readable and useful to the average observer.

With the cost of computers decreasing so that the technology is within the reach of the average individual, all sorts of computer capabilities are available to private citizens as well. Some personal uses for computer graphics include creating pictures for fun and creating bulletins or flyers for individual or family ventures. Many people are members of private or civic groups where a personal computer can be used to generate graphics that can be incorporated into newsletters or other documents.

For all these reasons and more, computer graphics is one of the fastest growing computer applications. In the next section, we discuss the three graphics categories available for computer applications: *presentation, design,* and *entertainment* graphics.

PRESENTATION GRAPHICS

Presentation graphics are used to present numerical data in an easy-to-comprehend diagram. The data can be input directly or called up from a spreadsheet or database (see Chapter 9 on integrated software) and a graph created from it. Some word processing programs can also transfer data to a graph.

Financial and other numerical data is often presented in columns and rows of numbers. However, a much more interesting and understandable format is a graph representing those same numbers. Such a display is not only more likely to hold the interest of the reader or audience, but it can

This graphics program displays pie, bar, and line graphs simultaneously for comparison.

be designed to emphasize the point being made. In the following section, we discuss the different types of graphs and features of each.

Types of Graphs   There are five basic types of two-dimensional graphs commonly used in graphics software programs: *XY graphs, line graphs, bar charts, stacked bar charts,* and *pie charts.* Two-dimensional graphs show two data values and their connecting point. For example, such a graph might show changes in grade point averages over a specified time period. More sophisticated programs sometimes offer three-dimensional graphs. The added dimension for our example might be, in addition to grade point averages and time periods, various subject grade averages.

The type of graph that you choose to represent a given block of information will depend on whether the data involved is *quantitative* or *qualitative.* Quantitative data is a measurement or count and is most often represented by an XY or line graph. Qualitative data is a classification, or category, and is usually displayed in a bar or pie chart. Each category of qualitative data can be expressed or displayed as a percentage of the total of all the categories. Percentages may then be compared for purposes of evaluation.

Graphics have their place in all areas of the curriculum. Bar, line, and pie graphs, as well as design graphics (all discussed below), are useful in mathematics, science, social studies, and physical education. Graphics can be used to represent such diverse elements as populations, pollution, finances, algebraic relationships, and student physical fitness. Easy Graph II (Houghton Mifflin), MECC Graph (MECC), and Exploring Tables and Graphs I and II (Optimum Resource) are popular elementary graphics programs that produce picture, bar, line, and pie graphics. Most statistics programs provide many additional graphics capabilities.

XY Graph   The XY graph is the one used in conventional mathematics and therefore probably the most familiar type. The XY graph is so named because it consists of an **X axis** and a **Y axis**. These terms simply mean that X represents a horizontal line on which a data value is placed and Y indicates the vertical line. One data item has both an X value and a Y value. Where these two values meet on the graph is a data point. Thus the graph displays scattered points, called **coordinates**, where data points occur. The points can be connected with a line, which is how a line graph is created.

Line Graph   A **line graph** shows relative up and down movements, or trends, of data values, and for this reason is sometimes referred to as a *trend graph.* A line graph is often used for time-related values because it can show changes over time. The time function may also be extended into the future, which makes the line graph an excellent tool for projections. Obviously, a trend graph serves this function and for that reason is widely used in all sorts of educational applications.

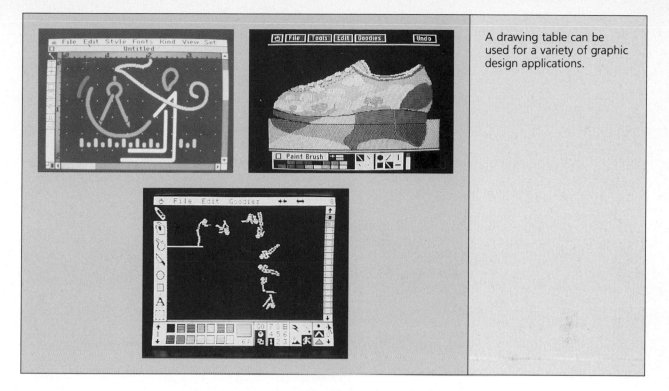

A drawing table can be used for a variety of graphic design applications.

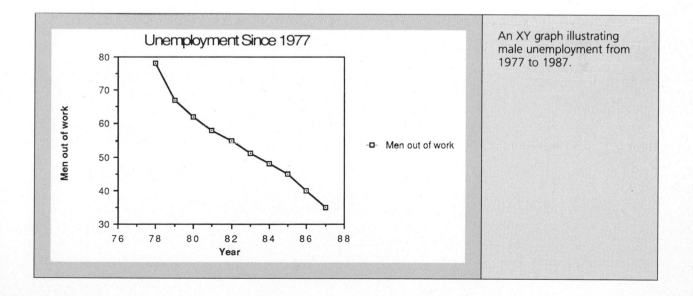

An XY graph illustrating male unemployment from 1977 to 1987.

One such application for a trend graph might be a graphic presentation of how student population has increased over a number of years and a projection of future changes. Planning for building programs, classroom space, hiring of teachers and administrators, money allocated for textbooks, and many other decisions depend on the accurate projection of student population in the future.

Bar Chart and Stacked Bar Chart · The bar chart, also called a **histogram**, is one of the types of graphs used to display qualitative data and one that most of us are familiar with. Each bar represents a data value; when displayed side by side in a chart, the bars allow rapid and easy comparison. A simple bar chart is one-dimensional and appropriate when there are only a few data values to be displayed. A rule of thumb is that a simple bar chart is adequate for displaying values of fifteen or less.

For information containing more data values, there are advanced versions of the bar chart. For example, the **stacked bar chart** shows a number of segments stacked one on top of another, forming a bar. Each segment

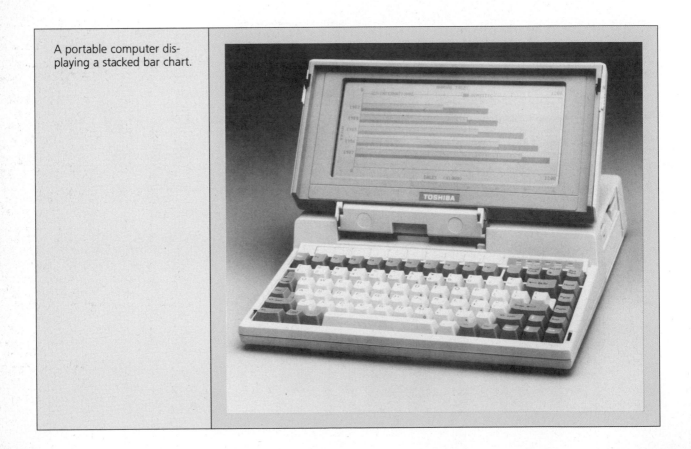

A portable computer displaying a stacked bar chart.

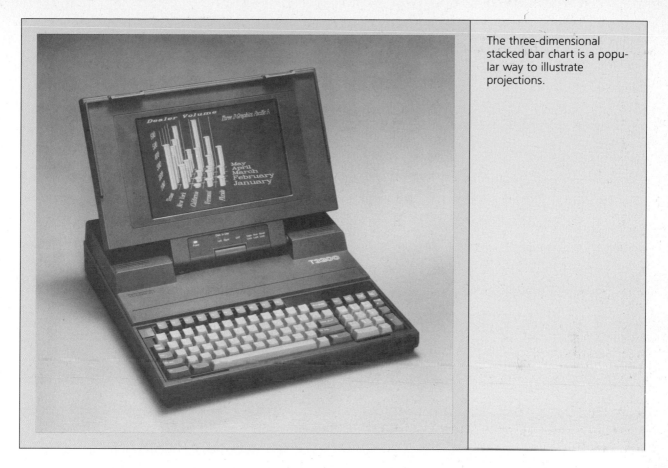

The three-dimensional stacked bar chart is a popular way to illustrate projections.

represents a different element of what the total bar represents. The multiple bar chart is similar to the stacked bar but is displayed differently. Here, the segments are displayed side by side forming a bar. Again, each segment represents a part of the whole.

Pie Chart   The pie chart is another way to display and compare qualitative data. One of the advantages of a pie chart is that percentages are represented by "pieces" of the pie. By viewing the whole pie and the size of each labeled piece, the user can see at a glance the relationship of component parts to the whole.

A refinement of the pie chart is one in which the segments are separated or one segment is pulled away from the rest. This is called the **exploded pie chart**. The purpose of separation is to emphasize one or more segments and still display the entire picture.

The exploded pie chart focuses attention on a particular piece of the pie.

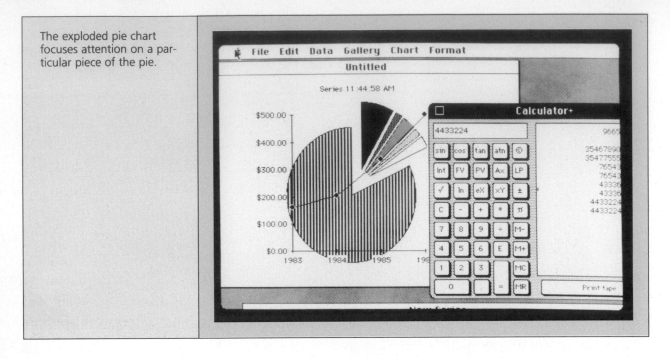

DESIGN GRAPHICS

Everything that is produced for human use or consumption is related in some way to a design procedure. The first thing we as consumers see when shopping for any product is the package. The impact of that first impression plays a large part in determining which product we choose. Even food, which is produced through natural processes, must be packaged for distribution, and there are thousands upon thousands of manufactured products that must be contained in some sort of package. Much planning and preparation goes into the design of any packaging material.

In the past, graphic artists spent much time at the drawing board, creating and revising designs that would catch the eye and imagination of the consumer. With the advent of computer-generated graphics, artists now can create, submit for approval, revising, and finalizing a design in a small amount of the time it took before, when each version was created by hand.

Packaging is only our first contact with the results of design graphics. The products themselves must be designed and made attractive enough to create a demand for them in the marketplace. The number and variety of products available in a free and open society such as ours is overwhelming. From the smallest baby toy to household appliances to automobiles, planes,

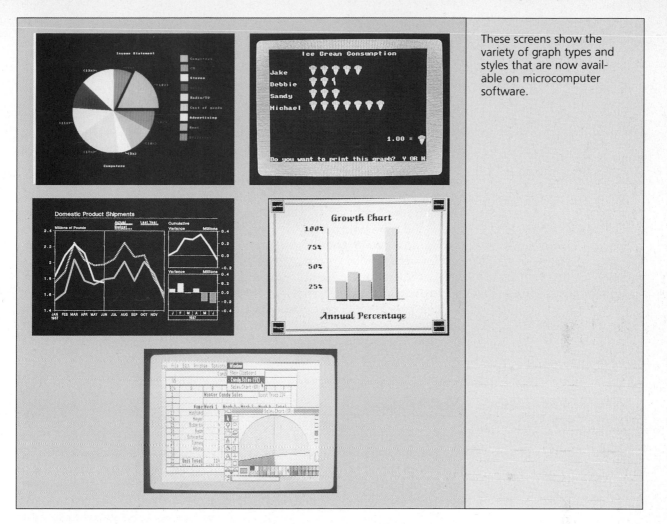

These screens show the variety of graph types and styles that are now available on microcomputer software.

and ships—all must first be generated in the mind of the designer. From that mental picture, the designer's job is to translate the image to a concrete medium from which the product can be created.

Computer-aided design (CAD) is the newest technology available to assist in this task. Computers are used by engineers, architects, and other designers to create and refine designs for automobiles, boats, planes, tools, furniture, appliances, and computers themselves.

Electronic circuits, essential components of computers, are extremely complex and precise arrangements, requiring rigorous design. In addition, they are used in many other products besides what we normally think of as computers. For example, in the past several years automobile designers and manufacturers have computerized functions of the family automobile and other vehicles as well. Stereophonic equipment, many television receivers, video cassette recorders, and other similar equipment have computerized components that consist of electronic circuitry, the design of which is enhanced and expedited by the intricate capabilities of CAD programs.

Other products that require design include personal items: from the world of fashion (for instance, clothing, jewelry, and cosmetics) to health care (for instance, prosthetic devices such as hearing aids). All these things, which are important to our health and well-being, can now be designed with the aid of graphics software.

In addition to product design, other functions of design graphics have an impact on our daily lives. Television commercials are a good example. They are often created by computer-aided design. As with the design of packaging material, the impression made upon the potential consumer through the use of graphics in commercials is most important to the marketing success of the product.

Because education is preparation for living and working in the grownup world, with design graphics the classroom teacher can provide students with various design tasks. Students may discover an attraction for a specific design area and get a preview of what it might be like to perform that kind of work.

ENTERTAINMENT GRAPHICS

Animated cartoons are enjoyed universally. They are one of the most basic and familiar forms of film entertainment. In the past, animation was created by the extremely laborious process of creating hundreds, sometimes thousands, of individual drawings in order to show movement. As the many drawings were photographed, each showing characters in a slightly changed position, it appeared that the characters were moving. Needless to say, the creation of this huge number of drawings took graphic artists many working hours to complete.

However, with the advent of computer graphics, the process was simplified and expedited. By simply copying and modifying each subsequent drawing, many of them are now completed in a small portion of the time it previously took. With the added capability of programming the individual drawings to appear on a screen at timed intervals, almost any action or behavior can be simulated in an animated cartoon. (Since computer animation simulates change and movement, it can be used to demonstrate real-life activities for education or entertainment: for instance, it can simulate time-related drawings of changes in a plant or mineral substance, or the action of robots or other mechanical devices.)

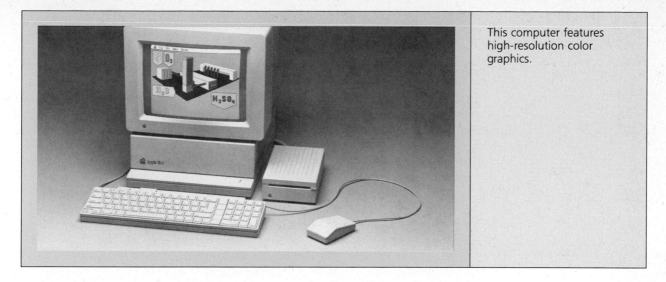

This computer features high-resolution color graphics.

Entertainment graphics are also used to create special effects for live-action movies. For instance, the movie *Star Wars* used graphics very effectively to portray interstellar combat. Computer-generated special effects cover the spectrum from horror movies with their unspeakably ugly characters to fantasy movies with attractive and appealing beings. Whatever the human mind can conceive and the hands can execute can be produced on a viewing screen.

Disneyland is another exciting and familiar example of the use of entertainment graphics, even to those of us who have never been there. The many fantasy experiences offered to the public in this environment are the result of computer graphics technology. For instance, one exhibit simulates the experience of space travel, something which most of us will never actually experience. Others simulate a haunted house, a safari, and flying like Peter Pan. Of course, video games use entertainment graphics extensively. The graphics give the player targets, characters, or situations to compete against. The Pac-Man graphics character is an example.

The above examples are only a few of the numerous ways in which computer-generated graphics affect our lives. As individuals, there are other ways in which we can use entertainment graphics.

A simple graphics package on a home computer allows the user to create pictures just for fun or to create bulletins and flyers for personal events. For example, personalized birth announcements can be produced on the family computer. You can also create invitations for birthdays, anniversaries, graduations, or any family celebration.

In the classroom, entertainment graphics play an important role in educational software. Because television and movies are an enjoyable part of children's lives, students respond well to programs that employ entertaining graphics techniques. Graphic presentations capture students' interest and help to lengthen students' attention span. In addition, because computer graphics are especially good at simulating the real world, they are well suited to certain subjects; for instance, in science to show the growth of plants and animals or the movement of planets and stars.

Popular classroom education graphics packages include TOP Draw (Styleware), MacDraw and MacPaint (Claris), SuperPaint (Silicon Beach Software), Videoworks II (Broderbund), Mouse Paint (Claris), Create with Garfield (DLM), and Print Shop (Broderbund), which is one of the most popular programs. Print Shop allows the user to create signs, posters, greeting cards, and banners. Many choices of graphics and fonts are available, which makes Print Shop ideal for bulletin-board preparation. Other programs such as Print Magic (Epyx), Professional Sign Maker (Sunburst Communications), and Graphicsworks (Mindscape) have similar capabilities.

In whatever way these visuals are used—for presentation, design, or entertainment—users must interact with the computer to create the graphics. In the following section, we describe some of the input and output devices and graphics enhancements that are used to produce computer graphics.

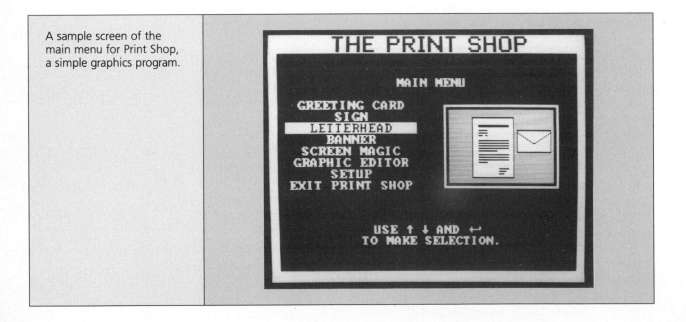

A sample screen of the main menu for Print Shop, a simple graphics program.

INPUT DEVICES

Cursor control keys on a keyboard can direct movement only in a straight line and in only four directions: left, right, up, and down. On very sophisticated systems, straight-line, diagonal movement is possible, which still limits movement to eight directions only.

Cursor control devices, on the other hand, permit movement of the cursor in any direction, at any angle. Movement with these devices is limited only by the dexterity of the human hand.

Joystick   The best-known input device is the joystick. Although we are familiar with its use with video games, it was originally created to guide a graphics character or icon through a maze or direct an object to a target. It was the first such device and has been in use since the earliest video screens were developed. By tilting the joystick in one direction or another, positional signals are sent to the computer. This primitive pointer was the forerunner of more complex input devices.

Mouse   The *mouse* is a small device with a roller ball on the bottom that is moved around on a flat surface by hand. There are two types of mice, **optical** and **digital**; the optical mouse uses a special electronic pad while the digital mouse can be rolled on any flat surface. As the mouse is rolled along, the ball moves devices inside that send signals to the computer. The signals act in the same way as cursor control keys in directing cursor movement. As the mouse is moved, the cursor moves on the display screen in the same way and in the same direction.

In addition, the mouse has one or more buttons on the top that send other signals to the computer. For example, if the user wishes to draw a line where the cursor is being moved, a button will transmit that information to the computer and the line is drawn.

Trac-Ball   A device similar to the mouse but less sophisticated is the **trac-ball**, which is often used with home computers. Basically, it's a simpler, upside-down version of the mouse, with the ball on the top. The user activates the transmission of directional signals to the computer by rubbing a hand over the ball.

Puck   Similar to the mouse but more sophisticated is the puck. The puck is different from the mouse in that it contains a small magnifying glass with cross hairs that intersect at right angles allowing very precise cursor movement. The puck, used in conjunction with a digitizer pad, selects points with the magnifying glass and tracks drawings by following the lines.

Digitizer Pad   A **digitizer pad** is a large, flat tablet made up of fine wire mesh covered by a drawing surface. When touched by a puck or a special

The digital mouse uses a rolling ball to send signals to the computer to move the cursor in the same direction as the ball is moved.

type of pen, the wires make contact and send signals to the computer. What action this causes depends upon the type of software being used.

Digitizer pads are used for many different applications. One program even allows handwritten data to be entered in this way. When information is written on the drawing surface, it is input the same as if it were key-punched. This is especially helpful for users who are unfamiliar with a keyboard.

Touch-Tablet Another type of pad that can be written on is the touch-tablet. No special device is needed for writing; any pointed instrument can be used, even a finger. For this reason and because they are inexpensive, touch-tablets are popular for use with home computers. Many programs

A digitizer pad enables the user to transfer images to the computer.

for young children require a touch-tablet. The Koala pad (PTI-Koala) is popular in education. The software program Koala Painter (PTI-Koala) is an example of an application. Koala Painter produces graphics used with nursery rhymes.

Light Pen   Another simple device for sending signals to the computer is the **light pen**, which has a light sensor on the end of it. When touched to the display screen, signals are transmitted to the computer. In this way, the cursor may be positioned, an item may be selected, or a line may be drawn.

Exactly what is accomplished with the use of a light pen depends on the software being used.

Image Digitizer   The **image digitizer** is another simple way to transfer images to the computer. (A digitizer converts sound or images into binary code, which is made up of the digits zero and one, also called bits. All forms of information are digitized before the computer can use them.) Some image digitizers resemble cameras, others look like copy machines; however, they function in much the same way by capturing the image, digitizing it, and sending those signals to the computer. With the proper hardware, an ordinary video camera can be connected to the computer. The video camera then performs the same function of digitizing the image and transmitting it to the computer.

Graphics Editors   There are also software programs to make the use of graphics easier. Generally called **graphics editors**, these simplified programs allow the user to easily create personalized pictures and designs. They are created with the use of a mouse, light pen, digitizer pad, or even cursor movement keys. Some systems also have predrawn images that can be combined in varied ways to create many different designs. For the user with little artistic talent, predrawn images open up a world of creativity never before experienced.

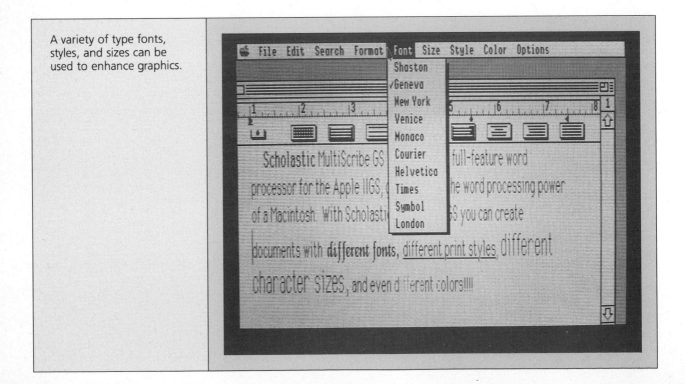

A variety of type fonts, styles, and sizes can be used to enhance graphics.

Some graphics editors use small images, called **icons**, to represent special options within the program. Following is a list of a few icons that are representative of those available:

- *Lasso*   The lasso can be used to encircle a drawing, or parts of a drawing, to be moved.
- *Dotted Box*   The dotted box can be used in a similar way, to encircle parts or all of a drawing to be copied in another area.
- *Pencil*   The pencil allows freehand drawing. Other options are line widths or patterns of lines.
- *Eraser*   The eraser allows erasing all or part of a drawing.

Other icons provide different choices. The user can create circles and boxes, either empty or filled, boxes with rounded corners, and other symbols. Enclosed areas may be filled in with preselected designs.

Text may also be added to drawings with the use of icons. A variety of styles, fonts, and sizes of type are offered with the text option. Text may be positioned anywhere in the drawing using any of the different type styles available with the software program in use.

The icons appear in one corner of the screen and are activated by pointing to a specific one with a pointing device. That particular icon remains active until changed in the same way. MacDraw and MacPaint (Claris) are two of the most popular graphics editor programs.

Other Graphics Enhancements

Other enhancements can be used by the graphics designer to emphasize strategic elements, or simply to create an aesthetically pleasing picture. For example, different colors can be used to represent different values or combined to group together similar values. We only have to envision the difference between color TV and the older black-and-white version to recognize the difference that color can make in a finished product.

Fonts   Another method for enhancing graphics is to use different **fonts** when specifying printing parameters. Fonts are the different typefaces in which characters will print. For instance, the labels and headings of a graph can be printed in different kinds of type by designating a different font. A heading might be printed in EXTRA LARGE TYPE or in *italics*. A fancy design such as script or Old English might be used to set apart the most critical information or that which is meant to be eye-catching.

OUTPUT DEVICES

The devices described thus far input information and images to the computer. To view the graphics that were entered, an output device is needed. An example is the display screen, which shows the user what has been

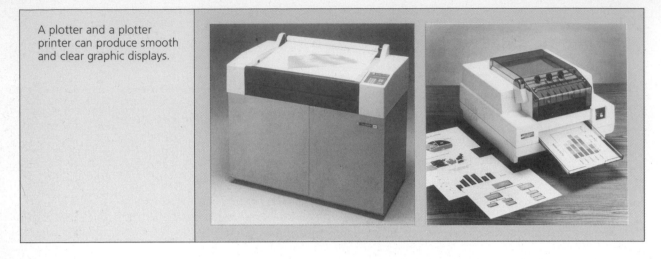

A plotter and a plotter printer can produce smooth and clear graphic displays.

input. Other output devices permit the transfer of that picture to paper, or what is called a *hard copy*. These devices are printers and plotters.

Printer   A graphics printer is very similar to an ordinary printer except that it can print graphics including designs and drawings as well as characters and numbers. Dot matrix and laser printers can print graphics, but the daisy wheel printer cannot. As with all other computer applications, there are many different options. Both hardware and software should be chosen with the user's requirements as the primary guide.

Plotter   An alternative to the graphics printer is the **plotter**, which can produce diagonal lines, curved lines, and circles. A plotter uses small pens and actually draws a picture of what is contained in the computer signals. The display plotted on paper is often clearer and smoother than that produced by a printer.

DISPLAY METHODS

Once designed, you must decide how to distribute or display your graphics. The method you choose depends on several factors—number of people who must see them, where these people are, and whether your work is to be presented at a formal meeting—to name just a few.

Let's assume that you've designed a graph that a large number of people scattered over a wide geographic area need to see. The most reasonable and cost-effective method is to print a hard copy (printed on paper), have duplicates made, and mail them to the necessary locations.

Transparency   Another method for presenting a hard copy is to create transparencies for use on an overhead projector. The graph is copied onto transparent material using an ordinary copier. The transparent copy, when placed in an overhead projector, projects the image onto a screen (like a movie screen) that can be seen by a room full of people.

Display Screen   However, suppose that only one other person in the same office is interested in the information. In this situation, the most feasible method is to simply call up the graph on a computer screen for the person to view.

Slide Show   Now, for illustration purposes, let's imagine that there are several graphs related to the same subject and one or two people want to view them. Instead of requiring that each graph be called up separately on the computer display screen, many presentation graphics programs offer the capability of creating a *slide show*.

Slide show is a command structure that allows the user to specify a number of graphs to be displayed in sequence. In addition, the user can choose whether the program will move automatically through, one slide after another, or if it will need to be prompted. If a speaker is presenting detailed information about the graphs, he or she will want to choose the prompted option. This allows the speaker to change the display on the screen when ready.

On the other hand, if the user chooses to have the program change the display automatically, the time that each slide is to be shown can be preset. A more complicated graph can be shown for the necessary time it takes to explain, and a simpler one for less time.

Slides   Another method of presenting graphs during a presentation is by using a conventional slide projector. Photographs can be taken of the display screen as each graph is displayed. The film is then developed into slides and shown with a slide projector on a movie screen. As with the computerized slide show, the projector can be set to change slides automatically or when prompted by the user.

CREATING A GRAPH

Now that we have explored the ways in which drawings and graphs can be used and the various methods for displaying and distributing them, we will describe how to create a presentation graph. As stated earlier, many spreadsheet software programs incorporate graphics. Usually, the option appears in the main menu of the spreadsheet.

Following are some of the commands that are likely to appear in spreadsheet graphics and a description of what they will do when implemented. As we've said before, not all software programs use the same language for commands. Those presented here are an approximation of what you can expect. However, you will quickly become familiar with the command structure of your particular program.

Graph   The Graph command switches the system to graphics mode and displays the next menu.

Type   The **Type** command allows the user to specify the type of graph to be created—line, bar, or pie.

Data Range   Data Range asks the user to identify the data in the spreadsheet to be included in the graph. This is done by identifying the cell locations in the spreadsheet that contain the data to be used. (See Chapter 6 on spreadsheets.)

The user must be cautious and precise when defining the data range, for obvious reasons. If the data specified is incomplete, or if unwanted data is included in error, the resulting graph will present an erroneous picture, which will not be readily apparent to viewers. Therefore, when setting the boundaries for which data are to be translated to a graph, take utmost care to ensure accuracy.

Title   The Title command allows the user to create headings to describe what the graph represents. Within the space limitations of the command, give careful consideration to the heading, so that it is obvious to the viewer what the graph contains.

Label   The Label command tells the system what the labels should be for the X and Y axes.

Legend   The **Legend** command allows the user to assign names to each value represented in the graph. Legends are used because, generally, there is not enough space on the printed graph to permit an adequate description of the value.

Most people are familiar with the use of legends on geographical maps. There is so much information contained on a map that it would create utter confusion if a map maker attempted to print it all on the face of the map. Therefore, legends are used to identify certain things, and a list of the legends and their meanings appears in one corner of the page. In the same way, graph creators use legends to mark and explain what the different areas of the graph represent.

Display   The Display command brings up on the display screen the graph you've designed, which is the result of choices you made when prompted by the Type, Data Range, Title, Label, and Legend commands.

Print   The Print command causes the computer to print a hard copy of the finished graph.

SOFTWARE AND HARDWARE CONSIDERATIONS

Of course, not all graphics packages are created equal. What is adequate for family entertainment on a home computer would not serve well in a more complex and demanding operation. For that reason, users must determine exactly what their needs are and how they will use the graphics. Graphics software packages come in all price ranges and all degrees of complexity. The one chosen should be adequate to the tasks it will be asked to perform. On the other hand, if it offers capabilities far beyond the user's needs, such capabilities are superfluous and not worth paying for. The key, then, is to match needs with capabilities when making a decision about software purchases.

Users must also consider hardware capabilities to meet their needs. What is important to efficient on-screen graphics display is called **resolution**. Resolution relates to the number of *pixels* that are accessible. (The term **pixel** is derived from *picture element*.) Simply defined, a pixel is one of the display points of light on a display screen. The information given to the computer from the monitor regarding the display is stored in the portion of the computer's memory known as **screen memory**. Different computers have varying amounts of screen memory (as well as total memory). To deal with this, there are three types of resolution available. The type of resolution a computer can use, then, is based on the amount of screen memory available as well as the capability of the monitor.

The three types of resolution are text resolution, low resolution, and high resolution. **Text resolution** allows the computer to use only the number of pixels necessary to generate characters. A special circuit, called a *character generator*, defines how characters are to be displayed.

Characters include letters A through Z, and numbers zero through nine. Instructions for displaying special characters or symbols such as asterisks, ampersands, and dollar signs are also contained in the character generator. In addition, some predefined graphic characters are included, such as underlining. There is a limit of less than 256 characters for each computer.

Because characters are already defined, text resolution requires very little screen memory. However, there is no access to individual pixels; only the defined characters may be displayed. An advantage is that this allows space in screen memory for designation of color on those computers that have color capability.

Low resolution differs from text resolution in that it allows access to small groups of pixels. Access to pixels provides clearer images and still allows some color designation. Fewer colors will be available, however, because low resolution uses more screen memory.

The third type, **high resolution**, allows access to each individual pixel. Because this capability requires much more screen memory, availability of color can be affected. Depending on the computer, displays may be limited

Resolution

to black and white. The advantage of high resolution is that it provides much greater flexibility for creating images. With graphics, however, color is often considered essential; for that reason, most graphics programs use low resolution.

SUMMARY

In the past, graphic art, commonly called *graphics,* was created by hand by a person known as a graphic artist. Today, with a computer the same artist can create in minutes or hours what used to take days or weeks to create. The medium is used also in new product design, advertising, publishing, electronic media, and all forms of entertainment.

Graphics programs can also produce diagrams, or graphs, which are often used in presentations to make complicated information more understandable or comparisons among different items easier. Because they condense information, graphs can be projected on a screen or copied onto paper for distribution, allowing many people to view the same information at the same time.

Computer graphics benefits many segments of society. In education, the classroom teachers can make their subjects more comprehensible to a large group of students, while school administrators can use graphics for their many administrative tasks. In government, bulletins, pamphlets, newsletters, and instructional material often contain graphic illustrations to enlighten or educate citizens. Graphs can be put to administrative uses by government agencies as well. In personal life, individuals can create pictures for fun or create bulletins or flyers for individual or family ventures, or for private or civic groups.

Computer graphics is one of the fastest growing computer applications. Three categories of graphics are available for computer applications: presentation, design, and entertainment graphics.

Presentation graphics are used to present numerical data in easy-to-comprehend form. The data can be input directly or may be called up from a spreadsheet or database; some word processing programs can also transfer data to a graph.

There are five basic types of two-dimensional graphs commonly used in graphics software programs: XY graphs, line graphs, bar charts, stacked bar charts, and pie charts. The type of graph that you choose to represent a given block of information depends on whether the data involved is quantitative or qualitative.

Design graphics use computers to design various products. Designers can now create, submit for approval, revise, and finalize a design in a small portion of the time that it took when it was done by hand. Computer-aided design (CAD) is the newest technology available to assist in this task. Computers are used by engineers and architects to create and refine designs for automobiles, boats, planes, tools, furniture, appliances, and computers themselves.

Entertainment graphics is the use of computers to create pictures, animated cartoons, special effects for movies, and unique entertainment facilities, such as Disneyland.

Information is input into graphics programs with a variety of devices, including the joystick, mouse, and light pen. Information is output using a printer or a plotter. How graphics are displayed depends on how they are to be used and how many people must see them. The display can be as simple as viewing a graph on the monitor's display screen or as complicated as a slide show using slides photographed from copies printed on paper (using a printer or plotter).

With the use of a home computer and a graphics editor, family activities can result in many useful, entertaining, and decorative productions. Graphics editor programs allow you to create personalized pictures and designs. Some graphics editors use small images, called icons, to represent special options within the program. The icons appear in one corner of the screen and are activated by pointing to a specific one with a pointing device.

Users must consider their needs and the purposes for which they intend to use graphics when deciding to buy graphics software. In addition, they must make certain that their hardware can perform well with the graphics program. Especially important is their computer's resolution, which is made up of pixels, or the points of light on a monitor screen. If users are careful in their choices, they will find that the graphics software meets their needs and indeed makes many tasks easier and quicker.

REVIEW EXERCISES

Multiple Choice

1. Graphs are often used
   a. in presentations
   b. to make complicated information more understandable
   c. to make easy comparisons among different items
   d. all of the above
2. Which of the following is not a graphics application?
   a. database
   b. presentation
   c. design
   d. entertainment
3. Scattered points on a graph that show where data points occur are called
   a. data items
   b. coordinates
   c. X-Y axes
   d. none of the above
4. A line graph is also called a(n)
   a. qualitative graph
   b. XY graph
   c. trend graph
   d. none of the above
5. A simple bar chart is adequate for displaying
   a. values of fifteen or less
   b. two coordinates at a time
   c. ten data points or less
   d. all of the above
6. With integrated software, graphs can be created from
   a. spreadsheet data
   b. a database
   c. word processing data
   d. all of the above
7. CAD stands for
   a. computer and data
   b. computer-aided drawing

c. computer-aided design

d. none of the above

8. Creating graphics is easier with input devices, such as a
    a. mouse
    b. joystick
    c. trac-ball
    d. all of the above

9. An example of computer graphics in entertainment is
    a. *Star Wars*
    b. Disneyland
    c. a and b
    d. none of the above

10. A small image used to represent special options in a graphics program is called a(n)
    a. image digitizer
    b. icon
    c. lasso
    d. none of the above

True/False

1. Artists can create images in minutes or hours on the computer that would take days or weeks to create by hand.
2. Graphs are used to display large amounts of text or spreadsheet data.
3. Computer graphics applications are useful in teaching social studies as well as math and science.
4. It is not yet practical for individuals to use computer graphics.
5. Presentation graphics are used to present numerical data in an easy-to-comprehend form.
6. Line graphs cannot be used to show changes over time or projections for the future.
7. Bar charts are also called histograms.
8. An exploded pie chart may occur if the computer malfunctions while running a graphics program.
9. Slide show is a command structure that allows the user to specify a number of graphs to be displayed in sequence.
10. The three types of resolution are text resolution, low resolution, and high resolution.

Short Answer

1. What are the advantages of displaying data in graph form?
2. What are the five types of two-dimensional graphs?
3. Define the term *pie chart*.

4. How can fonts be used to enhance graphs?
5. Define the term *design graphics*.

Activities

1. Choose one curriculum area and research ways in which graphics applications are used to teach in that area.
2. Visit a local computer retail or teaching supply store to see several popular graphics packages.
3. List several purposes for which you might use computer graphics on a home computer.
4. Invite an architect or engineer to speak to your class about computer-aided design.
5. Research ways in which graphics is used to enhance educational software, such as simulation programs.
6. Use a commercial software program such as Print Shop to create a bulletin board for a classroom.
7. List several occupations that require a graphics background.
8. Choose one curriculum area (for example, language arts, social studies, science, math, and so on) to research how graphics can be used to teach the subject.
9. Make a list of all the ways in which graphics software can be used in the classroom.

BIBLIOGRAPHY

Adams, Richard C. "Low-Cost Graphics Tablets." *The Computing Teacher* 11 (no. 5, December-January 1984): 65–66.

Bitter, Gary G. *Computers in Today's World*. New York: John Wiley, 1984.

Coburn, Edward J. *Learn to Compute!* Albany, N.Y.: Delmar, 1988.

Ettinger, Linda F. "Talk About Teaching Computer Art Graphics." *The Computing Teacher* (October 1983): 16–18.

Grauer, Robert T., and Paul Sugrue. *Microcomputer Applications*. New York: McGraw-Hill, 1987.

Hiatt, Richard R. "CHARTWORKS." *Nibble* 9 (no. 10, October 1988): 22–47.

"Innovation in Graphics." *T.H.E. Journal* (special issue) 15 (no. 6, February 1988).

Johnston, Randolph. *Microcomputers: Concepts and Applications*. Santa Cruz, Calif.: Mitchell, 1987.

Lewis, R., and E. D. Tagg (eds.) *Trends in Computer-Assisted Education*. Palo Alto, Calif.: Blackwell Scientific Publications, 1987.

Marcus, Aaron. "Graphic Design for Computer Graphics: Implications for Art and Design Educators." *The Computing Teacher* (April 1984): 59–61.

Savage, James R. "Speed Draw." *Nibble* 9 (no. 11, November 1988): 67–84.

Smeltzer, Dennis. "The Microcomputer and the Media Center—Computerized Graphics Production." *Tech Trends* 33 (no. 2, March 1988): 19–21.

Solomon, Cynthia. *Computer Environments for Children.* Cambridge: MIT Press, 1986.

SOFTWARE PUBLISHERS

Apple Computer, Inc.
20525 Mariani Ave.
Cupertino, CA 95014

Baudville, Inc.
1001 Medical Park Dr., S.E.
Grand Rapids, MI 49506

Broderbund Software
17 Paul Dr.
San Rafael, CA 94903-2101

Claris Corp.
440 Clyde Ave.
Mtn. View, CA 94043

DLM
One DLM Park
Allen, TX 75002

Epyx, Inc.
680 Galveston Dr.
Redwood City, CA 94063

Houghton Mifflin Co.
Dept. 67
Mount Support Rd./CN 9000
Lebanon, NH 03766–9000

MECC (Minnesota Education Computing Corporation)
3490 Lexington Ave. No.
St. Paul, MN 55112–8097

Mindscape
3444 Dundee Rd.
Northbrook, IL 60062

Optimum Resource, Inc.
10 Station Pl.
Norfolk, CT 06058

PTI-Koala
269 Mt. Hermon Rd.
Scotts Valley, CA 95066

Silicon Beach Software
P.O. Box 261430
San Diego, CA 92126

Spinnaker Software Corp.
1 Kendall Square
Cambridge, MA 02139

Styleware
5250 Gulton, Ste. 2E
Houston, TX 77081

Sunburst Communications
39 Washington Ave.
Pleasantville, NY 10570–9970

REVIEW ANSWER KEY

Multiple Choice

1. d
2. a
3. b
4. c
5. a
6. d
7. c
8. d
9. c
10. b

True/False

1. T
2. T
3. T
4. F
5. T
6. F
7. T
8. F
9. T
10. T

Short Answer

1. To make complicated information more understandable and to make comparison easier.
2. XY graphs, line graphs, bar charts, stacked bar charts, and pie charts.
3. A circle in which percentages of a whole are represented by "pieces" of the pie.
4. By printing labels and headings in different type styles or fancy designs.
5. Computer-aided design of manufactured and marketed products.

CHAPTER 9

TELECOMMUNICATIONS AND INTEGRATED SOFTWARE

Objectives

- Define the term *telecommunications*
- List uses of telecommunications and integrated software in education
- Describe a *modem* and what it does
- Define the term *integrated software*
- Define *desktop publishing*

Key Terms

acoustic coupler
analog
ASCII
asynchronous
baud rate
bit
bulletin board
desktop manager
desktop publishing
downloading
full-duplex
half-duplex
integrated software
LAN (local area network)
modem
network
parity
pull-down menu
simplex
synchronous
system integrator
telecommunications
teleconferencing
uploading
window

Imagine living without a radio, television, or telephone. We constantly use these devices to find out what is happening in the world. We are now beginning to experience other forms of communication, such as FAX machines, bulletin boards, and various mobile telephone systems.

Communication is a crucial element in the interaction between individuals, groups of individuals, and structured organizations. First with the telegraph and then with the telephone, much progress has been made over the past century to improve our means of communication. The latest innovation in this area has evolved because of the computer.

TELECOMMUNICATIONS

Computers originally were used to store information. They rapidly became more sophisticated, stored larger amounts of data, and manipulated the data in various and useful ways. It soon became apparent that users needed to share their computer information with other computers and users in remote locations.

For example, a school district with schools in widespread locations needs to share the data contained in the mainframe computer with smaller computers located in individual schools. Conversely, the information input into on-site computers is needed by the mainframe in order for administrators to have at their fingertips comprehensive and current information. **Telecommunications**—the process of transferring data from one point to another without changing the data as it travels—answers this need.

With telecommunications, a school district can have a large database of information in a centrally located mainframe computer that can be accessed by microcomputers in remote school locations. If all schools in the district can access this information, then the district gets the maximum benefit from the money it spent for the resource and reference material in the database.

Schools can also access commercial information services through telecommunications. In this way, teachers can locate reference materials that are not contained in the school's own computer system. Most information services offer a bibliographical search that the classroom teacher could initiate via telecommunications and a microcomputer in the classroom.

Telecommunications allows teachers to bring into the classroom volumes of information that previously could only be obtained at the local public library. As a matter of fact, students can be taught to use the library by using a computerized catalog. Books, periodicals, and audio materials can then be ordered from the library through telecommunications.

The flow of communications goes both ways. Teachers can send information from a microcomputer to the mainframe. Student records can be updated and maintained in this manner. Curriculum information and lesson plans can be shared with other classroom teachers with the use of telecommunications between microcomputers in different locations.

Telecommunications can also provide a new type of instructional environment. Consider the advantages of using **teleconferencing** (three or more people meeting electronically between two or more locations) to impart knowledge usually given in a classroom. Experts in various fields could be contacted and their valuable input included at lower fees. In this way, handicapped and homebound persons could be educated at home, and parents with young children could attend classes in their homes, at the same time fulfilling their child-care responsibilities. Continuing education could be arranged to accommodate working students' schedules. Campus locations could be used to initiate instruction with branch campuses at remote sites.

The University of Wisconsin and the University of Illinois have done extensive work with telecommunications. The Bell System's PICTURE-PHONE Meeting Service (PMS) has been linked to many different cities in an effort to provide communication between off-campus sites with participants being heard and seen, and to present visual aids to other participants.

Research in many disciplines is one of the major efforts of most universities. With telecommunications as a tool, research can be conducted in diverse and remote locations with continuous exchange of information and monitoring of results. Research is also conducted at various levels of government, which is another institution that can benefit greatly from the capability of computers to communicate.

Government, by the very nature of its structure, is a widespread network of agencies, offices, and individuals. At its most basic level, small city government, it still covers a wide geographic area. At its highest level, the

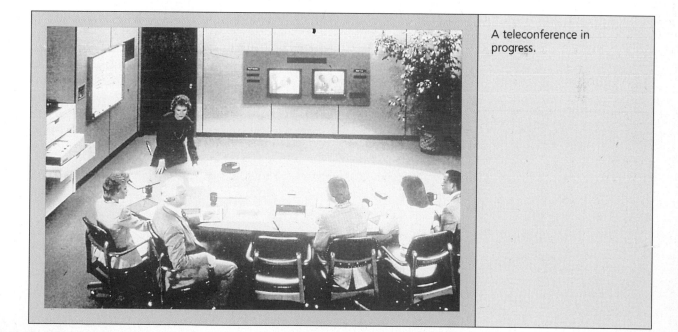

A teleconference in progress.

federal government, it covers the entire nation, with federal offices in almost every community.

Telecommunications creates an environment of interchange between the levels of government, as well as individual departments within each level. Not only is communication established in this way, but exchange and sharing of data can save many tax dollars by eliminating the need for duplication. For instance, by increasing and accelerating the exchange of information between law enforcement agencies through telecommunications, every citizen benefits, both in a more secure societal environment and in tax money saved.

In business, telecommunications has improved access to information. For instance, because large corporations can receive input daily from all their branches, they can monitor their profits and losses more efficiently. The most common business applications are ordering, travel arrangements, inventory control, employee contact, and financial transactions.

As individuals, we receive benefits from telecommunications, some of which have been mentioned previously. A few examples are in-home services such as banking, shopping, travel, entertainment, reference information, education, free computer software, message services, and electronic games. As the technology develops and becomes more affordable for the individual, the possibilities for telecommunications to change our daily lives are enormous.

Telecommunications is also referred to as data communications, and the data is most commonly transmitted via telephone lines or cables. Telecommunications comprises four basic elements: the sender, the message, the transmission line, and the receiver.

Sender

Telecommunications can be facilitated between mainframes, between personal computers, from mainframe to personal computer, or from personal computer to mainframe. This flexibility allows one computer to communicate with another without regard to distance or location. The sender is the computer from which the data originates. The data can be keyed in as it is being transmitted or files can be called up from storage and sent all at once. The process of sending data from files on a microcomputer to databases on a host or a central computer is called **uploading**. **Downloading** is the transfer of data from the database on a host or central computer to a microcomputer for use or storage on disk. To accomplish this feat, the following discussion covers some of the hardware and software requirements.

Message

The data cannot be transmitted as it is output from the computer because it is in a different form than information relayed by telephone. In most cases, the telephone is an **analog** device, which means that the information is sent in a continuous, smooth signal (sound waves). The computer, on the other hand, is a digital device that uses on/off signals, also referred to as *binary digits* or **bits**. Bits represent the absence or presence of electric voltage. Presence of voltage is denoted by one and absence by zero.

When the sender enters information via a CRT, the data goes to a **modem**, or *modulator-dem*odulator. Modulation means to convert digital data to analog; demodulation is just the opposite, converting analog to digital. The modem converts binary signals in the computer to voicelike waves that travel over telephone lines in the same way that your voice travels from telephone to telephone.

Modems   There are three types of modems. The first one developed was the **acoustic coupler**, which is a telephone handset that is placed in rubber cups and attached to the computer. The information is sent through the telephone to a transmission line.

The second type is called *direct connect*. This one directly accesses the telephone line (without a handset). This avoids the interference from environmental noise that you have with the acoustic coupler.

Because the acoustic coupler and the direct connect modem are external to the computer, they are interchangeable from one computer to another; they often have blinking lights that allow the transmission to be monitored. However, they require extra desk space and may sometimes be in the way.

The third type of modem, a simplification of the direct connect, is the *internal modem*. It is plugged into slots inside the computer. The internal

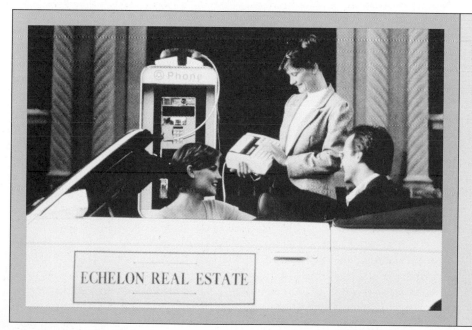

Using an acoustic coupler to connect the computer to the telephone.

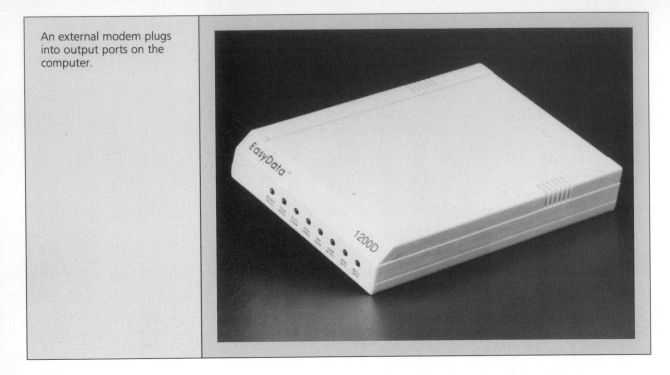

An external modem plugs into output ports on the computer.

modem is usually less expensive, provides more security for data, and requires no space outside the computer. In addition, it is called a "smart" modem because it can use the memory and processing capabilities of the host computer. There are also several other advantages—for example, the smart modem provides an on-line telephone directory and can dial outgoing calls as well as answer incoming calls automatically. Internal modems are often used to set up a bulletin-board system with a microcomputer since they can answer incoming calls automatically.

Speed   Modems vary in price and capabilities. Capability is judged by the speed of data transmission, which is called the **baud rate**. Baud rate is measured in bits per second (bps). One alphanumeric character consists of eight bits. A speed of 300 or less bits per second is considered low; 1,200 to 9,600 bits per second is medium speed; over 9,600 bits per second is high-speed transmission.

For a general idea of what these rates mean, consider that a typical computer screen of information consists of twenty-four rows and eighty columns. At 300 bps, one screen full of data is transmitted in one minute. At 1,200 bps, it takes sixteen seconds, and at 2,400 bps, it is sent in eight seconds. However, high-speed modems require special data communications lines and therefore are usually not feasible for use with personal computers. Faster baud rate devices are also more costly; however, if large amounts of data are being transmitted, the higher-rate devices may be more cost-effective in the long run. The modem, then, is the connection between the computer and the transmission line.

The transmission line, also referred to as a link, is a communication channel through which the data is transmitted. Because the modem and link work together, the baud rate of the channel should match the baud rate of the modem. It will do the sender no good to have a high-speed modem and a low-speed transmission line, or vice versa.

Transmission Line

In addition to speed, there are two other important features of the communication channel: direction and sequencing.

Direction   Direction refers to the direction in which the data is being sent. Three types of channels define the directions.

If the lines can be used in only one direction, the transmission is **simplex**. In simplex telecommunications, data can be sent, but no answer can be received. This system is used, for example, where payroll reports are sent by telecommunications to a parent company each pay period. Paychecks are mailed later by the parent company, but the telecommunications occurred in one direction only.

Since the simplex line carries information in only one direction, it is used by devices that either send or receive information but do not perform both functions. For example, the point-of-sale terminal (the now-familiar computerized cash register) only sends information; it does not receive. On the other hand, a printer only receives information; it does not send any. Since the simplex is a one-way line, it is not used to connect two computers, because computers can both send and receive.

The most widely used system of telecommunications is the **half-duplex** system, in which data is sent and received on the same lines, but not simultaneously. (This process is analogous to a two-way radio system in which the user can only send or receive messages at one time.) Payroll reports are sent and then an answer is sent back after all information has been received. In this situation, one computer cannot respond until the other has completed its message.

The most refined system uses **full-duplex**, in which data can be transmitted in two directions at the same time. This is accomplished by assigning different frequencies so there is no interference. There are obvious advantages to using this system, one of which is time saved, which is important to large organizations.

Sequencing   Once direction capability is established, another consideration is sequencing, which refers to how the message is sent. For instance, **asynchronous** transmission sends one character at a time, as from a keyboard.

Each character is preceded by a start bit and followed by a stop bit. This tells the receiving computer that a character is coming and also tells it when the character ends. The result is that each character consists of ten bits, rather than eight, when being transmitted.

The time interval between characters can vary with asynchronous transmission. This is a necessary feature when data is entered from a keyboard and is being sent at the operator's discretion and convenience.

Synchronous transmission, on the other hand, requires more sophisticated equipment because, as the name implies, it must be synchronized. For this reason, it is more often used for mainframe-to-mainframe communication. However, it does offer faster transmission because it's not necessary to use the start and stop bits that signify the beginning and end of a character.

Parity   Another reason for adding a bit to each character is for **parity** checking. When data is transmitted over communications lines, it is subject to alteration due to distortion on the lines. By adding the bit for parity checking, both sending and receiving computers can check to see if the data has been changed in any way.

Receiver   When downloading data from the host or central computer, the receiving computer must be contacted and a means of communication established with the sending computer. This is accomplished with software. The software establishes a common protocol that defines the rules for communication. It provides for one device to "listen" while the other is "talking." A familiar form of protocol establishes rules of order for a meeting, conference, or hearing. Protocol establishes who can speak and when.

When this initial communication has been set up between two or more computers, it is called "handshaking." Once the protocol has been established and handshaking has occurred, most software packages store the protocol information in a file for future reference. Consequently, the file can be retrieved for future communication without reestablishing the rules of order.

In order for the receiver to receive and understand the information being sent, the data must be converted back to digital form, since the receiver (a computer or various peripheral devices) uses digital information while the transmission line uses analog. Therefore, the receiver must have a modem that converts the analog signal to digital. Again, the baud rate of the modem determines the speed at which data is received. The receiver then verifies through parity checking that the message was received.

How is this method different from simply calling on the telephone to relay information? Because entire files can be sent, if necessary, much more detail is available in the form of graphs, lists of statistics, and other items to be printed out at the receiving end. Decisions can be made with more confidence, based on complicated and detailed information, without sending a representative to check each small piece of information. In addition, information can be received more quickly than by more conventional means (shipping, hand carrying).

A large organization may cover a broad geographical area. In order to take full advantage of telecommunications, a network can be established. A **network** is two or more computers linked together as described above for the purpose of sharing data. Networks offer an efficient use of expensive equipment.

Networks

The latest version of a network is called a **LAN** (**local area network**). A LAN is so named because it usually consists of several computers linked

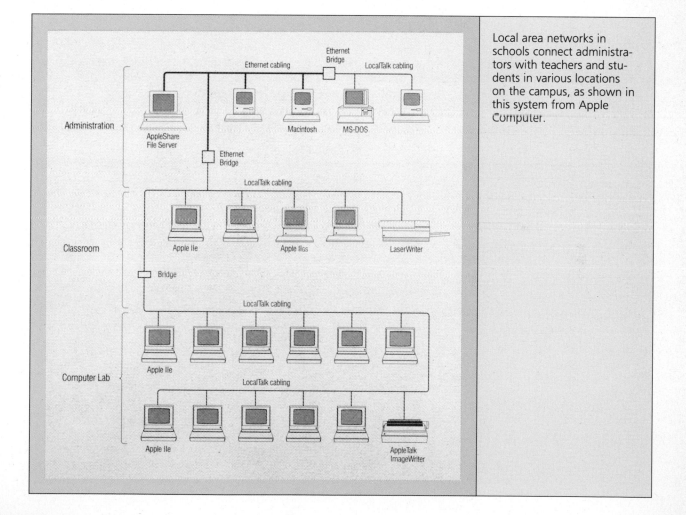

Local area networks in schools connect administrators with teachers and students in various locations on the campus, as shown in this system from Apple Computer.

in a network and housed in one building, or at least in a relatively small area. A LAN can consist of microcomputers only or can include a mainframe as well. The exchange of information made possible by a LAN makes it an ideal configuration to connect classrooms or schools. California, for example, has a computer network with a bulletin board set up for its schools and is inviting school systems in California and in other states to follow suit.

The advantages of using LANs are several. High cost peripheral devices, especially those that are used infrequently, may be linked to several computers to maximize their use and productivity. Information is available to smaller-capacity computers that otherwise would not be able to access it. In this way, a large mainframe can share its data with a number of users whose computers could not store such massive volumes of information. Another useful feature of networking is the ability to send and receive messages, which is called *electronic mail.*

Electronic Mail   An *electronic mailbox* is an area of the computer's memory where messages can be sent, received, and stored. Messages can be addressed to individuals or to groups. For example, a personal message can be addressed to the one person for whom it is meaningful, or a meeting notice can be sent to everyone who will attend the meeting.

When received by the addressee, messages can be displayed on the screen for viewing, can be forwarded to other users, can be directed to the

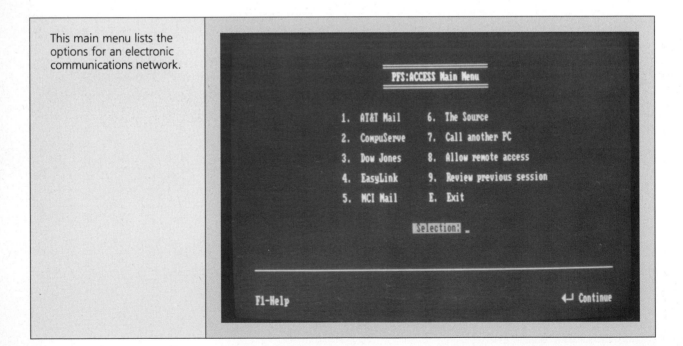

This main menu lists the options for an electronic communications network.

printer to produce a hard copy, or all these choices can be implemented. Most systems provide a storage area for messages so that they can be retained and reviewed as needed. While electronic mail serves the needs of individuals or groups of individuals within a specific organization, there is a similar service available to the public in the form of bulletin boards.

Bulletin Boards   A **bulletin board** is an electronic mailbox shared by people who may not be connected in any way other than that they are able to access the bulletin board. Just like any other public bulletin board, an electronic one is used for posting notices, advertising items for sale, and disseminating any other information of interest to its users.

One very effective use of the bulletin board is the sharing of information within a special interest group. For instance, user groups for specific types of computers often share tips in this way. Another way bulletin boards benefit users is in the sharing of software written by individuals and groups. Called public domain programs, these are often offered free of charge, or for a nominal contribution. Most software applications that are available in commercial programs are also available through this medium.

Examples of public domain software are FrEdWriter, a word processing program, and FrEdMail, an electronic mail program. The prefix FrEd derives from *free ed*ucational software. These are only two of hundreds of public domain programs available.

In education, the global classroom is fast becoming a reality with the use of electronic bulletin boards. Students can send letters and information

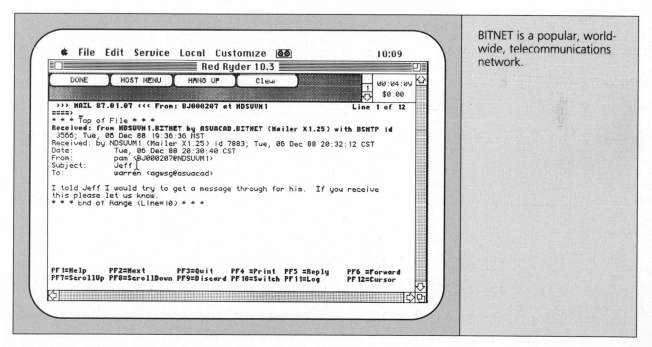

BITNET is a popular, worldwide, telecommunications network.

to classes all over the world. For example, a group of students in the United States can send weather information to students in Canada, Australia, or Europe. In a collaborative project at the National Graphic Society called the NGS Kids Network Project, elementary school students collect and share scientific data nationally using telecommunications. Information includes measurements of rainfall, studies of bird migration, and daylight astronomy. In all cases the students are participating in active, ongoing scientific research.

Many bulletin boards also offer a system for sending and receiving private messages as well. This service can be used on an individual basis or within a group of people with similar interests. As with any electronic mail, users check their mailboxes on a regular basis to receive their messages.

In addition to private mail and information appropriate to special interest groups, there is a large body of more formal and structured data that is made available to the public through information services.

Information Services   Information services are commercial telecommunications ventures whereby the user can access large bodies of information and reference material. These services offer a wide variety of information including news stories, financial information, entertainment information, travel information, library and reference information—even an on-line encyclopedia.

Users can make reservations for train and airline travel, hotels, restaurants, and theaters. Some services even offer movie reviews.

Banking transactions also can be accomplished through a computerized information service, transferring funds and making payments electronically. Some services offer shopping by computer; the user chooses among items described, then pays for them by charging to a credit card or transferring funds from a personal bank account.

Stock and bond market information is available to users who are interested in this specialized kind of information. Wall Street ticker tape machines are a familiar sight in old movies. The same sort of service is now available to the personal computer user. Information can be updated almost instantaneously through the speed of telecommunications.

Other types of investment information, including tax information, can be accessed in this manner, giving the user a direct line to the business world from wherever the computer is located. In the same way, all types of business information can be relayed by telecommunications, connecting all areas of an organization no matter how far-flung they are.

The Future of Telecommunications

A giant leap forward is being accomplished with improvements in the amount of data transmitted, the use of satellites, the increasing number of organizations using data communications, and improvement in the means of transmitting data, such as using fiber optics.

Changes in regulations by the FCC (Federal Communications Commission) have opened up opportunities to expand the communications networks beyond the one carrier available in the 1960s—American Telephone and Telegraph (AT&T). With other companies developing and selling systems, expansion has been rapid. Since travel costs are increasing, installation of a telecommunications system has become a cost-effective means for companies, school districts, other educational institutions, government agencies, and all types of organizations to conduct conferences and transmit large amounts of data.

Telecommunications is a link between individuals, groups, and organizations as well as a means of transferring or sharing data. As such, telecommunications is only one of several components of integrated software. The data to be transmitted comprise other components that are discussed in the following section.

INTEGRATED SOFTWARE

While telecommunications enables computers to communicate with each other, **integrated software** allows different software programs to interact. Integrated software made its appearance when it became obvious that there was a need for programming that would allow a user to access more than one application at a time. For example, when preparing a document using a word processor, it is often necessary to include information from a spreadsheet or database. However, many software applications use programming techniques so different from other programs that they are incompatible and cannot share information. Even with programs that allow information to be accessed from one program to another, the method is cumbersome: The user must exit from the one program in order to access the other; frequently, moving in and out of different programs necessitates switching disks, which can be tedious and time-consuming. In addition, although they may be compatible, applications often have their own specific commands and other terminology, so that the user must switch to a new mode of operation when switching to another application.

It became apparent, then, that there was a need for software that would combine, or *integrate,* different types of applications. Essentially what was needed was the ability to share and transfer data among various applications. The applications most often needed in combination were word processing, spreadsheets, databases, presentation graphics, and communications.

As with telecommunications, integrated software is an innovation in computer technology that adapts very well to the classroom. One of the disadvantages of software used in the classroom has been the time required for teachers to instruct and students to learn to use various applications.

With integrated software, each application uses the same or similar commands, thus reducing the time for students to become comfortable and proficient in their use.

Integration also allows the teacher to present a more comprehensive view of a subject and show its relevancy and relationship to other subjects or demonstrate practical applications of material learned.

Several methods were developed to achieve integration. Each of them is discussed in the following sections.

File Transfer Software

File transfer software converts files from one format to another that can be used by a different application. The format most commonly used in conversion operations is **ASCII** (American Standard Code for Information Interchange). A simplified explanation of ASCII is that it is a coding scheme that assigns a specific combination of binary digits (ones and zeros) to each key on the keyboard.

Each alphanumeric character on the keyboard, as well as commonly used symbols, is assigned its own ASCII code. In other words, as a standard method for data representation, ASCII is a commonly understood coding system that facilitates conversion of data from one program format to another.

For this reason, most printers receive data in ASCII, thus necessitating that output to printers be in this format. Some word processing packages store data in ASCII format. Others use their own unique representations of data and sometimes offer an option of converting data to ASCII for use with other programs. However, not all programs have this option, which is why file transfer software was created. Almost any type of conversion can be done with the appropriate file transfer software. The operation of these programs is fairly simple and straightforward and increases the user's capabilities.

File transfer software has solved some problems, but it does not address the inconvenience of having to move in and out of various applications. Originally, another distinct disadvantage involved graphics software packages that did not use standard formats for storing graphics; this made them difficult or impossible to convert. Obviously a more sophisticated and complex system of software was needed for tasks that required data sharing and interaction among several applications. Integrated software was created to fill this need.

Integrated Software Programs

Integrated software combines several or all five of the applications most commonly needed to produce a specific result. Word processing, spreadsheets, databases, graphics, and communications, or some combination of these, meet the needs of most users or required tasks.

In an integrated software package, text and other data are stored in the same format for all applications. There is no need to convert from one format to another, or to enter data more than once—the data entered can be accessed for any of the operations contained in the program.

In addition, all applications use the same command structure. This eliminates the need to learn different commands for each application and then recall which apply to the current operation. For example, the Move and Copy commands are used in most applications. Word processing moves and copies blocks of text. Databases move and copy basic information to be sorted and tabulated in various ways. Spreadsheets move and copy rows and columns of figures. Integrated software uses the same commands and keystrokes for these functions no matter which application is in use. Microsoft Works is an example of a program that integrates telecommunications, a word processor, a database, and a spreadsheet.

Microsoft Works Command Summary

Key	WP	DB	SS	COM
A		Sort	Absolute Cell Ref	
B	Bold		Bold	
C	Copy	Copy	Copy	Copy
D	Draw	Enter Date	Fill Down	
F	Find	Find Field	Find Cell	
G	Go To Page #		Go To Cell	
I	Italics	Insert Record	Insert	
K	Copy Format			
L		Show List/Form		
M	Prepare to Merge	Match Records		
N	Normal Text		Normal Text	
O	Open	Open	Open	Open
P	Print	Print	Print	Print
Q	Quit	Quit	Quit	Quit
R	Replace		Fill Right	
S	Save	Save	Save	Save
T		Enter Time		
U	Underline		Underline	
V	Paste	Paste	Paste	Paste
W	Small/Full Window	Small/Full Window	Small/Full Window	Small/Full Window
X	Cut	Cut	Cut	Cut
Y	Paste Format			
Z	Undo	Undo	Undo	
=			Calculate Now	Hang Up
"		Duplicate field in previous record		
+				Hang Up
	Activate last document in Window menu	Activate last document in Window menu	Activate last document in Window menu	Activate last document in Window menu

For even greater flexibility, many integrated software packages allow two or more applications to be operated simultaneously. This is done by opening windows on the display screen. A **window** is a portion of the screen that displays data from another application.

For instance, when a report is being prepared using the word processing application and the user wishes to include information from a spreadsheet, the spreadsheet can be accessed and displayed in a window. The user can then locate the specific data needed, format it as desired, and copy the result into the body of the report being prepared. Likewise, spreadsheet data can be converted into a graph, and the graph placed in the report.

In some integrated software programs, these operations can be performed at the same time. That is, a database file can be sorted while a spreadsheet is being reformatted, or a graph can be created from spreadsheet data while the printer is producing a printed copy of word processing text.

Obviously performing multiple operations from different applications requires a more complex method of accessing data and implementing commands than does a single application. To serve this purpose, integrated software packages have a sophisticated system of menus.

Menus   Each integrated software package establishes its own system for menus, which display the program's options. Many programs, however, use some version of pull-down menus, although they may have a different

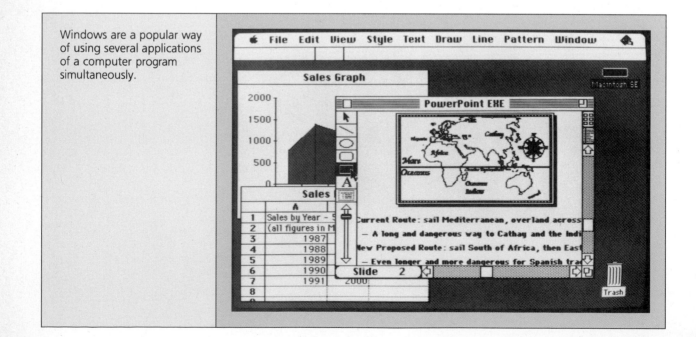

Windows are a popular way of using several applications of a computer program simultaneously.

name for them. **Pull-down menus** are main menus offering a number of choices, each of which offers a group of further choices, or *submenus.*

The pull-down menu solves the problem of displaying the options provided by the different applications in integrated software packages; because there is no room for all of them to appear on the screen at once, the menus are structured in a multilevel fashion. When an option is selected, a submenu "pulls down" to display subsequent options until the user arrives at the application and data needed for a specific task. From the initiation of the task, through the use and integration of various options, to the final output—screen display or printed copy—the operation is guided and controlled by menus and the user's menu selections.

System Integrators

Many school districts already have expensive software in place and are satisfied with its performance. Except for the inconvenience of having to move in and out of various programs to access different applications, the software serves its purpose and meets the needs of the user. Although an integrated software program would solve the problem of having to exit and reenter programs, it would also require that users learn a whole new command structure. The ideal solution is to use the existing software like an integrated package. It was for this purpose that system integrators came into being.

A **system integrator** allows the user to open a new program without leaving the program already in use. There are different ways in which this can be accomplished. Some integrators use windows very similar to those used by integrated software programs. Others use memory partitions, which are spaces in the computer's memory set aside for specific purposes. Since partitions cannot be accessed simultaneously, this method is more limited than windows; you can view only one program at a time. (However, moving from one to another is accomplished easily and quickly.)

There are other disadvantages; while system integrators may be an easier solution than purchasing an entirely new software package, they require extensive computer memory. This can result in slower response time and less storage for data files. In addition, system integrators are designed to interface with specific software. Thus, depending on the software in use, an integrator might require additional utilities to support standard functions.

As discussed in earlier sections of this chapter, another need in the process of sharing data is telecommunications. Many system integrators as well as integrated software programs encompass this capability along with combining other applications. This allows the user to share data with computers in other locations as well as to access data for reports and other documents.

A system integrator for an auto supply company allows users to window detailed graphics and stock information from a menu.

National Auto Supply Catalog

Nut—
Washer—
Element
Cover

Auto: Honda Civic 1975

Fuel   [Engine]   Cooling/Heating
Cylinders   Gaskets   [Air Cleaner]

Gasket

Gasket, cleaner case

Gasket

Part No. 17258-634-300
Price per item: $ 6.45

Installation

Location: Aisle 3, Shelf 12, Bin 4

(Inventory)   (Add/Pick List)
(Suppliers)   (Print Pick List)

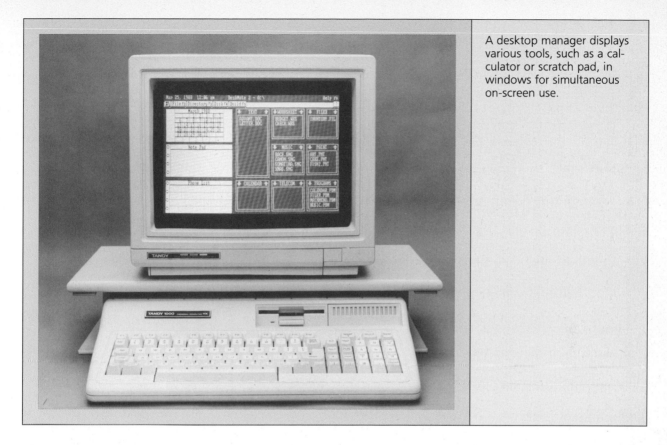

A desktop manager displays various tools, such as a calculator or scratch pad, in windows for simultaneous on-screen use.

Desktop Manager

Another feature often incorporated in both integrated software and system integrators is the desktop manager, which generally operates on the window technique. The **desktop manager** functions like the instruments commonly found on a desktop, from which it gets its name. Calculators, scratch pads, and telephone directories are some of the tools used daily for personal productivity. The desktop manager combines these functions, which can be accessed through windows without leaving another application program.

For example, a scratch pad can be called up on the display screen for making quick notes that come to mind while preparing another document or report. The pad then can be stored for future reference or copied to another document.

A calculator, which appears on screen and looks just like a desktop calculator, can be used for mathematical computation and included in a present document or copied to the scratch pad for later use. If the computer's keyboard includes a numeric keypad, using the on-screen calculator is very similar to using a regular calculator.

The telephone directory can be accessed to look up a number without interrupting the current operation. If the computer has a modem attached, the desktop manager can even automatically dial the number.

All files created by the desktop manager can be copied to disk and used over and over again. In addition, data can be moved from one function of the desktop manager to another just as with other applications of integrated software.

The functions of a desktop manager are also some of the tasks that a classroom teacher performs daily. Therefore, it is an ideal set of tools that can be useful and conserve time for a teacher.

Desktop publishing allows the user to produce publication-quality printed documents quickly and without having to use services outside the school or office.

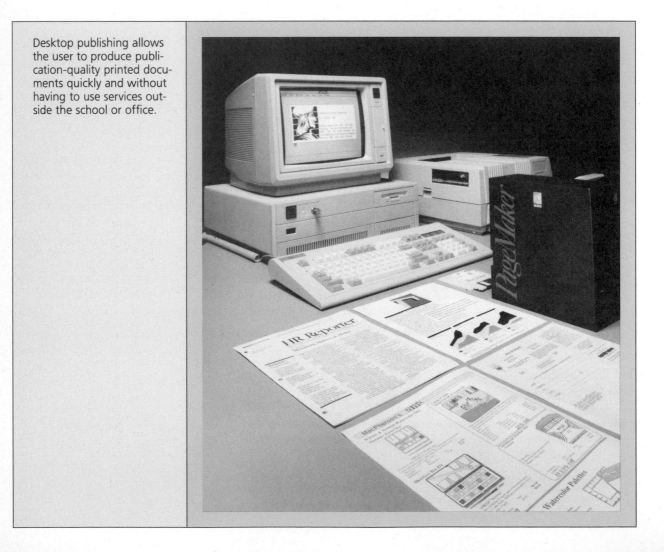

Desktop publishing is a new application made possible by integrated software. It allows the user to produce publication-quality printed documents. Quality of this level used to be achieved only by typesetting equipment. While the computerized desktop publisher is not currently capable of delivering the *same degree* of quality as a typesetter, the quality is acceptable for many publications. The cost savings resulting from in-house desktop publishing makes this alternative a very attractive one for many users.

Many different kinds of publications are used in schools, some for public distribution and others for internal use. Clearly, those intended for parents and other members of the community require a more professional and polished appearance than ones for school employees. Desktop publishing fills the gap that lies between computer printer output and professionally typeset publications.

Desktop publishing can also be used for instruction of various subjects in the classroom. A school or class newspaper can be produced, giving students an opportunity to learn a number of things about journalism, language usage, public communication, as well as publishing itself. Public relations, advertising, and document formatting are other subjects that might be learned from desktop publishing. The list is long and teachers can use their creativity and imagination to expand it as technology stretches the potential.

Desktop publishing systems rely on microcomputers and laser printers to produce near-typeset quality images. They are capable of extensive typesetting and document design functions. A hard-disk drive is required because

Desktop publishing can result in substantial cost savings over traditional typesetting.

of the large amounts of both external storage and main memory that are necessary for desktop publishing. Of course, a laser printer is recommended for better-quality productions. (More detailed information regarding desktop publishing is available in Chapter 15 about the future of computers in society.) Popular educational desktop publishing packages include Graphics Writer 2.0 (Seven Hills Software), Personal Newsletter (SoftSync), Publish It! (Timeworks), and Springboard Publisher (Springboard Publisher). (Addresses for software publishers are listed at the end of this chapter.)

SUMMARY

A developing area of computer applications, telecommunications refers to the process of transferring data from one point to another without changing the data as it travels. Telecommunications—which can be facilitated between mainframes or personal computers, or a combination thereof—consists of four basic elements: the sender, the message, the transmission line, and the receiver. The sender is the computer from which the data originates. The process of sending data to a central computer is called uploading.

For data transmission to occur, computer information, which is digital (a succession of on/off signals called binary digits, or bits), must be converted to analog (sound waves) in order to travel on the transmission line, which is a telephone line. This is done with a modem.

There are three types of modems: the acoustic coupler (a telephone handset attached to the computer), the direct connect (which directly accesses the telephone line without a handset), and the internal modem (which is plugged into slots inside the computer).

Modem capability is based on the speed of transmission, or baud rate. A speed of 300 or less bits per second is considered low; 1,200 to 9,600 bits per second is medium speed; over 9,600 bits per second is high-speed transmission.

Speed is also important to the transmission line, which is the communication channel through which the data is sent. In addition to speed, there are two other important features of the communication channel: direction and sequencing.

Three types of channels define the direction in which data is sent. If the line can be used in only one direction (to send or receive), the transmission is simplex. If the line can be used in both directions, but not simultaneously, the transmission is half-duplex. If the line can be used in both directions at the same time, the transmission is full-duplex.

Sequencing refers to how the message is sent. Asynchronous transmission sends one character at a time, as from a keyboard. Synchronous transmission, on the other hand, requires more sophisticated equipment because the sender and receiver must be synchronized.

To initiate telecommunications, the receiving computer must be contacted and a means of communication established with the sending computer. This is accomplished by the use of software that establishes a common protocol for this purpose. Downloading is the process of receiving data from a host or central computer. The receiving computer verifies that the information is received. Then, by parity checking, both the sending and the receiving computers determine whether the data has been changed in any way.

A network is two or more computers or peripheral devices linked together by telecommunications for the purpose of sharing data. A LAN (local area network) connects computers housed in one building or small area.

A common feature of a network is electronic mail. An electronic mailbox is an area of the computer's memory where messages can be sent, received, and stored. A bulletin board is an electronic mailbox shared by people who may not be connected in any way other than that they are able to access the bulletin board. Through bulletin boards, users may share free programs called public domain software.

Information services are more formal and extensive methods of receiving information through networks. An information service is a commercial telecommunications venture whereby the user can access large bodies of information and reference material. Some of the services offered are banking, shopping, travel, entertainment, reference information, education, free computer software, message service, and electronic games.

Telecommunications benefits teachers and educational administrators. In the classroom, teachers can access volumes of reference and research materials from bibliographic information services and can share curriculum information and lesson plans with other teachers at different locations. Outside the class, teleconferencing (two or more people connected via computers in different locations) provides a new educational environment especially convenient for the handicapped or parents at home with children. With networking, administrators can centralize their financial and managerial tasks and share resources with all schools in their district.

Telecommunications is only one of several components of integrated software; the data to be transmitted and the applications for formatting it are others. Additional features of integrated software assist the user in everyday office operations and increase personal efficiency.

Integrated software made its appearance when it became obvious that there was a need for programming that would allow a user to access more than one application at a time. Essentially what was needed was the ability to share and transfer data among various applications.

Developed for this purpose, file transfer software converts files from one format to another for use by a different application. File transfer software has solved some problems, but it does not address the inconvenience of having to move in and out of various applications.

Integrated software packages were created to solve this problem. Integrated software combines several or all five of the applications most commonly needed: word processing, spreadsheets, data bases, graphics, and telecommunications. Text and other data share the same format for all applications with no need to convert from one format to another. In addition, all applications use the same command structure.

For even greater flexibility, many integrated software packages allow two or more applications to be operated simultaneously. This is done by opening windows on the display screen. (A window is a portion of the screen that displays data from another application.)

Users pleased with their large and expensive applications program may not want to switch to an integrated software program. Instead, with system integrators they can access other programs without leaving the present one. However, systems integration programs take up a lot of memory and are usually designed for specific software, which can limit their flexibility.

Another feature often incorporated in both integrated software and system integrators is the desktop manager. Calculators, scratch pads, and telephone directories are some of the tools found on a desktop and used daily for personal productivity. The desktop manager combines these functions, which can be accessed through windows without leaving another application program.

A new application made possible by integrated software is desktop publishing. While the quality is not yet as good as that of typesetting, the cost savings resulting from in-house desktop publishing makes this alternative very attractive for most users.

Desktop publishing systems rely on microcomputers and laser printers to produce near-typeset quality images. They are capable of extensive typesetting and document design functions. A hard-disk drive is a requirement because of the large amounts of both external storage and main memory necessary for desktop publishing.

REVIEW EXERCISES

Multiple Choice

1. Telecommunications is also referred to as
   a. journalism
   b. management information systems
   c. data communications
   d. none of the above
2. The process of transmitting data to a host or central computer is called

   a. uploading
   b. downloading
   c. data verification
   d. none of the above
3. The first modem developed was called a(n)
   a. acoustic coupler
   b. compiler
   c. internal modem
   d. none of the above
4. The speed at which data is transmitted is the
   a. characters-per-second (cps) rate
   b. baud rate

c. real-time rate

d. none of the above

5. When data is sent one character at a time, the transmission is

a. more reliable

b. synchronous

c. asynchronous

d. none of the above

6. When two or more computers establish initial communication, the process is known as

a. sign-on

b. initial operating procedure (IOP)

c. handshaking

d. none of the above

7. Two or more computers linked through telecommunications are referred to as a

a. cluster

b. network

c. work station

d. all of the above

8. Integrated software allows computer programs to

a. be copied legally

b. transfer data among various applications

c. be accessible to all computer users

d. all of the above

9. A system integrator enables the user to

a. write integrated programs

b. open a new program without leaving the program already in use

c. combine various types of systems software

d. all of the above

10. Desktop managers can function as

a. calculators

b. scratch pads

c. telephone directories

d. all of the above

True/False

1. At present, telecommunications is available only for mainframe computers.

2. A modem converts digital data to analog and analog data to digital.

3. The internal modem is referred to as a "smart" modem.

4. In simplex telecommunications, data is transmitted in only one direction.

5. Downloading is the process of reloading software after the computer has malfunctioned.

6. Electronic mail messages can be displayed on the screen but not printed.

7. File transfer software provides for conversion of files from one format to another.

8. A window is a portion of the screen that displays data from another application.

9. Some system integrators use memory partitions.

10. Desktop publishing cannot be used with laser printers.

Short Answer

1. What are the four basic elements of telecommunications?

2. What are the three types of modems?

3. Define the three types of channels by which data can be sent.

4. What are the differences among simplex, half-duplex, and full-duplex data transmission?

5. Define the term *desktop publishing*.

Activities

1. Visit a local computer retail store to see some of the popular telecommunications software packages on the market.

2. Given your academic major, hobbies, or career field, make a list of bulletin boards or information services that would be useful to you.

3. Research how integrated software is being used to teach across the curriculum.

4. List as many ways as you can in which a classroom teacher might use a desktop manager.

5. Use a desktop publishing system to create a brochure showing the proper handling of disks or another topic of interest to you.

6. List as many ways as you can in which a school could use desktop publishing.

7. List all the educational electronic bulletin boards in your area.

8. Develop a lesson plan for an academic area like science or social studies that uses an electronic bulletin board to communicate with classes from other countries.

9. List the costs of setting up an electronic bulletin board in a classroom. Include modem costs, telephone line costs, and so on.

10. Write a summary of several national/international projects that have used telecommunications to share data.
11. Describe telecommunications, sometimes called distance education, and list the advantages and disadvantages.

BIBLIOGRAPHY

Apple Desktop Communications Solutions Reference Guide. Apple Computer, 1987.

Arcellana, J. E. "Is Desktop Publishing Worth It?" *MacWorld* 5 (no. 10, October 1988): 107–115.

Azarmsa, Reza. "Teleconferencing: How to Be a Successful Host." *Tech Trends* 32 (no. 4, September 1987): 19–23.

Baumbach, Donna. "Desktop Publishing." *Tech Trends* 32 (no. 5, October 1987): 13–15.

Bensen, Greg M., Jr., and William Hirschen. "Distance Learning: New Windows in Education." *T.H.E. Journal* 15 (no. 1, August 1987): 63–67.

Bitter, Gary G. *Computers in Today's World.* New York: John Wiley, 1984.

Bitter, Gary G., and Norm Higgins. "Computer Control of Mediated Instructional Presentation." *Monitor* 12 (no. 3, 1973): 6–8.

Bove, Tony, et al. *The Art of Desktop Publishing.* New York: Bantam Books, 1986.

Clark, Chris. "Telecommunications Is Here and Now." *The Computing Teacher* 15 (no. 8): 24.

Coburn, Edward J. *Learn to Compute!* Albany, N.Y.: Delmar, 1988.

Cunningham, Pat, and Joan Gose. "Telecommunications: A New Horizon for the Handicapped." In *8th Annual Microcomputers in Education Conference Proceedings*, 65–73. Tempe: Arizona State University, 1988.

Edyburn, D. L. "An Evaluation of the Information Retrieval Skills of Students With and Without Learning Handicaps." *The Computing Teacher* 15 (no. 7): 8.

FrEdMail News 2 (no. 3, Spring 1988).

Goldberg, Fred S. "Telecommunications in the Classroom: Where We've Been and Where We Should Be Going." *The Computing Teacher* 15 (no. 8): 26.

Grauer, Robert T., and Paul Sugrue. *Microcomputer Applications.* New York: McGraw-Hill, 1987.

Hurly, Paul, et al. *The Videotex and Teletext Handbook.* New York: Harper and Row, 1985.

Itzkan, Seth J. "The Emergence of the Global Classroom." *The Early Adolescence Magazine* 2 (no. 4, March 1988): 4–9.

Johnston, Randolph. *Microcomputers: Concepts and Applications.* Santa Cruz, Calif.: Mitchell, 1987.

Jones, Pamela. "Online Research at the Secondary Level: Access to a World of Information." *Tech Trends* 33 (no. 3, April-May 1988): 22–23.

Lehrer, Ariella. "A Networking Primer: When Is a Network Not a Network?" *Classroom Computer Learning* 8 (no. 5, February 1988): 39–47.

Pollack, Richard A., and Gene Breault. "On-Line Contemporary Issues Bring Today's World to Social Studies Classrooms." *The Computing Teacher* 12 (no. 8, May 1985): 10–11.

Roach, Debra B. "Roll the Desktop Presses!" *Teaching and Computers* 6 (no. 3, October 1988): 12–16.

Scrogen, Len. "Telecomputing: How to Overcome the Roadblocks." *Classroom Computer Learning* 7 (no. 5, February 1987): 40–45.

Thompson, Diane P. "Teaching Writing on a Local Area Network." *T.H.E. Journal* 15 (no. 2, September 1987): 92–97.

Tinker, Robert F. "Educational Technology and the Future of Science Education." *School Science and Mathematics* 87 (no. 6, October 1987): 466–476.

Will-Harris, Daniel and Toni. "Communicate by Design." *Compute!* 10 (no. 11, issue 102, November 1988): 30–43.

SOFTWARE PUBLISHERS

Microsoft Corp.
Box 77017
Redmond, WA 98073

Seven Hills Software
2310 Oxford Rd.
Tallahassee, FL 32304

SoftSync, Inc.
182 Madison Ave.
New York, NY 10016

Springboard Publisher
7808 Creekridge Cir.
Minneapolis, MN 55435

Timeworks
444 Lake Cook Rd.
Deerfield, IL 60015

REVIEW ANSWER KEY

Multiple Choice

1. c	5. c	9. b
2. a	6. c	10. d
3. a	7. b	
4. b	8. b	

True/False

1. F	5. F	9. T
2. T	6. F	10. F
3. T	7. T	
4. T	8. T	

Short Answer

1. Sender, message, transmission line, and receiver.
2. Acoustic coupler, direct connect, and internal.
3. Simplex, half-duplex, and full-duplex.
4. Simplex carries information in only one direction. Half-duplex carries information in two directions but not simultaneously. Full-duplex transmits data in two directions at the same time.
5. Desktop publishing is a system using microcomputers and laser printers to produce near-typeset quality publications.

CHAPTER 10

COMPUTER-ASSISTED INSTRUCTION

Objectives

- Describe the four major types of CAI software on the market—drill and practice, tutorial, simulation, and problem-solving
- List some of the characteristics of effective CAI
- List the benefits of CAI
- Explain how CAI can be used in special education
- Understand general guidelines for selecting CAI software

Key Terms

authoring language
branching tutorial
CAI (computer-assisted instruction)
computer literacy
computerphobia
courseware
drill-and-practice software
linear tutorial
problem-solving software
simulation software
tool software
tutorial software

Computers are changing almost every aspect of our daily lives. It should come as no surprise, then, to discover that computers have caused many people to rethink the very philosophy and methods that underlie our educational system. In order to prepare young students today for productive and fulfilling lives as adults in a highly technical society, schools have begun to tap into computer power to improve their teaching.

The use of computers to educate people is known as computer-assisted **instruction (CAI)**. Another commonly used term for computers in education is *computer-based instruction* (CBI). Whichever term is used, the process is the same: computers are used to teach, drill, and test students of all ages and abilities on a virtually unlimited range of subjects. In this chapter, we explore why schools are installing computer systems in classrooms, what types of CAI software are being designed, and how educators can make the most of the computer in the classroom.

ADVANTAGES OF COMPUTER-ASSISTED INSTRUCTION (CAI)

A teacher providing computer-assisted instruction in a computer laboratory.

CAI is a relatively new application of computer power. In Chapter 2, we saw that the early generations of computers were designed and used by government and industrial users who could afford to pay the huge costs of developing, maintaining, and programming complex and cumbersome computer systems. Not until the middle and late 1970s did computers become small, convenient, and affordable enough to be practical for installation in schools. In fact, some school budgets today do not permit the purchase of extensive computer hardware and software. But, fortunately, this condition is changing as prices decrease and the desirability of teaching with computers becomes increasingly apparent.

Because of its relatively recent appearance on the scene, CAI is in its infancy. Educators, programmers, and software publishers are still in the process of learning by experience. Nevertheless, it's already possible to see some of the benefits of using computers as teaching tools in the classroom.

Computers involve the student actively in the learning process   In traditional classrooms where teachers present new material through lectures, visual aids, group discussions, and so on, it's possible for students to become too passive. We know that learning doesn't occur by osmosis. Rather, the most lasting kind of learning occurs when students are highly motivated to *participate* in activities that promote learning. In other words, students who work with a hammer, nails, and saw will probably learn more about carpentry than students who merely read a book on the subject.

Teachers today face perhaps a larger challenge than ever before in motivating their students to take an active role in their own education. Because of television, many students are used to watching video images that require

Students are increasingly using computers at home or in their rooms at college.

no action from the viewer. Some educators feel this produces a lethargy in students that teachers must overcome if they are to teach effectively. How can they do this? Computers provide an important alternative to more traditional methods.

First of all, computers include video screens. Like the popular music videos on television, computers can also provide interesting, entertaining, and even informative visual images that help to keep students' attention. Second, computers require action from the user before they can perform. During a lecture, no one may notice that a student's mind is wandering, but during a computer session, the computer always notices. It cannot operate until the student gives it the necessary commands.

The ability of the computer to interact with the user suits it well to education. While it can never replace one-on-one human interaction, it can make a dull subject more interesting or encourage students to practice longer than they would do if working on a worksheet. Some sophisticated computer systems come close to replicating human interaction. With voice synthesis, they "talk." With children who are too young to read or who are visually impaired, this is an excellent feature.

Computers provide fast and systematic feedback   Whether teaching a math student long division or housebreaking a pet, we know that to be effective, feedback must be delivered quickly and consistently. One way the computer interacts with the student is to respond to answers as the student keys them in. The computer keeps a tally of student performance, rewards correct answers, and encourages the student who answers incorrectly to try again. All this communication enhances the learning process.

In a more traditional setting, students are expected to learn new concepts and then demonstrate mastery of skills through pencil-and-paper tests. Those tests must then be graded by teachers who are often already overburdened with paper work. Thus, students must sometimes wait a long time to receive any feedback, and when they do, it may be no more than a numeric score or letter grade. Consequently, they don't have a chance to try again or see what areas they need to improve.

The computer can actually follow each student on his or her path of learning, pointing out pitfalls and suggesting shortcuts along the way. This is simply not possible for the human teacher, who is responsible for the progress of many students at the same time. Well-written CAI software provides fast and systematic feedback that encourages the student to progress and assists in the process by providing patient and timely review of weak areas.

Computers allow all students—slow and gifted alike—to learn at their own pace   We hinted in the last few paragraphs that the computer is able to individualize instruction to a degree that is not always possible for the human teacher to accomplish. In a traditional classroom, the class as a group must progress at a given rate. Even though teachers recognize that slower students have fallen behind while gifted students are growing bored, they still must gear the pace of their teaching to the average learner. The computer is free from this limitation. Each student works at the computer individually—the computer is oblivious to whether he or she takes an hour or a month to complete a lesson.

The computer is also quite egalitarian in its dealings with students. That is, it does not favor one over another. Well-designed CAI software is written so that it responds to incorrect answers with positive, nonthreatening, and encouraging messages. It also does not (or certainly should not) embarrass the student who answers incorrectly. Thus, students may be more willing to answer a computer-generated question than to volunteer to answer questions posed by the teacher during a lecture. By the same token, the computer congratulates fast learners and may even reward them by allowing them to skip parts of lessons that are not challenging enough.

Individualized instruction has been an important trend in the schools in recent years. The computer may well be one of the most expedient methods of achieving this goal.

The computer facilitates and sometimes even manages remediation   Part of the reason for individualizing instruction is to recognize and meet the need for remediation as soon as possible. For teachers who oversee many students, this is not always an easy or manageable task. For the computer, it is a much simpler matter. Many CAI programs are written to keep score, as it were, of each student's performance. Records of student performance are then available to the teacher for the purpose of assessing how well the class and individual students are doing.

Students who need remediation can be assigned additional work or given extra computer time to practice concepts and skills. The computer may give the student only a certain number of tries before returning to earlier routines so that students can review information they do not fully understand. This process is consistent; review will be provided *every* time a student demonstrates a need for it. It is also immediate, since the computer provides the information at the time it is needed.

When the computer is used for remediation, other classroom activities can go on without interruption. Teachers can proceed with their plans for other groups of students, knowing that those who require remediation are getting the help they need from a patient, consistent, and reliable "teacher."

The computer frees teachers for more "human" tasks, such as helping individual students, listening to student concerns, and providing pats on the shoulder for work well done There is no need to fear that computers will ever replace human teachers. In fact, it is more accurate to call them teaching tools rather

Cooperative group learning is a popular approach to utilizing one computer in a classroom.

than teachers. Not until computers grow arms for hugging and hearts for caring will they ever come close to providing the warmth and concern that a human teacher can. Unfortunately, teachers currently spend a lot of their hugging time on mundane tasks instead, such as typing up tests, recording grades, and keeping attendance records. The more of these routine and time-consuming tasks they can delegate to the computer, the more time they have for uniquely human activities and the better their time is spent.

Just as the computer patiently teaches individual students, it can also tutor groups of students at one time. Provided there are enough computers and software available, an entire class can work on a lesson at the same time. While this is taking place, the teacher has an opportunity to work one-on-one with students who need additional tutoring or attention.

In Chapter 12, on computer-managed instruction, we examine some of the other activities besides teaching with which computers can assist teachers, freeing even more time for teachers to do what they do best: teach. These activities include record keeping, grading, word processing, and generating tests, worksheets, and handouts.

The computer can bring real-world conditions into the classroom   Through computer simulations, students can observe a nuclear reaction or fly jets in the classroom. With a little assistance from their imaginations, they can

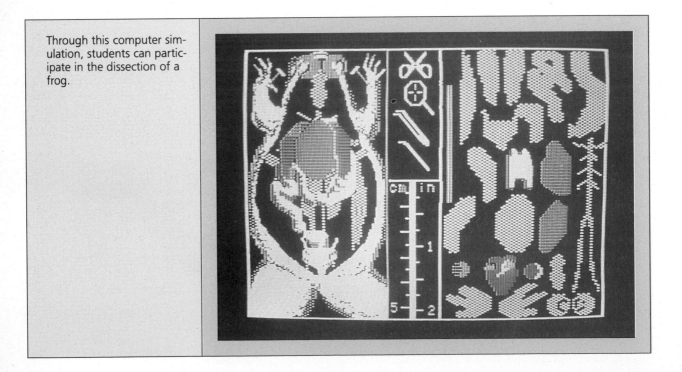

Through this computer simulation, students can participate in the dissection of a frog.

experience all sorts of conditions that would be dangerous or impractical for them to try in reality. They can test their reactions in life-threatening situations or relive historical events of long ago. With **tool software** such as word processing, database, graphics, and spreadsheet programs, students also learn specific skills that will help them in the workplace. Thus, computers can go a long way toward making education more relevant to students.

Not only does the computer present, drill, and test concepts and skills in all areas of the curriculum, but it teaches students computer literacy as well   This does not mean that students become computer experts capable of writing complex programs. It simply means that they feel fairly comfortable talking about, working around, and operating computers. In our highly technological society, **computer literacy** may become as important as the ability to read and write.

Young children can use the microcomputer as an educational tool.

How to promote computer literacy in our schools and throughout society at large is a great challenge. It is perhaps easier to accomplish in education than elsewhere, through the use of CAI. With computer-assisted instruction students learn basic computer skills, such as turning the computer on, loading a program into the computer's memory, entering information through the keyboard, using peripherals such as printers, and sometimes even writing simple programs. Often, they learn all these things without being consciously aware that they are becoming computer literate. Instead, they think they are simply practicing math or just having fun. But the ease with which they use the computer and the language they develop for discussing the computer are skills that will last a lifetime.

In a similar fashion, CAI can prevent or help to overcome **computerphobia**, or the fear of working with computers. Very young students have not yet formulated fearful ideas about computers. In fact, to them computers may seem like exciting toys. Therefore, they don't resist being introduced to computers; they enjoy the experience. Who knows? They may even help their parents and grandparents to feel more comfortable with computers as well.

DISADVANTAGES OF COMPUTER-ASSISTED INSTRUCTION

Encouraging as the scenario of computers in classrooms may be, there are some considerable challenges to overcome in bringing CAI into the schools. Some of these challenges arise from people's attitudes while others have to do with the state of the art of educational software. Educational software is changing rapidly, and many of the disadvantages of CAI are being resolved. Still, let's consider some of the obstacles that must be faced as computers are brought into classrooms in ever greater numbers.

Some people fear that computers will dehumanize education   These people are afraid that computers will eventually replace human teachers, just as robots have assumed some manufacturing and industrial tasks once performed by human workers. They don't want education to become a mechanical process of answering computer-generated questions without the caring touch of a human teacher. Others foresee a time when students will not attend schools, but instead will communicate with central computers from their homes to acquire information. In this situation, students would miss out on the very important social experience that takes place in the classroom.

Perhaps the best way to overcome these fears is through education itself. As people become more aware of what computers can and cannot do, they will find computers less intimidating. Viewing the computer as a teaching *tool* rather than as a teacher gives a more accurate perspective on CAI. Computers cannot replace teachers, but they can help teachers enhance

The teacher is an integral part of the instruction process in a computer-oriented classroom.

the educational experience of their students. Just as computers require humans to program them, students require teachers to help them learn to work with computers.

For CAI to be effective, many teachers will have to be trained in the use of computers   In-service teachers are charged with many responsibilities, including classroom instruction, discipline, reporting, and record keeping.

Their time is very valuable indeed, and for this reason, some teachers may feel overwhelmed by the prospect of computer training. They may believe that they must be computer experts themselves before they can teach their students to operate computers. Even those who are eager to use computers in their classrooms may not know how or where to get the training they need.

Here again, education is a positive solution. Seminars, workshops, conferences, and college and university courses must be offered to help teachers use CAI effectively. Once they see how the computer can save time rather than strain their schedules, teachers are more likely to take advantage of computer power. (For a more detailed discussion of how computers assist teachers with classroom management tasks, see Chapter 11 on computer-managed instruction.) It is also important to stress that teachers do not have to be computer experts before they can use CAI. Rather, teachers can learn how to work with computers right along with their students. In fact, the teacher who demonstrates an eagerness to learn more about computers sets up a positive attitude toward computers in the classroom. This attitude may be more beneficial to students in the long run than extensive computer expertise.

Young students can learn many basic skills on a computer.

The cost of computer hardware and software can dictate how widely computers are used in the classroom As mentioned at the beginning of this chapter, early computers were developed and used by those few who could afford them. Schools and personal users had to wait until computer technology became affordable to users on limited budgets. Therefore, some people— teachers and school administrators among them—may still believe that computers and software are beyond the reach of schools suffering from budget cutbacks or fiscal limitations. In most cases, this is not true.

The cost of computer power has fallen drastically in the more than forty years since the first generation of computers. In the mid-1970s, the microcomputer, for example, made electronic computing available to a wider range of users than ever before. And costs have declined steadily since then. Whether installing a single computer or a network of microcomputers in a lab, most schools can afford to purchase computer equipment.

The same holds true for CAI software. When computers were first introduced into the classroom, there was little educational software on the market. Much of what was available was simply not very effective, and because of limited competition, the cost was high. Today this is changing. As more educational software publishers appear on the scene, competition heats up and costs are reduced. The obvious winner is the CAI user who now can afford to purchase more software with fewer dollars than ever before. Therefore, costs associated with CAI are becoming less of an obstacle all the time.

CAI software is just coming into its own, and some users prefer to wait for further development In the early days of educational computing, some teachers experienced the disappointment of purchasing expensive CAI packages only to discover that they did not meet their students' needs. The software was so simple in its design that it was boring to students or did not make the most of the expensive computer equipment. In some cases the software was designed by programmers who didn't understand educational methodology. After spending precious funds on these "lemons," some teachers gave up hope of ever locating truly effective software. Simply put, there were not enough choices.

The picture is much brighter now. Recognizing the great potential market of educational users, software publishers are devoting more time and money to designing high-quality CAI software. They are hiring experts in education to work with programmers so that CAI software is both educationally sound and technically sophisticated. They are also actively listening to what classroom teachers have to say about the needs of their students. These actions result in software that teaches what it is intended to teach and does so in a way that holds students' attention and motivates them to work with computers.

Another option available to teachers who want better software for their students is to learn to use an **authoring language**. An authoring language

Software is available for most topics in education using many modes of instruction.

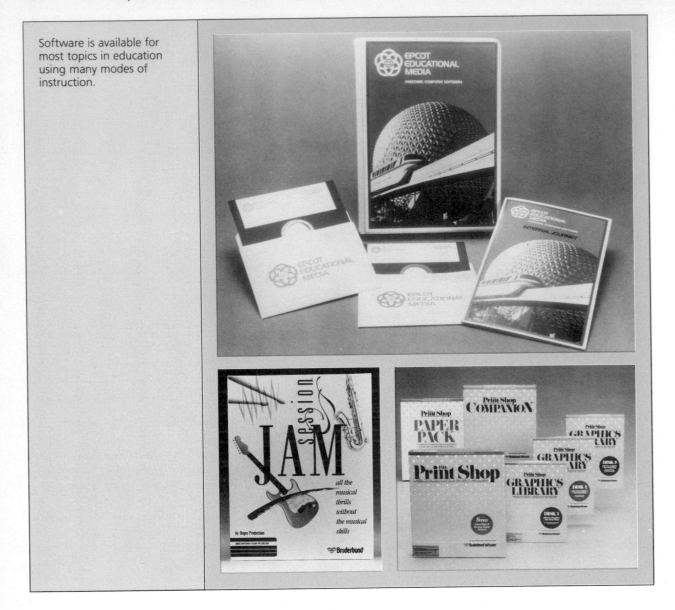

is a special, user-friendly language that allows a teacher to design customized software to meet the needs of individual classes. One common authoring language is PILOT. Some prepackaged CAI software is designed to enable teachers to change the content of lessons and exercises to match the curriculum they are teaching, thus making the software more relevant to their students. These packages are said to have *authoring capabilities*.

TYPES OF CAI SOFTWARE

Thumb through a catalog of educational software or browse through a retail store that markets **courseware**, which refers to CAI software and related materials such as workbooks, teacher guides, and posters, and you will be impressed by the wide range of packages available. Computers can teach almost any subject a student wishes to learn.

Nearly every CAI package on the market falls into one of four categories: *drill-and-practice, simulation, tutorial,* and *problem-solving* software. These terms refer to the way in which the software is designed and written and the way in which concepts and skills are presented to the student. In this section, we discuss the differences among these four types of CAI software.

Drill-and-Practice Software

Perhaps the earliest form of CAI, drill-and-practice programs still dominate the educational market today. **Drill-and-practice software** does exactly what its name implies: It offers students unlimited opportunities to practice concepts and skills that they have already learned through other, usually more traditional methods (textbooks, lectures, and class discussions). It is most often associated with rote-memory learning, similar to the type of learning that flash cards provide.

In other words, with drill-and-practice software, the computer functions more like a worksheet than a teacher. The classroom teacher must already have presented concepts and skills, because typical drill-and-practice software makes no provisions for teaching these. It is only a means by which students can practice what they already know and increase speed and proficiency. The benefits of this are obvious—students reinforce their knowledge. Drill-and-practice software also helps students memorize information.

Most drill-and-practice software follows a simple path:

1. The computer asks the student a question.
2. The student enters an answer.
3. The computer checks its memory to see whether the answer is correct.
4. The computer gives the student feedback.

A frequent application of drill-and-practice software is in the teaching of mathematics. Being essentially a mathematical tool, the computer can present problems that students must solve based on their knowledge of mathematical facts. It is relatively easy to reinforce multiplication tables, for example, with drill-and-practice programs. Even much higher levels of math can be reinforced. The computer can be programmed to generate problems randomly, so that students are continually challenged to practice their skills.

In the early days of CAI, much of the software available was drill-and-practice for mathematics because it is relatively simple to design and write.

(In fact, with a limited knowledge of programming techniques, students can write their own drill-and-practice programs.) But drill-and-practice software is not limited to math. It can also be very effective in other areas, such as vocabulary development and spelling. Because it lends itself to simple question-and-answer formats, the computer can present vocabulary words, definitions, and correct spellings until students have mastered the words they need to learn. Adults learning English as a second language or learning a foreign language can also benefit from drill-and-practice vocabulary programs.

Some educators feel that drill-and-practice is a waste of valuable computer time. Others find it most useful with students who need extra reinforcement rather than with an entire class. There are some well-designed

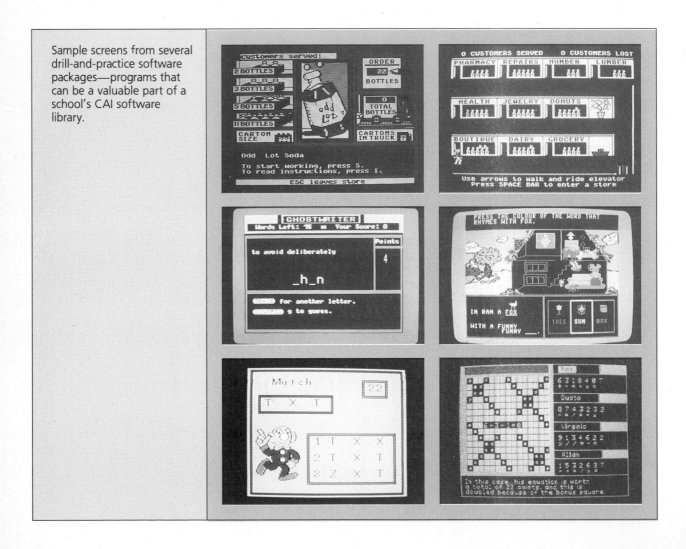

Sample screens from several drill-and-practice software packages—programs that can be a valuable part of a school's CAI software library.

drill-and-practice packages on the market. The challenge to the classroom teacher is to locate good software and integrate it into the curriculum.

How can a teacher judge the quality of drill-and-practice software? Following are several criteria to consider:

1. *Can students choose how many questions will be presented and control when to end the drill-and-practice session?* In general, several short drill-and-practice sessions produce better results than a single long session that outlasts the student's attention span.

2. *Does the software anticipate a range of incorrect answers and provide appropriate and helpful feedback?* Good drill-and-practice software is able to predict most common incorrect responses and then offer review material and hints, about correct answers.

3. *Does the software use game formats, puzzles, riddles, rhymes, clues, and so on to gain and hold the student's attention?* A major complaint about drill-and-practice software is that the format does not encourage students to use the software repeatedly. This means that the software is not nearly as cost-effective as software that attracts students time and again, expanding their opportunity to learn and review the material presented. Thus, even though the purchase price of a drill-and-practice program may be substantially less than that of a simulation program, for example, the simulation that holds student interest may be a better long-term investment.

4. *Can the teacher customize lessons and exercises to match the goals of the curriculum?* Unless the drill-and-practice software tests specific skills that have been presented as part of the regular curriculum, the value of the software is severely limited. On the other hand, software that can be customized is usually more relevant and more varied than its "canned" counterpart.

Well-designed drill-and-practice software can be a valuable part of a school's CAI software library. The benefit that it offers in terms of practicing lower-level skills is certainly worth the time and effort of locating effective software packages.

Tutorial Software

As its name implies, **tutorial software** casts the computer in the role of tutor. The computer presents new concepts and skills through text, illustrations, descriptions, questions, and problems. This is different from drill-and-practice software, which requires that students have already learned concepts through more traditional teaching methods such as lectures, reading, and class discussions. Because tutorial software actually teaches concepts, its design is more complicated and it is often more expensive.

In many cases, tutorial software comes with pretests, done either on paper or on the computer, to determine the point at which students should start in the program. An advanced student might skip over introductory lessons while a less experienced student begins with the first lesson and proceeds through all that follow. This flexibility helps to prevent students from becoming bored with lessons that are too basic or frustrated with lessons that are too challenging.

The tutorial presents a series of lessons followed by drill-and-practice exercises that test whether a student has mastered the lesson and is ready to progress. Often posttests are included to verify that students have accomplished the objectives of the tutorial.

Tutorial software must lead the student through the entire process required to learn concepts and skills. Gagne and Briggs (1979) have identified nine instruction events that can be applied to tutorial software:

1. *Capturing attention.* All effective CAI software must be able to capture and hold the attention of the people intended to use it. Otherwise, students are not motivated to spend the time necessary to learn concepts and skills.

2. *Stating objectives.* It is important that tutorial software be based on a set of meaningful and clearly stated objectives. This makes it easier to determine when students have mastered the material they need to learn.

3. *Reviewing prerequisite skills and knowledge.* When a certain body of knowledge or set of skills is required to use tutorial software to its best advantage, this should be indicated explicitly. Review material can be presented in the tutorial itself, or the student may be directed to other sources of review, such as textbooks.

4. *Providing stimuli.* All the unique capabilities of the computer— graphics, animation, color, and sound, for example—should be called into play to provide students with a variety of interesting and motivational stimuli. Tutorials that rely solely on long passages of text displayed on the screen are little more than overpriced textbooks, and students will lose interest in them quickly.

5. *Offering guidance.* Helpful guidance in the form of hints and review of pertinent information will assist the student in completing the tutorial successfully. It also helps prevent students from becoming frustrated when they don't understand material immediately.

6. *Monitoring performance.* Good tutorials monitor the student's performance throughout the learning session, not just at the end of the session. The software should predict a range of incorrect responses and then point the student in the right direction through effective feedback.

7. *Providing timely and useful feedback.* Students need to receive feedback at the time that they make an error or answer incorrectly. Learning is maximized through immediate and systematic feedback.

8. *Measuring performance.* At the end of each learning session, a well-designed tutorial presents a score or other measure of the student's

performance. This can be used to motivate the student to improve performance or to recommend areas in which the student needs further work. The software may also provide a measure of the performance of the class as a whole to help the teacher judge the rate at which the group is progressing.

9. *Helping the student retain and transfer skills.* Through reviews and practice exercises, tutorials can promote retention of the concepts and skills presented. They can also encourage students to apply concepts to a wide range of situations (as does simulation software).

There are two types of tutorial software: linear and branching. With the **linear tutorial**, all students must follow the same straight path through the lessons in the order in which they are presented. It's not possible to attempt lesson 5, for example, without first working through lessons 1 through 4. The linear tutorial makes individualized instruction of students difficult at best. It also prevents the teacher from choosing several lessons out of sequence, even though some of the lessons may not apply to the curriculum being taught.

In contrast, the **branching tutorial** allows students to follow different paths through the program, depending on their ability. An advanced student can skip over lessons that contain material he or she has already mastered. When a student answers incorrectly, the computer can interpret the incorrect response and suggest appropriate review. Teachers can select only the lessons that apply to the concepts in their curriculum, which makes the tutorial more relevant to the class.

At its best, the tutorial can do far more than textbook tutorials do. It can incorporate interesting and motivational formats not possible on a printed page. Thus, tutorials can be used to teach concepts and skills in areas where students have demonstrated a lack of interest. They can also provide specialized instruction in areas where teachers are not available or only a few students want to learn about the subject. Tutorials can be a very cost-effective means of providing special-interest education.

In evaluating tutorial software, teachers should look for programs that include as much interaction with the user as possible. This will help to weed out tutorials that are little more than "electronic textbooks" with long passages of text for the student to read.

Simulation

Imagine entering a classroom where students are working diligently at their lessons. As you stroll from desk to desk, you note an amazing range of activities going on. One student is learning to fly an airplane, another is directing a Shakespearean play, while a third dissects a frog. Across the room, a student accompanies George Washington across the Delaware while another takes a quick trip to Africa. How is all this possible, you may well ask?

Tutorial programs can incorporate interesting and motivational formats not possible on a printed page.

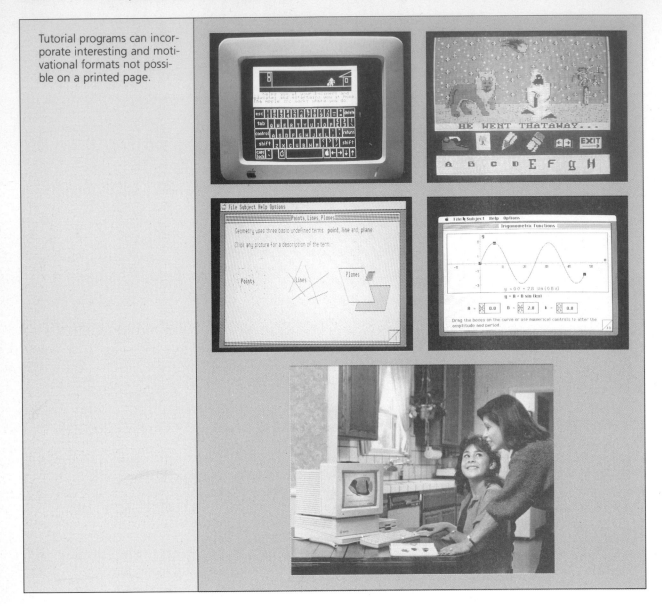

The answer is **simulation software**. Simulation is the re-creation of realistic conditions. Simulation software is used in the classroom to present situations that are impossible, dangerous, or too expensive for students to experience in reality. It allows students to apply the abstract concepts that they've learned to specific situations that they might never have the chance to experience otherwise.

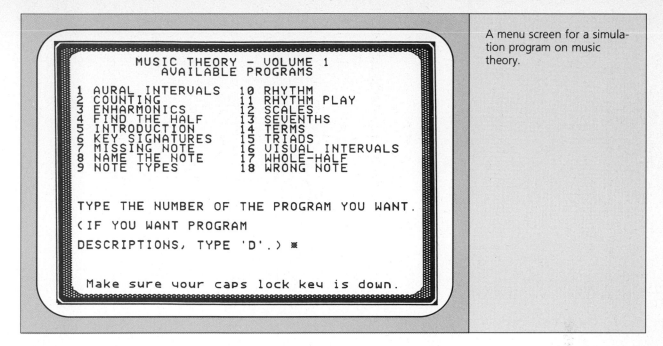

A menu screen for a simulation program on music theory.

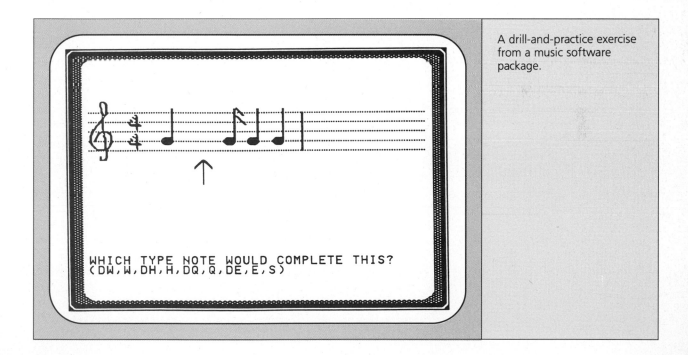

A drill-and-practice exercise from a music software package.

Two simulation programs. The software on the left screen simulates the positions of sun, earth, and moon. The right screen simulates a plane in flight.

Like drill-and-practice software, simulation software is supplemental to other teaching methods. That is, most simulation packages require that students have already mastered certain prerequisite concepts or skills through more traditional means (such as lectures, reading, watching films, and participating in class discussions).

Simulation software depends on a high degree of student interaction. The student controls the simulation experience through strategy and input. In other words, students make decisions and then see what effects their decisions have on the outcome. In some cases, variable conditions outside the student's control also determine the outcome of the simulation. Because simulations depend on student involvement, they are usually highly motivational.

According to Merrill et al. (1986), there are six characteristics of simulation software that make it especially valuable in the classroom:

1. *There is no risk involved in simulation.* For example, a common application of simulation software teaches people to operate equipment that is potentially dangerous to a novice. Pilots in training try their wings at a computer terminal before risking their lives in airplanes. The same is true of science education, where students can experiment with dangerous chemicals and conditions while they remain completely safe.
2. *There is less expense involved in simulation.* Some laboratory experiments, for example, require expensive equipment and supplies that schools cannot afford to purchase. With simulation software, students can perform these experiments repeatedly—the only cost to the school is the software and hardware involved.
3. *Simulated experiences are more convenient than real experiences.* Simulation software does not require that the student travel to a distant site or wait for certain conditions in order to experience a certain situation. Rather, the situation can be re-created in the classroom by simply loading the software into the computer.

4. *Simulation overcomes the limitations of time.* Students do not have to wait long periods of time for certain conditions to develop before seeing the results of their experimentation. For instance, they do not have to wait for several generations of bean plants to grow before observing the effects of crossbreeding. Regarding past events, simulation software can give students a realistic picture of an event that occurred a hundred or ten thousand years ago. Also, simulation can create and display events that occur too quickly for human observation.

5. *Simulation software makes it possible to focus on specific aspects of a topic or event.* Because it is by nature unreal, simulation offers a unique opportunity to highlight only parts of an event or situation. This is not usually possible with real experiences.

6. *Simulated experiences can be repeated as many times as the user wishes.* If a student misses a simulation because of absence or merely wishes to relive a simulated experience, he or she can do so with simulation software. In contrast, real experiences generally happen only once—and not always at times that are convenient for learning to take place. In re-creating simulated experiences, students can ask "what if" and try different combinations of variable conditions. Each student can try out his or her own solution.

As with other types of CAI software, simulation software should be evaluated on the basis of how well it uses the computer's attributes, such as graphics, color, animation, and sound. Effective use of these can make the simulated experience appear very real indeed—and the more realistic the simulation, the more effective it is.

Teachers also need to determine whether a particular simulation package fits into the curriculum. Even a very well-designed simulation package offers little if it is not related to other activities that occur in the classroom. Other factors that teachers should consider are how realistic the simulation is, whether it leads to valid conclusions about the material presented, and whether the knowledge gained can be applied to real-life situations.

Problem-Solving Software

In recent years, educators have given much attention to the development of problem solving skills. Many are interested in the potential of **problem-solving software**, including educational games, to foster such skills in students. Problem-solving software is closely related to simulation software in that it requires student strategy and input. Indeed, it is often rather difficult to distinguish between simulation and problem-solving software.

Problem-solving programs can be used to present math and word problems, puzzles, riddles, and so on. With math, the computer can be programmed to generate problems randomly, providing an infinite number of exercises to the student. In fact, one of the greatest benefits of problem-solving software is that it can provide as much opportunity for practicing problem-solving skills as an individual student requires. Most of these programs enable the user to select varying degrees of difficulty so that all learners are challenged according to their own abilities.

Some problem-solving software, like simulation software, permits the student to assign variables and then watch the results of different conditions. Programs can be designed to analyze incorrect responses and then provide meaningful feedback to direct the student in solving problems correctly.

Depending on their design, problem-solving packages offer varying degrees of learner control. In some cases, only the software or the teacher can determine the rate and sequence of presentation. With other packages, students exert more control over the learning session. As a general rule, problem-solving software that offers greater learner control is preferable to that in which students have fewer options.

Frequently, problem-solving programs are more interesting and more attractive to students than either drill-and-practice or tutorial software. They are more likely to want to work with problem-solving software repeatedly, which can make it a better investment. Students appreciate problem-solving programs for a number of reasons. They are an entertaining change from more standard teaching methods, such as lectures or workbooks. Also, they challenge students to score more points or capture more aliens. The student's imagination is engaged—or it should be.

Problem-solving software, especially that which follows a game format, gives students a chance to work in teams or small groups. An obvious advantage of this is that students learn to cooperate with others. At the same time, problem solving can foster healthy competition among students or teams.

Because of its highly motivational nature, some teachers use problem-solving software or educational games as a classroom reward. Students who behave well or progress quickly through other material earn extra computer time to play educational games that teach them to solve problems.

A Note on CAI in Special Education

While all the types of software discussed in this chapter are useful for students with special needs and abilities, it is important to note some unique considerations in using CAI to teach exceptional students. Computers in general and CAI software in particular have the potential to expand the availability of high-quality education to all segments of our society.

With appropriate software, the computer is especially valuable in special education for three reasons. First, it is infinitely patient. It can wait as long as required for a student's response without growing frustrated, and it can explain a concept with equal enthusiasm the first or the hundredth time. The computer offers the exceptional student all the practice he or she needs to master concepts and skills.

Second, the computer aids the special education teacher in individualizing instruction. Based on student performance, the computer can provide as much remediation as required or place the more advanced student appropriately within a lesson. Thus, students can be challenged without becoming frustrated or embarrassed.

Third, the computer can be customized by adding special hardware devices to help students overcome some physical limitations. Almost all CAI software packages on the market can be adapted for the unique requirements of special education. In addition, some educational software publishers offer packages specially designed for this application. When choosing software for special education, teachers need to analyze the amount and type of input that students must enter into the computer. Programs that require extensive data entry are not appropriate for students who have not learned to type or who are physically unable to use a standard keyboard.

One way to alleviate this problem is to consider alternate forms of data entry. There are several hardware devices on the market—and many more in the developmental stages—that assist the handicapped and others in working with computers. For example, using a light pen, the student need only touch an area on the screen to enter a response. Joysticks and paddles also offer easy data input as does the hand-held mouse, which requires only the touch of a button to enter a response into the computer.

But what about students who cannot manipulate a light pen or a mouse?

Special hardware devices allow the handicapped to use computers. This girl is using a lightbeam to hit the keys.

Special communications boards that respond to spoken commands or even the blink of an eye have been developed to enable handicapped persons to interact with computers. Though these devices are usually fairly expensive to purchase, they offer tremendous benefits to those who want to learn and work with computers.

Even those who are not able to function in a traditional classroom setting can enjoy the advantages of CAI through specially designed or modified microcomputers. Homebound students can keep up with their classmates by using computer terminals or modems that keep them in touch with school computers. Thus, CAI promises equal and effective education to students of all levels of ability.

SUMMARY

The use of computers to educate people is known as computer-assisted instruction (CAI), also called computer-based instruction (CBI). Whichever term is used, the process is the same: computers teach, drill, and test students of all ages and abilities on a virtually unlimited range of subjects. CAI offers teachers a number of benefits:

1. Computers involve the student actively in the learning process.
2. Computers provide fast and systematic feedback.
3. Computers allow all students—slow and gifted alike—to learn at their own pace.
4. The computer facilitates and sometimes even manages remediation.
5. The computer frees teachers for more "human" tasks, such as helping individual students, listening to student concerns, and providing pats on the shoulder for work well done.
6. The computer can bring real-world conditions into the classroom.
7. Not only does the computer present, drill, and test concepts and skills in all areas of the curriculum, but students also learn computer literacy while working with the computer.

Encouraging as the scenario of computers in classrooms may be, there are some considerable challenges to overcome in bringing CAI into the schools:

1. Some people fear that computers will dehumanize education.
2. In order for CAI to be effective, many teachers will have to be trained to use computers.
3. The cost of computer hardware and software can dictate how widely computers are used in the classroom.
4. CAI software is just coming into its own, and some users prefer to wait for further development.

Nearly every CAI package on the market falls into one of four categories: drill-and-practice, simulation, tutorial, and problem-solving software. These terms refer to the way in which the software is designed and written and the way in which concepts and skills are presented to the student. Drill-and-practice software offers students unlimited opportunities to practice concepts and skills that they have already learned through other, usually more traditional methods such as textbooks, lectures, and class discussions. Tutorial software presents new concepts and skills through text, illustrations, descriptions, questions, and problems.

Simulation is the re-creation of realistic conditions. Simulation software is used in the classroom to present situations that are impossible, dangerous, or too expensive for students to experience in reality. Problem-solving software is closely related to simulation software in that it requires student strategy and input. Indeed, it is often rather difficult to distinguish between simulation and problem-solving software.

The computer is especially valuable in special education for three reasons. First, it is infinitely patient. Second, the computer aids the special education teacher in individualizing instruction. Based on student performance, the computer can provide as much remediation as required or place the more advanced student appropriately within a lesson. Third, specially designed hardware devices can also be used to make it easier for handicapped persons to interact with computers.

REVIEW EXERCISES

Multiple Choice

1. CAI stands for
   a. computers and instructors
   b. computerized artificial intelligence
   c. computer-assisted instruction
   d. none of the above
2. Computers are used in schools to
   a. teach
   b. drill
   c. test
   d. all of the above
3. CAI is effective when
   a. each student has a computer
   b. it provides fast and systematic feedback
   c. textbooks are not available
   d. all of the above
4. By what year are computers expected to replace human teachers?
   a. 1990
   b. 2000
   c. 2100
   d. none of the above
5. One major obstacle to implementing CAI in our schools is
   a. the need to train teachers to use computers
   b. wiring classrooms for electronic equipment
   c. the rising cost of microcomputers
   d. a and b
6. Drill-and-practice software
   a. presents questions to the student
   b. indicates whether the student responds correctly or incorrectly
   c. provides feedback to the student
   d. all of the above
7. Students are placed at the proper point in tutorials through the use of
   a. pretests
   b. posttests
   c. teacher aides
   d. a and b

8. Which type of CAI software actually *teaches* new concepts?
   a. simulation
   b. tutorial
   c. drill-and-practice
   d. problem solving
9. Which is *not* a feature of simulation software?
   a. It involves less risk than real experience
   b. It costs less than drill-and-practice software
   c. It overcomes the limitations of time
   d. all of the above
10. Which type of CAI software is most closely associated with simulation software?
    a. tutorial
    b. CMI
    c. problem solving
    d. drill-and-practice

True/False

1. Computers involve the student actively in the learning process.
2. Computers encourage all students to progress at the same rate.
3. Only human teachers can provide remediation.
4. Computers free teachers to give more individual attention to students.
5. Computers have already begun to dehumanize education.
6. The quality of CAI software on the market is decreasing at an alarming rate.
7. Authoring languages prevent users from pirating software.
8. Probably the earliest form of CAI software was the tutorial.
9. Drill-and-practice software is usually associated with rote-memory learning.
10. Simulation software helps re-create realistic situations in the classroom.

Short Answer

1. List several advantages of using CAI.
2. What tasks can a human teacher perform that the computer cannot?
3. List several disadvantages of using CAI.
4. Why is some drill-and-practice software considered a waste of computer time?

5. How do peripheral devices such as light pens, joysticks, paddles, and communications boards aid in using CAI in special education?

Activities

1. Visit a local computer retail or teaching supply store to see some CAI packages currently on the market.
2. Choose one curriculum area and research what CAI software is available for teaching that subject.
3. Invite a teacher to speak to your class about how he or she uses CAI in the classroom.
4. Visit a rehabilitation center or special education classroom to see how computers are used to assist exceptional students.
5. Choose a popular CAI software package and look up several reviews of the package in educational journals.
6. List several commercial drill-and-practice software programs.
7. List several commercial tutorial software packages.
8. List several commercial simulation software packages.
9. List several commercial problem-solving software packages.
10. List the most popular CAI software packages today.

BIBLIOGRAPHY

Bitter, Gary G. "Computer Assisted Mathematics— Awareness, Applications and Programming." *Dimensions in Mathematics Quarterly 7*, (no. 1, February 1987): 17–22.

———. "Microcomputers and Problem Solving." *Technology in the Classroom*, NCTM, Reston, Va., Spring 1981.

———. "Understanding the Potentials Of Microcomputers in Education." *Educational Computer* (March-April 1982): 14.

Bitter, Gary G., and Ruth Camuse. *Using a Microcomputer in the Classroom.* 2d ed. Englewood Cliffs, N.J.: Prentice-Hall, 1988.

Davis, Kristie Younghans, and Milton Budoff. *Using Authoring in Education.* Cambridge, Mass.: Brookline Books, 1986.

Gagne, R. M., and L. J. Briggs. *Principles of Instructional Design.* 2d ed. New York: Holt, Rinehart & Winston, 1979.

Godfrey, David, and Sharon Sterling. *The Elements of CAI.* Reston, Va.: Reston, 1982.

Harper, Dennis O., and James H. Stewart. *RUN: Computer Education.* Monterey, Calif.: Brooks/Cole Publishing, 1983.

Heimler, Charles, et al. *Authoring Educational Software.* Santa Cruz, Calif.: Mitchell, 1987.

Hertz, Robert M. "Problems of Computer-Assisted Instruction in Composition." *The Computing Teacher,* 11 (no. 2, September 1983): 33–34.

Merrill, Paul F., et al. *Computers in Education.* Englewood Cliffs, N.J.: Prentice-Hall, 1986.

Miller, Maurene. "Touching the Right Keys." *The Computing Teacher* (August 1983): 33–34.

Nave, Gary, et al. *Computer Technology for the Handicapped in Special Education and Rehabilitation: A Resource Guide.* Vols. 1 and 2. The International Council for Computers in Education, University of Oregon, 1983, 1985.

Signer, Barbara. "How Do Teacher and Student Evaluations of CAI Software Compare?" *The Computing Teacher,* 11 (no. 3, October 1983): 34–46.

Solomon, Cynthia. *Computer Environments for Children.* Cambridge: MIT Press, 1986.

Taylor, Robert P. *The Computer in the School: Tutor, Tool, Tutee.* New York: Teachers College Press, Columbia University, 1980.

True/False

1. T	5. F	9. T
2. F	6. F	10. T
3. F	7. F	
4. T	8. F	

Short Answer

1. Involves student in learning process; provides fast and systematic feedback; allows students to progress at their own pace; facilitates remediation; frees teachers for more human tasks; brings real-world conditions into the classroom; teaches computer literacy.
2. Listening, touching, caring, assisting with personal problems, and so on.
3. Fear that computers will dehumanize education; need to train teachers to work with computers; costs; primitive state of the art.
4. Since students can use worksheets and other more traditional methods for the same benefits, the computer is underutilized.
5. Such devices facilitate interaction by making it easier for handicapped persons or those who cannot type to enter data in the computer.

REVIEW ANSWER KEY

Multiple Choice

1. c	5. a	9. b
2. d	6. d	10. c
3. b	7. d	
4. d	8. b	

CHAPTER 11

COMPUTER-MANAGED INSTRUCTION

Objectives

- Define the term *computer-managed instruction (CMI)*
- Describe the major functions of CMI programs
- Understand guidelines for selecting CMI software
- Describe the use of CMI to generate and score tests, and to provide immediate feedback to students
- Recommend effective measures for choosing and implementing a CMI system

Key Terms

backup
CMI (computer–managed instruction)
electronic gradebook
integrate
mean score
median score
mode score
network
objective
optical scanning
password
security
test generation
test item

In the last chapter, we saw how computers can be used to teach new concepts and skills to students and to provide drill-and-practice of skills learned by other means. The use of computers to teach students is called computer-assisted instruction (CAI). Effective use of CAI can free teachers from routine tasks and enable them to spend more time planning lessons and giving individualized instruction to students who need it.

But this is not the only way that teachers use computers in the classroom. In the past few decades, teachers have been overwhelmed with a great deal of paperwork in addition to their teaching duties. Federal, state, and local requirements mandate that teachers maintain mountains of reports and documentation of student progress. Of course, teachers must also keep records of grades, write tests, keep attendance records, maintain accurate class rosters . . . the list goes on and on. The average teacher spends an enormous amount of time trying to keep current records that are either required by law or simply necessary to organize and manage a classroom.

Because of its unique ability to process, store, and report information, the computer is proving to be a teacher's best management tool. Database and spreadsheet applications in particular can help teachers keep records that are updated whenever necessary. (For a detailed discussion of spreadsheet and database applications, see Chapters 6 and 7.) Timely and accurate information is the basis for wise decision making about lesson plans, student and class progress, and remediation. The use of the computer to manage instruction is known as *computer-managed instruction*.

A DEFINITION OF COMPUTER-MANAGED INSTRUCTION (CMI)

Computer-managed instruction (CMI) refers to the use of computer power to perform a wide range of tasks that have traditionally been done manually by teachers. These tasks include keeping student and class records, writing and scoring tests, calculating and recording grades, and prescribing and monitoring individualized instruction for students. When you consider the number of students in an average classroom, you can easily see how the computer can organize and facilitate the teacher's management tasks. CMI can be accomplished through a single program or a series of programs that perform different tasks. Most CAI packages include CMI components.

With CAI software, the student interacts with the computer to learn or practice skills and concepts. With CMI, the teacher or a support staff member may use the computer to perform administrative functions. Many CAI software packages include limited CMI features. For example, a drill-and-practice package that performs vocabulary improvement may include a function that keeps track of how well each student is doing and prints a report for the teacher's reference. In fact, teachers considering the purchase of CAI software usually prefer software that includes CMI components that

A teacher can use a micro-computer to plan lessons and monitor student progress.

can track progress and report it automatically. In this chapter, we explore CMI systems that are designed not only to teach but to aid in administering education.

Forman (1982) has identified five characteristics of CMI packages. CMI software can perform the following functions:

1. *Organizing curricula and student data.* Since almost all CMI packages are database management tools designed specifically for educational applications, teachers can store large amounts of data on CMI systems. Some of the types of data that can be stored this way are student records, class rosters, tests, lesson plans, assignments, and even inventories of classroom supplies. Data such as lesson plans can be revised and updated whenever the teacher wishes, eliminating the need to start from scratch each term or school year. Similarly, student records can be updated either by the teacher or by the computer.

2. *Monitoring student progress.* Like a traditional gradebook, the computer can be used to store records of student progress. Unlike a traditional gradebook, CMI software enables the computer to calculate grades almost instantaneously at any point during the term. Thus, teachers can quickly determine how an individual student or the class as a whole is performing at any given point without having to spend hours averaging grades on paper or with a calculator.

3. *Diagnosing and prescribing instruction.* With timely and accurate monitoring of student progress comes the ability to diagnose problems as they arise. Immediate feedback allows the teacher to intervene in

the learning process by providing extra assistance to students who are having trouble mastering skills and concepts. Used in conjunction with computer-assisted instruction, CMI software enhances individualized instruction to a degree not possible with manual record-keeping systems.

4. *Evaluating learning outcomes.* It is sometimes difficult for a teacher to determine when a particular method of presentation has been effective. Historically teachers have had to rely on intuition and hindsight to evaluate how effectively learning has occurred. CMI, on the other hand, provides timely information to help teachers determine when learning has been successful. In this way, remediation can be done quickly to correct any deficiencies that may exist.

5. *Providing information for teachers to use in planning lessons.* After teachers have evaluated the effectiveness of a lesson or unit, they can plan future lessons more efficiently. If most of the class has mastered the **objectives** (educational goals) of a given lesson, then the teacher will move on to another lesson. If a large number of students have been unsuccessful at mastering objectives, then the teacher can provide review or try a different method of presenting information. CMI makes it possible for teachers to meet the unique needs of individual students or groups of students.

CMI software is also capable of generating an endless variety of reports. Teachers can compile and print reports to use in advising students of their performance. These same reports can be used to keep parents informed and to recommend ways in which they can assist their children in performing better. Some systems allow teachers and administrators to format reports according to federal, state, or local requirements. This capability saves enormous amounts of time in compiling and producing reports for the government.

Like all types of computer software, CMI systems range from the very simple to the highly sophisticated. Some packages perform a single function, such as generating tests. Others are more comprehensive and may also score tests, calculate grades, maintain records, and print reports. In the next section, we explore some of the major functions performed by CMI software.

The Electronic Gradebook

In the past, teachers typically had two major record-keeping tools: the gradebook and the filing cabinet. Teachers have had to spend long hours recording grades, calculating averages, transferring grade records to reports for students to take home, tracking absences and tardiness, maintaining accurate class rosters, and so on. The larger the class size, the bigger the headache this can be for the teacher. Also, teachers who spend a great deal of time performing these record-keeping functions by hand have less time and energy to devote to the real task at hand—teaching students.

A teacher assisting students using microcomputers.

CMI software turns the computer into an **electronic gradebook**. Using spreadsheet or database technology, the computer stores vast amounts of information in a small amount of space. Computer-stored information can be retrieved quickly whenever it is needed, and it can be changed or deleted when circumstances change. In short, it is far more efficient than manual record keeping. Typically, gradebook programs offer the options discussed below.

The first step in creating an electronic gradebook is to *create a file*. This is comparable to a drawer in a filing cabinet where all student records for a single class will be kept. The program asks the teacher to give the class file a name and to set other parameters or characteristics. For example, the teacher may indicate how many grades will be included and to what percentage of the final grade each grade will contribute. In this way, the teacher can determine that quizzes count for ten percent of the grade while the final exam is worth forty percent. Should any changes to the file become necessary, the file can be revised with the *edit an existing file* option.

Now that the contents of the class file have been defined, the teacher is ready to *add student records to the class file*. For each student, a record is created to hold all the information the teacher wishes to store in the gradebook. This might include student name, student number, class hour, address,

The menu of this grade-book allows access to a student's record by class.

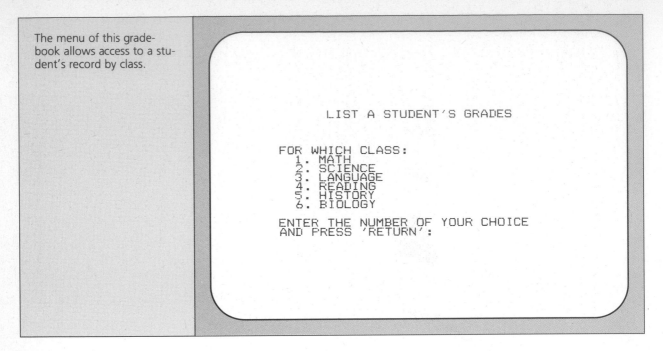

```
                    LIST A STUDENT'S GRADES


        FOR WHICH CLASS:
            1. MATH
            2. SCIENCE
            3. LANGUAGE
            4. READING
            5. HISTORY
            6. BIOLOGY

        ENTER THE NUMBER OF YOUR CHOICE
        AND PRESS 'RETURN':
```

telephone number, parent name(s) or emergency contact, special interests or problems, teacher comments, and so on. Setting up a record for each student on the computer is a time-consuming task, but in the long run the teacher saves a great deal of time compared to manual record-keeping procedures. Also, once created, student records can be changed, updated, or deleted with the *edit student records* and *delete student records* options.

The *edit student records* option is also used to enter grades throughout the term. This is true only when the gradebook software is not **integrated** (or linked) to software that scores tests and automatically enters the results into the gradebook. It is also used to record grades on assignments such as essays or oral presentations that cannot be scored automatically by the computer.

Whenever the teacher wishes to read information stored in the electronic gradebook, he or she can select the *print records or reports* option. Records and reports can be displayed on the screen for quick reference or printed out as hard copies that can be displayed on the screen for quick reference or printed out as hard copies that can be filed or sent home with students. Most systems enable teachers to design the format of these reports, determining what information will be included and in what order the information will appear. Others may offer a selection of preformatted reports.

In 1983, the Minnesota Educational Computing Consortium (MECC) introduced the Grade Manager, which is an exemplary gradebook program. The Grade Manager stores records for up to fifteen classes, or a total of more than 1,000 student records per diskette. For each student, up to fifty scores can be recorded. Depending on teacher preference, grades can be based either on percentages or on a curve. The Grade Manager also provides space for teacher comments.

The electronic gradebook has several obvious advantages over its paper predecessor. First, it can calculate grades automatically at any point in the term. This is cumbersome and time-consuming to do with a manual gradebook. Second, at the end of the term, actual grades are computed more quickly and accurately than can be done by hand. Assuming that all data has been entered correctly by human operators, the gradebook program produces correct grade averages in a small portion of the time required to compute grades with paper and pencil. Finally, the electronic gradebook can be used to generate class reports that include summary information to let the teacher know when learning has succeeded. With this information, the teacher can plan to move ahead or to review problematic areas. Thus, the electronic gradebook is a planning tool as well as a record keeper.

A word of caution is advisable here, though. As with any information stored on computers, gradebook data is subject to loss through power failure, loss or damage of disks, or vandalism. Therefore, it is critical that teachers make **backup** copies of grade information. In addition, teachers may want to keep printed copies of grades in case data must be reentered into the computer.

```
File: Class Grades            REVIEW/ADD/CHANGE              Escape: Main Menu
================A================M====N====O====P==Q===R===S===T===U===V===W==
 1|Subject:   Mathematics   Weights    Asgm  .80  Scale  A  90   C  70
 2|Class:     Grade 5                  Tests .20         B  80   D  60
 3|Year:      First Qtr 1989
 4|                         Tot  Wt  Tot  Wt
 5|Name                     Asgm Asgm Test Test  Score  A  B  C  D  F
 6|------------------------------------------------------------------
 7|Bakker, Donna            234 68.1  182 18.2  86.3   0  1  0  0  0
 8|Bitter, Gary             208 60.5  162 16.2  76.7   0  0  1  0  0
 9|Farrington, Don          162 47.1  132 13.2  60.3   0  0  0  1  0
10|Foster, David            201 58.5  147 14.7  73.2   0  0  1  0  0
11|Lane, Susan              219 63.7  170 17.0  80.7   0  1  0  0  0
12|Lang, Janet              196 57.0  185 18.5  75.5   0  0  1  0  0
13|Martinez, Jesse          212 61.7  150 15.0  76.7   0  0  1  0  0
14|Michael, James           234 68.1  187 18.7  86.8   0  1  0  0  0
15|Shore, Mary              230 66.9  173 17.3  84.2   0  1  0  0  0
16|Thomas, Mary             216 62.8  168 16.8  79.6   0  0  1  0  0
17|                                          ---Total Grades-----
18|                         211 61.4  166 16.6  78.0   0  4  5  1  0
```

An electronic gradebook can compute grades quickly and accurately.

Another reason for handling gradebook information with the utmost care is to prevent unauthorized persons from gaining access to it. Students generally consider their grades to be confidential information, and their privacy should be protected. Also, most of us have heard stories about unethical persons breaking into a computer system and changing grades of friends or enemies. There are **security** measures that can be taken to prevent this from occurring. Limiting access to the computer through the use of **passwords** (a privileged code that allows a user to work on the computer) is one effective means of making sure that grade information remains correct and confidential.

Test Generation

Another CMI function that uses database capability is **test generation**. When the computer "writes" or generates a test, it simply makes random choices from a database of test items that the teacher has composed and stored in the computer. A **test item** is a single question on a test, such as a true/false question. The typical test-generating program offers the options discussed below.

Before creating a file of test items, the teacher must write the test items and categorize them according to the topics they cover, the level of difficulty, the objectives they test for, and so on. Then the teacher selects the *create file of test items* option of the test generator. At this point, the computer

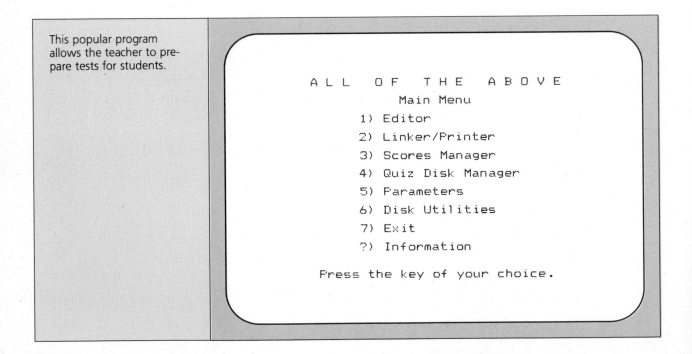

This popular program allows the teacher to prepare tests for students.

```
A L   O F   T H E   A B O V E
          Main Menu
      1) Editor
      2) Linker/Printer
      3) Scores Manager
      4) Quiz Disk Manager
      5) Parameters
      6) Disk Utilities
      7) Exit
      ?) Information

   Press the key of your choice.
```

requires the teacher to name the file and define its characteristics. Each category of test items must be named. Then the test items themselves are keyed into the computer along with their correct answers. The database of test items can be revised and updated at any time with the *edit file of test items* function.

When generating tests, the teacher has many alternatives for tailoring test forms to the needs of individual students or whole classes. The test generator allows the teacher to choose the file or files from which test items will be chosen as well as how many items are to be selected from each file or category. The computer will also ask how many different test forms are to be generated and how many copies of each test form are required, with the *print test forms* function. Finally, the teacher can include instructions to the student to be printed on each test form.

In this manner, the test generator enables the teacher to stress certain objectives more than others. Those objectives considered more important can be weighted more heavily by including a greater number of questions that refer to them. As the computer generates test forms according to teacher specifications, it also generates corresponding answer keys to facilitate scoring.

MECC's Study Guide Teaching Utility Programs for the Apple II, introduced in 1984, includes a test generator that stores up to 200 questions. The questions may be matching, completion, multiple choice, or true/false. Each question can be linked to one or more objectives, up to a maximum of fifteen

```
      Multiple Choice (without feedback)
Item.                              Item No. 1
What famous actress starred in the
award winning movie "Terms of
Endearment"?

     A) Glenn Close
     B) Carol Burnett
     C) Shirley McClain
     D) Meryl Streep
     E) Bette Davis




Correct Response: C
?:  Information about this format
```

An example of a test generator that provides a format for developing multiple-choice test items.

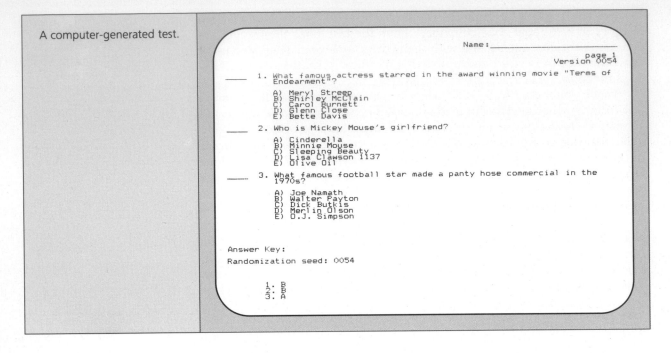

A computer-generated test.

```
                                               Name :_____
                                                                page 1
                                                       Version 0054
        ____  1. What famous actress starred in the award winning movie "Terms of
                 Endearment"?

                 A) Meryl Streep
                 B) Shirley McClain
                 C) Carol Burnett
                 D) Glenn Close
                 E) Bette Davis

        ____  2. Who is Mickey Mouse's girlfriend?

                 A) Cinderella
                 B) Minnie Mouse
                 C) Sleeping Beauty
                 D) Lisa Clawson 1137
                 E) Olive Oil

        ____  3. What famous football star made a panty hose commercial in the
                 1970s?

                 A) Joe Namath
                 B) Walter Payton
                 C) Dick Butkis
                 D) Merlin Olson
                 E) O.J. Simpson




      Answer Key:

      Randomization seed: 0054


          1. B
          2. B
          3. A
```

objectives. Many teachers have found this program to be an invaluable aid in generating objectives-referenced tests.

The most obvious benefit of the test generation is that various test forms reduce the opportunity for cheating. Other advantages are perhaps more subtle. Teachers appreciate the fact that tests can be individualized for particular students. Test generators also allow students to work at their own pace. Linked to CAI programs, for example, test generators allow students to test and retest whenever they feel they have mastered the objectives of a given lesson. Different test forms ensure that students are progressing because they have mastered objectives, not because they have memorized a particular test form. Test generators can be integrated with gradebook and test-scoring software to maximize benefits to teachers.

Though minor, there are two disadvantages of test generators that should be considered. First, some teachers may feel that test generators are more work than simply writing tests on paper. This feeling arises from the fact that the teacher must write more test items than are actually required for a single test. Also, if teachers do not have access to automated test scoring, they may feel that grading different test forms is too complicated to manage.

Test Scoring

CMI offers a solution to the problem of scoring tests and other exercises and reporting the results. Computerized test scoring is not new to education. In fact, it was one of the earliest applications of computer technology in education. Most college students have taken standardized aptitude or college placement tests that were scored by computer. Such tests, administered nationally, would be a nightmare to score and record were it not for the use of computers.

Test scoring relies on several computer capabilities: database, spreadsheet, and optical scanning. **Optical scanning** devices are able to detect and interpret marks on a paper test form and send the data to the computer for processing. The computer then refers to its database of correct answers to determine whether the response is correct or incorrect. Results of tests are then submitted to mathematical and statistical processing and the results are reported.

Indeed, the analysis and reporting features of computerized test scoring account for its real superiority over manual grading of tests. The computer can analyze test results for more than a student's final score. It can also report the scores of large or small groups of students, either alphabetically by name or numerically by test score.

CMI test-scoring programs perform statistical analysis of scores for an entire class or group of students to provide the teacher with important information. These statistics include:

1. **mean score**, the group average
2. **mode score**, the score most commonly achieved
3. **median score**, the dividing line between high and low scores
4. range of scores
5. standard deviation

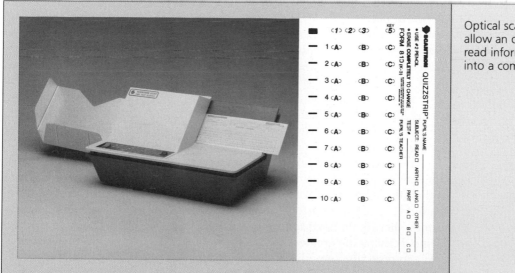

Optical scanning forms allow an optical scanner to read information directly into a computer program.

Teachers can use these statistics to judge whether a group of students has mastered the intended objectives. The same statistics can be used to evaluate how reliable the test instrument is in demonstrating mastery of objectives.

Another compilation by test-scoring software is an analysis of test items. For each item, the computer reports how often the item was answered correctly and how often incorrectly. When tests are administered by computer, the report can even include the average length of time students take to answer both correctly and incorrectly. This information is very useful in revising tests to make sure they are as effective as possible.

Test-scoring functions can be integrated with test-generation and gradebook functions so that student and class records are updated automatically after a test. Thus, teachers are relieved of the chores of compiling tests, scoring them, and calculating grades afterwards.

CMI ON NETWORK SYSTEMS

CMI packages are available for all types and sizes of computer systems. An individual teacher can use a single microcomputer to perform CMI tasks. A school district, however, may use a mainframe computer and terminals to perform CMI districtwide. Universities often have testing centers where students report to take tests; these tests can be generated, scored, and the results reported by a mainframe that is also used to perform other computer functions on campus.

In a classroom setting, computers used by students can be **networked** to communicate with the teacher's computer. In this case, the teacher's CMI software collects data from student computers or terminals and processes that data as the teacher requires. In a system like this, students can take tests on microcomputers that are linked to the central computer used by the teacher. Students' performance is then monitored by the teacher's computer through the use of CMI software. Thus, tests are scored and results reported practically instantaneously. Students do not have to wait for busy teachers to grade papers before finding out how they have done. In fact, the computer can display correct answers to students immediately after testing is completed.

There are several distinct advantages to using CMI and CAI on network systems. First, CMI performs administrative functions in a small amount of the time required to do the same work manually. Students can see immediate results of their performance. Also, when students take tests on computers, there is no need for anyone to produce, handle, and grade printed forms. Perhaps the greatest advantage is that CMI used in conjunction with CAI can prescribe remediation for individual students in a timely fashion.

Network systems provide a convenient way to share software, printers, and files.

Teachers who use network systems find that their role in the classroom changes. Rather than being the focal point and feeling pressured to present all the information that students receive, the teacher functions more as a facilitator. The computer presents and tests information, while the teacher helps the student make the most effective use of the computer for learning.

One obstacle to implementing this type of system widely in public schools is that network systems require a considerable amount of hardware. Where computer budgets are limited, it may be impossible to purchase enough hardware to make the system practical. Too few computers for the number of students who want to use them means that students will have to wait for computer time, and testing may be postponed.

Another consideration is that someone must be responsible for overseeing computer-administered testing. Unless a responsible proctor ensures that the student taking the test is indeed the correct student, it's possible for students to take tests for each other.

Finally, CMI test generation and test scoring does not allow the use of essay questions. With essays, student responses vary so widely that the computer's yes/no decision capability is at a loss. Yet essay questions are a valid means of testing for mastery. To overcome this limitation, teachers can score essays manually and then key the results into the electronic gradebook for calculation with other grades.

CMI IN ACTION

So far we have limited our discussion to the use of CMI by classroom teachers to write and score tests and to maintain student and class records. But this is actually a rather narrow view of the ways in which CMI can be used to manage, administer, and improve the educational process. Let's consider some very specific examples of how schools across the country are using CMI capabilities.

Teachers are not the only persons who use CMI. In the Genesee Intermediate School District in Michigan, school board members are using a computerized rating system to improve their performance as school board members. Working with the superintendent, school board members designed their own evaluation system that allows them to rate themselves and the entire board in eleven different areas. The computer summarizes and reports the results to the board. The superintendent of the district says that the evaluation system has indeed improved the performance of the school board.

Another Michigan school district, the Southfield Public Schools, is coping with high student turnover by using computers to enroll students quickly. A central computer is used to analyze where a student lives and how he or she has performed on standardized tests. Based on this information, students are placed in appropriate schools and grade levels. The computer also keeps a record of the student's class schedule at the new school.

CMI has also been sent to the principal's office. At least three principals in the Greenburgh Central School District 7 (New York) now use microcomputers to keep on top of the information needed to run their schools smoothly. This information includes biographical data and standardized test scores for each student in the school. The data is used to prescribe lessons for students, whole classes, and even the entire school. More mundane tasks can also be done, including compiling class rosters, making class assignments, and keeping attendance.

Principals can also use computer systems to reach parents who are not available during the day. Other uses include schedule changes performed by school counselors and a software program used to determine whether students who are planning to attend college are eligible for financial aid at the institutions they want to attend.

One of the earliest computer-based systems, PLATO, is used in many school districts to educate students who have dropped out or are considered high risks for dropping out. The CMI functions of PLATO effectively manage the instruction of these students. Thus, they are given another chance for education. School districts employing PLATO for this purpose find this system to be cost-effective since they are able to recapture federal funding that is lost when students drop out.

CMI can help to manage computer labs where a large number of students gather to perform a variety of tasks. For example, the Dearborn Public Schools in Michigan have a large computer lab that consists of thirty work stations. Students come here for highly individualized computer-managed instruction in the areas of math, reading, and English. They spend several hours per week working with computers in the lab.

Schools can even use CMI systems to plan for the future. In the Trumbull School District in Connecticut, Superintendent Edwin T. Merritt designed a computerized five-year plan that covers curriculum, staff development, testing, support services, and even extracurricular activities. The system enables the district to project its needs and its budget five years at a time.

Clearly, the definition of computer-managed instruction is broadening daily as teachers, administrators, and staff persons invent new ways of using the computer to organize and manage education.

CHOOSING AND IMPLEMENTING CMI PROGRAMS

As we noted earlier, there are a substantial number of CMI packages on the market, ranging from the fairly simple to the very sophisticated and powerful. Teachers, principals, and administrators who wish to use CMI will have to conduct a search and review process similar to that described in Chapter 12 on choosing classroom software. Following are some hints that should prove useful in making wise CMI purchases for a single classroom or an entire school district.

1. *Involve teachers and support staff in the review process from the very beginning.* Those people who will actually use the system are the experts: They know what they need and how they will use it. Also, they may already be familiar with some packages on the market and may be in touch with colleagues who are currently using CMI software. Teachers and support staff who are involved in the review process are likely to be more receptive to automating time-consuming reporting and administrative functions. Those who are not involved may resent having changes imposed on them from above.

2. *Consider how powerful the CMI program needs to be.* On one hand, a program used only to keep a gradebook for a class of twenty students can be relatively simple and inexpensive. On the other hand, a program that will be used for a wide variety of CMI functions throughout a school or an entire district will be complex and costly. It must be capable of handling a greater number of records. In general, the more sophisticated the software, the more computer memory it will require to operate efficiently.

3. *Consider what type of hardware the CMI package requires.* CMI packages are available for all computers, from micros to mainframes. If a school or district cannot afford to revamp an existing computer system, then the range of CMI choices may be limited. Again, the guidelines to consider are how many people will use the system, how many

records it must store, and how many different functions it must perform.

4. *Can the CMI package be integrated with other software?* A test generator is of limited value unless it can be linked with test-scoring and grade-book functions. It may also be possible to integrate CMI functions with the CAI software that a teacher wishes to use, thereby expanding the usefulness of the CMI package.

5. *Does the CMI package come with clear and complete documentation?* Especially in applications where more than one teacher or staff member is expected to create and maintain records, good documentation is essential. Documentation that is hard to read or understand or—even worse—nonexistent increases the time required to implement the CMI system. Users may become frustrated and give up if they cannot get clear answers to questions that arise.

6. *Is the program relatively free of bugs?* Most software packages undergo some amount of testing before they are released on the market. Testing allows the designers to locate and correct errors, or bugs, in the software. However, in today's competitive software market, testing is rarely as thorough as it should be. When this is the case, users may find that the software they purchase does not operate as promised. Serious bugs may even result in data loss. Therefore, it's important to evaluate how efficiently the software runs before purchasing it. A good way to do this is to request from the publisher a list of school districts that use the package currently.

Once the available CMI software has been reviewed and a program purchased, the process of implementation begins. This may be a small task undertaken by a classroom teacher or a districtwide effort requiring the participation of a large number of people. In either case, training and patience are required. The following recommendations should help to make CMI implementation as smooth as possible:

1. *Expect the transition to take some time.* Rome wasn't built in a day, as the saying goes. When tasks that have always been performed manually are automated, there is bound to be a period when teachers and staff are uncertain and sometimes even mistrustful of the new computerized system. Staff members who have never worked with a computer may resist the automation of familiar tasks. Given time and adequate training, though, they usually come to appreciate the time and drudgery that CMI saves them. Under the best of circumstances, those who use the system will need time to learn to use the software and to key in the considerable amount of data required by most CMI systems.

2. *Teachers and staff members may need to be trained to operate computer hardware.* If the CMI system involves the introduction of new computer equipment, those who are going to use it will have to become familiar with it as well as with the software.

3. *Anyone who uses the CMI system should receive copies of training manuals and other documentation.* Even after the best training, staff members still encounter problems and raise questions about their CMI system. These problems should be addressed in the documentation, and each person using the system should have access to a copy. Otherwise, users may give up when they become confused or frustrated by what the computer is doing.

4. *Data should always be verified at the time of entry.* It is a good policy to check the accuracy of data when it is entered into the system. Incorrect data keyed in at the beginning of the school year affects the data entered later and may be hard to locate. To verify data, the teacher or staff member can request a printed copy of data after it is keyed in. This printed copy can be compared against the original data to make sure that no mistakes have been made.

5. *Teachers and staff members who use the CMI system should be asked to provide feedback.* Again, those who actually use the system are the real CMI experts, and their opinions should be taken seriously. Periodic evaluations of how well the system is working help administrators determine whether CMI is being used successfully. Feedback can also indicate when further training or enhancements to the system are required.

SUMMARY

The average teacher spends an enormous amount of time trying to keep records current that are either required by law or simply necessary to organize and manage a classroom. CMI refers to the use of computer power to perform this wide range of tasks, which have traditionally been done by teachers manually. These tasks include keeping student and class records, writing and scoring tests, calculating and recording grades, and prescribing and monitoring individualized instruction for students.

Like all types of computer software, CMI systems range from the very simple to the highly sophisticated. Some packages perform a single function, such as generating tests. Others are more comprehensive and may also score tests, calculate grades, maintain records, and print reports. Most CAI packages include some CMI components to track student and class progress.

One CMI component, the electronic gradebook, has several obvious advantages over its paper predecessor. First, it can calculate grades automatically at any point in the term. Second, at the end of the term, actual grades are computed more quickly and accurately than can be done by hand. Assuming that all data has been entered correctly by human operators, the gradebook program produces correct grade averages in a small portion of the time required to compute grades with paper and pencil.

Finally, the electronic gradebook can be used to generate class reports that include information to let the teachers know when learning has succeeded. With this information, the teacher can plan to move ahead or to review problematic areas. Thus, the electronic gradebook is a planning as well as a record-keeping tool.

Another CMI function is test generation. When the computer "writes," or generates, a test, it simply makes random choices from a database of test items that the teacher has composed and stored in the computer. A test item is a single question on a test, such as a true/false question.

CMI offers a solution to the problem of scoring tests and other exercises and reporting the results. Test scoring relies on several computer capabilities: database, spreadsheet, and optical scanning. Optical scanning devices are able to detect and interpret marks on a paper test form and send the data to the computer for processing. The computer then refers to its database of correct answers to determine whether the response is correct or incorrect. Results of tests are then submitted to mathematical and statistical processing and the results are reported.

CMI packages are available for all types and sizes of computer systems. An individual teacher can use a single microcomputer to perform CMI tasks, whereas a school district may use a mainframe computer and terminals to perform CMI districtwide. In a classroom setting, computers used by students can be networked to communicate with the teacher's computer. In this case, the teacher's CMI software collects data from the students' computers or terminals and processes that data as the teacher requires.

Following are some hints that should prove useful in making wise CMI purchases for a single classroom or an entire school district:

1. Involve teachers and support staff in the review process from the very beginning.
2. Consider how powerful the CMI program needs to be.
3. Consider what type of hardware the CMI package requires.
4. Can the CMI package be integrated with other software?
5. Does the CMI package come with clear and complete documentation?
6. Is the program relatively free of bugs?

Once the available CMI software has been reviewed and a program purchased, the process of implementation begins. The following recommendations should help to make CMI implementation as smooth as possible:

1. Expect the transition to take some time.
2. Teachers and staff members may need to be trained to operate computer hardware.
3. Anyone who uses the CMI system should receive copies of training manuals and other documentation.
4. Data should always be verified at the time of entry.
5. Teachers and staff members who use the CMI system should be asked to provide feedback.

REVIEW EXERCISES

Multiple Choice

1. CMI stands for
   a. computers mean instruction
   b. computer-maintained instruction
   c. computer-managed instruction
   d. none of the above
2. CMI software relies primarily on which computer application(s)?
   a. database
   b. spreadsheet
   c. word processing
   d. a and b
3. CMI software helps teachers and administrators perform
   a. reporting
   b. inventory
   c. grading
   d. all of the above
4. The first step in creating an electronic gradebook is to
   a. add students to the class file
   b. print student records
   c. create a new class file
   d. none of the above
5. Which of the following is *not* an advantage of the electronic gradebook?
   a. Students can access their records at any time
   b. Grades can be calculated at any time
   c. Grades can be calculated quickly and accurately
   d. none of the above
6. Reports generated by electronic gradebooks help teachers determine
   a. when students have mastered objectives
   b. when students need individual assistance
   c. which lessons are most effective
   d. all of the above
7. A test generator makes random choices from a database of
   a. essay questions
   b. test items
   c. math problems
   d. none of the above
8. The most time-consuming task for a teacher who uses a test generator is
   a. writing answer keys
   b. writing test items
   c. creating different test forms
   d. none of the above
9. Computerized test scoring relies on which computer capability (capabilities)?
   a. database
   b. spreadsheet
   c. optical scanning
   d. all of the above
10. Persons reviewing CMI software should consider
    a. hardware requirements
    b. whether it can be integrated with other software
    c. the quality of documentation included in the package
    d. all of the above

True/False

1. With CMI software, teachers or support staff members can use the computer to perform administrative functions.
2. Many CAI software packages include limited CMI functions.
3. CMI makes it possible for teachers to track the progress of individual students.
4. The electronic gradebook calculates grades only at the end of an academic term.
5. Data stored in an electronic gradebook cannot be lost.
6. Test generators are useful in creating essay questions.
7. Students use optical scanning devices to mark answers on tests.
8. At present, CMI software is available only for mainframe computers.
9. A major benefit of CMI is that it provides immediate feedback on student performance.
10. Since most teachers and support staff members are not computer experts, it is not advisable to involve them in the process of reviewing CMI.

Short Answer

1. List some of the tasks that can be automated with CMI.
2. According to Forman (1982), what are the five characteristics of CMI packages?
3. How does the electronic gradebook save teachers' time?
4. Name two disadvantages of using a test generator.
5. List several hints for implementing CMI successfully.

Activities

1. Research current applications of CMI and report your findings to the class.
2. Visit a local computer retail or teaching supply store to see what CMI software is available.
3. Research uses of CMI in special education.
4. Discuss some of the limitations of standardized tests. Why are they used so widely?
5. Invite a computer professional on your campus to speak to your class about how CMI is used at your college or university.
6. Determine which are the three most popular CMI systems. List their advantages and disadvantages.
7. Determine which of the three CMI systems is the most popular. List its manufacturer, the equipment required, and the approximate cost per student.
8. Summarize the research findings on CMI systems in 1969.

BIBLIOGRAPHY

Bitter, Gary G. "Computer Assisted Mathematics — A Model Approach. *Computers in the Schools* 4 (no. 2, Summer 1987): 37–47.

———— . "Migrant Student Math Skills Computerized." *The Computing Teacher* 7 (no. 6, 1980): 36–37.

Bitter, Gary G., and Julian R. Aguilu. "A Computer Assisted Management System for the Teacher." *Journal of Educational Data Processing* 10 (no. 7, 1972): 8–9.

Bitter, Gary G., and Allan Cameron. "Mathematics Skills Screening of Preservice Teachers." *Journal of Computers in Mathematics and Science Teaching* 6 (no. 4, Summer 1987): 22–27.

———— . "Mathematics Skills Screening of Preservice Teachers at Arizona State University College of Education." In *Microcomputers in Education Conference Proceedings* 35–42. Rockville, Md.: Computer Science Press, 1986.

———— ."Microcomputer Assisted Mathematics Diagnosis and Remediation Program." *Computers in Adult Education and Training* (May 1988): 15–24.

Bitter, Gary G., and Ruth Camuse. *Using a Microcomputer in the Classroom.* Englewood Cliffs, N.J.: Prentice-Hall, 1988.

Burrowes, Ted and Sharon. "It's the End of the Marking Period—And There Goes My Weekend!" *The Computing Teacher* 11 (no. 6, February 1984): 31 – 32.

"The Electronic School." *The American School Board Journal* 174 (no. 7, July 1987): A23–A27.

Forman, D. "Search of the Literature." *The Computing Teacher* 9 (no. 5, 1982): 37–51.

Fuchs, L.S. "CMI and Special Education Monitoring." *The Computing Teacher* 15 (no. 1): 59.

Harper, Dennis O., and James H. Stewart. *RUN: Computer Education.* Monterey, Calif.: Brooks/Cole, 1983.

Merrill, Paul F., et al. *Computers in Education.* Englewood Cliffs, N.J.: Prentice-Hall, 1986.

Reid, Ivan, and James Rushton (eds.). *Teachers, Computers and the Classroom.* United Kingdom: Manchester University Press, 1985.

Watson, James, Jr. "General Multiple Choice Quiz." *The Computing Teacher* 11 (no. 3, October 1983): 54–56.

REVIEW ANSWER KEY

Multiple Choice

1. c
2. d
3. d
4. c
5. a
6. d
7. b
8. b
9. d
10. d

True/False

1. T
2. T
3. T
4. F
5. F
6. F
7. F
8. F
9. T
10. F

Short Answer

1. Keeping student and class records; writing and scoring tests, calculating and recording grades; prescribing individual instruction.

2. Organizing curricula and student data; monitoring student progress; diagnosing and prescribing instruction; evaluating learning outcomes; and providing information for teachers to use in planning lessons.

3. Automatically records and calculates grades, reports grades, tracks absences and tardiness, maintains class rosters, and so on.

4. Teachers must write more questions than required for a single exam; grading different test forms may be difficult to manage.

5. Expect the transition to take some time; train teachers and staff to operate hardware; give copies of documentation to all persons who will use the system; verify data at time of entry; ask teachers and other CMI users for feedback.

CHAPTER 12

CHOOSING SOFTWARE FOR THE CLASSROOM

Objectives

- List several sources of information about educational software
- Contact a software publishing house about review copies of software
- Use checklists to compare features of similar software packages

- Evaluate drill-and-practice, problem solving, tutorial, simulation, and application software
- Recognize sources of public domain software and software reviews

Key Terms

compatible
copy-protect
courseware
documentation
drill-and-practice
help screen
K (kilobytes)
menu
mnemonic
peripherals
piracy
pirated
public domain software
simulation
tutorial
user groups

As computers become more visible and more accessible in our society, teachers have begun to realize the many benefits of computerized education. As we have seen in earlier chapters, the computer is a versatile tool for the teacher. Some of the functions it performs are:

1. Teaching new skills and testing skills already learned
2. Helping the teacher conquer mountains of paper work
3. Freeing the teacher to devote more time to individual students
4. Preparing students for adulthood in a computerized society

Recognizing what computers are capable of doing for them and for their students, many teachers search enthusiastically for a way to introduce computers into their classrooms. Unless there is already a collection of useful educational software available in the school or the district, the teacher typically faces the hurdle of locating software that will meet the needs of his or her students as well as perform administrative tasks that the teacher wishes to automate.

Another term for educational software is **courseware**. Courseware includes the software program as well as additional classroom materials. Some of these are textbooks, workbooks, teacher guides, visuals, tests, and so on. Courseware eliminates the problem of trying to coordinate computer learning with more traditional materials, such as textbooks.

We have become accustomed to hearing, seeing, and reading advertisements for computer hardware and software every day. From this, we might deduce that the teacher's task of locating software is a simple one. Merely consult the local telephone directory under "computer retailers," and the problem is half-solved. Not so—educational computer applications require special considerations that may not apply to software designed for business or personal use. So where does the teacher begin in the search for effective and dynamic educational software?

SOURCES OF EDUCATIONAL SOFTWARE

The local telephone directory may indeed be a starting point in the search for educational software. In most cities, computer retail stores offer a wide range of software for many applications and computer systems. A teacher who is looking for a specific software package or a particular type of package can save time by calling local stores and asking whether the software is available locally.

However, most computer retail stores still cater primarily to business and personal computer needs, since this is where most of their market lies. Of course, teachers who are looking for applications software (such as word processing, database, spreadsheet, or telecommunications) can review a variety of software packages at local computer retail stores. Many such packages designed for business or home use can be adapted for the classroom, depending on the skill level of the students who will use the software. In this way, for example, high school students in business classes would gain experience with real-world software. They may also be using similar packages on computers at home or at work.

While consulting the telephone directory, look for stores that specialize in educational supplies and materials. Many such stores exist, and if they do not stock educational software, they may be able to order it. They are also likely to offer a selection of books and periodicals that help teachers learn about new packages on the market and innovative ways to use all types of software in the classroom.

When visiting computer stores, be sure to ask about computer clubs in your area. For the cost of annual membership dues, computer club members have access to the club's library of software. The clubs may even own computer hardware for reviewing software, and some offer training for the new user. Look for clubs that concentrate on hardware commonly found in schools. Business computer clubs may have little or no expertise in educational software.

In many areas, computer users have banded together to form **user groups** to exchange information about computers and software. Again, they usually have a library of software owned or perhaps even created by club members. Try to find club members who are also teachers or who are interested in educational applications of computers. These people are often excellent sources of ideas for finding and using software. Computer retail stores can usually put you in touch with user groups in the area. You may be fortunate enough to locate a user group specifically for teachers.

Yet another source of good educational software is a local college or university. Most have software libraries you can visit to try out software products that you may be considering for your classroom. Along with software, these libraries usually subscribe to popular computer and educational journals that keep readings up to date on software availability. Also at the local college or university you will probably find instructors and staff members who are quite knowledgeable in the field of educational computing. Talking with them can point you to tried-and-true educational packages.

While visiting these campuses, think about signing up for a class in educational computing. Many schools offer such classes. You will benefit from the instructor's expertise, and you will also meet other people who share your interest in teaching with computers.

Consider attending workshops and conferences that deal with the topic of computers in education. Not only will you meet people who are experts in this field, but you can also meet other teachers who are just starting out with whom you can share your experiences in searching for software. In addition, software publishing houses often send representatives to educational conferences across the country to demonstrate software and inform teachers of how to obtain review copies or make purchases. At large conferences, a wide selection of educational software is displayed in a small space. This makes it fast and easy for teachers to compare features of similar packages.

You may not need to travel at all to locate resources. Find out which other teachers in your district are using computers in their classrooms. They have been through the process of selecting and installing computer hardware and software, and their advice can help you avoid pitfalls in your own search. You can also write to the department of education in your state and request any materials they have on using computers in the classroom. They may also provide you with information about computer use in districts other than your own. Thus, you have another list of "experts" to consult during your search.

Don't overlook the possibility of finding free or inexpensive software available in the public domain. **Public domain software** has been developed by individuals or groups who offer their software to users without charge or sometimes for the price of a disk for copying the software. The quality of the software may be excellent or poor, but the price is always right. One organized effort to help teachers obtain public domain software is the California Computer-Using Educator's "Softswap" software collections, available at no cost or at minimal cost.

How can teachers locate public domain software? Often, information about such packages is published in educational journals and newsletters. Other teachers may also be aware of sources of free or inexpensive software. Public domain software can enhance the teacher's software collection without biting into often limited software budgets. (See the end of this chapter for a list of sources of public domain software.)

Finally, one of the best sources of information about educational software is the people who make their living writing and publishing it. They are always interested in demonstrating the products their companies have developed. Teachers should keep in mind that software publishers have a vested interest in representing their products as the best available. It is up to the teacher to compare as many packages as possible before choosing one. Also, it is wise to make sure that the publisher has a favorable return policy for software that does not meet the teacher's needs. In general, it is a good policy to try out a software package before purchasing it.

The basic question the teacher must ask before contacting software publishers is whether he or she is limited by the type or brand of computer that will be used. If computers have already been purchased, it is a waste of time to contact publishers whose software is not **compatible** with that particular hardware. On the other hand, if no hardware has been bought, the teacher may find it more useful to look for software *before* choosing hardware for the classroom. Whenever possible, it is almost always best to shop for software before committing to a specific computer.

Software publishers are listed in software directories available in computer retail stores or in libraries. Also included are available packages, hardware requirements, prices, and ordering information. In most cases, the directories are impartial. That is, they do not review the software they list. That is left to the buyer. Once you have located a number of software publishers, you can contact them to request any information they offer, including brochures, catalogs, and reviews of their software.

In some cases, software publishers offer copies of their software for review. This is especially true if a school or school district wants to purchase a large number of copies of the software. The publisher will naturally want assurance that the software will not be copied unlawfully, or **pirated**. The publisher has invested a great deal of time and money in developing, producing, and marketing the software. The only way to recover this investment is to make sure that the software is not pirated. Therefore, it may be necessary to guarantee that you will not make unauthorized copies of any software you receive for review.

Software **piracy** is a major problem in all areas of software publishing because those who develop software must make a profit in order to stay in business. If they go out of business, all users will suffer from a lack of good software on the market. This is of special concern to teachers, who rely on new and better software packages to benefit their students. To avoid the possibility of pirating, many publishers offer special demonstration disks. These disks are designed to show off the features of the program, but either they do not contain all the functions of the software or they cannot be copied by the user. Some companies **copy-protect** their software, which means they restrict the number of copies that can be made by the user even *after* purchase. It is a good idea to find out how many backup copies can be made, especially in the classroom where rough handling, chalk dust, and other factors may ruin disks.

REVIEWING EDUCATIONAL SOFTWARE

Now that the teacher has located sources of educational software, the review process can begin. To save time and avoid duplicating effort, teachers should consult books and journals that publish reviews of educational software. These publications are available in libraries, bookstores, and computer retail stores. Some are devoted to software review, but others are special-interest publications, such as education journals, that regularly feature columns in which software packages are reviewed. If a package has received many good reviews, it is probably a good candidate for purchase. In contrast, a package that has gotten several bad reviews may not live up to the user's expectations.

In addition to publications, there are numerous organizations that specialize in software review. These groups are often excellent sources of information about the quality of educational software on the market. For example, the federal government funded a project called Microsift to review software and to publish the results. The result is a newsletter that keeps teachers informed of state-of-the-art software for the classroom. Another review source is the Educational Software Evaluation Consortium which publishes the Educational Software Preview Guide (available from the International Council for Computers in Education). This preview guide lists software that educators should consider. The guide includes academic area, computer requirements, software company, type of software, price, and suggested grade levels. (See the end of this chapter for a list of sources of software review.)

The more time and thought a teacher puts into the review process, the more likely it is that he or she will locate the right package. Sometimes, a group of teachers in a school or a group of schools within a district review software packages. In this case, it's important that the members of the evaluation team try to keep careful written records of their findings. This makes it simpler to compare opinions and helps prevent duplicated effort.

Many factors besides computer compatibility must be taken into consideration when selecting software. For example, the amount of memory a computer has determines what software can be used. Some educational software, such as simulation programs, require more memory than simpler programs do. With most computers, it is possible to expand the memory by purchasing more from the computer manufacturer. However, the cost of expanding memory may be too expensive for some budgets.

Educational software may also require that certain **peripherals** be attached to the computer, such as printers, cassette recorders, disk drives, mice (hand-held data entry devices), special touch tablets, card readers, or voice synthesizers. Without this equipment—which can be more expensive than the school's budget permits— the software may not live up to its potential.

Some software, especially educational packages designed for young children, rely on colorful graphic displays to keep students interested and motivated. If the classroom computer does not display color, an important feature of the software is lost; in this case, another program may be more effective.

Software publishers furnish brochures that list the hardware requirements of their packages, and they are always happy to answer inquiries from customers as well. Hardware needs should be taken into consideration before any further decisions are made about a specific software package.

Once the software prospects have been limited to those designed for use with the computer equipment available, the review process can begin. Of course, reviewing software is like reviewing a movie or a best-selling novel. Everyone has an opinion, and more often than not those opinions vary widely. A program that is perfect for one teacher's classroom may fail miserably in another's. Therefore, teachers should consider their teaching styles and their students when choosing software.

Just as teachers may disagree with each other, so may teachers and students disagree about the kind of software that works best. Therefore, whenever possible, it's a good idea to involve students in the review process, by allowing them to try out software when review copies are available. After all, students are the ultimate users of educational software.

Before discussing the mechanics of reviewing software, let's look at some philosophical and methodological concerns about CAI software. Before it is deemed worthy, it must meet certain basic educational standards. When selecting software for review, teachers should keep in mind the following criteria:

What Makes Computer-Assisted Instruction (CAI) Software Effective?

1. *Is the program based on sound educational theory and methodology?* This criterion will be judged differently by different teachers, but it's important that the teacher feel that the software is compatible with his or her educational philosophy and style.
2. *Is the program based on accurate content?* No matter how appealing an educational program or game, it is of little value if it conveys incorrect or inadequate information to students.
3. *Does the program show discrimination on the basis of sex, race, and so on?*
4. *Does the program assume that students are experienced computer users?* If so, new users may become frustrated when they don't understand instructions and options. Is assistance available through on-screen prompts, help screens, and so on?
5. *Does the program manage to keep the student's attention?* Students must feel motivated and involved in the program, or they will not want to use it repeatedly. Software that allows competition, presents interesting stories and games, or permits more than one student to participate at a time is more attractive to students than software that is limited in performance.
6. *Does the program give appropriate responses to the student for correct and incorrect answers?* Correct answers should be rewarded, and incorrect answers should prompt the software to provide help instead of criticism. Phrases that belittle or insult the student are harmful. However, responses to correct answers must be more attractive than responses to incorrect answers; software that encourages students to answer incorrectly so that they can see the response defeats the purpose for which it was intended.
7. *Does the program allow students or teachers to control the lesson?* Can students choose how fast to do a lesson, how difficult the lesson will be, when to review previous screens, and so on? If so, all students can work at their own pace, which is a major benefit of computer learning; the computer is patient with beginners and challenging to more advanced users.

8. *Is the program based on clearly stated and educationally sound objectives?* Both teacher and students should understand the purpose of the software.
9. *Does the program allow students to work independently?* This allows the teacher to give more individual attention to other students.
10. *Is the program flexible?* That is, teachers should be able to change the content and level of difficulty of the material presented. For example, a program that teaches vocabulary should allow the teacher to change vocabulary lists from time to time or for different groups of students.
11. *Does the program include helpful auxiliary materials* such as workbooks, charts, tests, lesson plans, follow-up activities? Such materials expand the uses of software and make it a more cost-effective learning tool.
12. *Does the program include a good management system?* Such a system enables the teacher to track student progress, change class lists, and see reports of student performance.

Different types of software require different methods of evaluation. The most common types of educational software are drill-and-practice, simulation, problem-solving, tutorial, and applications (tool) software. (For a more complete discussion of these types of software, refer to Chapter 10 on computer-assisted instruction.) When reviewing drill-and-practice programs, for instance, teachers will consider different features than when reviewing simulation programs. Later in this chapter, we discuss some specific questions to ask when reviewing the various types of software.

First, though, let's look at some common characteristics of all educational software. These general features provide a starting point in the review process, since they apply to all kinds of software packages. A good software review checklist includes these characteristics, which are vital in the decision-making process.

Backup Policies

In the typical classroom, many conditions threaten the life of a program disk. Among these are dust, magnetic objects, bright light, and hands that may be less than gentle with computer disks. So one extremely important characteristic to consider is the software publisher's policy about making backup copies of program disks. Publishers must try to strike a balance between protecting themselves from piracy and making sure their customers can protect themselves from damaged or lost disks. Policies vary widely from company to company, but usually they fall into one of the following categories:

1. *Software comes with only a master program disk.* In this case, no backup copies are provided. The publisher may charge a replacement fee if disks are damaged. Sometimes a backup disk is sent to the person

registering the software. (Registering software is similar to returning a warranty card for a household appliance.) If the publisher makes no provisions for backup copies, it may be a good idea to consider buying from another publisher. It is a fact of life that disks get lost or damaged when used by a number of people.

2. *Software comes with a master program disk as well as a backup disk.* In this case, the teacher can file one disk away for safekeeping and use the other in the classroom. Of course, if both disks are damaged, it may be necessary to pay a replacement fee to the publisher or buy another copy of the program.

3. *Software is not copy-protected.* Often, publishers permit teachers to make their own backup copies of master disks. Sometimes teachers can make as many copies as they want as long as the copies are used only by the buyer. In other cases, the number of copies that can be made from the master is limited by special codes written into the software. A counter in the software keeps track of backup copies as they are made, and the copies themselves cannot be copied.

Understanding the publisher's policy on copying disks can help avoid difficulties and delays when disks are lost or damaged. A program that is affordably priced may become quite expensive if additional copies must be purchased because of an unfavorable backup policy.

When reviewing more than one software package at a time or when more than one person is involved in the review process, it is a good idea to use a checklist or evaluation form to keep track of reviews. See the sample evaluation form that follows. Many school districts that purchase large amounts of educational software have developed their own forms for this purpose. Evaluation forms should include space for recording the following general features of software. In addition, there should always be a space for software *reviewer(s) name(s)*. This is especially important when teachers and administrators are reviewing software as a group.

Using a Software Evaluation Form

Name of program. Publisher. Address. Price. Ordering information. This information not only identifies the package being reviewed, but it is also vital once the buying decision has been made.

Subject area. For what curriculum area(s) is the program designed? What skills is it intended to teach?

Topic(s). What specific topics and skills within the subject area are taught by the program?

Grade level. For what grade level or ages is the program designed? Brochures or manuals that come with the software usually indicate this. Sometimes, however, it is useful to have students try out software to make sure that it is neither too simple nor too difficult for the targeted grade level.

Type of program. The reviewer should note whether the program is drill-and-practice, tutorial, simulation, problem-solving, or an applications pro-

This sample form can be used when evaluating software for purchase.

SOFTWARE EVALUATION FORM

Reviewer _____ Date of review _____

Name of program _____

Publisher _____

Address _____

City _____ State _____ Zip _____

Price $_____

Ordering instructions: _____
_____

Subject area(s): _____

Topic(s): _____

Grade level: _____ Type of program: _____

Brief description of the program: _____
_____
_____

Computer: _____ Memory required: _____ K

Type of storage: _____

Other hardware required: _____
_____

Other software required: _____
_____

Auxiliary materials available: _____
_____
_____

Features   Yes   No

  1. Is software easy to load?   ____   ____

  2. Does software run as promised?   ____   ____

  3. Does software make good use of the computer?   ____   ____

  4. Are manuals and on-screen text clear and easy to read? ____   ____

  5. Are screen displays clear and attractive?   ____   ____

  6. Do menus make the software user-friendly?   ____   ____

  7. Can students skip over instructions?   ____   ____

  8. Can students correct errors easily?   ____   ____

  9. Are commands simple to enter and easy to remember? ____   ____

10. Do you recommend purchase of this software?   ____   ____

(NOTE: Reviewers can add any features they wish to this evaluation form.)

Additional comments: _____
_____

gram. (These are discussed in detail later in this chapter.) A brief description of the program, including the features that make it unique and attractive, is also helpful.

Computer. This allows the reviewer to indicate on which computers the software can run. Both brand name and model should be identified since not all models of the same computer can run the same software. If the software is available in different formats, that is, for different brands and models of computers, it is a good idea to note that also.

Memory requirements. How much memory is required to run the program? Remember that the cost of expanding memory to run a program may make the program a very expensive purchase. Memory is expressed in **K**, or **kilobytes** (1,000 bytes of information).

Type of storage. The most common types of storage are disk, cartridge, or cassette tape. If the software is available on different media, it may be helpful to note this. Cartridges, for example, are safer in small hands that have not yet been trained to handle disks carefully.

Other hardware required. Does the software require that extra equipment be attached to the computer? Some programs cannot be run effectively without a mouse, color monitor, special keypad, printer, or voice synthesizer. Reviewers need to be aware of this before recommending the purchase of software.

Other software required. Sometimes, though rarely, a program may require the presence of other software in order to run. The availability and cost of other programs is an important factor to consider when reviewing software.

Auxiliary materials available. Does the software publisher offer related software, textbooks, workbooks, tests, teacher guides, and so on? It is often easier to coordinate lessons with such auxiliary courseware than with unrelated materials.

Most of the above information can be obtained from brochures and manuals supplied by the publisher. This forms the basis of the evaluation. Other characteristics of the software are reviewed by actually running the program. Questions about the effectiveness of the software can be answered best when the reviewer tries out the software. The reviewer should attempt to answer the questions that follow.

Is the software easy to load? If the teacher wishes for students to work at the computer independently, the software must be easy to load, or start up. Is it simple to figure out how to load the program and begin working with it?

Does the software run as promised? A program that is full of bugs is frustrating to students.

Does the program make good use of the computer? In other words, can students learn more from using the program than they could from more traditional paper-and-pencil methods? If not, then the software wastes valuable computer time.

Are manuals and on-screen text clear and easy to read? Especially when students will be working individually, it is necessary to have clear **docu-**

mentation (instructions either in a manual or on the screen) that students can read and understand on their own. Be sure that all of the text uses good grammar and spelling. Otherwise, the software may reinforce poor writing skills. Also indicate whether the readability level of the documentation is appropriate for the students targeted to use the software.

Are screen displays clear and attractive? Young children especially can be motivated by visually exciting screen displays. Are the screens inviting to the eye? Can students see important information at a glance, or must they search each screen to see what to do next?

Do menus on the screen make the software user-friendly? A **menu** is simply a list of helpful instructions displayed on screen to show the user what actions can be taken. Students choose an action from the menu, just as they might choose a hamburger or pizza from a restaurant menu. Menus must be clearly written and displayed on the screen in order to be useful. Also consider whether the student can request the program to display a **help screen** (more detailed instructions displayed on screen) when he or she is confused about how to run the program.

Can students skip over instructions once they are familiar with the software? Many programs allow students to choose a skill level from beginning to advanced. Beginners are given the most on-screen help and instructions, whereas advanced users are given shorter explanations. Some programs also have shortcuts, such as abbreviated commands, to speed the use of the program by more advanced users.

Can students correct errors easily? Usually, typing errors can be corrected by backspacing and retyping. If a program does not allow fast and simple correction of errors, it may frustrate students. Some poorly designed programs even stop in the middle if the user makes an error.

Are commands simple to enter and easy to remember? Many programmers use **mnemonic** codes for commands because they are easy to remember. Some common examples of mnemonic codes are Y for Yes, N for No, E for Exit, and S for Save. When commands are complicated or difficult to remember, students may have trouble learning to operate the program.

The above characteristics apply to all types of CAI programs. However, when reviewing specific types of CAI software, teachers must consider a number of other factors. Let's take a look at special criteria that must be met by drill-and-practice, tutorial, simulation, problem-solving, and applications software.

Drill-and-Practice Software

Drill-and-practice programs present sets of questions or exercises for students to complete. By completing drill-and-practice exercises successfully, students demonstrate their mastery of skills and concepts that have already been taught through textbooks, classroom discussions, and so on. Therefore, the thrust of the drill-and-practice program is to reinforce and test skills, rather than to teach concepts.

Much of the educational software on the market falls under the heading of drill-and-practice. One explanation for this is that this software is perhaps the easiest type to design and write. A series of exercises is presented and the number of appropriate responses is relatively limited. Drill-and-practice software is useful when it encourages students to practice skills they have already mastered.

But it has several drawbacks as well. If students can complete exercises on a worksheet just as easily as on a computer, then the software wastes valuable computer time. Also, when drill-and-practice software is too repetitive, students are not motivated to use it more than once or a few times at most. This may mean that a drill-and-practice program is not a good investment in the long run if it gathers dust on a shelf.

To avoid making an unwise purchase, reviewers of drill-and-practice software need to answer the questions that follow.

Does the software make use of an interesting game format? Students may become so interested in playing the game that they do not mind repeating exercises and practicing skills. However, if exercises are simply flashed on the screen, students won't become as involved in the software.

Are sound, color, and graphics used in such a way to make the screen attractive to students?

Do incorrect answers cause the software to display tutorial lessons? While drill-and-practice software is based on students already having learned concepts, it is helpful to students who answer incorrectly to see on-screen tutorials that refresh their memories or further explain basic concepts.

Does the program tell a student how he or she has done? After completing a lesson, students need to know how they have performed. This will motivate them to compete against themselves to improve performance in the future.

Does the program generate problems randomly? If exercises always appear in the same order, students may be able to memorize the correct answers in sequence rather than actually figuring them out. Also, students find it boring to use a program that operates in only one predetermined way.

Can the teacher change problems and exercises? The more flexible a drill-and-practice program is, the better investment it will be. Also, when problems and exercises are varied, students are more interested in working with the program repeatedly.

Does the program include a good management system? This is more important to some teachers than to others, but many want a program that reports student and class performance. From such reports, the teacher can determine when the class has mastered certain concepts and skills and when additional help is needed.

Tutorial Software

Tutorial software not only tests skills but actually presents and reinforces concepts through a teaching format. Many tutorial programs also contain drill-and-practice exercises that test how well students have learned the

To avoid making an unwise purchase, drill-and-practice software should be reviewed.

Software Evaluation Form - Drill and Practice   Student   _____

Program   _____   Date Published   _____
Publisher   _____   Version Number   _____
Subject area: _____

Grade Level: Elementary   _____   Sp Ed: _____ Specify area: _____
                Jr. High   _____   Other: _____
                Secondary   _____

	Yes	No
1. Are the drills appropriate for the age/grade of the student?	____	____
2. Is the subject matter of the program well organized?	____	____
3. Does the author present the material in a logical order?	____	____
4. Are the practice sessions of proper length?	____	____
5. Do the drills advance in difficulty at an appropriate rate?	____	____
6. Are there any graphics in the tutorial?	____	____
7. Is the student provided feedback about his/her progress?	____	____
8. Do the lessons provide remedial reinforcement for errors?	____	____
9. Can the teacher add customized drill material to the program?	____	____
10. Are the instructions for the tutorial clear for the student?	____	____

11. Describe some of the good and/or unique features about this program.

_____

_____

_____

12. List any program weaknesses.

_____

_____

13. When would you use this drill/practice program in your class or with a particular student? Why?

_____

_____

_____

Reviewer   _____
Date   _____

concepts presented in the tutorial. Tutorials are available on a virtually unlimited range of topics. Individual students can often be placed at different points in the tutorial based on their level of knowledge and skill.

Tutorials can be used to supplement more traditional teaching methods, or they may be used alone to present lessons. They can also be used to challenge advanced students who wish to explore areas not included in the regular curriculum. Special factors to consider when reviewing tutorial software are highlighted in the questions that follow.

Does the tutorial encourage the student to become actively involved? A computer screen is not a textbook, and tutorials are not effective when they merely present screens full of text. Concepts should be presented creatively, and the program should encourage student interaction to avoid boredom.

Does the tutorial tell students how they have done? Some students may be able to skip over introductory lessons, while others may require review. Performance evaluations let students know how they are doing and motivate them to improve.

Can students choose to review sections of the tutorial when they wish to? A student who needs to return to an earlier lesson for review may become frustrated if the program doesn't allow this.

Is the length of each lesson appropriate? Younger students have shorter attention spans than older students do. If the tutorial doesn't take this into account, students may not benefit as much as when lessons are geared to their age and skill level.

Are the topics presented relevant? Tutorials are only valuable when the concepts they present are useful and not trivial.

Can students complete the tutorial independently? If students must constantly ask the teacher for help, then perhaps the material could be presented better through more traditional means, such as lecture or discussion. A well-designed tutorial enables the computer to act as teacher and frees the teacher for other important tasks, such as providing individual attention to students.

Does the tutorial come with useful materials such as workbooks, teacher guides, filmstrips, and so on? These materials help teachers integrate the tutorial into the curriculum and provide reinforcement of concepts and skills.

Is the tutorial based on sound educational theory and methodology? Does it rely too heavily on rote memorization or multiple-choice questions?

Does the tutorial use effective color, graphics, and sound to hold students' attention? Attractive screen displays keep students interested in the material being presented. Dull screen displays have the opposite effect.

Simulation and Problem-Solving Software

One of the most popular types of CAI software is simulation. **Simulation** software presents students with realistic situations in which they must make decisions and practice skills. The computer presents a set of conditions to which the student must respond, thereby actually applying skills in real-world situations. Well-written simulation programs stimulate students' imagination and allow them to have experiences they may never have in reality.

Simulation software often includes tutorial and drill-and-practice segments to present concepts and test mastery of skills. It is perhaps the most

An evaluation form specifically designed to review tutorial software.

Software Evaluation Form - Tutorials   Student   _____

Program   _____   Date Published   _____
Publisher   _____   Version Number   _____
Subject area: _____

Grade Level: Elementary   _____   Sp Ed _____ Specify area: _____
                    Jr. High   _____   Other: _____
                    Secondary   _____

                                                                    Yes   No

1. Is the tutorial appropriate for the age/grade of the student?   ____   ____
2. Is the subject matter of the tutorial well organized?   ____   ____
3. Does the author present the material in a logical order?   ____   ____
4. Are the lessons of proper length?   ____   ____
5. Do the lessons advance in difficulty at an appropriate rate?   ____   ____
6. Are there any graphics in the tutorial?   ____   ____
7. Is the student provided feedback about his/her progress?   ____   ____
8. Do the lessons provide remedial reinforcement for errors?   ____   ____
9. Are the instructions for the tutorial clear for the teacher?   ____   ____
10. Are the instructions for the tutorial clear for the student?   ____   ____
11. Describe some of the good and/or unique features about this tutorial.

    _____
    _____
    _____
    _____

12. List any program weaknesses.

    _____
    _____
    _____

13. Would you use this tutorial in your class or with a particular student?   Why?
    Why not?

    _____
    _____
    _____

                                                Reviewer   _____
                                                Date   _____

difficult type of CAI software to design and write, which accounts for its relatively high price tag. But good simulation software motivates students to become actively involved in the learning process so that, in most cases, the money is well spent. To help make a purchasing decision, simulation software should be reviewed with the questions that follow in mind. Most of these considerations can apply to problem-solving software as well, since it shares many characteristics with simulation software.

Is the simulation realistic? The goal of simulation software is to re-create conditions that exist in the real world and to show students how their decisions will affect those conditions. Therefore, a simulation must be realistic to be effective.

Does the simulation cause the student to become involved in the experience? Does the student care whether the spaceship gets to Pluto, for example?

Does the simulation allow students to work cooperatively? A major advantage of simulation software is that it often works best when teams of students compete against each other. Students learn about cooperation as well as about the content of the simulation itself. In addition, team members motivate each other to improve their performance.

Can students control the speed of the lesson? Some students take longer to read and respond to instructions. They become frustrated when the lesson appears to fly by them and they are pressured into making choices without enough time to consider all the options. Many simulations allow users to select a level of difficulty at the outset.

Is the length of the simulation appropriate? Even exciting simulations may be ineffective if they are so long that they cannot hold students' attention. If the simulation is too long to be completed within a single class period, does the program allow students to save their work in progress?

Does the simulation state what skills a student must possess before operating the program? Simulation relies on certain concepts and skills having been learned already, and these prerequisites should be stated clearly. Otherwise, students will have to stop in midstream to learn new material.

Does the simulation include helpful materials such as workbooks, teacher guides, videotapes, filmstrips, and so on? These help reinforce skills and integrate the simulation into the curriculum.

Does the simulation use color, graphics, and sound to hold students' attention? Exciting screen displays and sound effects lend realism to the simulation.

Applications (Tool) Software

Applications, or tool, software (such as word processing, database, spreadsheet, and graphics) has usually been developed for business or home computer systems. So why would a teacher purchase tool software for classroom use? One reason is that tool software can perform a wider range of functions than, say, a tutorial designed only to teach Civil War history. A word processor, for example, can be used to write essays, design a class newsletter, or practice grammar skills. Since one software package does many tasks, students learn many valuable computer skills that they can apply in the future.

Because applications software is not designed with education in mind, teachers are often left to their own devices in selecting appropriate software and integrating it into the curriculum. All the general criteria for selecting

A sample evaluation form
for simulation software.

Software Evaluation Form - Simulations   Student _____

Program   _____   Date Published _____
Publisher   _____   Version Number _____
Simulation area: _____

Grade Level: Elementary _____   Sp Ed _____ Specify area _____
                     Jr. High   _____   Other: _____

                                                                          Yes   No

1. Is the simulation appropriate for the age/grade of the student?   ____   ____
2. Is the simulation well organized?   ____   ____
3. Does the simulation present a realistic "picture" of the activity?   ____   ____
4. Are the simulation sessions of proper length?   ____   ____
5. Do the simulations advance in difficulty at an appropriate rate?   ____   ____
6. Are there any graphics in the simulation?   ____   ____
7. Is the student provided feedback about his/her progress?   ____   ____
8. Does the simulation provide remedial reinforcement?   ____   ____
9. Are the simulations factually correct?   ____   ____
10. Are the instructions for the simulation clear for the student?   ____   ____
11. Describe some of the good and/or unique features about this simulation program.

_____
_____
_____
_____

12. List any program weaknesses.

_____
_____
_____

13. When would you use this simulation in your class or with a particular student?
      Why? Why not?

_____
_____
_____

                                                        Reviewer _____
                                                        Date   _____

good CAI software apply to applications software. For example, the package
chosen must be compatible with hardware that is used in the classroom.
When reviewing tool software for classroom use, teachers should try to
answer the questions that follow.

What functions does the software perform? A simple word processor may

Software Evaluation Form - Tool and Applications   Student _____

Program   _____   Date Published   _____
Publisher   _____   Version Number   _____
Type program: _____

Grade Level: Elementary ____   Sp Ed: _____ Specify area: _____
                 Jr. High   ____   Other: _____
                 Secondary   ____

                                                       Yes   No

1. Is the program appropriate for the age/grade of the student?   ____ ____
2. Is the program well organized?   ____ ____
3. Are the commands in the program presented in a logical way?   ____ ____
4. Will the program help the student save time in getting work done?   ____ ____
5. Are the instruction manuals thorough and easy to use?   ____ ____
6. Can the student work on the program by him/herself?   ____ ____
7. Is there a tutorial with the application or tool?   ____ ____
8. Is there an on-line help system when the student has problems?   ____ ____
9. Does the student need to memorize program command sequences?   ____ ____
10. Can the material created in the program be used in other programs?   ____ ____
11. Describe some of the good and/or unique features about this program.

_____
_____
_____
_____

12. List any program weaknesses.

_____
_____
_____

13. When would you use this program in your class or with a particular student?
    Why?

_____
_____
_____

                                      Reviewer _____
                                      Date   _____

Tool and applications software can provide a wide range of functions, but needs a careful evaluation before purchase.

be appropriate for third graders. High school students, on the other hand, may require a more sophisticated package with advanced features, such as footnoting.

Is the program used widely outside the school? A program that has enjoyed success in the business and personal computer market is probably a reliable program. Also, there are likely to be many books and articles available on how to use the program.

Is the program simple to learn and easy to use? Some applications software is difficult to learn to operate. The documentation may be poorly written or the software design may assume that the user is a computer expert. How much computer experience is required to operate the software?

For what areas of the curriculum can the software be used? A database program, for example, can store information on any subject under the sun. This makes it a versatile tool in almost any classroom. Since applications software is not designed especially for classroom use, it is up to the teacher to decide how it will be integrated into the curriculum.

SUMMARY

As computers are used more widely in schools, the selection of educational software available to teachers improves. There are a number of sources where teachers can find CAI software for their classrooms. Some computer retail stores carry lines of educational software, especially stores that specialize in teaching tools. There are also computer clubs and user groups that maintain collections of software for their members to use. Local universities and colleges are another source of information about educational software. Teachers can attend seminars and workshops where software is demonstrated and sold.

Many teachers turn to their colleagues and administrators for advice about choosing and purchasing software. In this way, they can benefit from the experiences of others. Teachers may also choose to contact software publishers directly for brochures and review copies of software on the market.

Once they locate software, teachers must evaluate its effectiveness for their students. The first consideration must be whether the software can be run on computer equipment that is available in the classroom. If no computer equipment has been purchased, it's a good idea to review software before choosing which brand of computer to buy.

When reviewing software packages, teachers should consider the following questions:

- Is the software based on sound educational theory and practice?
- Is the program based on accurate content?
- Does the program show discrimination on the basis of sex, race, and so on?
- Is the program suitable to the students' level of computer literacy?
- Does the program hold students' attention?
- Does the program provide appropriate responses for correct and incorrect answers?
- Does the program allow students or teachers to control the lesson?

- Is the program based on clearly stated and educationally sound objectives?
- Does the program allow students to work independently?
- Is the program flexible?
- Does the program include helpful auxiliary materials?
- Does the software include a good management system?

In addition, the reviewer should consider the following:

- What are the publisher's backup policies?
- What computer does the program run on? Does the program require any additional hardware or software?
- Does the program run as promised?
- Does the program make good use of the computer?
- Is the program user-friendly? Can students correct errors easily? Are commands mnemonic?

These questions, along with more specific concerns about CAI software packages, form the basis of the software review process. When more than one person is involved in the process, it is often a good idea to design an evaluation form to keep from duplicating effort. Such forms can be customized to include the features that a teacher or school district considers most important.

Specific types of CAI packages, such as drill-and-practice, tutorial, simulation, problem-solving, and applications software, must meet different criteria in order to be judged effective. Drill-and-practice software, for example, must use innovative formats to avoid boredom. Simulation software must present realistic conditions in which students can make meaningful choices.

The time and energy that teachers spend in reviewing and selecting educational software definitely pays off. Careful selection is the best way to guarantee that students benefit from the time they spend working with computers.

REVIEW EXERCISES

Multiple Choice

1. Good sources of information about educational software are
   a. colleges and universities
   b. computer retail stores
   c. educational journals
   d. all of the above

2. Computers in the classroom cannot
   a. teach new concepts
   b. test students' skills
   c. provide a caring environment for learning
   d. help teachers keep records

3. Software that is available to users at no charge is called
   a. courseware
   b. firmware
   c. public domain software
   d. drill-and-practice

4. Software directories usually do not include
   a. software reviews
   b. software publishers
   c. prices
   d. ordering information
5. When reviewing software, the teacher's first consideration should be
   a. price
   b. other teachers' advice
   c. students' age
   d. the kind of computer to be used
6. Some software requires the presence of additional hardware, such as
   a. voice synthesizers
   b. printers
   c. card readers
   d. all of the above
7. Which type of software is *not* designed especially for educational uses?
   a. simulation
   b. application
   c. drill-and-practice
   d. tutorial
8. When a group of people is involved in reviewing software, it is a good idea to use
   a. similar computers
   b. deadlines
   c. a democratic voting system
   d. software evaluation forms
9. Software evaluation forms usually include
   a. a brief description of the program
   b. reviewer's name
   c. price
   d. all of the above
10. What is the simplest type of CAI software to design and write?
    a. applications
    b. drill-and-practice
    c. tutorial
    d. simulation

True/False

1. CAI software should never show any racial, sexual, or other bias.
2. Drill-and-practice software presents realistic situations in which students can make meaningful choices.
3. Compatible software can be run on any brand of computer.
4. Teachers should not purchase software on disks for classroom use.
5. Teachers should keep backup copies of CAI software on file.
6. Software piracy is not actually illegal.
7. Whenever possible, students should be involved in the process of selecting educational software.
8. Students often benefit from teamwork on the computer.
9. It is usually not necessary to read documentation when reviewing software.
10. Effective use of color, graphics, and sound motivates students to use educational software.

Short Answer

1. How is computer memory measured?
2. Why is it important to consider the length of lessons in tutorial software?
3. What are the limitations of drill-and-practice software?
4. Why do some teachers use applications software in the classroom?
5. Why do software publishers copy-protect their products?

Activities

1. Visit a local computer retail store to see what educational software is available.
2. Visit a classroom to see how CAI software is being used.
3. Choose a CAI software package and look up several reviews in journals. Report on your findings.
4. Consult a software directory and locate several software packages for a particular grade level and subject area.
5. Choose one type of applications software and make a list of ways it could be used in the classroom.
6. Evaluate a public domain software disk. List the advantages and disadvantages of public domain software.
7. Prepare a software review using the software review forms in this chapter for drill-and-practice, simulation and problem-solving, tutorial, and applications tool software programs.

8. Collect software review forms from several school districts. Write a comparison review of the forms (for instance, what is similar, what is different, what is unique, and so on).

9. Visit a software library and write a detailed description of their cataloging system.

10. Compare a software program that runs on several different microcomputers. Did you find any differences in the software from computer to computer?

BIBLIOGRAPHY

Bitter, Gary G. "Choosing the Proper Tools." *The McGill Journal of Education* 18 (no. 3, Fall 1983): 219–225.

————. "Evaluating Hardware and Software." *Computers in the Schools* 1 (no. 1, Spring 1984): 13–28.

————. " 'Games' Aren't All Bad." *Educational Computer* 3 (no. 4, July-August 1983): 20.

Bitter, Gary G. (with K. Gore). "Expanding Your Microcomputer Center." *Computers in the Schools* 1 (no. 3, Fall 1984): 19–31.

Bitter, Gary G. (with Patricia Mulligan). "Microcomputer Feedback to the Student Learner." *IDEAL* 2 (Summer 1987): 75–90.

Bitter, Gary G. (with David Wighton). "The Most Important Criteria Used by the Educational Software Evaluation Consortium." *The Computing Teacher* 14 (no. 6, March 1987): 7–9.

Bitter, Gary G., and Ruth Camuse. *Using a Microcomputer in the Classroom.* 2d ed. Reston, Va.: Reston, 1984.

Brooks, Susan. "Using Integrated Software to Create Simulations for the Classroom." In *8th Annual Microcomputers in Education—Emerging Frontier.* Tempe: Arizona State University, 1988: 32–33.

Callison, D., and G. Haycock. "Students as Software Evaluators." *The Computing Teacher* 15 (no. 6): 23.

Hannafin, Michael S., and Kyle L. Peck. *The Design, Development and Evaluation of Instructional Software.* New York: Macmillan, 1988.

Heck, William P., et al. *Guidelines to Evaluating Computerized Instructional Materials.* Reston, Va.: National Council of Teachers of Mathematics, 1981.

International Council for Computers in Education. *Educational Software Preview Guide.* Eugene: University of Oregon, 1988.

Jaeger, Michael. "Zaps, Booms, and Whistles in Educational Software." *The Computing Teacher* 15 (no. 6): 20.

Keller, Arnold. *When Machines Teach: Designing Computer Software.* New York: Harper and Row, 1987.

Lathrop, Ann, and Bobby Goodson. *Courseware in the Classroom.* Menlo Park, Calif.: Addison-Wesley, 1983.

Reed, W. Michael. "Problem Solving, Writing Theory and Composing Process Software." *Computers in the Schools* 4 (nos. 3–4, Fall–Winter 1987–1988): 179–189.

Rivers, R. H., and E. Vockell. "Problem Solving and Simulations." *The Computing Teacher* 15 (no. 2): 42.

SOURCES FOR PUBLIC DOMAIN SOFTWARE

There are many sources for public domain software. Apple users groups are usually a good local source. It may be worth your while to contact your local group (the local Apple dealer probably has their phone number) to see what they can tell you about public domain software.

There are also several larger national or regional organizations that collect and disseminate public domain software. You may want to contact these groups, some of which are listed below:

The Public Domain Exchange (Apple and Macintosh)
2074C Walsh Ave., Dept. 634
Santa Clara, CA 95060
1-800-331-8125
In California: (408) 496-0624

Public Brand Software (IBM)
P.O. Box 51478
Indianapolis, IN 46251
1-800-426-DISK
In Indiana: (317) 856-7571

CUE SoftSwap
P.O. Box 271704
Concord, CA 94527-1704
(415) 685-7289

TCEA Public Domain Software
c/o Lane Scott
Box 1295
Ozona, TX 76943

SOURCES OF SOFTWARE REVIEW

Software Directories and Guides for Education

1988–89 Educational Software Preview Guide
ICCE, University of Oregon
1787 Agate Street
Eugene, OR 97403
(503) 686-4414

Apple Curriculum Software Reference Guides
Science, Language Arts K–6, Language Arts 6–12,
Mathematics K–6, and Mathematics 6–12.

Educational Computing Newwork
Courseware Catalog
Dept. EE, P.O. Box 8236-SC
Riverside, CA 92515
(714) 687-3333

The Educational Software Catalog
Soft-Kat, Inc.
16130 Stagg Street
Van Nuys, CA 91406
(818) 781-5280

The Educational Software Selector
(T.E.S.S.)
EPIE Institute, P.O. Box 839
Water Mill, NY 11876

K–12 MicroMedia
Dept. EE, 172 Broadway
Woodcliff Lake, NJ 07675

Library Software Review
520 Riverside Avenue
Westport, CT 06880

Directory of Microcomputer Software
DataPro Research Corp.
1805 Underwood Blvd.
Delran, NJ 08075

Micros for Managers: A Software Guide for School
Administrators
New Jersey School Boards Assoc.
413 West State Street
Trenton, NJ 08605
(609) 695-7600

Only the Best: The Discriminating Software Guide for
Preschool–Grade 12
Education News Service
P.O. Box 1789
Carmichael, CA 95609
(916) 488-4623

Queue: The Best in Educational Software
798 North Avenue, Queue, Inc.
Bridgeport, CT 06606
800-232-2244

Selected Microcomputer Software Catalog (Elementary)
Opportunities for Learning, Inc.
8950 Lurline Avenue
Chatsworth, CA 91311

Software Directories

Apple Software Directory
R.R. Bowker Company
205 E. 42nd Street
New York, NY 10017

Book of Apple Software
Arrays, Inc.
6711 Valjean Avenue
Van Nuys, CA 91406
(818) 994-1899

Educomp's Macintosh Public Domain Software Catalog
2429 Oxford Street
Cardiff-by-the-Sea, CA 92007

Kinko's Academic Courseware Exchange
4141 State Street
Santa Barbara, CA 93110
800-292-6640 (outside California)
800-235-6919 (in California)
(catalog information also available on the AppleLink®
network)

MacGuide
The Delta Group, Inc.
818 17th Street, Suite 210
Denver, CO 80202
(303) 935-8100

Macintosh Buyer's Guide
Redgate Communications Corp.
660 Beachland Blvd.
Vero Beach, FL 32963
(407) 231-6904

Personal Computer Software Directory for Apple
Micro Information Publishing
4730 Dakota Street, SE
Prior Lake, MN 55372
(612) 447-6959

Wheels for the Mind
Apple Computer, Inc.
P.O. Box 1834
Escondido, CA 92025

Apple II® Magazines and Newsletters

A + Magazine
One Park Avenue
New York, NY 10016
(212) 503-3500

Access: Apple
Boston Publishing Company
314 Dartmouth Street
Boston, MA 02116
(617) 267-7100

Apple Bits
NEO Apple Corps
1935 Mattingly Road
Hinckley, OH 44233
(216) 225-1097

Apple Index
B P Publications
Box 617
Southbury, CT 06488
(203) 264-2143

Apple Library User Group Newsletter
10381 Bandley Drive
Cupertino, CA 95014
(408) 973-2552

Apple II Review
Redgate Communications Corp.
660 Beachland Blvd.
Vero Beach, FL 32963
(407) 231-6904

Apple User
Database Publications Ltd.
Europa House
68 Chester Road, Hazel Grove
Stockport SK7 5NY, England

Apple's Apprentice
Emerald City Publishing, Inc.
Box 582-AA
Santee, CA 92071
(619) 562-7785

InCider
CW Communications/Peterborough, Inc.
80 Elm Street
Peterborough, NH 03458
(603) 924-9471

On Three
(The reverence resource for the Apple III)
P.O. Box 3824
Ventura, CA 93006
(805) 644-3514

Education Periodicals and Newsletters

Apple Education News
Apple Computer, Inc.
20525 Mariani Avenue, M/S 23TB
Cupertino, CA 95014
(408) 996-1010

Apple Educator's Newsletter
9525 Lucerne Street
Ventura, CA 93004

Apple Library User Group Newsletter
10381 Bandley Drive
Cupertino, CA 95014
(408) 973-2552

Classroom Computer Learning
2451 E. River Road
Dayton, OH 45439
(513) 294-5785
800-543-4838

Computer Student
(The Apple Computer Clubs newsletter)
Computer Publishing Services, Inc.
217 Jackson Street, Box 948
Lowell, MA 01853
(617) 459-7181

The Computing Teacher
University of Oregon
1787 Agate Street
Eugene, OR 97403
(503) 686-4414

Educational Marketer
Knowledge Industries Publications, Inc.
701 Westchester Avenue
White Plains, NY 10604
800-248-KIPI (outside New York)
(914) 328-9157 (in New York)

Electronic Learning
Scholastic, Inc.
730 Broadway
New York, NY 10003
(212) 505-3000

Teaching and Computing
Scholastic, Inc.
730 Broadway
New York, NY 10003
(212) 505-3000

Technology on Campus
2451 E. River Road
Dayton, OH 45439
(513) 294-5785
(800) 543-4838

Information Services

ARPANET
U.S. Dept. of Defense
Defense Communications Agency
Attn: B6-46
Washington, DC 20305
(202) 694-4001
Note: *Only for universities with U.S. Defense Advanced Research Projects Agency (DARPA) projects.*

BITNET
P.O. Box 364
Princeton, NJ 08540
(609) 734-1878
Note: *Your institution must be a degree-granting college or university.*

CompuServe
5000 Arlington Center Boulevard
P.O. Box 20212
Columbus, OH 43220
800-848-8199 (outside Ohio)
(614) 457-0802 (in Ohio)

DELPHI
3 Blackstone Street
Cambridge, MA 02139
800-544-4005

DIALOG Information Services
3460 Hillview Avenue
Palo Alto, CA 94304
(415) 858-3810

GEnie
GEISCO
401 N. Washington Street
Rockville, MD 20850
800-638-9636

The Source
1616 Anderson Road
McLean, VA 22102
800-336-3366

SpecialNet
2021 K Street, NW, Suite 315
Washington, DC 20006

Desktop Publishing

Personal Publishing
The Renegade Company
P.O. Box 390
Itasca, IL 60143

Publish!
P.O. Box 51966
Boulder, CO 80321
800-222-2990

Showpage
1044 Howard Street
San Francisco, CA 94103

REVIEW ANSWER KEY

Multiple Choice

1. d
2. c
3. c
4. a
5. d
6. d
7. b
8. d
9. d
10. b

True/False

1. T
2. F
3. F
4. F
5. T
6. F
7. T
8. T
9. F
10. T

Short Answer

1. K (kilobytes), approximately 1,000 bytes.
2. Students do not learn if the lesson is longer than their attention span.
3. It may be repetitive; it may not maximize computer time; students may find it boring after a few uses.
4. Applications software has many general uses. It is a flexible tool. Students learn real-world computer skills.
5. To protect themselves against piracy.

CHAPTER 13

ETHICS AND SOCIAL CONCERNS

Objectives

- Identify several types of computer fraud, citing examples of theft involving money, goods, information, time, and software
- Identify security measures for access to computers, data processing centers, and confidential records
- Define *technological elitism* and its social ramifications
- Identify the role of the teacher in promoting the ethical use of computers among students
- Describe the concept of the electronic cottage

Key Terms

bootlegging
computer fraud
demagnetization
electronic cottage
elitism
hacker
password
piracy
rounding
security measures
software license
Trojan horse
vaccine
virus

We have only to look around us to see the myriad daily applications of computers in our lives. Computers are now so pervasive in our society that the question of how they can be used most wisely, efficiently, and ethically is no longer academic. Instead, it is a lively issue that demands the attention of anyone interested in computer use. Although many of the purposes for which computers are used are extremely beneficial to the individual and to society, there is an unfortunately wide range of misuse as well. For the past several decades, science fiction writers, philosophers, educators, and many others have been warning us about the dramatic changes that computers will cause in our lives. What will these changes be? How will we adapt to such drastic reorganization of our routines?

Current research seems to offer more questions than answers about these issues, which we must grapple with now if we are to shape a productive and humane future. Indeed, issues such as computer fraud and invasion of individual privacy are no longer matters of speculation: They are immediate concerns that must be addressed as we move further into our technological future. In this chapter, we examine the contemporary problems of computer fraud, invasion of privacy, technological elitism, long-range concerns of shifts in the work force, and the role teachers will play in promoting ethical use of computers in the future.

COMPUTER FRAUD AND MISUSE

Hundreds of thousands of large mainframe computers are used in the United States alone. People directly involved with these systems number in the millions. Many others have access to mainframes through microcomputers. These figures add up to an alarming increase in the incidents of computer abuse, especially computer-related crime—a trend that will likely continue into the future.

Let's look briefly at two examples of **computer fraud** before examining some ingenious schemes.

> A computer analyst at a Wall Street brokerage house programmed a computer to sell nonexistent securities through fictitious accounts. The analyst pocketed $832,000 before the fraud was discovered.
>
> A computer security consultant defrauded a Los Angeles bank of $10.2 million by requesting a funds transfer to an account in a Soviet bank in Switzerland through a computerized system.

What is the cost of this type of theft? The most recent estimate is $4 billion annually, and this may be conservative. Computer crime is big business.

One ingenious case of computer-related theft involved a bank employee whose only computer training was operating a terminal. The employee selected accounts with large amounts of money and few transactions and

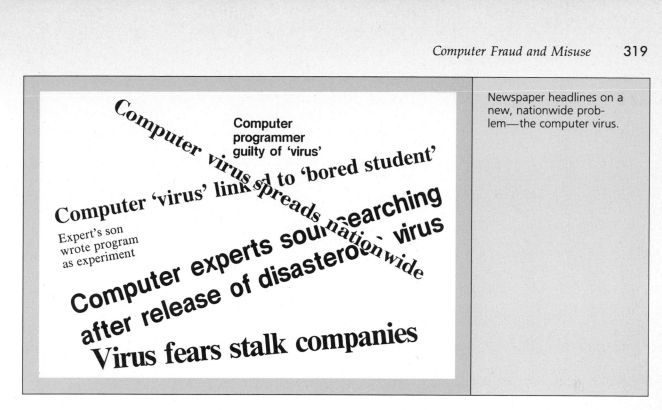

Computer
programmer
guilty of 'virus'

Computer virus linked to 'bored student'

Computer 'virus' spreads nationwide

Expert's son
wrote program
as experiment

Computer experts soul searching
after release of disaster virus

Virus fears stalk companies

used a computer terminal to change the balance figures. Pocketing the difference, he then made sure that the computer quickly "corrected" the error. Using his position as a chief teller to receive advance notice of audits and inspections, he was able to prevent the bank and the customers from becoming suspicious. During a period of three years, he transferred $1.5 million, enabling him to spend up to $30,000 per day to support his gambling habit.

In another case the perpetrator never even touched a computer, although he apparently understood the computer system. After being granted a twelve-month installment loan, he noted the codes on the installment payment forms he received from the bank. Instead of including the top form with his first payment, he sent the bottom form. The bank's computer generated a form thanking him for paying off the loan so promptly. He did not literally steal the money and when the error was finally discovered, he was not prosecuted since he claimed that he had simply made a mistake by sending in the wrong form.

Other cases involve indirect interaction with the computer as well. Several crimes have been committed by using the magnetic or specially shaped character codes placed on checks and deposit slips. In one such case, a man opened an account in the usual fashion and deposited several thousand dollars. After receiving his personalized checks and deposit slips on which his account number was printed, he obtained the blank courtesy deposit slips that are left on the bank's counters. Then he had his magnetic ink code printed on these deposit slips and returned them to the counters in the bank. A number of depositors unwittingly used these fraudulently imprinted deposit slips, expecting the money to be credited to their own accounts. However, the fraudulent coding was read by the computer and the money sent to the thief's account instead. The error was noticed when customers complained that their checks were bouncing after they made deposits to their accounts. By this time, $250,000 had been diverted and $100,000 had disappeared.

Rounding is another technique for diverting funds from one account to another. Banks routinely round interest amounts up or down. Dishonest programmers can instruct the computer to place the rounded-down amounts into a separate account that they created for this purpose. If there are discrepancies, depositors often blame their own mathematical errors and do not complain to the bank.

Theft of Goods

Not only money but also goods are stolen via the computer. Often, goods are ordered in some way through the computer and are sent to a pickup point. For example, one case involved 217 railroad boxcars owned by a bankrupt railroad. Federal agents investigating the case found that a computer program had been altered to show that these cars had been sold to a fictitious company. This company would later "resell" or rent the cars, returning the profit to the owners of the bankrupt company.

Another story of computer-stolen goods began on a young man's way home from school. While rummaging through various trash cans owned by the telephone company, he acquired a library of operating manuals for telephone equipment, not especially valuable then but worth keeping. By this means, he also obtained discarded telephone equipment as well as the instructions for ordering new equipment. Through various ruses he succeeded in getting the codes to access the ordering system. He then set up the telephone equipment in his home, in conjunction with an automatic remote dialer and his own terminal and began ordering new equipment for resale. This project increased to such a grandiose scale that he hired several employees and organized a company to sell the equipment to private suppliers and users until he was caught.

Private industries and individuals are not the only victims of computer-related crime. There are numerous cases on record involving theft of government goods. It is a relatively simple matter for dishonest personnel to adjust computerized supply records so that huge quantities of food, vehicles, parts, fuel, and clothing are delivered to the wrong hands for later resale.

Theft of Information

Items less tangible than money and goods are also stolen or tampered with. Stealing information from a computer and using a computer to market stolen information illegally are not uncommon practices. Many private companies and government agencies maintain computerized lists of their customers and clients. Once these lists are accessed by unauthorized personnel, the information can be sold to others for various uses. For example, a department of motor vehicles employee was charged with adding more than a thousand names to a computerized list of approved applicants for driver's licenses. The employee then sold the licenses to unqualified drivers for a profit of more than $300,000.

Police personnel have been known to sell computerized lists of criminal records to be used as bribery or for blackmail. Tax calculation methods have been sold to those in high tax brackets who benefit from legally claiming deductions. Even health records have been sold. Some information has been held for ransom. The list goes on and on.

This is a serious concern to school personnel who store student records on computers. With access to a computer and the determination to break into confidential records, students have been known to alter the grades of their friends and enemies. Also, students or others can destroy data that is critical to school administrators. Even if the data can be recovered, school personnel must spend a great deal of time and money recreating lost records.

Theft of Time

The theft of computer time is another computer-related crime on the increase. In one case, a high school student who was an electronics enthusiast gained access to a company's computer system to play computer games. People who invade computer systems without authorization are called **hackers**, and their escapades are not always so innocent. In another case, a man used secret passwords to gain access to the computer owned by his former employer. Over long-distance phone lines, he used the computer to direct the operation of machines owned by his present employer. The total commercial value of the time consumed was $15,000. Another case of time theft involved an illegal bookmaker who used a university computer to make his betting calculations.

We have seen how computers can be used to commit crimes against individuals, banks, industries, and government agencies. Computers can also be used to commit crimes against other computer companies. This includes getting access to new computer specifications, future product details, customer lists, and marketing information.

Since computers can be very expensive to buy, rent, operate, and maintain, some users share computers to reduce cost. However, once users gain access to a computer, they have the potential to raid the computer's memory.

Some cases on record involve millions of dollars in business and information stolen in this manner.

Theft of Programs

Software **piracy**, another very serious problem, is the theft of computer programs. Software piracy occurs whenever a person purchases a computer program and then copies it for friends or resale. However, piracy is not limited to individuals: It has spread to microcomputer users' clubs as well, some of which maintain libraries of programs. New members can copy or use these programs rather than purchase them from software retailers.

Some retailers are major perpetrators of software piracy. They buy copies of programs and then duplicate them for resale. These programs are either sold separately or offered as added sales incentives. Some unscrupulous retailers purchase programs at special group rates and then duplicate the programs and resell them, either at the individual rate or at a discount (which is less than the average retailer pays for the product wholesale). This is known as **bootlegging** software.

Software bootlegging occurs on such a large scale that it costs an estimated $2.5 million each month—$1 million in actual losses and $1.5 million in lost sales opportunities. Its success lies in the fact that it is quite easy to copy computer programs. Because of the wear and tear on program disks, most computer programs are written with the capability to copy programs onto tape or disk as backup to be used in case of loss of the original.

Unfortunately, piracy also occurs in the classroom. Many teachers are caught in a bind: They have a class full of students who want to use the same software at the same time, but there's not enough software to go around (usually because of budget limitations). Given the ease with which software can be pirated, it is tempting to make unauthorized copies. Although the act of piracy takes only a few minutes, the ramifications are long term. First, piracy sets a poor example for students, who are, after all, the computer users of the future. Second, it ultimately results in higher prices of CAI software since publishers must raise prices to compensate for losses through piracy.

The International Council for Computers in Education (ICCE) has issued its *Policy Statement on Network and Multiple Machine Software* (1983) that defines the teacher's role in checking piracy in the classroom.

Computer piracy results in higher software prices for the user. Software developers must divide the cost of writing, packaging, and marketing software among the many potential buyers of prepackaged software. Piracy results in fewer legitimate customers and, consequently, higher-priced software packages to guarantee a profit to the developer. Thus, software piracy affects all computer users.

An ethical alternative to piracy is to purchase a **software license**, which permits the purchaser to make a designated number of copies of a program

Publishers of **The Computing Teacher** journal.

[Permission to reproduce is granted.]

ICCE Policy Statement on Network and Multiple Machine Software

Just as there has been shared responsibility in the development of this policy, so should there be shared responsibility for resolution of the problems inherent in providing and securing good educational software. Educators have a valid need for quality software and reasonable prices. Hardware developers and/or vendors also must share in the effort to enable educators to make maximum cost-effective use of that equipment. Software authors, developers and vendors are entitled to a fair return on their investment.

Educators' Responsibilities

Educators need to face the legal and ethical issues involved in copyright laws and publisher license agreements and must accept the responsibility for enforcing adherence to these laws and agreements. Budget constraints do not excuse illegal use of software.

Educators should be prepared to provide software developers or their agents with a district-level approved written policy statement including as a minimum:

1. A clear requirement that copyright laws and publisher license agreements be observed;

2. A statement making teachers who use school equipment responsible for taking all reasonable precautions to prevent copying or the use of unauthorized copies on school equipment;

3. An explanation of the steps taken to prevent unauthorized copying or the use of unauthorized copies on school equipment;

4. A designation of who is authorized to sign software license agreements for the school (or district);

5. A designation at the school site level of who is responsible for enforcing the terms of the district policy and terms of licensing agreements;

6. A statement indicating teacher responsibility for educating students about the legal, ethical and practical problems caused by illegal use of software.

Hardware Vendors' Responsibilities

Hardware vendors should assist educators in making maximum cost effective use of the hardware and help in enforcing software copyright laws and license agreements. They should as a minimum:

1. Make efforts to see that illegal copies of programs are not being distributed by their employees and agents;

2. Work cooperatively with interested software developers to provide an encryption process which avoids inflexibility but discourages theft.

Software Developers'/Vendors' Responsibilities

Software developers and their agents can share responsibility for helping educators observe copyright laws and publishers' license agreements by developing sales and pricing policies. Software developers and vendors should as a minimum:

1. Provide for all software a back-up copy to be used for archival purposes, to be included with every purchase;

2. Provide for on-approval purchases to allow schools to preview the software to ensure that it meets the needs and expectations of the educational institution. Additionally, software developers are encouraged to provide regional or area centers with software for demonstration purposes. The ICCE encourages educators to develop regional centers for this purpose;

3. Work in cooperation with hardware vendors to provide an encryption process which avoids inflexibility but discourages theft;

4. Provide for, and note in advertisements, multiple-copy pricing for school sites with several machines and recognize that multiple copies do not necessarily call for multiple documentation;

5. Provide for, and note in advertisements, network-compatible versions of software with pricing structures that recognize the extra costs of development to secure compatibility and recognize the buyer's need for only a single copy of the software.

The Board of Directors of The International Council for Computers in Education approved this policy statement, with attachments, June 5, 1983.

The International Council for Computers in Education (ICCE) released this policy statement on June 5, 1983, regarding educators' responsibilities in stopping software piracy in the classroom.

ICCE Policy Statement on
Network and Multiple
Machine Software
(continued).

The committee that drafted this policy included:

Jenny Better, Director of Curriculum, Cupertino Union Elementary District
LeRoy Finkel, San Mateo County Office of Education
Pennie Gallant, Apple Computer, Inc.
John Hazelwood/Jeffrey Armstrong, Corvus Systems, Inc.
Marion B. Kenworthy, Saratoga High School
Richard R. Monnard, Addison-Wesley Publishing Co.
Henry Vigil/Cliff Godwin, Cybertronics International
William Wagner, Santa Clara County Office of Education

ATTACHMENT 1
Suggested District Policy on Software Copyright

It is the intent of _____ to adhere to the provisions of copyright laws in the area of microcomputer programs. Though there continues to be controversy regarding interpretation of those copyright laws, the following procedures represent a sincere effort to operate legally. We recognize that computer software piracy is a major problem for the industry and that violations of computer copyright laws contribute to higher costs and greater efforts to prevent copies and/or lessen incentives for the development of good educational software. All of these results are detrimental to the development of effective educational uses of microcomputers. Therefore, in an effort to discourage violation of copyright laws and to prevent such illegal activities:

1. The ethical and practical problems caused by software piracy will be taught in all schools in the District.

2. District employees will be expected to adhere to the provisions of Public Law 96-517, Section 7(b) which amends Section 117 of Title 17 of the United States Code to allow for the making of a back-up copy of computer programs. This states that "... it is not an infringement for the owner of a copy of a computer program to make or authorize the making of another copy or adaptation of that computer program provided:

   a. that such a new copy or adaptation is created as an essential step in the utilization of the computer program in conjunction with a machine and that it is used in no other manner, or

   b. that such a new copy and adaptation is for archival purposes only and that all archival copies are destroyed in the event that continued possession of the computer program should cease to be rightful."

3. When software is to be used on a disk sharing system, efforts will be made to secure this software from copying.

4. Illegal copies of copyrighted programs may not be made or used on school equipment.

5. The legal or insurance protection of the District will not be extended to employees who violate copyright laws.

6. _____ of this school district is designated as the only individual who may sign license agreements for software for schools in the district. (Each school using the software also should have a signature on a copy of the software agreement for local control.)

7. The principal of each school site is responsible for establishing practices which will enforce this policy at the school level.

ATTACHMENT 2
Sample Software Policy of a Community College with a Large Microcomputer Lab

It is the policy of this college that no person shall use or cause to be used in the college's microcomputer laboratories any software which does not fall into one of the following categories:

1. It is in the public domain.

2. It is covered by a licensing agreement with the software author, authors, vendor or developer, whichever is applicable.

3. It has been donated to the college and a written record of a bona fide contribution exists.

4. It has been purchased by the college and a record of a bona fide purchase exists.

5. It has been purchased by the user and a record of a bona fide purchase exists and can be produced by the user upon demand.

6. It is being reviewed or demonstrated by the users in order to reach a decision about possible future purchase or request for contribution or licensing.

7. It has been written or developed by _____ (college employee) for the specific purpose of being used in the _____ (college) microcomputer laboratory.

It is also the policy of the college that there be no copying of copyrighted or proprietary programs on computers belonging to the college.

Source: De Anza College, Cupertino, California.

ATTACHMENT 3
Suggested Format of Software Licenses

1. Designated on a per site, district-wide or other geographic basis.

2. Requires the signature of a responsible school employee.

3. Includes provisions for a single copy purchase (with archival back-up copy) at full price.

4. Multiple-machine pricing:

   Includes provisions for a quantity discount for subsequent purchases of the same software provided:

   a. the purchase discount applies to a single purchase order.
   b. the purchase discount is noncumulative.
   c. the software is for the same computer type.

   i.e.: Radio Shack presently offers a 50% discount for purchases of 10 or more sets of the same software; Gregg/McGraw-Hill offers a discount schedule with incremental increases—buy 2, pay 10% less; 3—20% less; 4—30% less; 5 or more, 40% less.

5. Network Pricing:

   May be offered as per school site or with quantity discount for school districts with multiple sites.

   Provide for a flat license fee for network-compatible versions of the software.

   • flat fee provision is preferred over any variable rate based on number of computers or number of student users.

   • network-compatibility, not just an unlocked version of the software, is required to eliminate the need for local reprogramming of copyrighted and licensed software.

   Include provision for purchase of multiple copies of documentation and accompanying materials.

   i.e.: A flat fee of two times the single copy retail price is offered to network users of Random House software.

ATTACHMENT 4
Some Technical Notes on Software Encryption for Software/Hardware Vendors

1. Single Machine Encryption

Explanation:

The purchased disk is not copiable by ordinary means. The software cannot be transferred to a network system or used on several computers at once. This scheme is the most common, especially for inexpensive software.

Technical notes:

The protected disk is usually formatted in a non-standard way which will defeat standard disk copy programs such as COPYA on the Apple or TRSDOS BACKUP on the TRS-80. Alternatively, the publisher may write special information on the disk in places which the standard disk copy programs do not check. The copy program proceeds to completion, but the special information is not transferred to the duplicate disk. When the duplicate is used, the software checks for the special information, fails to find it, and stops.

Implications:

Schools will need to purchase many copies of the same program and should expect significant volume discounts. The customer is entitled to an archival backup and should expect the publisher to include a backup disk with every purchase.

Manufacturers of network systems should recognize that single machine encryption (which is incompatible with their products) will remain the software industry standard unless they actively support software protection on their systems.

2. Single Site Encryption

Explanation:

A single product can serve all the machines at a site. This scheme applies to VisiCalc™ and Logo.

Technical Notes:

Software which loads initially into memory and subsequently interacts only with data disks is de facto "single site encrypted," even though the program disk may be uncopiable. A single program disk can be used to initialize all the computers in a room, after which each user operates with his or her own data disks. VisiCalc™ and Logo operate in this way.

A functionally equivalent alternative is referred to as "master and slave" or "lock and key" encryption. This scheme is common where a program is too large to fit it in memory all at once. Frequent disk access is needed as different parts of the software are brought into play.

In the "lock and key" scheme, the program modules which are routinely needed can be freely copied. A "slave" disk containing these modules is duplicated for each computer (or even for each student). The slave will not operate, however, unless the computer has been cold started with the (uncopiable) master disk.

ICCE Policy Statement on
Network and Multiple
Machine Software
(continued).

Implications:
Since the "master" disk is uncopiable, the publisher still bears the burden of providing an archival backup. The protection on the "master" disk normally makes the software incompatible with network systems, so the above comments again apply.

Single site encryption reduces the dependence on volume discounts to facilitate multiple machine use. However, volume discounts should still be made available at the district level to encourage district level adoption of software.

3. Hard Disk/Network Compatible Versions of Software
Explanation:
Floppy disks containing network compatible software must be copiable since the software is copied as it is transferred onto the network. The problem of protecting network compatible software is how to allow this legitimate copying while preventing illegal copying.

One solution is to abandon software protection altogether and to rely on license agreements to prevent illegal use of the program(s). The problem with this solution is that freely copiable software may be freely copied.

Other solutions rely on publishing special versions of the software for the various network systems available. These versions do not run on stand-alone computers.

A publisher can also take steps to discourage people from installing the network software at sites other than the intended site.

Technical Notes:
A publisher can prevent network software from running on a stand-alone computer by using a device check. The software senses whether it is running on a network system and stops if it is not. The device check is specific to the network system involved. Software with a device check could be installed at many network sites, not just the one for which it was licensed.

To discourage use at non-licensed sites, the publisher can embed the name of the licensee in the software. This requires that the publisher customize each network-compatible version sold. Although such customization discourages porting the software to another network site, it does not physically prevent it.

To prevent porting of the software to another network, the publisher might implement what is essentially single machine encryption on the network level. This protection scheme would work by checking the serial number or other unique identifier in the network hardware. If the software encountered a change in identifier, it would fail to operate. This has the disadvantages that a licensee would have to be a single network installation and that normal activities such as replacing or upgrading one's network system would disable the software.

Implications:
Use of a device check or serial number check requires a publisher to maintain a separate inventory item for each device to be supported. The time required for a publisher to embed the customer's name in each product sold for use on networks can become prohibitive.

These protection schemes may prove economically unfeasible for inexpensive software.

These protection schemes require close working relationships and sharing of information between publishers and network system manufacturers.

University of Oregon   1787 Agate St.   Eugene, OR 97403 USA   503/686-4414

for multiple users. The license is more cost-effective than purchasing individual copies of a program.

We have discussed how people use computers illegally for personal gain and how these schemes victimize everyone. Now, we turn our attention to crimes in which the computer itself is a victim. We examine some of the reasons behind these attacks and then explore some of the methods of abuse.

PHYSICAL ABUSE OF COMPUTERS

Recently several books and articles have attempted to explain the motivation behind physical abuse of computers. Many attacks result from persons who view the computer as a destroyer of personal identity. Some people regard the computer as a detested symbol of corporate capitalism. Other acts are committed by computer users in moments of frustrated, irrational outbursts. Sometimes attacks are planned for political reasons.

Computer equipment can be damaged in many ways. Instruments used to damage computers include guns, pointed objects, fire, and magnets. In 1986, students at a high school in Sacramento fired numerous shots into a computer used to notify parents of student absences. Computer sabotage has also been used by radical and revolutionary groups to express protest. During the war in Vietnam, a number of computers at American universities were targets of abuse, especially those thought to be connected with Defense Department research. Many other examples have been cited. In 1970 in a bombing at the University of Wisconsin, one person was fatally injured; damage to the computer was estimated at more that $500,000. During the same year, a Molotov cocktail damaged a computer at Fresno State University in California, costing the school $1 million. In 1973, in Melbourne, Australia, antiwar demonstrators used a double-barrelled shotgun to extensively damage a computer in the offices of an American computer manufacturer.

Demagnetization is another commonly used method of destroying data stored magnetically, as on magnetic tape and floppy and hard disks. By passing any magnetic material near the storage media, the data will be erased. In 1970, an antiwar group attacked data processing facilities, destroying equipment, punch cards, and magnetic tape. Several magnets were found in the rubble, and since some of the tapes had been erased by demagnetization, it is safe to assume that these magnets were used to destroy the data. Reconstructing the lost information cost more than $100,000.

The latest danger to befall computers is called a **virus**, which is a destructive program that causes an undesirable action to occur, such as data loss. Programmer saboteurs bury virus programs within other harmless programs called **Trojan horses**. A user purchases a Trojan horse without realizing that it contains a virus.

It may take a considerable length of time to detect a virus in the computer. Virus programs are usually designed to lie dormant until triggered by a certain sequence of keystrokes or a particular date. But this is not

An illustration of how a computer virus works.

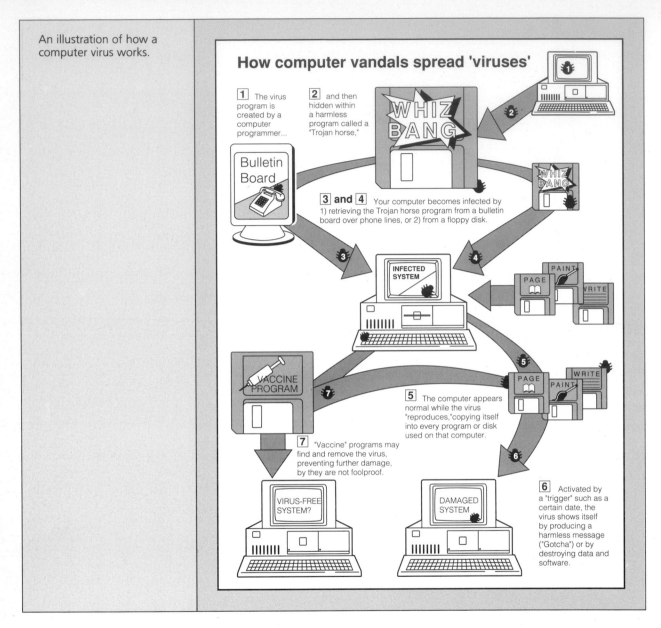

How computer vandals spread 'viruses'

1 The virus program is created by a computer programmer...

2 and then hidden within a harmless program called a "Trojan horse,"

Bulletin Board

3 and **4** Your computer becomes infected by 1) retrieving the Trojan horse program from a bulletin board over phone lines, or 2) from a floppy disk.

INFECTED SYSTEM

VACCINE PROGRAM

7 "Vaccine" programs may find and remove the virus, preventing further damage, by they are not foolproof.

5 The computer appears normal while the virus "reproduces,"copying itself into every program or disk used on that computer.

VIRUS-FREE SYSTEM?

DAMAGED SYSTEM

6 Activated by a "trigger" such as a certain date, the virus shows itself by producing a harmless message ("Gotcha") or by destroying data and software.

always the case. For example, on November 1, 1988 a person entered into the computer a virus which was intended to live innocently and undetected in ARPANET, the U.S. Department of Defense computer network. But a design error in the virus caused it to replicate out of control. This virus ultimately jammed more than 6,000 computers nationwide, including computers at the Rand Corporation, SRI International, Lawrence Livermore Laboratories, the Massachusetts Institute of Technology, and military bases all over the United States. The virus spread by "mailing" itself to other computers under the auspices of a legitimate user. Since the program continued to replicate itself, it slowed down and then eventually shut down all the computers to which it gained access. In a case like this, the potential threat of a computer virus is no laughing matter, as it could have compromised the defense of the country.

To solve the problem, **vaccine** programs are being written to detect and eradicate virus programs. Though they are not always effective, vaccines help alleviate the problem. Apple Computer recently offered a program called Virus Rx to its customers after learning that certain Macintosh computers owned by NASA had fallen victim to a virus. At the same time, Apple began an investigation with the hope of prosecuting the programmer who created the virus, pointing out that virus programming is a serious and intolerable computer crime.

MAINTAINING SECURITY

There is a definite need for security of computer equipment and its data. This is true for a computer system of any size, from a large mainframe system with extensive peripheral equipment to a microcomputer on a stu-

A computer virus composed of "sh" files.

Computer virus contamination across the United States.

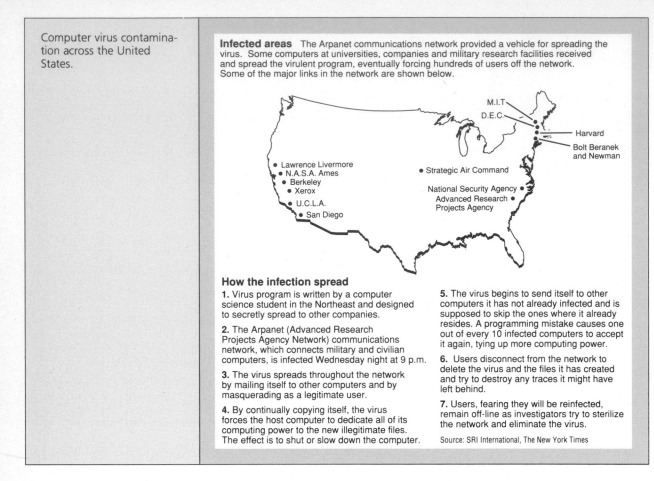

Infected areas The Arpanet communications network provided a vehicle for spreading the virus. Some computers at universities, companies and military research facilities received and spread the virulent program, eventually forcing hundreds of users off the network. Some of the major links in the network are shown below.

How the infection spread

1. Virus program is written by a computer science student in the Northeast and designed to secretly spread to other companies.

2. The Arpanet (Advanced Research Projects Agency Network) communications network, which connects military and civilian computers, is infected Wednesday night at 9 p.m.

3. The virus spreads throughout the network by mailing itself to other computers and by masquerading as a legitimate user.

4. By continually copying itself, the virus forces the host computer to dedicate all of its computing power to the new illegitimate files. The effect is to shut or slow down the computer.

5. The virus begins to send itself to other computers it has not already infected and is supposed to skip the ones where it already resides. A programming mistake causes one out of every 10 infected computers to accept it again, tying up more computing power.

6. Users disconnect from the network to delete the virus and the files it has created and try to destroy any traces it might have left behind.

7. Users, fearing they will be reinfected, remain off-line as investigators try to sterilize the network and eliminate the virus.

Source: SRI International, The New York Times

dent's desk. While it is reasonable in large organizations to allow only authorized personnel to enter the computer room, in most schools such a security measure would be unrealistic. However, access to the administrative computer containing confidential records should be limited. Security measures in the computer lab and in individual classes would be necessarily broader.

Security Measures   **Security measures** are actions taken to prevent the fraudulent use or destruction of computer equipment. These measures include something a person has (a key or badge), something a person knows (a password), or something about a person (a fingerprint, a voice print, a facial feature).

Most large companies have security systems that one must pass through to gain access to the computer room. These systems may use special cards to insert or buttons to press on the outer door of the computer room.

However, according to many computer security experts, security needs to be even tighter. They advocate the use of many logical but frequently overlooked security measures.

One measure allows only the personnel necessary to perform certain functions to be in a certain place, for instance, in the computer room. Therefore, once programs are written and in place, computer programmers should not be allowed to go into the computer room and should never be allowed to run their programs. Another measure requires the investigation of staff and security clearances for those who work with confidential information. A third measure establishes a system for efficiently investigating suspected breaches of security.

No system is ever foolproof, but every effort should be made to ensure the security of both computer and data. Setting up controls helps to prevent unauthorized and fraudulent modification of data during processing and ensures the validity, integrity, and accuracy of applications and system software during design, programming, testing, and implementation.

Computer centers commonly use another popular measure—the **password**, which usually is a coded sequence. Passwords are frequently used to gain access to the computer via a computer terminal or a telephone hookup. Most users have limited access that allows them to perform specific functions. Other users require more flexible access. Authorization is granted to particular users at different levels, ranging from a particular group of items in the database to an entire data file, database, or program.

For example, student files set up for the teacher's use should not be accessible to students. By the same token, the teacher should not be able to access the personnel files available to the principal.

One effective security measure that organizations can use to minimize the possibility of computer crime is to screen potential employees carefully during the hiring process. Many private detective agencies have investigators who specialize in this area.

Although the security risks covered here threaten large computer systems, microcomputers are also at risk. These systems are even more vulnerable because they are transportable and more easily hidden. For instance, data files and programs can be stolen by simply slipping a floppy disk into a coat pocket or a briefcase. In addition, disks can be destroyed easily by magnets or fire.

An effective security system drastically reduces computer crime. But, as we have seen in the beginning of this chapter, it is not always easy to eliminate fraud. Computer crimes have been discovered in a number of ways, including accidental exposure, careful audits, inside informants, and unfortunate circumstances (unfortunate, that is, for the perpetrator). Detection of crime is one matter; reporting crime is often quite another.

Reporting Crime

Teaching and regulating ethics are extremely difficult. Once breaks in security are discovered, many organizations become very reluctant to admit them. Consider what happens when a company reveals a fraud scheme involving its computer.

First, if customers see how easy it is to tap the company's records and accounts, the trust and integrity of the company might easily be undermined. Large amounts of business could be lost, costing the company more than the original theft. Second, the case would be reported in newspapers. The company executives would be embarrassed and seem foolish; they might even lose their jobs. Third, losses not covered by insurance would have to be made up from company profits, which would certainly displease stockholders and owners. Therefore, the reasons for keeping computer crimes secret are easy to understand. Fortunately, many industries, especially the banking industry, have federal controls that encourage reporting of such crimes.

Other factors cause businesses to hide computer crimes. Proving that someone has stolen materials or money using the computer is often difficult and, consequently, costly. It is sometimes cheaper to write off losses and then work to prevent such situations from occurring again. Indeed, it may even be cheaper to keep the crime a secret than to prosecute.

August Bequai (1978) and other authors state that part of the problem associated with computer crime stems from the relative newness of handling large amounts of data by computer. In the past, data were handled in ways that provided physical evidence. Nowadays, computer-generated physical evidence—printouts—must be authenticated by experts. Sometimes the originals must be located. The legal system is currently wrestling with this and other evidential issues.

SAFEGUARDING INDIVIDUAL PRIVACY

Thus far, we have discussed crimes and abuses committed by individuals for their own personal gain. Many of these crimes affect us only indirectly, through increased prices and lowered standards of quality. However, one aspect of computer crime may have an impact on each and every one of us: invasion of privacy resulting from improper use of databases.

Until 1974, there was little concern about privacy with regard to data banks. Few data banks shared their information, since manual access was slow and inefficient. However, as technology has advanced and data banks evolved into databases, so has concern for privacy of the individual increased. In 1974, President Gerald Ford signed the Privacy Act into law. Its purpose was to protect confidentiality of files generated by the federal government. Its principles are paraphased below:

- There must be no personal-data record-keeping systems whose very existence is secret.

- There must be a way for individuals to find out what information about them is in a record and how it is used.
- There must be a way for individuals to prevent information about them obtained for one purpose from being used or made available for other purposes without their consent.
- There must be a way for individuals to correct or amend records of identifiable information about them.
- Organizations creating, maintaining, using, or disseminating records of identifiable personal data must assure the reliability of the data for their intended use and must take reasonable precautions to prevent misuse of the data.

Let's examine the privacy issue with regard to several situations. First, consider credit checks. Today, we are a nation of borrowers. In fact, we have become so dependent upon credit that much business probably could not exist without it. Cars are bought on time payments, merchandise is charged to credit cards, and homes are mortgaged. All these items are bought on deferred payment plans requiring the establishment of credit.

Problems always arise whenever there is access to credit information. Questions range from who is authorized to access the information to how much information that person is entitled to know. In addition, the information available may or may not be accurate. For example, data might have been entered incorrectly, resulting in denial of credit purchases. Often, information is entered into a system but is never removed. A record of an arrest in a law enforcement database may be entered without indication of whether or not the person was acquitted of the charge. This same information may result in a university refusing an applicant admission.

Another problem results from the unrestricted use of data. The large amounts of data available today often become accessible to more people than originally intended. The growth of government obviously increases the amount of data collected. In addition, data collected by one agency is often shared and used by other agencies for other purposes.

We submit tax forms to the Internal Revenue Service each year. The Census Bureau gathers information. Law enforcement data banks compile criminal records. Motor vehicle departments contain registrations of car ownerships and licenses. There are voter registration lists. With this wide range of information available, the possibility exists to merge these databases. Such a merger could produce a detailed picture of an individual, threatening the individual's right to privacy. Many doctors and other professionals are reluctant to store client information in computer systems because of such a threat.

With such capability, privacy has become a major issue that must be resolved by a thorough understanding of the implications of access to databases. The computer is invaluable in the proper collection and distribution of information. It is up to those with access to use this information legally, wisely, and ethically.

THE CHANGING LABOR FORCE

Yet another issue of primary concern to our society in the years ahead is the dramatic shift in the labor force that will result from automation of functions that human workers now perform. Experts predict that by 1990 we will experience a shift of fifty percent of the labor force away from industrial jobs and toward technological jobs. Of course, a movement of this magnitude brings with it many concerns.

The major problem our society will face is to find jobs for the workers displaced by the anticipated shift. It is now apparent that the jobs of the future will be much more technologically oriented than are the jobs of today. Those people who are computer literate will be in a far better position to step into these jobs than will those who have no such training. The demand for trained professionals to work with computers is expected to double, and perhaps even triple, in the next decade.

The people who will be displaced are those performing routine manufacturing tasks that can readily be automated. How will we accomplish the vast amount of training necessary to prepare these displaced workers for technical jobs? What about people who resist education or are intimidated by the idea of working with computers? These are large questions of great consequence that must be addressed by leaders and educators today so that we may handle this change successfully.

The Electronic Cottage   In his landmark book *The Third Wave*, Alvin Toffler points out another change soon to occur in the working habits of our society. Toffler, echoing the sentiments of many futurists, suggests that we may very soon perform most of our work in our homes on remote terminals or microcomputers. Thus, in the future we will find ourselves living in what Toffler terms **electronic cottages**. This trend will bring about a number of social changes.

One reason the concept of the electronic cottage is so appealing to many is that it offers a viable alternative to the problems faced by commuters. If people didn't have to drive long distances to the work place, vast amounts of time and energy would be saved. Problems such as finding a parking space and coping with rush-hour traffic would be virtually unknown, and the level of pollution would decrease dramatically.

Yet another effect of this trend would be to broaden the work force substantially. People who, for some reason, have not wanted or been able to leave their homes would be able to stay at home to work. Handicapped people and parents of small children have often been hard pressed to maintain employment. The electronic cottage is a solution for these people.

However, with this scenario, many people fear that the people in the computerized society of tomorrow will be alienated from each other and

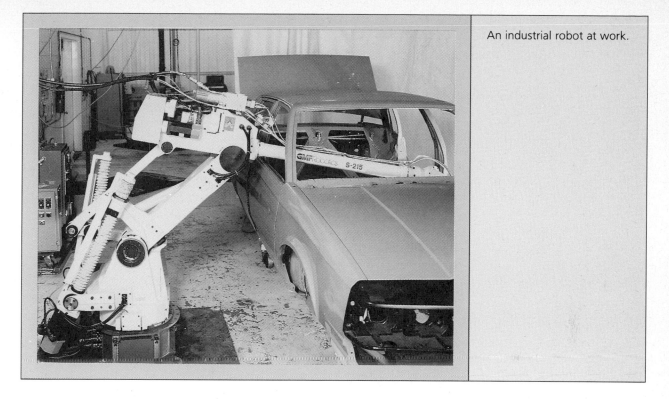

An industrial robot at work.

dehumanized by constant contact with electronic entities. Toffler believes that this will *not* occur. In fact, he suggests that a society comprised of electronic cottages would be far more stable than the communities of today. A worker would no longer need to relocate across the country to change jobs: Instead, that worker would simply connect with a different mainframe computer! This would certainly encourage people to become more actively involved in communities in which they expect to live for long periods of time.

The electronic cottage concept may also serve to reinforce family ties, since parents could work in their homes and be more available to their children. The time and energy that these people would otherwise spend in commuting could well be spent interacting with their children. Married couples might choose to share jobs, both working in the home. This could encourage the sharing of other tasks as well as help to bond relationships further. Toffler even suggests that children may be capable of sharing jobs with their parents, which would not only bond parent and child but would also teach children a sense of responsibility.

ETHICAL CONCERNS IN EDUCATION

So far our discussion of computer crime and the drastic changes that computers are causing in our society have pointed up some of the new responsibilities that teachers are facing. Two questions in particular demand immediate answers.

First, how can we ensure equal computer access to all students? Educators are concerned that only students in more affluent school districts are receiving adequate computer literacy training. Those in areas where funding is more limited may receive little or no hands-on experience with computers. This creates a dangerous form of technological **elitism**. In a society where most desirable employment is technologically oriented, those with more computer training will enjoy higher salaries, better fringe benefits, and a generally superior lifestyle. Conversely, those who receive little or no computer training will be severely disadvantaged in a computerized society.

Educators have a responsibility to make certain that all students have sufficient access to computers, regardless of ethnic or socioeconomic background. To do less is to doom underprivileged children to an underprivileged adulthood. It is necessary to create and support programs that reach out to all students and prepare them equally for productive citizenship in our increasingly technological world. This issue and other ethical concerns are addressed by the ICCE in their *Code of Ethical Conduct for Computer-Using Educators* (1986).

Second, how can we teach our students to use computers in an ethical manner? Educators share with parents and society at large the task of teaching ethical use of computers. There are two effective methods of accomplishing this. First, the teacher must set an example of ethical behavior whenever using or discussing the computer in the classroom. A lecture on the evils of software piracy becomes meaningless if the teacher practices piracy.

Also, the teacher can spend class time discussing ethical issues with students. There are many role-playing models that cast students as software pirates, software publishers, and so on. This gives students an opportunity to consider computer crime from all angles and can spark discussions that help students develop and clarify their own ethical codes.

There are also simulations available to encourage students to tackle ethical questions. Two such simulations were designed by Larry Hannah (1985). The Senate Committee Hearing on Software Copyright Laws simulation divides students into senators, lobbyists, and reporters. Students learn about how Senate committee hearings are conducted while at the same time debating ethical ramifications of software piracy. Voyage to Planet Ecco gives students an opportunity to participate in deciding what kind of society they want to create on the never-before-inhabited Planet Ecco. Work-

Code of Ethical Conduct for Computer-Using Educators

An ICCE Policy Statement

Permission to reproduce all or part of this document is granted.
Please acknowledge the ICCE Ethics and Equity Committee.

Preamble

Educators should believe in the essential importance of knowledge, morality, skill and understanding to the dignity and worth of human beings, individually and collectively. Educators develop the dignity and worth of their students through organized learning. As they do, they should defend the freedom to teach and to learn, and recognize that everybody should have an equal opportunity to learn. The duty to support these beliefs is not limited by the particular educator's role.

As an educator using computers, I work with an instrument that is changing the ways people teach and learn. I will use the computer and help learners and my colleagues use the computer only in ways that promote the dignity and worth of the learners. I accept the following code of ethics and will look to it when faced with unanticipated situations. I am willing to evaluate others and be evaluated on the basis of this code.

Principle I. Curriculum Issues

I have some responsibility for defining the roles of computers in the school curriculum and for assessing significant and likely intended and unintended consequences of those roles. In fulfilling these goals, I will:

a. Evaluate the type of computer instruction being given and to whom it is being given. The evaluation will examine planned and unplanned outcomes, including changes in the roles of teachers, students and administrators.

b. Judge where computers are and are not desirable in learning environments.

c. Strive toward integrating use of the computer, where appropriate, at all levels and throughout the curriculum.

d. Constantly evaluate the effectiveness of computer use toward achieving my goals.

e. When appropriate, provide teacher training for integrating computers into the curriculum and for the changes in curriculum that computer use brings.

f. Evaluate software covering controversial activities or using a controversial methodology or paradigm to determine its appropriateness for my students.

g. Ensure that my use of computers adequately reflects uses the student will have outside school now or in the future.

h. Ensure that the curriculum addresses topics related to information technology.

Principle II. Issues Relating to Computer Access

I support and encourage policies that extend equitable computer access to all students, and I will actively support well-reasoned programs and policies that promote such use. In fulfilling these goals, I will:

a. Strive to see that all students have equal access to computers and computer-related experiences. I will see that students have such access no matter what their academic potential, ethnicity, gender, socio-economic group, or special education status.

b. Support and encourage equity among schools in terms of availability and breadth of computer technology use.

c. Support and encourage equitable computer use among departments and subject areas.

d. Attempt to provide curriculum materials for computer use that will have meaning and appeal to all learning styles.

Principle III. Privacy/Confidentiality Issues

I have varying degrees of responsibility for the development of policy that guarantees the proper use of computerized and non-computerized information in the school's possession. In fulfilling these goals, I will:

a. Respect the privacy of others and exercise this respect when handling computer-stored information.

b. Review the use of computer systems and networks to ensure appropriate confidentiality and privacy for all.

c. Ensure that access to data bases does not exceed the limitations of use granted at the time the data were provided.

d. Teach to those I supervise the legal and social responsibilities that attend collecting, manipulating and disclosing data—in school and in society.

The ICCE Code of Ethical Conduct, which addresses the issue of equal access to computers for all students, was developed in December 1986.

The ICCE Code of Ethical Conduct (continued).

Principle IV. Teacher-Related Issues

Administrators and curriculum supervisors are responsible for overseeing the proper use of computers in the school setting, whether as a tool for teachers or as a multipurpose technology for students. In order to redefine the teacher's role in light of the integration of computers into classrooms, each teacher must have a minimum level of general computer literacy, including skills and knowledge about computers appropriate to the classroom setting and subject area. In addition, each teacher must accept the responsibility to practice as a professional according to the highest ethical standards. In fulfilling these goals, administrators and curriculum supervisors will:

a. Strive to obtain teacher training appropriate to needs for classroom use of computers.

b. Include planning for equitable management of computer resources.

c. Participate in evaluation of results of educational computer use.

d. Strive to provide teachers with release time for computer training to a level of competency consistent with their projected use of computers.

e. Give attention to teaching students the ethics of computer use.

f. Participate in the selection of computer use goals.

g. Strive to provide opportunities for teachers to learn about future situations when making decisions about the pace and nature of computer integration.

h. Strive for computer literacy for both teachers and students.

i. Consider likely future situations when making decisions about the pace and nature of computer integration.

j. Help teachers keep up with current trends, research and literature related to computer developments affecting education and with the curricular implications of these developments.

Principle V. Student Issues

One way to measure success is by the progress of each student toward realization of potential as a worthy and effective citizen. To help fulfill this goal, I will:

a. Help students learn about future trends and possible impacts and consequences of a computerized society.

b. Demonstrate respect for computer ethics in the school, which includes not permitting unauthorized duplication of software by my students.

c. Ensure that students have opportunities to evaluate their current and future roles and the impact their actions can have on future consequences in a computerized society.

d. Help students learn to evaluate the models which underlie simulations on which major societal decisions are made.

e. Help students examine issues that relate to computer ethics.

Principle VI. The Community

The general community, parents and educators share responsibility for creating learning environments. In fulfilling responsibilities to the community, I will:

a. Provide training to members of the educational or general community when asked and when practical.

   1. Increase parental and community knowledge of possible educational goals that involve computers and of how these goals can be realized.

   2. Encourage parental involvement in long-term planning of computer use.

   3. Coordinate expectations for computer use between home and school.

b. Extend the standards of respect for copyright into school/community interactions.

c. Evaluate what control donors should have over the use of hardware and software they provide.

Principle VII. School Organizational Issues

Effective and efficient use of computers in education requires organizational support. In fulfilling this responsibility, I will:

a. Participate in short- and long-range plans to introduce and manage hardware and software in schools.

b. Encourage the development and maintenance of adequate support structures within the school district and region.

c. Encourage funding for computers in schools according to a planned strategy for their integration.

Principle VIII. Software Issues

I have some responsibility for the acquisition, development and dissemination of software in the school environment. In fulfilling these responsibilities, I will:

a. Discourage and refuse to support unauthorized duplication of software by students or educators.

b. Discourage and refuse to support unauthorized duplication of printed material related to copyrighted software.

c. Evaluate the quality of software for classroom use.

b. Discourage and refuse to support unauthorized duplication of printed material related to copyrighted software.

c. Evaluate the quality of software for classroom use.

d. Analyze software for equitable gender and ethnic representation.

e. Acknowledge the ethics of developers and vendors who adhere to truth in advertising and marketing, who deliver a product that serves learners' interests and needs, and who promote equity.

f. Encourage, through purchasing decisions, those vendors who make reasonable provisions for backup copies and multiple access.

g. Evaluate software in the light of the needs of prospective users and the goals of school and community.

Principle IX. Hardware Issues

I share responsibility for the quality and improvement of hardware used by educators and students. In fulfilling this responsibility, I will:

a. Set standards for the acquisition, development and dissemination of hardware used in education.

b. Respect the efforts and expertise of hardware developers and vendors, particularly when they risk extending the uses of the computer.

c. Acknowledge the ethics of developers and vendors who adhere to truth in advertising and marketing, who deliver a product that serves learners' interests and needs, who make provision for after-sale maintenance and training, and who promote equity.

d. Allow for cooperative participation of teachers and administrators in the selection of equipment.

e. Develop and communicate criteria for hardware used in education.

f. Plan hardware purchases that address longitudinal strategies for computer use in schools.

The Board of Directors of the International Council for Computers in Education approved this policy statement December, 1986.

The members of the ICCE Ethics and Equity Committee are:

Chair, Daniel T. Shere, Director of Finance, Employment Readiness Support Center
Lana Bernhardt, Principal, Kibbutz Hanita Elementary School
Larry Hannah, Professor, Sacramento State University
Deryn Watson, Computers in the Curriculum, Chelsea College
Doris Ray, Project Director, Maine Computer Consortium
Brent E. Wholeben, Professor, University of Texas at El Paso
Jo Ann Wilton, Coordinator of Computer Education, Peel Board of Education, Mississauga, Ontario

For more information contact Daniel T. Shere, 7890 E. Spring #2G, Long Beach, CA 90815.

The ICCE Code of Ethical Conduct (continued).

ing cooperatively, they decide how computers will be used on the planet, enabling them to examine the long-term implications of computer use and the changes that accompany it. (Further information on these simulations is available from Larry Hannah, Post Office Box 119, Shingle Springs, California 95682.)

We have only begun to experience the radical changes that computers will effect on society as we know it. Computer scientists and sociologists differ in their estimates of our technological future: Some foresee a stark 1984-type world of humanoid robots and mechanized human beings; others, Toffler among them, predict a bright future in which humans, aided by advanced technology, function with greater freedom than ever before. Who is right remains to be seen, but this much is certain: Computers are bound to change our lives and our society in dramatic and irrevocable ways.

SUMMARY

Computer fraud and abuse take many forms: theft of money and goods, unlawful use of information stored in computers' memories, and unauthorized use of computer time. Sometimes computers themselves are victims of sabotage. Hackers enter computer systems without authorization. Software piracy, which is the theft of computer programs, can cause software prices to increase. (The software license is an incentive to discourage piracy.) The computer virus is another major concern of computer security. The entry of a virus can destroy or damage records and shut down computers. Generally, viruses are difficult to detect, but vaccines are available to overcome them.

Computer crimes are on the increase partly because of the increasing number of computers in society. Computers affect more and more lives every day in many ways. Some people feel intimidated by a machine with so much influence. Perhaps with the advent of microcomputers, more people will see that the computer is a beneficial tool that can be controlled.

There are various methods of maintaining security in the computer room, primarily by limiting access to the room to authorized personnel. The password is the most popular method of controlling entry into a computer system and limiting access to records. In addition, many organizations screen potential employees in the hiring process. However, computer crime is often difficult to detect. In many instances, the crime is not reported to law enforcement agencies for fear of losing customer confidence in the company and its services.

In addition to concerns for the security of organizations, there is concern for the rights of individuals. The Federal Privacy Act of 1974 was made into law to protect the confidentiality of files generated by federal government computers. Several state governments have passed laws to further protect the average citizen from illegal use of computer information.

Besides computer crime, the issue of changes in the labor force is another major concern. Experts predict a fifty percent shift in the labor force from industrial jobs toward more technologically oriented jobs. We must prepare for this shift by planning ways of training the displaced workers, many of whom may be resistant to change, for new and redefined careers.

Yet another significant change in the labor force will occur as increasing numbers of workers perform work tasks from home computers. The electronic cottage may well be the workplace of tomorrow, bringing with it vast changes in our society.

Teachers face new challenges in computer-based education. First, they must strive to provide equal access to computers to all students, regardless of ethnic and socioeconomic background. Second, they must promote computer ethics in their classrooms. They can do this by setting an example of ethical computer use and by using tools such as role-playing and simulations to examine ethical questions.

REVIEW EXERCISES

Multiple Choice

1. Passwords are a
   a. common security control device used to gain access to a computer
   b. means of controlling who enters the building in which the computer is located
   c. special name given to each employee in a computer center
   d. special name given to all employees of a particular company
2. Much computer crime is discovered
   a. by accident
   b. easily
   c. only by the police
   d. by a lawyer
3. Magnets can
   a. destroy files of data
   b. do no harm to computer data
   c. do only marginal damage to the surface of magnetic tape
   d. be used to hold the tape reel on the tape drive
4. A common form of computer crime is
   a. arson
   b. fraud
   c. shooting a gun at the computer
   d. pouring coffee on the computer
5. Privacy of computer records
   a. is of the same concern today as it has always been
   b. has little importance in our society
   c. is not as important today as it was when data was all on cards
   d. is a growing concern
6. What percentage of our labor force is expected to shift from industrial to technologically oriented jobs in the next decade?
   a. 10 percent
   b. 25 percent
   c. 50 percent
   d. 75 percent
7. According to Alvin Toffler, workers of the future will perform work at home in
   a. electronic cottages
   b. databases
   c. intelligent terminals
   d. computer rooms
8. People who have sufficient access to computer power are known as
   a. technologically elite
   b. geniuses
   c. computer programmers
   d. hackers
9. A _____ is a destructive computer program that results in undesirable outcomes.
   a. bug
   b. hacker
   c. virus
   d. password
10. A common form of computer fraud in schools is
    a. destroying library records
    b. grade tampering
    c. creating imaginary students
    d. stealing lunch money

True/False

1. Security measures ensure that only authorized people have access to the computer and its various files.
2. The 1974 Privacy Act was signed by Gerald Ford to provide greater privacy of vital records.
3. Computer crime is a diminishing problem.
4. Computer criminals are easy to prosecute.
5. Only computer experts can use computers to steal information and money.
6. Workers displaced from industrial jobs during the next decade can readily be placed into technological jobs.
7. Toffler believes that electronic cottages are likely to result in more stable, smaller communities.
8. Hackers are people who destroy computers with guns, magnets, and fire.
9. Computer programs that allow unscrupulous people to gain access to credit records are called Trojan horses.
10. Teachers can promote ethical conduct through class discussions, role-playing, and simulations.

Short Answer

1. Name two types of computer fraud and give examples.
2. Why do some people physically abuse computers?

3. How does Toffler see interpersonal relationships changing in a society of electronic cottages? How would these changes affect our views and expectations of society?
4. Do the five principles of fair information practice cited in this chapter seem reasonable? How might they be changed to be more effective?
5. What are the dangers of technological elitism?

Activities

1. Describe recent cases of fraudulent uses of computers.
2. Discuss security measures necessary for a computer center.
3. Research violations of individual rights to privacy through unauthorized access to records.
4. Research the problem of training displaced industrial workers and suggest several methods of accomplishing such training.
5. Obtain a simulation dealing with computer ethics. Lead your classmates in completing the simulation.
6. List several recent cases of viruses and what was done to remove them.
7. Describe how the U.S. government maintains security on all records pertaining to individuals.
8. Visit a local credit bureau and list the steps necessary for accessing your personal credit information.
9. List all the local, state, and national government databases that contain data about you. Be as specific as possible.
10. Describe how a person could be characterized using all the information about them stored in computer systems.

BIBLIOGRAPHY

Apcar, Leonard M. "Old Computers Jeopardizing Work at IRS." *Wall Street Journal* 108 (no. 57, March 23, 1983).

Bequai, August. *Computer Crime*. Lexington, Mass.: D. C. Heath, 1978.

Bitter, Gary G. (with K. Gore). "Curricular Implications of a 'Computer for Every Student'." *Computers in the Schools* 3 (no. 2, Summer 1986): 15–21.

Bitter, Gary G. (with Shelly Davis). "Measuring the Development of Computer Literacy Among Teachers." *AEDS Journal* (Fall 1985): 243–253.

Collis, Betty. "Building a Global Village." *The Computing Teacher* 15 (no. 2): 5.

_____ . "Sex Related Differences in Attitude Toward Computers: Implications for Counselors." *The School Counselor* (November 1985): 120–130.

Dietz, Lawrence D. "Computer Security: Not Just for Mainframes." *Mini-Micro Systems* 15 (no. 6, June 1982): 251–256.

"Ethics in Computer Use." *The Computing Teacher* 12 (no. 1, August-September 1984).

Gordon, Al. " 'Viruses' Pose Tricky Threat to Computers." *Arizona Republic* (June 19, 1988): AA–1.

Hannah, L. S., and C. B. Matus. "A Question of Ethics." *The Computing Teacher* 12 (no. 1): 11–14.

International Council for Computers in Education. *Code of Ethical Conduct for Computer-Using Educators*. Eugene: University of Oregon, 1986.

_____ . *Policy Statement on Network and Multiple Machine Software*. Eugene: University of Oregon, 1983.

"Keyboard Bandits Who Steal Your Money." *U.S. News & World Report* (December 27, 1982–January 3, 1983): 68–69.

Lockheed, M. E., and S. B. Frant. "Sex Equity: Increasing Girls' Use of Computers." *The Computing Teacher* 11 (no. 8): 16–18.

Logsdon, Tom. *Computers Today and Tomorrow*. Rockville, Md.: Computer Science Press, 1985.

Lyon, D. "From 'Pacman' to 'Homelink': Information Technology and Social Ethics." *Faith and Thought* 3 (no. 1): 13–21.

Markoff, John. "Computer 'Virus' Linked To 'Bored Students'." *The Arizona Republic* 99 (no. 171, November 5, 1988): 1–2.

_____ . "Security Expert's Son Created 'Virus'." *The Scottsdale Progress* 28 (no. 224, November 5, 1988): 1,7.

Marshall, Jon C., and Susan Bannon. "Race and Sex Equity in Computer Advertising." *Journal of Research on Computing in Education* 21 (no. 1, Fall 1988): 15–27.

Morris, J. M. "Hacker Meets Star Wars." *Datamation* 31 (no. 8): 161–162.

Ognibene, Pete. "The Keeper of the Secrets." *OMNI* 5 (no. 6, March 1983): 52–112.

Parker, Donn B. *Computer Security Management*. Reston, Va.: Reston, 1981.

————. *Fighting Computer Crime.* New York: Scribner's, 1983.

Ragsdale, Ronald. *Permissible Computing and Education: Values, Assumptions and Needs.* New York: Praeger, 1988.

Ricketts, Dick. "Software Piracy—A Diminishing Problem?" *The Computing Teacher* 11 (no. 9, May 1984): 5.

Sennett, M. L. "Teach Your Students To Be Friendly." *The Computing Teacher* 11 (no. 4, November 1983): 18–19.

Sturdivant, P. "Access to Technology: The Equity Paradox." *The Computing Teacher* 11 (no. 8): 65–67.

Toffler, Alvin. *The Third Wave.* New York: Bantam Books, 1981.

Turkle, S. *The Second Self: Computers and the Human Spirit.* New York: Simon and Schuster, 1984.

Using Software: A Guide to the Ethical and Legal Use of Software for Members for the Academic Community. Princeton, N.J.: EDUCOM, 1987.

Wholeben, Brent Edward. "Ethics and Equity in Educational Computing: Strategic Assessment of Policy Initiatives." *Journal of Research on Computing in Education* 21 (no. 1, Fall 1988): 36–50.

ADDITIONAL READING

Business Week
Byte
Computer Decisions
Computerworld
Communications of the ACM
Datamation
INFOworld
Information Week
Mini-Micro Systems
Newsweek
Personal Computing
Time
U.S. News & World Report
USA Today
Wall Street Journal

REVIEW ANSWER KEY

Multiple Choice

1. a	5. d	9. c
2. a	6. c	10. b
3. a	7. a	
4. b	8. a	

True/False

1. T	5. F	9. F
2. T	6. F	10. T
3. F	7. T	
4. F	8. F	

Short Answer

1. Diverting funds into a bank account; illegally ordering and selling goods; stealing information, time, or program (software piracy).
2. Fear, hatred, political activism, frustration.
3. Relationships would be closer because there would be more contact; children could become more productive members of society by participating in parents' jobs; society would become decentralized.
4. Answers will vary according to individual opinion.
5. Economically disadvantaged students will not be prepared for life in our computerized society.

CHAPTER 14

TRENDS IN TEACHING WITH COMPUTERS

Objectives

- Predict the role of computers in the classroom of the future
- List the benefits of computerized education
- Explain how computers can assist disabled students
- Discuss the criticisms of computerized education and their validity
- Describe the teacher's role in the computerized classroom

Key Terms

AI (artificial intelligence)
CD-ROM disk
desktop publishing
DVI (digital video interactive) software
expert systems
HyperCard
hypertext
idea processor
optical disk
portable software
robots
stacks
supercomputers
video disks
videoencyclopedia

As the printing press made written words inexpensive enough to duplicate for the average person, the computer has made interactive, individualized education cost-effective for the classroom. It did not happen as quickly as the experts predicted at the beginning. However, there were valid reasons for the delay of computer technology's impact on education, some of which we've covered, such as a lack of software programs that worked well for education and the high price of computer equipment. As we've seen, for the most part these obstacles have been successfully overcome and computers play a bigger role in classrooms every year. However, there is still room for improvement, and in this chapter we focus on the technological advances that will have an effect on computerized education in the future.

NEW TECHNOLOGY AND COMPUTERIZED EDUCATION

It's clear that computers in the classroom have come a long way. Nowadays, there are many well-written, affordable CAI and CMI programs that meet the needs of teachers, students, and administrators. In addition, computer equipment is more sophisticated yet cheaper than ever before, so that most school districts can afford to computerize, even if only in a small way.

As exciting as these advances have been, there are more waiting in the wings. Development of robots, artificial intelligence, and sophisticated simulation software will take computerized education into the future. In addition, strides have been made in data storage, which up until now has been one of the knottier problems confronting computer scientists.

Data Storage   For many years now, floppy disks have been the standard device for data and program storage. Although small and portable, recently their limitations have overshadowed these advantages. They are fragile—subject to damage from dust, heat, and improper handling—all of which puts them at risk, especially when used by a large number of students in a classroom. But more importantly, their storage capacity is limited.

Because of the small amount of memory available on an individual floppy disk, teachers would need to use a large number of disks on which to store the curriculum for just one class. In addition, to make computerized teaching feasible, each student would require a copy of each disk. The logistics of storing, maintaining, and updating so many disks is overwhelming, and hence has severely circumscribed the role that computers play in the classroom curriculum. Up until now, that role has been limited to the purchase of individual programs that teachers had to fit into their curriculum, a curriculum that is still based on traditional methods of manual organization and teaching techniques. However, changes in curriculum management may be in sight because of advances in expanded data storage capacity.

Optical Disks   Microcomputer memory capacity has been increased greatly by the development of **optical disks**, one of which can store many times the amount of data that can be stored on a standard floppy disk. For example, the read/write, three-and-one-half-inch optical disk (called an optical cartridge) for the NEXT computer can hold 356 megabytes of data. The optical disk has 10,000 to 20,000 tracks per inch as compared to less than fifty for a magnetic floppy disk. In addition, optical disks provide random access (as do floppies), which means that the user has ready access to any information on the disk at any time. (An example given by a manufacturer states that a single high-density optical disk can hold the dictionaries of all the languages in the world and access any word in less than a second!) In addition to the large memory, optical disks are small and lightweight; they are impervious to dust, heat, and normal handling; they have a lower error rate than magnetic tape storage; they can store digitized data from image, audio, text, and graphics sources; and they are easily duplicated by mechanical stamping. With such capabilities, the entire curriculum for a class could be contained on one small, rugged, easy-to-store optical disk.

The optical disk is read by a low-powered laser beam in very much the same way that a phonograph needle tracks the grooves of a record. However, because the beam simply scans the disk optically (without physical contact), the disk does not wear out with repeated use. The information that the beam reads is electronically converted from binary digits to analog signals—audio, video, or data. Optical audio disks (compact disks, or CDs) are already familiar to music lovers, having gained rapid popularity because they produce a vastly superior sound.

Video Disks   **Video disks** offer the broadest applications of optical disks. They can be written to and read from; they allow random access. They're cost-effective because they can be easily duplicated. They can hold a high density of images, audio, and text; and they allow text or graphics to be placed over a video image. These capabilities plus their ruggedness makes them especially good for educational and training applications. In addition, the user has extensive control over the medium and the data it contains, which is vital to the success of CAI software.

It's projected that in the 1990s, the video disk will skyrocket in popularity and use, as the audio disk already has done. We can expect to see video disks in education, training and development, science, and business.

CD-ROM Disks   Compact disks with read-only memory are called **CD-ROM disks**. These disks share all the features of optical disks save one: They cannot be written to or erased; the data contained on them is permanent. In addition, they can store up to 600 megabytes of data—or as much as can

Optical disks have large memories yet are small and lightweight.

The optical disk is read by a low-power laser beam in very much the same way that a phonograph needle tracks the grooves of a record.

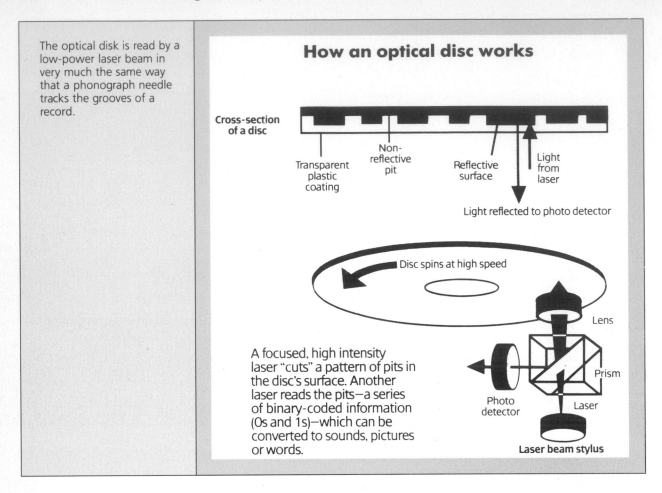

How an optical disc works

Cross-section of a disc

Transparent plastic coating

Non-reflective pit

Reflective surface

Light from laser

Light reflected to photo detector

Disc spins at high speed

Lens

Prism

Photo detector

Laser

Laser beam stylus

A focused, high intensity laser "cuts" a pattern of pits in the disc's surface. Another laser reads the pits—a series of binary-coded information (0s and 1s)—which can be converted to sounds, pictures or words.

The sleek-looking NEXT computer uses an optical disk.

be stored on 1,500 360K, $5\frac{1}{4}$-inch floppy disks. This is roughly equivalent to 275,000 typed page. Because of their ruggedness, their storage capacity, and the security of their data, these disks are especially useful for storing reference materials and other types of data that do not need to be updated or altered in any way.

Another version of a CD-ROM disk is the WORM (write once, read many times). This high-performance disk can contain a huge volume of data; therefore it is ideal for business and industry, as well as government agencies.

Telecommunications

Telecommunications using fiber optics will extend the regular classroom into the home. Just as books are required for students, in the future individual computers will be a necessity and their low cost will enable students to have them at home. Students will be able to send their lessons from home into the classroom and to access any classroom program from their home computer.

Many of the programs accessed will be educational games, which will train students to think logically, sequentially, and strategically. New patterns of thinking will strengthen mathematics principles, reinforce grammar concepts, and improve spelling techniques. Games of this kind will make computer learning more attractive and desirable to the reluctant learner. Because of the vast capabilities present in the computers and software of the future, the programs and games will be sophisticated, intricate, and graphic.

With the expansion of computer technology into the home—bringing with it the classroom—learning will be even more of an ongoing process. The classroom will then become the hub of the telecommunications network whereby information is distributed. In essence, it will be a multimedia resource center. Students will be able to access information from their home computer or spend time in the classroom itself.

Telecommunications systems will be interact with weather satellites to teach students the dynamics of weather patterns. Students located in different geographic areas will share information about bird migration. Phenomena such as acid rain will be studied and data compiled for access by students. Students from all over the nation will be able to share environmental and ecological data from their individual areas, via satellite.

Digital Video Interactive (DVI) Software, HyperCards, and Idea Processors

Another addition to the classroom of the future will be **digital video interactive (DVI) software**, which simulates real-world experiences and situations. Developed by RCA Laboratories in the 1980s, DVI expands video beyond the capabilities of the video disk. Today DVI provides digital full-motion, full-screen video, three-dimensional motion graphics, and high-quality audio.

DVI can provide experiential, lifelike situations with which students can interact. Therefore, it's excellent for teaching about other cultures, languages, and experiences that many students might not otherwise encounter. Through simulation, students will participate in the American Revolution, agonize with Abraham Lincoln in his history-making decisions, or stand beside MacArthur, Patton, Bradley, Eisenhower, Wainwright, and other military leaders during World War II. In the classroom of the future, students will interact with famous writers such as Charlotte Brontë, George Sand, Emerson, and Thoreau; with scientists like Ohm, Edison, Darwin, Galileo, and Watts; and with mathematicians such as Blaise Pascal, Pierre de Fermat, Eratosthenes, and even Thomas Jefferson.

Because of the experiential capabilities of DVI, it has the potential to be used widely for training programs. It therefore will be extremely useful in vocational education where hands-on training can be simulated by computer to give the student the equivalent of actual experience.

Another new technology that performs in a similar manner is called **HyperCard**. HyperCard is a personal software toolkit that gives the user the power to create, customize, and manage information using text, sound, music, voice, and animation. An integral part of HyperCard is Hypertalk, an easy-to-use English-based programming language that provides computer users with the ability to design and write their own software. CD-ROM and videodisk can be interfaced as part of the HyperCard-based program. The interfacing of these technologies gives programs sound and graphics instead of simply text. HyperCard applications include simulation, presentation, reference materials, interactive games and stories, personal finances, instruction and training materials, and interactive encyclopedias. Teachers can generate their own HyperCard "stacks" (special files that HyperCard can access at any time) for use in presentation and creating classroom instruction materials. Administrators can use HyperCard to manage school and administration tasks.

Other valuable assistance to the teacher will come from **idea processors**, which will aid in the organization of writing. Just as a spelling checker or thesaurus aids in the mechanics of writing, an idea processor helps organize the student's thoughts. By helping the student present ideas in a logical and organized manner, the idea processor improves writing skills and teaches the student better communication techniques.

Robots   The classroom of the future will contain other aids as well, such as **robots**. Robots will teach sequential and logical ways of thinking; they will also be used in drill-and-practice situations that are boring and time-consuming for the teacher, such as math and spelling drills.

In addition, robots will act as lab assistants, performing repetitive, boring, or dangerous tasks, such as chemical experiments. They will also handle hazardous items, such as hot beakers and various acid experiments.

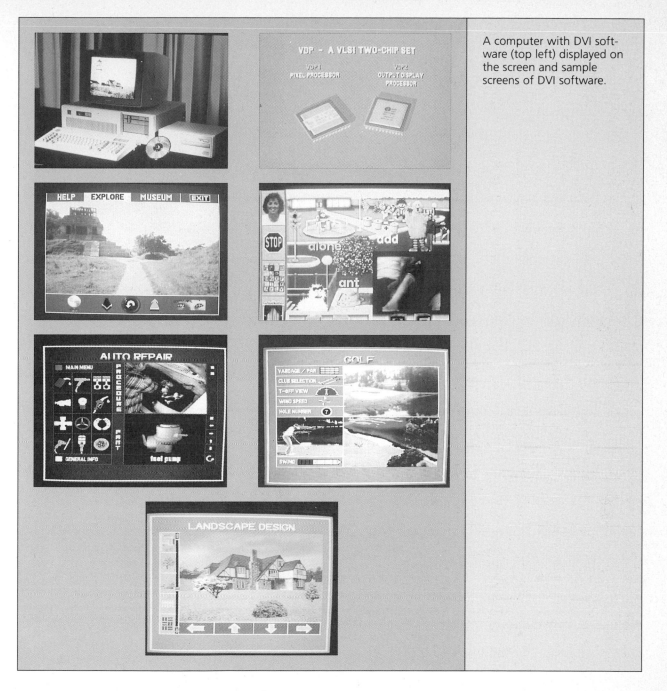

A computer with DVI software (top left) displayed on the screen and sample screens of DVI software.

A fully programmable electronic robot with articulated arm, wrist, hand, and head, and a detachable, motorized serving tray.

Artificial Intelligence (AI)

In the future, the classroom teacher will have **artificial intelligence (AI)** computers to help diagnose learning difficulties and assist in developing remedies. Artificial intelligence is a development of computer technology that imitates the working of the human brain. The processing of information based on knowledge stored previously in the computer and the capability to apply this knowledge (which includes past experiences) to a new situation allows artificial intelligence systems to make decisions, evaluations, and diagnoses.

With a program specially designed for diagnostic work, the teacher can input information, for instance, whether a student is inattentive, a daydreamer, or unable to read. The system will respond to the teacher's information, and teacher and computer will go back and forth until the system is able to diagnose a learning disability.

Students can also enter data into the AI computer about their interests, likes, and dislikes. This information will be used to help the teacher devise a viable method of motivating underachieving students.

The artificial intelligence tools used in the future classroom can help students develop a positive attitude toward learning by helping the teacher develop individualized lessons for students, taking into account each student's interests and study methods. Students will be more motivated because their interests, their capabilities, and their style of learning will all be considered.

Through continuing research in artificial intelligence, **expert systems** will be developed that will program the knowledge of experts and make it available on optical disk. When a student is studying a particular subject or area, expert knowledge will be accessible right in the classroom. For example, a Shakespearean scholar when studying Shakespeare, a renowned symphonic conductor when studying classical music, students of Freud, Jung, and Rogers when delving into psychotherapy, historians who have devoted their lives to the study of humankind's progress—the knowledge of these and countless others will be instantly available to students of the future. Not only from our own culture but from all over the world, expert information will be formatted for use in the classroom.

Expert Systems and Other Technological Developments

Another way in which students will be able to study other parts of the world is by satellite. Transmission of live images and sound from anywhere in the world (perhaps even from outer space!) will broaden the student's area of study far beyond what has been available in the past.

Supercomputers, which contain banks of many microprocessors, will provide the powerful hardware necessary to implement the sophisticated software currently being developed in research institutions. Supercomputers are the most powerful machines in the computer world. They can execute over a billion calculations a second and are used to model complex situations such as weather, space travel, or detailed research projects. Education must stay ahead of what is happening in the rest of society in order to equip graduates with the knowledge and skills they will need in the working world. Toward that goal, institutions of higher education are working hand in hand with business to develop software for the future.

Carnegie Mellon University, in conjunction with IBM, has developed software that adresses the needs of higher education. By allowing software to be used on computers from different manufacturers, it is said that educational software will be "as **portable** as textbooks." Brown University and the Massachusetts Institute of Technology are working on similar programs to standardize computing systems for higher education.

In addition to making software portable, the system developed at Carnegie Mellon can manage a campus network of terminals, accessing files and displaying and printing data from any one of them. It has an authoring language that allows professors, most of whom are not computer experts, to write educational software in the same format. For instance, inexperienced users can create graphics "backwards"—the user draws the pictures and the computer fills in the programming instructions. In addition, it has sophisticated versions of familiar applications, such as word processing, electronic mail, and bulletin boards.

Music education will be enhanced by a new computer-based pitch recognition system, developed in England, that can "hear" musical tones and translate them into musical notes on the display screen. It is projected that this system might also be used to monitor machinery by detecting changes in the sound it makes. This system could also be adapted to industrial security, necessitating recognition of a security sound code before allowing access to a computer system.

Software "assistants" are being developed that can browse through databases for specific information. These technological assistants can be most helpful and timesaving for professionals who need to remain current on information in their own fields but do not have the time to conduct their own computer searches.

Hypertext (sometimes referred to as a programming language of HyperCard) is the electronic equivalent of a reference library and was developed to aid classroom learning. Hypertext provides links to **stacks** of related information (similar to the book shelves, called stacks, in a library). The computer, assisted by hypertext, guides the user through many paths of relevant material once a particular subject has been accessed. In other words, the user can investigate a subject based upon specific interests rather than simply following a traditional fixed path. The impact of hypertext on research done in the classroom will be phenomenal.

Hypertext can also conduct bibliographical searches. You can identify the items you need and have them available to you on an optical disk immediately. This will be quite different from the present library system of locating a needed item in a card index only to find it is not on the shelf.

The school library of the future will be contained in each classroom on optical disks aided by hypertext. Students can access library materials available to all classrooms through a computerized central library catalogue. Familiarizing students with both the computer and the library makes using library resources more attractive to the student who has not yet developed the joy of reading.

Another development is the **videoencyclopedia**. This technology makes the contents of the encyclopedia come alive. Students can watch filmed reenactments of historical occurrences or observe a caterpillar turn into a butterfly. This as well as hypertext can be a stimulating enhancement to many different classroom subjects.

Through the implementation of all these new developments, the classroom computer will not only offer individualized education to students, but may also inspire the apathetic student as effectively as the printing press inspired the masses.

In the future, more classrooms will have microcomputer testing and tutoring, which means that the computer will quiz students on lesson material, then direct them to appropriate areas of further study based on the result. Students will be encouraged to work at their own pace, knowing that their areas of weakness can be identified and remedied.

CURRICULUM

The future of computerized education looks bright. The computer technology discussed in this chapter as well as that covered in earlier chapters will enrich the classroom curriculum of tomorrow, in all subjects.

In English classes, students will continue to use tool software such as word processing to write reports and essays in which they may include pictures and graphics, check the spelling, find words in a thesaurus, and use software specially designed to critique the grammar, sentence structure, logic patterns, and syntax of their writing. In addition, **desktop publishing** systems (including computers and peripherals, laser printers, and publishing software) will be available. Students can use these tools to write, edit, and print individual class newspapers. During the process of writing and revising, they will be improving their basic language skills as well.

The menu on this Hyper-Card™ screen allows both directed searches and exploratory browsing.

Microsoft Bookshelf contains the U.S. Zip Code Directory.

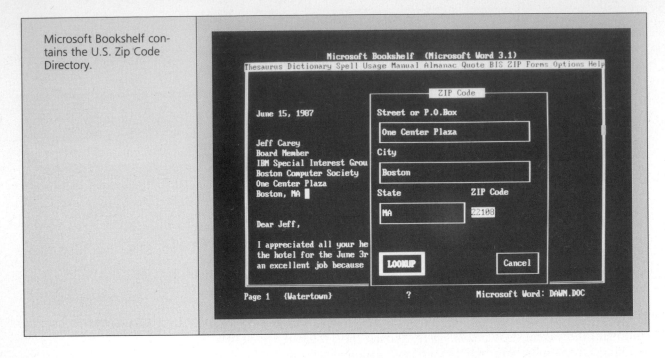

The study of literature can be enhanced by hypertext. For instance, students will use hypertext to research an author's life, locate other books relevant to the time period, or find material on related subjects. In addition, videoencyclopedia could allow students to see films that depict time and place relevant to the literature.

In math classes, the computer will continue to be a successful tool. With electronic spreadsheets automatically performing many of the repetitive, time-consuming numerical functions, students can create all sorts of financial and other numeric demonstrations of the concepts being learned. For instance, one school system has established computerized banking where, on a regular basis, students can make deposits and withdrawals of their own money. Thus, by using a computer to conduct their own personal banking students gain a deeper understanding of the world of finance.

Science is another subject that will continue to benefit from progress in computer technology. DVI software is an excellent tool in this area. It combines pictures, graphs, text, and sound to make complicated information more understandable and interesting. Students can simulate experiments on the computer that would be far too hazardous to actually perform in the classroom. For instance, the use of radioactive materials or explosives could never be permitted in the school environment. However, through simulation the computer can conduct an experiment and then help the student write a summary of the findings.

DVI software can also be used by business students. They can simulate the design, development, manufacture, and marketing of a product. In addition, they can use spreadsheets, graphics, and word processing to chart and document the financial support necessary for such a production.

In vocational education, hypertext will be a valuable tool. For instance, automotive students can use an actual automobile along with a video disk training program to learn about the inner workings of cars and how to maintain and repair them.

Typing, now called *keyboarding,* will be taught from the first grade on, giving students a skill that will be useful throughout their lives. Handwriting skills can also be taught by computer: With a graphics program, students can use a stylus to practice their penmanship.

Computer classes are a fairly recent development in the school system. In addition to learning how to operate and program computers, students are learning how to build them. They are taught not only how computers work but how to maintain and repair them. Teachers themselves often benefit from these classes. They can be retrained from low-demand areas, such as home economics and industrial arts, to the increasingly high-demand area of computer technology.

Robotics, the study of robots, is also a new development in schools. Students can learn, via the computer, about robots, how they are developed, what they are used for now and how they may be used in the future, and the care required to keep them operating efficiently.

COMPUTERS AND DISABLED STUDENTS

Computers can be of tremendous help to the disabled, in education as well as in other areas of life. The computer can operate special devices to help the disabled manage everyday but difficult tasks. Telephones, radios, heating and cooling controls, and microwave ovens are a few of the appliances that can be controlled by a disabled person with the aid of a computer. In addition, research is now being conducted on the ability of microprocessors to take over the function of disabled limbs where nerve and muscle systems remain intact. In the future, it's expected that continued research will lead to devices that take over the functions of limbs with damaged nerve and muscle systems as well.

One of the most exciting uses of computers in the field of health is in teaching deaf children to speak. Children deaf from birth or a very young age have no idea how their words should sound. By seeing on a display screen the sound waves created when words are spoken by a hearing person, children can compare the sound waves of their own words and can learn to match the correct sounds.

Computers can be of tremendous help to the disabled by operating special devices that help them manage everyday but difficult tasks.

By using this vocalization tool, the speech- or hearing-impaired can learn to communicate more effectively. This young student successfully moves a hot air balloon over a mountain by using his voice to make a sustaining sound.

By using the computer, students can learn to communicate without speaking or hearing. While graphics and visuals will assist the deaf in expanding their horizons, voice-activated programs will assist the blind. In addition, blind students will use computers with braille keyboards and printers. The printers will also convert to regular print so that teachers can receive the result of their students' work.

Students with other physical disabilities will learn to use robots for the various physical functions that they cannot otherwise perform. If their disabilities are too severe for them to attend school, telecommunications will allow them to communicate with their classroom from home.

Not all disabilities are physical. There is a large percentage of illiterate adults in this country. The computer can help them. Adults who might be intimidated or embarrassed to work with human teachers can spend time with a computer without any awkwardness. Studying by computer, these adults can begin with the very basics of education—reading and writing at the primary level. They can spend as much time on a particular lesson as they need and repeat it as many times as necessary without feeling insecure or unacceptable.

ADMINISTRATION

The computer has a place in other areas of the school besides the classroom or classroom-at-home. All sorts of administrative functions can be performed better and faster with a computer. Just as the classroom teacher uses the computer as an assistant, so can the administrator. Various paperwork, such as student and staff personnel records, attendance and payroll records, and warehouse inventories can be generated and maintained on a computer. Principals and superintendents can use computers to manage individual schools and districts more effectively.

Placement of new students can be a complicated procedure. Students of the future will be evaluated and placed by computers using an expert system, based on demographic data plus scores on computer-generated and scored, standardized tests.

Schools can produce public relations materials for distribution to the community they serve. Desktop publishing systems can be used to publish regular newsletters. Schools can also produce video disks to show the community what is going on within the school district.

The school board can benefit from the new technology as well. In some districts, school boards are already using computers to evaluate and assess building programs, curriculum, hiring procedures for teachers and other employees, and the funding to support it all. Such deliberations help school districts to plan for the future and to project budget allocations. By looking

A computer screen displaying the sound waves produced by a kazoo.

at the overall picture of a school's activities and present and future needs, the computer can assist in more efficient management of available resources.

For smaller school districts where funding is more difficult, telecommunications and interactive technology can offer curriculums that would otherwise be too expensive. For these schools, and larger ones as well, networking can take advantage of expertise available in the community. By networking with the professional environment, students can have on-the-job training while remaining in the classroom. In effect, the expert is brought to the students electronically.

INCORPORATING COMPUTERS INTO THE SCHOOLS

Incorporating computer technology into the schools will involve major tasks. The first challenge will be to convince the community that the school system needs this new and expensive technology. With the allocation and expenditure of public monies comes a grave responsibility to handle it wisely. For that reason there is reluctance on the part of those responsible to venture into new and untried territory.

Restructuring policy, curriculum, and administrative procedures is the next step toward obtaining computers for administrators, teachers, and students. In addition, planning for and providing the physical environment, such as buildings, classrooms, and electrical power systems, will require knowledge, funding, and personnel.

Training of personnel will be an important and costly task in setting up computer systems in the school. While experts may be brought in to install and initiate the use of computers, it will be essential to have well-trained, on-site personnel to maintain and update both hardware and software. To be performed efficiently, maintenance needs a broad base of support; one maintenance person per school district will not be sufficient. For instance, the classroom aide who now performs the teacher's more mundane duties must be able to maintain computer equipment and update software as needed.

In addition, all school personnel involved with computers should attempt to keep up with changes in the computer field. Because the technology changes so rapidly, this will require continuing education and training. However, it's the one way to ensure that advances in computerized education continue to be implemented in your school.

While keeping up with what is new and desirable, decision makers must not allow vendors to pressure them into purchases that do not satisfy educational needs. While new hardware or software may be impressive, the purchaser needs to evaluate its worth in the classroom to both the teacher and students.

Locating the appropriate software and course material will require the expertise of teachers as well as computer technicians. If the content of a program's course material is inadequate, it's of little importance that the program runs well. Much cooperative planning will be necessary for school districts to receive the very best in computerized education for their dollars spent.

Ethical issues of access and security must be considered also. School records contain a vast amount of very personal and private information about the student's entire family. Guarding that information and every family's right to privacy is an important consideration when designing a computer system. Again, the assistance of experts in areas other than computer technology will be needed to ensure adequate protection and security.

University students using computers in an engineering lab.

Funding is the foundation upon which the entire concept depends. Without adequate funding to support the project and equipment chosen, an experiment in computerized education could be a disaster for a school district. Therefore, conversion to computers in the classroom must be a cooperative decision of any school community. A commitment to support the system chosen is absolutely essential to the success of such a program.

CRITICISMS OF COMPUTERIZED EDUCATION

One of the primary concerns of educators when considering the impact of computerized education on those affected most—the students—is that a new form of elitism will be created. The elite, or information-advantaged, would consist of those students who have computers available to them in the home as well as at school. Another advantage accrues to those students who not only have a computer at home, but who also have computer-literate parents, who are interested and involved in their child's computer education. If they are willing and able to provide expensive software and peripheral equipment, then the student benefits further.

The disadvantaged, on the other hand, would be those students who have no access to a computer outside the classroom, and whose parents for whatever reason do not consider such access important to their children's development or cannot provide it.

One attempt to address this issue has taken place in a school district where computers are made available for children to take home. This enables the student to reinforce basic skills taught in the classroom. It might also involve the parents, giving them access to computers that they would not otherwise have. The exposure and familiarity acquired by having a computer in the home may motivate the parents who can afford it to provide one for the family.

In another school district, teachers are given the opportunity to take computers home to write lesson plans, communicate with parents, and complete other paperwork and tasks. The teachers' time saved in this manner can then be spent in more direct teaching activity.

Another solution may come about as computers and auxiliary equipment become less costly. It has been predicted that computers in the future will be considered as essential and affordable as books, paper, and pencils are in today's educational environment. If that occurs, anyone who wants one will be able to afford one.

Another important concern is that of guarding the privacy and confidentiality of personal information. Much attention must be given to this issue so that the public will believe that information will be kept secure and private. At present, the issue is being addressed by new security devices and capabilities developed for this specific purpose. Voice-activated entry is one method of limiting and defining who will have access to stored data. The protection of privacy also requires that new confidentiality laws be written and passed.

While educators, parents, and students themselves have some concern about the impact of computers on education, it seems obvious that the benefits far outweigh any potential disadvantages. Computerized education will enhance the learning process dramatically. All learning builds self-esteem; by allowing children to learn more effectively, the computer will further encourage this growth. The classroom teacher's ability to teach will likewise be enhanced by computerization. In addition, when our children leave school they will take with them not only academic but computer skills, which will help them in the workplace as well as other areas of their lives.

Although computers will inevitably change the way children are educated, they will not change the goals of education. We will still attempt to teach our children the knowledge and skills that will enrich their lives and make them capable adults. Computers offer us a way to do this more effectively.

SUMMARY

The computer has made interactive, individualized education cost-effective for the classroom. However, software and hardware were not always affordable or workable in the school environment. In addition, data storage capacity could not satisfy curriculum needs. Nowadays, however, software and hardware are well designed and less expensive; and data storage capacity has been increased with the development of optical disks.

One optical disk can contain many times the amount of information possible on one floppy disk. In addition, optical disks (which include video and CD-ROM disks) store digitized data from image, audio, text, and graphics sources; they are also small, lightweight, rugged, easy to store, and easy to duplicate. With these disks, there is no longer a storage or handling impediment to a fully computerized curriculum in the classroom. Other developments will also contribute to computerized education.

Telecommunications will extend the classroom into the home and home computers will become as necessary as books (and almost as affordable). Because the home and the classroom will be closely connected, education will become an even more ongoing process.

Other technological advances will have an impact as well. DVI (digital video interactive) software will make real-world simulations more sophisticated. The capabilities of DVI will allow students to experience decisive moments in history and to interact with famous authors, scientists, and mathematicians through lifelike, video re-creations. Idea processors will help students organize their thoughts for writing. Robots will have their place in the classroom, as teaching and lab assistants. Teachers will be able to use artificial intelligence (computers that learn by experience) to help diagnose and evaluate learning disabilities. With further AI development, expert systems will make the knowledge of experts in any field available to students for reference and research. Access to reference libraries will be available in the classroom by using hypertext (which contains stacks of reference materials, much like the stacks in a real library) stored on optical disks. Videoencyclopedias will make the contents of the encyclopedia come alive.

All areas of the curriculum will be enhanced and broadened because of these technological advances. In addition, new subjects in the curriculum will appear: Computer classes and robotics will teach students about these new technologies, and keyboarding (previously called typing) will be taught at early ages so that all students can use computer power.

In addition, computers will benefit the disabled. Telecommunications will allow students who are too severely disabled to attend school to communicate with their classroom from home. Computers will teach the deaf and the blind. They will also help those disabled by illiteracy: Illiterate adults, who might be intimidated or embarrassed by a human teacher, can be taught to read by the computer.

Computers have their place in school administration as well as in the classroom. Many administrative functions, such as student records and staff payroll, will be handled by the computer. Student placement, public relations, enrollment projections, and much more will also be accomplished by computer.

However, to implement computer use in the classroom and in the office, teachers and administrators will need to plan thoroughly: They must decide what their needs are and how best to implement them. They must be aware that computerization cannot be accomplished without thorough training of teachers and staff. Most importantly, they must have the funding to accomplish computerization: Their community must support them in their desire to computerize; they must then tailor their needs to their budget.

Although most agree that computerized education is a good thing, there are concerns about computers in the school environment. One is that an elite, or information-advantaged group, consisting of those students who have computers available to them in the home, will result. Another important concern is that of guarding the privacy and confidentiality of personal information. Much attention will need to be given to this issue in order for the public in general to trust that information will be kept secure and private. However, learning builds self-esteem, and making the world of knowledge accessible to everyone will be well worth the effort necessary to accomplish it.

REVIEW EXERCISES

Multiple Choice

1. Optical disks are a great improvement over floppy disks because optical disks
   a. are rugged
   b. have a large data storage capacity
   c. are easy to store
   d. all of the above
2. How much data can be stored on a CD-ROM?
   a. 600 M
   b. 128 K
   c. 1 M
   d. 5 M
3. Hypertext stores information on a wide range of subjects in
   a. volumes
   b. files
   c. stacks
   d. catalogs
4. Hypertext is a valuable tool in
   a. English classes
   b. teaching mathematics
   c. vocational education
   d. all of the above
5. Disabled students can use computers to
   a. interact with other students
   b. manipulate appliances
   c. communicate
   d. all of the above
6. The development in computer technology that imitates the workings of the human brain is
   a. artificial intelligence
   b. impossible
   c. a dangerous trend
   d. all of the above
7. Expert systems are
   a. groups of computer scientists
   b. computers programmed with the knowledge of experts

c. teachers who can program computers
d. students who have completed computer literacy classes

8. Telecommunications will allow future students to
   a. access school computers from home
   b. receive data via satellite
   c. both of the above
   d. neither of the above

9. Introducing computers in the schools requires a considerable amount of
   a. training
   b. planning
   c. funding
   d. all of the above

10. Protecting the confidentiality of information stored on the computer is the responsibility of
    a. the individual user
    b. school districts
    c. society
    d. all of the above

True/False

1. Computers have revolutionized classrooms faster than experts predicted in the beginning.
2. Computers will soon replace human teachers in the classroom.
3. A single CD-ROM disk could contain a twenty-four-volume encyclopedia.
4. Hypertext is the electronic equivalent of a reference library.
5. Disabled students cannot use computers effectively.
6. With artificial intelligence, the computer learns by experience.
7. Expert systems are useful only in managing large businesses.
8. Implementing computers in the schools requires careful planning.
9. Teachers should be involved in deciding what educational software to buy for classroom use.
10. In the future, only students who can afford personal computers will succeed.

Short Answer

1. What factors have slowed the impact of computers in the schools?
2. What are the advantages of optical disks as compared to floppy disks?

3. List several benefits of using DVI software in the classroom.
4. List some of the ways computers aid handicapped students.
5. List several criticisms of computerized education.

Activities

1. Visit a local computer store to see CD-ROM technology.
2. Research ways in which school administrators use computers to manage their schools.
3. Attend a workshop, seminar, or conference on computers in education.
4. Invite a school principal to speak to your class about how computerized education is being implemented in his or her school.
5. Consider the criticisms of computerized education mentioned in this chapter. Are they valid or invalid? Defend your position in an essay.
6. Write a detailed paper on your perspective of the classroom of the future.
7. List CD-ROM disks that are available for education. Explain curriculum applications for each.
8. Write a paper describing the present status of DVI. Include costs, availability, and applications.
9. Develop a language arts classroom scenario including word processing, idea processing, spell checking, grammar checking, and so on.
10. Write a detailed paper describing the research reports on using the computer in the classroom. Summarize the findings of the studies.

BIBLIOGRAPHY

Bank, Adrianne, and Richard G. Williams. *Information Systems and School Improvement: Inventing the Future.* New York: Teachers College Press, 1987.

Becker, Henry J. *The Impact of Computer Use on Children's Learning.* Baltimore, Md.: Johns Hopkins University, 1988.

Bitter, Gary G. "Classroom of the Future." Unpublished paper. Tempe: Arizona State University, 1987.

————. *Computers in Today's World.* New York: John Wiley, 1984.

_____ . "Future of Education in the Microcomputer Revolution." *ERIC* no. 10183 (1982).

_____ . "Microcomputer-Based Mathematics Fitness." *Technological Horizons in Education Journal* 15 (no. 4, November 1987): 106–109.

Bitter, Gary G. (with K. Gore). "Robots in the Classroom: Another of Tomorrow's Teaching Tools Today." *Computers in the Schools* 2 (no. 4, 1985): 15–20.

_____ . "Trends in Hardware/Software." *Computers in the Schools* 4 (no. 2, Summer 1987): 31–35.

Bitter, Gary G. (with Mei-Yan Lu). "Factors Influencing Success in a Junior High Computer Programming Course." *Journal of Educational Computing Research* 4 (no. 1, January 1988): 71–78.

Budin, Howard, et al. *Using Computers in Social Studies.* New York: Teachers College Press, 1986.

Coburn, Edward J. *Learn to Compute!* Albany, N.Y.: Delmar, 1988.

Collis, Betty. "An Evaluation of the Program II Severely Learning Disabled (Elementary) Computer Project." *The Computing Teacher* 15 (no. 7): 7.

"Computers of the World, Unite." Brochure. Cupertino, Calif.: Apple Computer, 1988.

Congress of the U.S. Office of Technology Assessment. *Power On! New Tools for Teaching and Learning.* Washington, D.C.: U.S. Government Printing Office, 1988.

"The Disabled Get Computer Ability." *Insight* 14 (no. 21, May 23, 1988): 42–43.

Dreyfus, H. L. *What Computers Can't Do.* New York: Harper Colophon, 1979.

"The Electronic School." *The American School Board Journal* 174 (no. 7, July 1987): A1–A27.

Forester, Tom (ed.). *The Information Technology Revolution.* Cambridge: MIT Press, 1985.

Forsyth, Richard, and Chris Naylor. *The Hitch-Hiker's Guide to Artificial Intelligence.* New York: Chapman and Hall/Methuen, 1985.

"A Futuristic Vision of High-Technology Classrooms." *Arizona Republic* (May 12, 1988).

Gilkinson, Carol. "Robots in the Curriculum." In *8th Annual Microcomputers in Education Conference.* Tempe: Arizona State University, 1988: 74–75.

Johnson-Laird, Philip N. *The Computer and the Mind.* Cambridge: Harvard University Press, 1988.

Lambert, Steve, and Suzanne Ropiequet (eds.). *CD-ROM: The New Papyrus.* Richmond, Va.: Microsoft Press, 1986.

Lindblom, Steven. *How to Build a Robot.* New York: Thomas Y. Crowell, 1985.

Lobello, Anthony J., and Jane D. Stahler. *Networking in the Educational Environment.* Atlanta, Ga.: IBM, 1988.

Mims, Ted, and James Poirot. "Computer Competencies for School Administrators." *The Computing Teacher* 11 (no. 7, March 1984): 38–39.

Pea, Roy D., and Karen Sheingold (eds.). *Mirrors of Minds: Patterns of Experience in Educational Computing.* Norwood, N.J.: Ablex Publishing, 1987.

Poirot, James L., and Cathleen A. Norris. "Artificial Intelligence Applications in Education." *The Computing Teacher* 15 (no. 1): 8.

Queisser, Hans. *The Conquest of the Microcomputer.* Cambridge: Harvard University Press, 1988.

Rosenberg, Jerry M. *Dictionary of Artificial Intelligence and Robotics.* New York: John Wiley, 1986.

"Six New Technologies That Will Change the Computer and Your Life." *Compute!* 10 (no. 2, issue 93, February 1988): 14–28.

Strickland, Dorothy S., et al. *Using Computers in the Teaching of Reading.* New York: Teachers College Press, 1987.

Wenger, Etienne. *Artificial Intelligence and Tutoring Systems.* Los Altos, Calif.: Morgan Kaufmann, 1987.

White, Mary Alice. *What Curriculum for the Information Age?* Hillsdale, N.J.: Lawrence Erlbaum, 1987.

REVIEW ANSWER KEY

Multiple Choice

1. d	5. d	9. d
2. a	6. a	10. d
3. c	7. b	
4. d	8. c	

True/False

1. F	5. F	9. T
2. F	6. T	10. F
3. T	7. F	
4. T	8. T	

Short Answer

1. Educational software often did not work well; computer software and hardware was expensive; data storage was inadequate for curriculum requirements.

2. Optical disks are small, rugged, easy to store, and can hold many times the amount of information that floppy disks can store.

3. Vast expansion of video capabilities; provides experiential, lifelike situations for interaction; is excellent for teaching about other cultures, languages, and experiences.

4. Computers can operate special devices; take over functions of limbs that are damaged; teach deaf children to speak; robots can help with physical disabilities.

5. No appropriate software; expensive, inadequate hardware; difficult to integrate into curriculum; ethical issues of access; threat to confidentiality and privacy.

PHOTO CREDITS

INDEX